# IUDÆA, seu TERRA SANCTA

quæ

## HEBRÆORUM sive ISRAELITARUM

in suas duodecim Tribus divisa;

secretis ab invicem Regnis

### IUDA et ISRAEL

expressis insuper sex ultimi temporis ejusdem Terræ Provincijs

*ex Conatibus Geographicis*

*Guilielmi Sanson Christianissimi Galliarum Regis Geographi*

SERENISSIMO PRINCIPI DELPHINO

*offerebat humillimus, Obsequentissimus ac fidelissimus servus*

HUBERTUS IAILLOT.

*Created and Directed by Hans Höfer*

## INSIGHT GUIDES

# ISRAEL

**INCLUDING THE WEST BANK AND GAZA STRIP**

Edited by George Melrod

Photography by Richard Nowitz and others

Updated by Simon Griver

Editorial Director: Brian Bell

HOUGHTON MIFFLIN COMPANY

APA PUBLICATIONS

# ISRAEL

*Third Edition (Revised)*
© 1994 APA PUBLICATIONS (HK) LTD
*All Rights Reserved*
Printed in Singapore by Höfer Press Pte Ltd

| Distributed in the United States by: | Distributed in Canada by: | Distributed in the UK & Ireland by: | Worldwide distribution enquiries: |
|---|---|---|---|
| **Houghton Mifflin Company** | **Thomas Allen & Son** | **GeoCenter International UK Ltd** | **Höfer Communications Pte Ltd** |
| 222 Berkeley Street | 390 Steelcase Road East | The Viables Center, Harrow Way | 38 Joo Koon Road |
| Boston, Massachusetts 02116-3764 | Markham, Ontario L3R 1G2 | Basingstoke, Hampshire RG22 4BJ | Singapore 2262 |
| ISBN: 0-395-66197-8 | ISBN: 0-395-66197-8 | ISBN: 9-62421-039-X | ISBN: 9-62421-039-X |

# ABOUT THIS BOOK

This is a completely revised edition of one of the most successful books in the 180-strong Insight Guides series. Such is the dynamic nature of the State of Israel that, even when peace reigns, nothing stays the same for long – except for the amazing energy of the Israelis – and new chapters have been added to bring the book decisively into the 1990s.

Such a country, of course, lends itself perfectly to the effective mix of hard-hitting journalism and stunning photography pioneered by Apa Publications more than 20 years ago. *Insight Guide: Israel* is much more than a guidebook, therefore: it delves behind the current headlines and daily crises to discuss the history and nature of this cradle of Christianity, Judaism and Islam.

The original book assembled an expert team of writers and photographers under the leadership of a single project editor, **George Melrod**. A native New Yorker and (by definition, therefore) a born critic, Melrod majored in visual and environmental studies at Harvard University and studied communications at Hebrew University. His contributions in this book include essays on the Southern, Central and Northern Coasts, and the New City of Jerusalem.

## An Expert Team

Providing almost half the colour photography in the book is **Richard Nowitz**, a regular contributor to Insight Guides. Based for many years in Jerusalem, he now lives in the United States but still travels the world with his camera and returns regularly to Israel to keep his portfolio up-to-date.

This edition was updated by **Simon Griver**, a writer who was born in England but who never really felt he had found his true home until he settled in Israel. The experience is typical of many immigrants to Israel and enabled Griver to contribute valuable insights into everyday life in his chapter on contemporary Israel.

The first three chapters of the history section are by **Geoffrey Wigoder**, editor-in-chief of the *Encyclopedia Judaica*. Educated at Trinity College in Dublin and Oriel College at Oxford, he has been living in Israel since 1949.

New York freelancer **Walter Jacob** contributed the chapters on the history of Zionism and the Yishuv. Jacob graduated *magna cum laude* from Yale University with a speciality in European intellectual history.

The modern history chapter was penned by **William M. Recant**, a political consultant based in Washington DC, who studied in both Jerusalem and Cairo, and received his PhD in political science from George Washington University.

Writing about Jews, Arabs and Christians alike, **Helen Davis** is the talent behind the People section. Born in New Zealand and now living in Israel, Davis has worked as a reporter and as foreign correspondent.

**Daniel Gavron**, a feature writer on the *Jerusalem Post*, contributed chapters to the Places section on the Negev Desert, Dead Sea and Central Crossroads regions, as well as shorter chapters on Druze and Bedouin in the People section. A native of London, he immigrated to Israel in 1961.

Our Tel Aviv correspondent, **Michal Yudelman**, was born in Beersheba, Israel, in 1950 and grew up on a kibbutz in Negev. A graduate of Hebrew University and the Uni-

*Melrod*

*Nowitz*

*Davis*

*Gavron*

versity of Chicago, she is a reporter for the *Jerusalem Post*.

The author of the Haifa chapter, **Muriel Moulton**, is a writer and teacher, and former lecturer at the University of Illinois at Chicago. She has lived in Haifa since 1978.

**Leora Frucht**, who wrote about kibbutzim and the impact of high technology, as well as a sprawling portrait of the Galilee, was educated at Montreal's Concordia University. She is assistant editor of *Israel Scene*.

**Bill Clark** spans the country with chapters on the Golan Heights and Eilat, and an essay on ecology. Born in New York and an Israeli resident since 1980, Clark works for the Society for the Protection of Nature in Israel.

**Matthew Nesvisky**, who contributed essays on the Old City of Jerusalem and on the role of the Army, was born in the US and made his pilgrimage to Jerusalem in 1971. He is on the staff of the *Jerusalem Post*.

Describing the controversial territories of the West Bank and Gaza Strip is American **Amy Kaslow**. A graduate of Vassar College, Kaslow lived for two years in Tel Aviv, and is an editor with the *Mid-East Report*.

The task of delineating the country's various religious groups was assigned to **Mordechai Beck,** who attended art school, yeshiva and university in London, and made his *aliyah* to Israel in 1973.

**Nancy Miller**, who describes the archaeology scene in Israel, was assistant to the editor of the *Biblical Archaeology Review*.

London-born **Asher Weill** moved to Israel in 1958. He is editor of *Israel Scene* and *Ariel*. His contributions to this volume include essays on Culture and Language, and an introductory English-Hebrew vocabulary.

**Barbara Gingold** is a freelance journalist, editor and photographer specialising in Jewish arts and crafts. Born in New York, she has lived in Israel for many years.

In addition to Richard Nowitz's work, photographs were also provided by, among others, **Werner Braun**, who was born in Germany and emigrated to Israel in the mid-1940s; **David Harris**, a graduate of the School of Modern Photography in New York and one of the best known names in Israeli photography; **Neil Folberg**, whose work is immensely graphic; **Bill Clark**, who is more fully represented in this volume as a writer; **Vivienne Silver**, who also contributed to the visual side of the book with historical material from her extensive SilverPrint collection; **Joel Fishmann**; and **Israel Hirshberg**.

## A World Leader

Insight Guides, with more than 180 titles in print in this series, plus an additional 50 Insight Pocket Guides, has become a truly international publishing operation, with offices in several continents, and its books now appear in as many as nine languages. Even in English, however, language poses a problem: which version of English? Insight Guides' pragmatic answer is to publish titles to North and South American destinations (and associated areas) in American English and titles to European destinations in British English. Colors look just as good in colour!

Keeping up with a dynamic country such as Israel is difficult at the best of times, and Insight Guides welcomes new information from readers which can be used in future editions. This edition was finalised in Insight Guides' London editorial office under the supervision of **Dorothy Stannard**. The index was compiled by **Brian Bell**.

*Clark*

*Nesvisky*

*Braun*

*Harris*

*Iuif de la Terre sainte.*

Ce Medecin a longue barbe      Qui d'vne dose de Rhubarde.
Est vn chymiste intelligent      Fait comme il veut l'or et l'argent.

chez Monnart vis a vis les Mathurins au coq auec priu

# *History*

# *People*

## Maps

# TRAVEL TIPS

**For detailed information
see page 321**

# SHALOM

The landscape below you passes from sparkling blue to dirty white (the metropolis of Tel Aviv) to verdant green. As you descend towards the runway, Ben-Gurion Airport comes into view, surrounded by lush greenery. At last the plane grinds to a halt. The door opens to a gust of warm, Mediterranean air. As you step up to the ramp, the stewardess extends her hand, smiles, and says "Shalom."

You have arrived in Israel.

Shalom means hello, goodbye, and above all, peace. It is equally a greeting and an exclamation, a catch-all and a prayer. It is a fitting introduction to this land of promise and prayer, where Abraham forged his convenant with God.

Described in the Bible as the Promised Land of the Hebrew nation, today Israel has arisen like a phoenix from the ashes of destruction and 2,000 years of exile. Canaanites, Philistines, Assyrians, Romans, Crusaders, Mamelukes – all made their stands here, briefly flourished, and were swept away. That the Jews have re-established their nation, dispersed at the dawn of recorded history, is an achievement on a par, some might say, with that of Moses.

Containing only 5 million people in an area slightly larger than New Jersey, Israel has emerged from its austere beginning as a beleaguered wasteland to join the circle of modern nations in less than 50 years. Throughout it all, it undertook two enormous tasks: the ingathering of Jews from around the world, and the irrigation of the desert that would be home.

Today, Israel is a land of dynamic contrasts: as new as yesterday's newspaper, as old as the Bible. Ragged desert, ripe farmland and cosmopolitan cities; fervent religious passion and cutting-edge technology; futuristic skyscrapers and age-old shrines – all coexist. At the crossroads of three continents – Asia, Africa and Europe – Israel is an amalgam of East and West, its culture and people a uniquely Israeli blend. At the crossroads of three great religions – Judaism, Christianity and Islam – Israel safeguards some of the world's most sacred shrines.

Politically, too, Israel has found itself at a crossroads time and again, and has fought five wars in less than four decades. Since 1967, Israel has had the mixed burden of occupying the West Bank and Gaza Strip, with their large Arab populations. The momentous negotiations in 1993 between Israeli prime minister Yitzhak Rabin and the chairman of the Palestine Liberation Organisation, Yasser Arafat, sought to find a permanent solution to the problem.

In short, Israel is a diverse and complex collection of states: the Land of Milk and Honey, once again overflowing with a vivid spectrum of resources; the Holy Land, timeless refuge of Abraham and Isaac, David and Solomon, Jesus and his disciples.

Welcome to Israel. Shalom.

Preceding pages: Cartouche from 1681 map featuring Moses and Aaron; 18th-century Jewish doctor; evening at the Dead Sea; Monastery of St George at Wadi Kelt; Bedouin shepherd; Jerusalem. Left, an Orthodox Jew at Jerusalem's Western Wall plays the *shofar* (ram's horn).

# GEOLOGY OF ERETZ ISRAEL

"Eretz Israel" is the Hebrew term for the Land of Israel, sometimes reduced simply to "Ha'aretz", the land. Yet the literal meaning conveys little of the deep emotional, religious and historical significance the term implies. The bond between the people of Israel and the land of Israel is enormous, all the more so for the 2,000 years that stood between them.

The return of the Jewish people to this soil in the 19th and 20th centuries inaugurated a new chapter in this relationship. Israeli general Moshe Dayan once recollected: "I set out to be a farmer – and I think I made quite a good farmer. Yet I have spent most of my adult life as a soldier." These two careers, so vital to contemporary Israeli society, represent the two spheres most influential on the landscape of this nation: redeveloping its productive resources and establishing its boundaries.

Geographically, Israel is situated at the gateway between Asia and Africa, along the great depression of the Jordan Rift Valley, which stretches from Eastern Africa up to the Amanos Mountains in southern Turkey, including the length of the Red Sea. The rift is believed to have been created millennia ago with the drifting apart of the continental masses of Africa and Arabia. More recently – that is, in the Middle Pleistocene Era – it was the site of a great lake that extended from the Hula Basin through to the Dead Sea.

The rift valley remains Israel's most important geological feature and the run-off channel for the lion's share of the country's precious water supply. Along its course lie the historic Sea of Galilee, the world's lowest fresh water lake; the winding Jordan River, the world's lowest river bed; and the desolate Dead Sea, the world's lowest point above water, at 400 metres (1,300 ft) below sea level.

Besides the rift valley, Israel's main geographic regions include the sandy, fertile coastal plain, interrupted in the north by the ridge of Mt Carmel, the rolling lowlands of the Galilee, and the empty loess flatlands and limestone peaks of the Negev desert, with its own brooding formations (among them three vast craters and impressive pillars of Nubian sandstone above Eilat). Since 1967 Israel has also been in possession of the Golan Heights, rich in underground streams and ancient lava, which extend Israel's sub-tropical bounds to the sub-alpine slopes of Mt Hermon, and the central range of hills spanning from Judea to Samaria.

The face of the land has changed dramatically in modern times, with such projects as the draining of swampy Lake Hula in the 1950s, the construction of the National Water Carrier between the Sea of Galilee and the northwest Negev, and the replanting of the desiccated forests outside Jerusalem and all over. Behind this pragmatism, however, a certain mysticism towards the land lingers. For, despite fluctuations in borders ancient and modern, Israel is nurturing the sands tilled by its forefathers centuries ago.

**Left**, Nahal Arugot, near the Dead Sea.

Hora itineris. Com─

Mons Arnon.    Arnon, Schi

Carvhar

Philadelphi
Rabbath

Vallis
Hermon.                                                                         Hic hodie multa et
Dara.                                                                           ruinata habiacula
                                                                                viuntur, sed deserta
                                                             Nabathæi.          et nominibus carentia

Emathitæ                  ITVRÆA.

Zoba   Tebrbath      Bodag           Thernan           Roma  Mahanaim          Sebeth    El
BASAN  Argob                              Bath enæi.  Geruy                Manaei
Adai   Badgad.           Ethatona          Asteroth                Iabis  Carnar  Fons Car  Iaboc  A
REG-        Phiala fons.               Echatona.             Masphath      næym          Pinel
NVM.   TERRA  HVS.  Asteroch.                              Dachemaan.  Iabbin  Casphor  Magpha
Separtchrum   Ganerela                                                 Gadern.  Ephrum
TRACHO-  Cedar.        ista           GERASAEORVM                Baru  Galaad  Pella
Arama   Seleuca.    NITIS             REGIO.               sa.  Pella  Anstoch.
Gedaana.   REGIO        Asaroch           Labis.              Gadara   Amma    us topar
Cæsarea  quæ Bellena   Gau             Iordanis flu  Caless.        Gadara        chia    MAN.
ior fons  Dan  Enbassa              Adama           Mare Galileæ, uel      Mageth    Illustris vallis
Bethsemes  Sinachonis lacus  Ievron  Meroth                Tiberiadis.  Debar  Dion        ACRAB
Roma   Hazuyph  TRI  Lekum  Anoth                                   Ammaus     Aera  T
Magdal.  Cha  Edrai         Tabur.  TALIM            Magdalum.            Arbel  Itaburi  Itabus  ut maior
Libanus  nan  æi.  Ahon  Hamath  Antiopia                             Genme  ar  bor.
mons   GALI    Asfor, uel Hyron.                                        Thabor  Enahis
Ilamon  Reluh  Horma          Hathy               Achan           Bethsan  Scyhopolis  Thyanc  Enahis
GALI-  GALI-  LEA  SVPE-RI-EN  GEN           Gouraym  Belina  Amita  tha       Magnus  Ca
Beritha  Cana  OR, SEV  Clat  Chabul  TIVM.  Iotapata           Belsa  fort       Ierusel Geri  num  S.
Haly   Spelua         Elien  Eleos  Hanachon  Dionem.  tha                Darnabe  Gerim  S.
Antilibanus  ber.fort.  fort.        Maa  Gadara.             Abell.  In  Sam  Gorim
mons   Beroa  Asaph.                           Romo  Guria.       LE  SAM
Sidon  Canana         TRIBVS  ASER.  Msfah  Theron.  TRIBVS  HEVAEI  A.  aben  TRI
Sarepta  Cidreba  Amrad  Mont.fort.  Tabulon.  ZABVLON.  Azareth.  IN FERIOR  Gabara  Hippon  Brixenese
PHOE  Dira  Amrad  Hoffa  Vallis leph  thael.  GALILEA  Azareth.     Phere  tæi
NI  Samdalum  Afor  Sihor torre.  Bethdagon  Sephora  Lakno  am.  Narbathæ toparchi
Arad  Canagalileo  SA
Arnon  Langeresh  CIA.   Sihor.  Chifon torrent  Carmelus mons  Aretha  Mont
Ptolemaci  Caps  Ga  SA.
Acna.     Prema  Doira  CHAR.

MARE

SYRIACVM.

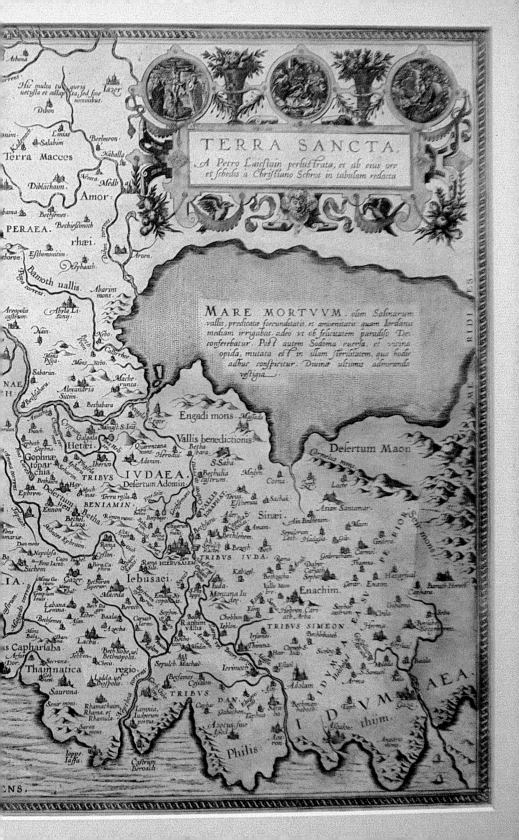

# TERRA SANCTA.

A Petro Lætstain perlustrata, et ab eius ore et schedis a Christiano Schrot in tabulam redacta.

MARE MORTVVM, olim Salinarum vallis, præditæ foecunditatis, et amœnitatis quam Iordanis mediam irrigabat, adeo vt ob felicitatem paradiso Dei conferebatur. Poſt autem Sodoma euerſa, et vicina opida, mutata eſt in illam ſterilitatem, qua hodie adhuc conſpicitur. Diuinæ vltionis admiranda veſtigia.

Athona
Hic multa tu quiris uetusta et collapsia, sed sine nominibus
Lazer
Dibon

Terra Macces
Beelmeon
Nabala
Lintas
Salabim
Medh
Nemen
Amor
Dibleraim

PERAEA.
Bethsemes
Bethiesmoth
rhæi.
Aroen

choron
Esthemonitin
Nephaath

Bamoth uallis
Abarim mons

Areopolis castrum
Abyla Lisaniæ
Nebo
Mons Nebo

Nain
Mons Pisga
Cabrrhæ

NAE H
Sabarim
Macherunta

Alexandria Sittim
Bethabara

Gophna toparchia
Hetæi
Engadi mons
Massada
Vallis benedictionis
Betha bara
Desertum Maon
Quarentana mons
Herodui
S.Saba
Corneliæ vinæ

TRIBVS
IVDAEA.
Desertum Adomin
Berhulia castrum
Mesyn
Coena

Ephrem
BENIAMIN
Betha
Terra rosla
Sinæi
Ain Bedhensin
Asan Sanramar

Ennon
Bethel Luza
Rama
Rimon mons
Bethlehem
Loch Hadufta
Maon

Napolosa
Sichem
Ramah
Eslhon
Rama HIERVSALEM
TRIBVS IVDA.
Rema
Enachim

Iebusaei
Bethoron Superior.
Iuda Montana Iu repolis
Hebron Cariath arb Arba
Gehirzi

Capharsaba
Thamnatica regio
Lachis
Raphim vallis
TRIBVS SIMEON
Hormæ

Saurona
Sepulch Machab
Ierimoth
Adolain

Thaïmnatica
Iamnia Iudœorum portus
TRIBVS DAN
Azotus siue Azod
Asaron
IDVMAEA

Ioppe Iaffa
Castrum Pervald.
Philis

NS.

Situated in the cradle of civilisation, the Land of Israel was destined to play a role in human history out of all proportion to its modest size. At the crossroads of three continents – Asia, Europe, and Africa – it lay along the great highways running from north to south and east to west. Until the realisation that the world was round, many cartographers depicted Jerusalem as the very centre of the world. However, Israel may still have been little more than a historical footnote were it not for the crucial role it played in the history and conscience of the three great monotheistic religions – Judaism, Christianity, and Islam. This was inextricably linked with its fate as a people who settled there over 3,000 years ago in the conviction that this land had been divinely assigned to them. Even during a 2,000-year exile, this belief and their yearning to return motivated their lives and their dreams, and was expressed in many ways ranging from their prayers to their belief in a Messiah whose first deed would be to return them to their home. These people, at first known as Hebrews or the Children of Israel, were later called the Jews, after the biblical kingdom of Judah.

The saga of the emergence of the Jewish people, their creation of their ancient state, and the message of their lawgivers and prophets passed down from generation to generation.

**In the beginning:** The Land of Israel was at the very heart of the region where human culture first developed. Artifacts found in and around the Holy Land provide evidence reaching back to prehistoric times. The spades of the archaeologists have turned up traces of the origins of homo sapiens, the beginning of agriculture and the domestication of animals, the emergence of religious beliefs and cults, and the consolidation of human settlements, growing from small family units into towns. The world's oldest known city was Jericho, in the Jordan Valley, whose first fortifications were built 9,000 years ago. The earliest people in this land resided mainly along the Mediterranean coast, in the Jordan Valley, on the hills of Judea, and in the northern Negev.

By 3000 BC, it was inhabited by Canaanite tribes who established city-kingdoms. Two super-powers dominated the Middle East – Assyria and Egypt – and the land of the Canaanites, lying along the land-bridge between them, took on strategic significance.

The armies and the commerce moved along two major routes: the coastal road linking Egypt and Syria and the "King's Highway" connecting Egypt and Assyria. Because of its location, the land of Canaan was the scene of many fierce battles between these powers.

In the course of time, the original inhabitants (known as the Amorites) were augmented by new elements, from Asia Minor, from Mesopotamia, and from the Greek isles, home of the Philistines before they set sail to capture and settle the southern coastal plain of Canaan. One of the new arrivals in the country was the patriarch Abraham, who left Ur (in modern Iraq) to cross the desert and to pitch his tent in Beersheba. Abraham lived early in the second millennium BC; it was about this time that Egypt became the ruling power in the area, until it faced a challenge from the north – the Hittite Empire. Warfare between the two in the 13th century sapped their strength and it was under these circumstances that the local rulers in Canaan were able to assert their independence and that the Israelites were able to make their appearance on the stage of history.

**The Hebrew nation:** The emergence of the Israelites is obscure and the only record is the Bible. This tells of the patriarchs Abraham, Isaac, and Jacob living in the land of Canaan and their revelation of monotheism which distinguished them from all the surrounding clans, tribes and peoples. It also relates the story of the sojourn of their descendants in Egypt, the miraculous exodus under the leadership of Moses, their 40-year journey across the wilderness where they received the revelation of the law at Mount Sinai, the return to Canaan, and their conquest of most of the land from the Amorite peoples. This conquest was a gradual process and at first succeeded in the areas east of the Jordan

**Preceding pages:** 1584 map of Israel, with Jonah and the whale on the lower left. **Left**, Chagall depiction of David playing his harp at the Knesset.

river, along the Jordan valley, and in the mountainous areas. The Mediterranean coastal plain remained in the hands of the Philistines. In the areas under their control, the Israelites now settled down and the former nomadic shepherds turned their hands to farming and crafts.

Their early leaders were "judges" – tribal heroes who led the Israelite tribes to victories against their enemies and strengthened their hold on the land. Although it was accepted that God was their ruler, the Israelites began to hanker for a human king, following the example of their neighbours, and pressured the prophet-judge, Samuel, to find them a candidate. His selection was Saul, who proved an outstanding military leader and administrator. He laid the groundwork for national unity by establishing the monarchy and bringing a close union among the tribes; he defeated the Philistines in battle and vanquished other peoples threatening the Israelites; he organised a trained standing army which guaranteed stability to the country and to his regime; and laid solid foundations on which his successors, David and Solomon, could consolidate and expand.

He was followed by David, a brilliant ruler and outstanding statesman, who after his death grew in the national memory to become a religious symbol of epic proportions. His first major action after his accession (c. 1000 BC) was to capture Jerusalem (a town which had remained a Canaanite enclave) and proclaim it his capital – an astute move in view of its central location and its neutral position outside the territories of the 12 Israelite tribes. Jerusalem was an acceptable centre for all, especially after David placed there the major object of the cult, the Ark of the Covenant, originally constructed in the wilderness under Moses' directions and containing the two Tablets of the Covenant on which were engraved the Ten Commandments. It was David who finally broke the military power of the Philistines and gave the Israelites uninterrupted access to the Mediterranean Sea. In the south, by defeating the Edomites, he extended his kingdom to the Red Sea at the port of Ezion-Geber (near today's Eilat). He crushed Ammon and Moab to the east and Aram (Syria) to the north, annexing large territories (including Damascus) as far as the Euphrates river. Only the Philistine cities along the southern coast

and the Phoenicians along the northern coast held on to their independence. David's domination of the great international highways in the region proved to be one of the most important factors in building up his kingdom's overall prosperity.

David's son and successor, Solomon, inherited a flourishing kingdom secured from external dangers. He formed alliances with neighbouring states including Egypt (an Egyptian princess was one of his many wives) and developed international commerce – both overland, reaching down to the Arabian peninsula from where the fabled Queen of Sheba sought him out, and overseas, for which he built a navy in the Red Sea. He also

completed the religious centralisation started by his father with the construction of an impressive Temple in Jerusalem which ensured the central role of that city.

This was Israel's greatest moment. Its bounds extended from the Red Sea in the south to the Euphrates river in the north, it was respected internationally, and its economic achievements were reflected in its external commerce and in its internal construction and development.

However, despite his reputation for wisdom, Solomon's political sagacity was faulty. Heavy taxation exacted from the people alienated them from the throne as did the regular periods of forced labour they had to contribute. General discontent led, towards the end of his reign, to an unsuccessful uprising and immediately after his death to a split in the kingdom.

**Two kingdoms:** Jealousies among the tribes, kept in check by the first three kings, could not be contained by their less effective successors, and the 10 northern tribes seceded to establish their own state – known as the kingdom of Israel. The remaining two tribes, Judah and Benjamin, remained faithful to the House of David and, with Jerusalem as their capital, maintained the southern kingdom of Judah. For more than 200 years the two kingdoms continued to live side by side,

Omri." He ruled from his new capital, Samaria, which he adorned with ivory palaces. His son and successor, Ahab, further expanded the country's boundaries. Under the influence of his notorious Phoenician wife, Jezebel, the worship of foreign gods became prevalent and evoked the wrath of the prophet Elijah who vigorously stamped out the cult of Baal. Throughout these centuries the prophets, such as Isaiah, Jeremiah and Amos, served as the conscience of the nation and their moral demands were listened to by ruler and people. In their written form, their words were to exert a profound influence on the religious beliefs and social ethics of the western world.

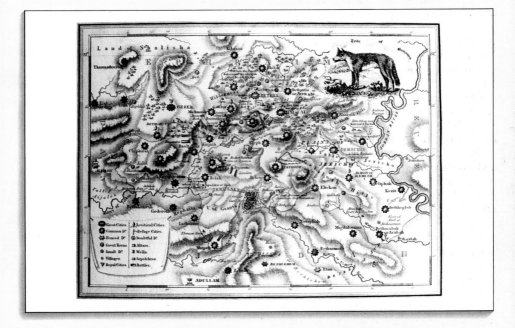

sometimes at peace with each other, sometimes at war, with the larger and more fertile northern kingdom tending to dominate. Thanks to the rule of the House of David, the southern kingdom enjoyed internal stability but its northern neighbour was rocked by frequent palace revolts and changes of ruler. Its outstanding king was Omri – called the "David of the North" – under whom the kingdom became a significant factor in the region and was long known as "the land of

**Left**, early shekels celebrate the fruit of the earth. **Above**, 1812 map of the tribe of Benjamin – note Jerusalem, lower centre.

The two small kingdoms often had to contract external alliances to survive. The northern kingdom came to an end when it joined its northern neighbour, Aram-Damascus, in daring to oppose the invading Assyrian army. After a three-year siege, Samaria fell in 722 BC. Assyria exiled many of the inhabitants to other parts of its extensive empire, replacing them with conquered peoples from faraway regions. The Israelites sent to distant lands were eventually assimilated into their new surroundings and all traces of them disappeared, although throughout the ages legends of the discovery of the "Lost Ten Tribes" – from east Africa and central Asia to North America – have aroused the imagination.

The southern kingdom escaped the fate of Israel by accepting Assyrian suzerainty. This afforded it a respite for a further century and a half. During this time, the Assyrian Empire was replaced by the Babylonian Empire and it was against the Babylonians, under Nebuchadnezzar, that Judah rose in rebellion, counting on Egyptian aid that never arrived. Nebuchadnezzar invaded the country, laid waste its cities, captured Jerusalem and destroyed its Temple in 586 BC, exiling many of the population, especially the elite, to Babylonia. Over the ruins of Jerusalem the author of lamentations bewailed "How doth

Judah where they patiently rebuilt the walls and the city of Jerusalem and reconstructed the Temple. This was no easy task as they were surrounded by unfriendly peoples. To the north, the foreign peoples brought by the Assyrians had intermarried with the remnants of the 10 tribes but the men of Judah did not accept their descendants as true Jews and tensions were high between the "Jews" (i.e., the people of Judah) and the "Samaritans" (i.e., the people of Samaria).

Judah was now a small and obscure Persian province and remained that way for two centuries. The incursion of Alexander the Great and his victory over the Persians in 333 BC brought a new era to the region, which for

the city sit solitary that was full of people," while the voice of the exiles was heard yearning for their homeland: "By the waters of Babylon we sat down and wept when we remembered Zion."

But soon other voices were heard. In the remote exile, the voice of the prophet rang out "Comfort ye, comfort ye, my people," foretelling the end of the people's tribulations. And so it happened that some 40 years after the fall of Jerusalem, the Babylonian Empire fell to the Persians under Cyrus the Great whose policy was to allow all exiled peoples to return to their homes. Many of the Jews in Babylonia eagerly went back to

the next nine centuries was to be part of the Greco-Roman orbit. Initially this meant considerable autonomy and continued religious liberty for the Jews with the Temple remaining at the focus of their national life. But there was also growing friction with the non-Jewish population of the country who had adopted Hellenistic customs and religion.

In the 2nd century BC, the country was ruled by the Syrian-based Seleucid dynasty which sought to enforce a policy of Hellenisation. The Jews were appalled at the regulations forbidding the practice of Judaism and outlawing the basic Jewish observances including Sabbath, circumcision and the dietary laws. The Jerusalem Temple was defiled by the sacrifice of a pig on its altar and its dedication to Zeus. The Jews reacted with a campaign of large-scale disobedience leading to martyrdom and to armed resistance led by a priest called Mattathias and his five sons known as the Maccabees or Hasmoneans. A brilliant guerrilla campaign directed by the eldest son, Judah the Maccabee (or Judas Maccabeus), inflicted successive defeats on the Syrian army, culminating in the capture of Jerusalem and the rededication of the Temple in 164 BC.

**Roman Judea:** For the next century Jewish sovereignty was re-established and under successive Hasmonean rulers, the country

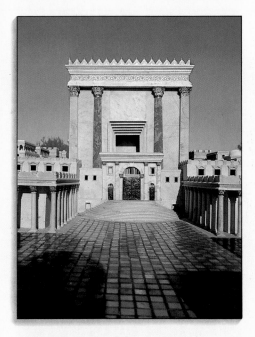

regained much of its former glory and reattained most of its former boundaries. However, internal quarrels and civil war undermined the kingdom, which fell easy prey to the Romans in 63 BC. It now became a vassal Roman state called Judea. Although subject to the Roman governor of Syria, it still enjoyed a limited autonomy under its own king. The outstanding ruler of the Roman period was Herod the Great (who reigned from 37 to 4 BC). The Romans recognised

**Left**, a medieval view of Solomon and Sheba. **Above**, a model of Solomon's Temple at Holy Land Hotel.

him as "a friend and ally" and rewarded him with grants of extra territory, including parts of Transjordan, which meant that he ruled over nearly all the historic Land of Israel. An energetic despot, he founded magnificent new cities such as Caesarea on the Mediterranean coast, and completely rebuilt the Temple, making it one of the most imposing structures of its day.

This was the world into which Jesus was born. The New Testament reflects the turmoil of its time. The Jews were divided into various groups: the aristocratic Sadducees who controlled the Temple cult and the priesthood; the scholarly Pharisees who interpreted the law for the masses and who determined the path of historic Judaism; the ascetic Essenes, an exclusive group whose way of life has been illumined by the recent discovery of the Dead Sea Scrolls; and the fanatical Zealots advocating armed struggle against the Roman overlords. Rome ruled the country through a succession of procurators, many of them inept and greedy, whose seat was in Caesarea. The Jews railed against the oppressive Roman rule. The country knew frequent uprisings with seething messianic ferment based on the growing hope that the Romans would be expelled and a sovereign Jewish state restored.

An attempt by the mad Roman emperor Caligula to have his image installed in the Temple goaded the Jews to fury. Growing unrest led to the strengthening of extremist groups who eventually terrorised the more moderate elements and stirred up the nation to total revolt against the Romans (AD 66). After the Jews scored a number of successes, the Romans brought large reinforcements under the command of the future emperors, Vespesian and his son Titus. Gradually they reconquered the country and by AD 69 only Jerusalem and one or two fortresses held out. The siege of Jerusalem was prolonged and bitter, with rival parties inside the besieged city fighting each other. Finally, in the summer of AD 70, Titus and his army broke through the defenses and captured the city. The Temple was burnt down and its sacred vessels carried off to Rome. Only the remote stronghold of Masada in the southern desert held out for three more years. The Jewish Revolt had been crushed, the religious centre of Judaism destroyed and the last vestiges of Jewish independence and sovereignty ended.

This tragedy could have been a death-blow to Judaism and the Jewish people, but the genius of the rabbis found the formula to ensure their continuity. The focus of the religion shifted from the Temple in Jerusalem to the synagogues, the house of worship established wherever a Jewish community existed (which in turn inspired the institutions of the church and the mosque). Heinrich Heine was to speak of the Jew with his "portable fatherland", and with his Bible, synagogues and religious traditions the Jew indeed acquired a flexibility that enabled him to maintain his identity anywhere in the world, independent of his location.

The authoritative Sanhedrin continued to meet and legislate – no longer in Jerusalem, but elsewhere in Palestine (the Roman name for the province, derived from the ancient Philistines). Many Jews had been exiled, but a large Jewish population remained: centreed mainly in the north of the country in Galilee.

The decree of the Roman emperor Hadrian forbidding circumcision sparked off a second Jewish Revolt in AD 132. Led by Simon Bar-Kochba, it was accompanied by a strong messianic motivation. Once again there were initial shock victories over the Romans, who had to bring in reinforcements from elsewhere; once again it took three years to suppress the rebellion. The punishment inflicted was severe: the spiritual leaders of the Jews were put to death, hundreds of villages were destroyed, and large numbers of Jews were sold into slavery. The cities with a Gentile population received added importance. The Jewish capacity for resistance had been effectively broken.

**Arabs and Crusaders:** In the following centuries, Christianity expanded throughout the Roman empire and in the 4th century became the state religion. Under the first Christian emperor, Constantine the Great (288–337), Palestine was recognised as the Holy Land. Great churches and shrines were erected on the sites associated with the events described in the New Testament, especially in Jerusalem, Bethlehem and Nazareth, and pilgrims began to flock to the country in homage. Monasteries and hospices proliferated and the Christian population increased rapidly. By the 5th century, there was a Christian majority, while anti-Jewish legislation and economic hardships led to a growing attrition of the Jewish population. Although at all times Jews were living in the country, their numbers were small, and were to remain so over the next 12 centuries.

The 7th century was a turbulent era for Palestine, marked by a brief Persian regime, the reinstatement of Byzantine Christian rule – and then in 640 the Arab invasion. The Arab army, fired by the new religion of Islam, swept out of the deserts of Arabia and swiftly conquered the region.

Under the Arabs, the country was part of the greater province of Syria. Efforts were made to Islamise the population, and Jerusalem became a Muslim Holy City, the object of particular veneration in the belief that it had been visited by the prophet Mohammed on his miraculous night journey which had taken him from Arabia to heaven. The great Dome of the Rock (or Mosque of Omar), completed in 691 on the ancient Temple mount, was built over a rock said to retain Mohammed's footprint. Jerusalem was now sacred to three monotheistic faiths – Judaism, Christianity and Islam – and attracted pilgrims from all three religions.

The Arabs built the city of Ramla as their administrative centre. Under their rule, the economy was mainly agricultural. Their domination of the Holy Land was seen by the Christian world as a sacrilege and a challenge. At the end of the 11th century the Pope inaugurated the first of a series of Crusades whose object was to wrest the control of the Holy Places from the "infidel". The Crusader armies crossed Europe and entered the Middle East.

By 1099 most of the Holy Land was in their hands. Their conquest of Jerusalem was accompanied by a massacre of its Muslim and Jewish inhabitants. The Crusaders established several principalities, but these were all subservient to the central Kingdom of Jerusalem which was responsible for overall

**Left, Crusader walls hug the Mediterranean coast at Acco, once known as St Jean d'Acre, the Crusaders' capital city.**

political and military policies. The two great mosques in Jerusalem were turned into headquarters for the Order of the Templars and a Christian church. The main structure of Crusader control collapsed in 1187, in a decisive battle at the Horns of Hittin near the Sea of Galilee by Saladin, the ruler of Egypt. They held out for another century, but the fall of Acre (today's Acco) in 1291 marked the end of the Crusader kingdom. The two centuries of its existence had been marked by frequent wars and widespread misery for the local inhabitants.

**Mamelukes and Turks:** During the next two to three centuries the country was governed by the Mamelukes, the slave-sultans of Egypt were only a small minority, often living under intolerable conditions, isolated and subject to oppressive taxation. The Mamelukes did, however, leave behind vestiges of their handsome and elaborate architecture, which remain to this day in parts of the Old City of Jerusalem.

Eventually the Mameluke Empire weakened and in 1516–17 was defeated by the Ottoman Turkish sultan, Selim. The Holy Land was to remain under Turkish control for four centuries. Selim's son, Suleiman the Magnificent, who ruled from 1520 to 1566, brought a new era of prosperity to the Holy Land. Under his firm hand, the economy revived, agriculture developed, and travel

who were brought over from Asia to be trained as an elite corps of soldiers, and who came in time to rule the country. This was a strict military regime, which maintained security and order through viceroys responsible to rulers in Egypt.

Palestine was now a backwater; the trade routes moved elsewhere (especially after the discovery of America), pilgrimage dropped to a trickle, the coastal areas reverted to grazing grounds for animals, and the population suffered severely as a result of their depressed economic status and the outbursts of Islamic fanaticism. It was a land of peasants and Bedouin; the Christians and Jews again became safe. The imposing walls he constructed around Jerusalem stand today as an awe-inspiring monument to his achievement. But this golden era soon faded and the decline of the Ottoman Empire in the 17th century was reflected in the deterioration of conditions in the Holy Land. The central government was unable to keep its grip on its outlying provinces, and local sheiks and small rulers asserted independence, leading to a general breakdown in authority.

The economic situation plummeted again while the minorities were often terrorised. The various Christian communities were preoccupied with their own internecine strife and rivalry for control of the Holy Places. While Europe was entering the modern era, the Ottoman Empire was floundering in corruption and inefficiency.

In 1799, Napoleon extended his imperial ambitions to include the Holy Land, including an abortive adventure against Acco, defended by the notorious sheik Al-Jazzar and a British flotilla under Sir Sidney Smith. Though the attempt was unsuccessful, it did reawaken European interest in the region. To secure a foothold, the different European powers took local minorities under their protection and opened consulates in Jerusalem. The symbolic importance associated with the area became such that, in 1854, one

Mary Magdalene on the Mount of Olives. The Western powers sought to protect the privileges of the Latin Christians, and established their own modest colonies.

The geopolitical and economic importance of the Middle East, transformed by the opening of the Suez Canal in 1869, turned the region once again into a major trade route, and intensified the competition for influence among the European powers as the days of the Ottoman Empire were obviously numbered. At the end of World War I, Britain at last wrested the control of Palestine from the Turks, and soon after received its mandate from the League of Nations. During this eventful period the Jewish presence began to

of the issues that touched off the Crimean War was the disappearance of a silver star marking the site of the nativity in the manger church in Bethlehem.

The Russians saw themselves as defenders of the rights of the Orthodox Christians, and built some of the first modern structures outside the city walls in Jerusalem to accommodate their pilgrims and mark their presence, including the Russian Complex in the western part of the city and the onion-domed

**Left**, idyllic view of 18th-century Jerusalem. **Above**, Turkish cavalry officers plot strategy in Palestine, 1917.

grow significantly. Although there had often been Jewish immigration – especially to the "Holy Cities" of Jerusalem, Hebron, Tiberius and Safed – circumstances had kept the numbers low. But many obstacles were removed in the course of the 19th century, and by the time of the First Zionist Congress in 1897 the Jews had already become the majority of the population in Jerusalem. Moreover, the newcomers were arriving not only for religious reasons, but out of ideological motivation, bent on reviving the glory of the Land of Israel. Unlike their fathers who had come to die in the Holy Land, the new generation was coming to live there.

Oval border text: FRANCISCVS AMENDOCA ARCH · MARG̃ · II · COMMI · IMPERIALI · COMVNI · TIENORICAL

Franciscus de Mendoça Admirael van Arragon Marcgrave van
Guadaleste, en van Iamaica, Comandor van Val de Pennas,
vander Orden van Calatrava Hofmeester en oꝑperste President des Conincx van Spaignen, opper Hofmeester des Aerts-
Hertochs Capiteyn van lichte peerden          N. de Clerck bxc.

de Hooft

During the 25 centuries Israel was being retaken by different conquering nations, the people of Israel were dispersed around the globe, and the word Diaspora – coming from the Greek word for "dispersion" and referring to the scattered community of Jews outside Israel – was born. But being Jewish is a complex identity, involving not only religion, but also an identification with a people, a way of life, and the land of Israel. The very existence of the Jewish people today attests to their persistence in maintaining these loyalties throughout their periods of achievement and duress in exile.

**From Babylonia to Spain:** Many of the Jews exiled to Babylonia in the 6th century BC elected to remain there permanently. Other Jews established a community in Egypt. By the 1st century Egyptian Jewry numbered 1 million, largely centred in the great port city of Alexandria. Inevitably, Jews in the Diaspora were influenced by the civilisations of the peoples among whom they lived, and in Egypt it was the Hellenistic (Greek) culture that attracted them. They sought to synthesise it with their Jewish traditions and the results included the first Greek translation of the Bible and works combining Jewish religion with Greek philosophy.

Jewish communities appeared in many other lands. St Paul's accounts of his travels bear witness to the existence of Jewish communities on the Greek mainland and isles, in Asia Minor and in Rome.

The first manifestations of anti-Semitism occurred in Alexandria. The Roman rulers of the region made the lives of the Jews miserable and in 115 AD the Jews in Egypt, Libya and Cyprus rose up in rebellion. The fighting lasted two years, involving heavy losses on both sides. The Roman legions conducted a battle of annihilation against the Jews, resulting in the decimation of the Egyptian community and the end of its period of greatness.

Following the destruction of the Second Temple, many Jews were sent as prisoners from Judea to be sold into slavery in Rome. In the course of time they won their freedom and eventually the Jewish community there numbered 40,000. They were tolerated by the Romans and spread out to many parts of the Empire, often as traders. However, the life of these Jews changed fatefully when Christianity became the state religion of the Empire. By the end of the 4th century AD, the Empire had split in two with most Jews living in the eastern half whose capital was Byzantium (today Istanbul). The Jews in the Byzantine Empire, mostly craftsmen and farmers, were soon the objects of hostile legislation aimed at their religious observance and economic wellbeing.

The situation was different in Babylonia (modern Iraq), which was outside the Christian sphere of influence. This became the focus of Jewish spiritual life, where the Babylonian Talmud, the great authoritative legal source book that would guide all future generations of Jews, was compiled. Jews in Babylonia enjoyed an honoured position; many worked in agriculture, others were engaged in occupations as diverse as commerce, shipbuilding and sailing.

Most Jews continued to live in and around the Mediterranean area. A Jewish centre flourished in Arabia but in the 7th century it suffered a tragic fate when Mohammed, founder of the new religion of Islam, destroyed many Arabian Jewish communities in his anger at their refusal to accept his teachings. The armies of his successors burst out of Arabia and conquered much of the known world including the Near East, North Africa and Spain. Jews, like Christians, were subject to many restrictions under Muslim rule, and suffered severely in periods of fanaticism. But as a "People of the Book" they were tolerated and allowed to practise their religion. Jews attained high positions in the political, economic and cultural life of Islamic countries. Moses Maimonides, greatest of medieval Jewish scholars, was physician to the Sultan of Egypt and other Jews held court appointments. Under Muslim rule in Spain, Jewish creativity reached unprecedented peaks in a two-century "Golden Age", expressed in the fields of

**Left**, Spanish-Dutch Jewish admiral, Franciscus de Mendoca, who served in the Caribbean, illustrates the range of Diaspora Jewry.

Bible study, Hebrew language, religious law, sacred and secular poetry, science and philosophy. Jewish translators from Arabic to Latin brought Muslim culture to the Christian world of Europe.

**Christian Intolerance:** Meanwhile in Christian Europe, Jews had been moving northward founding communities along the Rhine Valley and branching out to Germany, France and England. They were initially welcomed as merchants and craftsmen but under the influence of the Church became the object of hatred. The Church taught that Jews were "killers of Christ"; it subjected them to humiliating ordinances, such as the wearing of special clothing as a "mark of shame."

massacres of Jews. In a series of expulsions Jews were stripped of their possessions and driven out of England, France and the German states. In those places where they were allowed to live, they were subject to severe restrictions – they were forbidden to work on the land or engage in regular commerce and in most crafts. Often the Jews were confined to ghettos – restricted quarters in towns sometimes surrounded by a wall and gates that were locked at night. The Church portrayed the Jew as a satanic figure, killer of God, greedy for money.

Despite the unending oppression, the Jews succeeded in maintaining their internal cohesion, steadfastness and unity. They lived –

The Middle Ages were a period of growing horror. The Crusaders moved through Europe wiping out Jewish communities in a frenzy of religious violence. The Ritual Murder libel, accusing Jews of killing Christian children and using their blood for Passover preparations, started in England and spread throughout the continent, leading to regular persecution of Jewish communities. At the time of the Black Death (the bubonic plague) in 1348–49, the wrath of the masses was directed against the Jews, who were believed to have poisoned the wells to cause and spread the epidemic. All these libels were the occasions for attacks on and

and often died – with great dignity. In both Christian and Muslim worlds, the Jews always enjoyed considerable self-government and this enabled them to develop their own communal life and autonomous institutions. At all times they produced a rich literature: from the 12th and 13th centuries this was often written in Yiddish, a language of medieval German origin, written in Hebrew letters, widely used by the Jews in Central Europe and the new communities of Eastern Europe. The main trend of migration was to the east and communities developed over wide areas of Poland and Lithuania.

In Spain, the position of the Jews deteriorated as the Christians reconquered the country from the Muslims. In 1391, massacres destroyed more than 100 Spanish communities while tens of thousands of Jews were forced at sword point to convert to Christianity. Their adherence to Christianity was often only nominal and the infamous Spanish Inquisition was introduced to root out secret Jews, some of whom were burnt at the stake. In the 1490s all Jews who had not accepted Christianity were expelled from Spain and Portugal. Most of the refugees found new homes in Mediterranean lands. Many who remained in the Iberian peninsula later found freedom in Protestant lands – Holland, England, and the Baltic states of

Germany. Some followed the new trade routes to establish small communities in Brazil, under Dutch rule, and, later in the Caribbean. One group in 1654 reached New Amsterdam, later New York, inaugurating Jewish settlement in North America.

About this time the main concentration of Jews, now in Poland, was struck by disaster. They were the scapegoat of the 1648 Cossack rebellion in which tens of thousands were slaughtered, many communities destroyed, and the survivors impoverished. In utter despair, Jews turned to messianism. When the charismatic Shabbetai Tzevi from Izmir in the Ottoman Empire claimed to be the Messiah who would lead the Jews back to their own land, Jews the world over began to pack their bags. The disillusionment following his acceptance of the Sultan's demand that he convert to Islam engendered a spiritual crisis in Jewry. Out of it emerged Hasidism, teaching that Judaism should be an emotional, joyful experience as contrasted with the rabbinical emphasis on learning.

While eastern European Jewry was in turmoil, a new hope emerged in the West. In the dawn of Enlightenment, the small community of the newly independent United States became the first Jews to receive full civil rights, embodied in the Declaration of Independence. A few years later the French Revolution issued its "Declaration of Human Rights" stating that "all men are born and remain equal in right" and granted full citizenship to the Jews of France. The Revolutionary Armies conveyed this message of equality to all parts of Europe. Although the fall of Napoleon brought an era of reaction, the forces unleashed by the Revolution could not be held back and within a few decades the Jews of Central and Western Europe had attained civil rights. They entered energetically into all branches of society and culture and their names became household words, from Rothschild to Marx and, later, from Einstein to Freud and Kafka.

But this new freedom did not extend to eastern Europe where 80 percent of the world's Jews were then living under the oppressive regime of the Russian Czars. A series of harsh decrees confined Jews to a limited area (the Pale of Settlement) and subjected the Jews to occupational and economic restrictions. When in the early 1880s savage pogroms were instigated against the Jews, they left by the million – to the USA, to Latin America, Canada, South Africa, Australia and Israel.

With the coming of the 20th century, including the 1917 Bolshevik Revolution (which cut off the 3 million Jews of the USSR) and the Holocaust (in which 6 million Jews perished), Europe's central role to the Jews of the Diaspora would come to an abrupt end, its ashes contributing to the soil from which Israel would be reborn.

**Left**, interior of the synagogue at Worms, Germany. **Above**, the thoughtful gaze of Nathan Adler, Chief Rabbi of England in the 1800s.

# ZIONISM: THE DREAM REBORN

*"In Vienna, whence he had come, an Israel-ite, on whom the modern universe pressed, yet dreamed the old dream of a Jewish State – a modern State, incarnation of all the great principles won by the travail of the ages..."*
—Israel Zangwill, 1898:
Dreamers of the Ghetto

A look at today's Israeli – proud, opinion-ated, defiant – would never tell you that the early architects of the Jewish State under-took their work with great reluctance. Zion-ism, the fragmented and still controversial ideology of the Jewish homeland, was built slowly and almost always under duress. It is the product of a world that would not let the Jewish people live in peace.

The Jew's longing for the land of Zion survived millennia of turmoil, but by the 19th century it had begun to fade. After centuries of numbing religious persecution, the French Revolution and Enlightenment had brought a measure of liberty, equality and fraternity that slowly spread to Italy, Germany, Austria-Hungary and Scandina-via. The Jews stepped out of their ghettos into a world that was acutely aware of ethnic differences. Romantic nationalism was in its heyday, and as the Germans sought inde-pendence from the French, the Italians and Magyars from the Austrians and the Slavs from the Magyars, each people gained a new fascination with its own cultural heritage.

The response of the Jews to their new-found liberties was to immerse themselves joyfully in the various cultures which had excluded them for so long. Baptism and intermarriage became commonplace.

In Eastern Europe, time stood still. The region's autocratic rulers had no love for revolution or democracy, and their Jewish subjects were still the victims of discrimina-tion laws and arbitrary violence. Russia's 4 million Jews were confined in the 18th century and thereafter to a Pale of Settlement comprising the Western fringes of Russia and Russian-ruled Poland. Banned from major cities and many rural areas, they were jammed into towns where their dire poverty and disproportionate numbers provoked hostility within the non-Jewish population.

Eastern European Jewry's desperate plight fostered desperate notions. Many deeply re-ligious Jews advocated waiting and praying for the already long-awaited Messiah. To think of recapturing Zion for oneself, they warned, was tampering dangerously with divine will. Others burrowed themselves into Russia's revolutionary movements or tried to melt into Russian culture like their co-religionists in the West – to no avail.

**The Crucible:** The year 1881 jolted even the world's most disaffected Jews awake. Czar Alexander II, who had emancipated Russia's peasants and brought about some relaxation of anti-Jewish laws, was assassinated by a revolutionary's bomb. Unrest swept Russia, and both the government and the revolu-tionaries encouraged anti-Jewish riots or pogroms to win popular favour. Betrayed on both sides, Jews fled by the tens of thousands to Central and Western Europe and the US.

The pogroms had a profound effect on Jewish intellectuals. Many flocked to join Peretz Smolenskin, a Russian-born journal-ist in Vienna who borrowed ideas from other national movements to call for a secular Jewish state in Turkish-controlled Palestine, the ancient land of Zion. In 1890, the social-ist Nathan Birnbaum coined the term "Zion-ism" in a call for political action towards such a state. Societies to promote immediate emigration to Palestine sprang up in Russia and United States, calling themselves Hovevi Zion (Lovers of Zion). Affiliated groups were formed abroad, and small settlements were actually founded. Leon Pinsker, a phy-sician who had once advocated assimilation, produced a tract entitled *Autoemanzipation* (1882) that called on Jews to raise funds to buy themselves a safe homeland—in Pales-tine or anywhere else.

Even in the wake of the pogroms, only a rare individual could have united the dispa-rate, warring factions of 19th century Jewry. Theodor Herzl, born in May 1860 in Buda-pest, was an unlikely candidate.

He was as assimilated as a Jew of his day

could be. Herzl studied law in Vienna and was admitted to the Vienna bar, but embarked on a career as a journalist and playwright instead. Though he was troubled by the rise of an anti-Semitic movement in Vienna in the 1880s, and by the Russian pogroms, it was only as Paris correspondent for the *Neue Freie Presse* after 1891 that his head was turned – in large part by anti-Semitic agitation he witnessed while covering the Dreyfus Affair of the early 1890s.

Herzl's primary concern from the start was not in preserving the Jewish culture or faith, but in protecting Jews. He was not religious. In fact, one of his first ideas involved a mass baptism at St Stephen's Ca-

would not listen to him unless he had money and people behind him. With help from a close circle of followers, Herzl convened the first annual World Zionist Congress with 200 delegates in Basel, Switzerland, in 1897. There he succeeded in establishing a Jewish Colonial Trust as well as an official Zionist press in several languages. The Congress, which became the supreme body of the Zionist movement, brought Jews of all lands and beliefs together, publicised Zionist goals, and promoted Herzl as the leader of the Zionist cause. He wrote with characteristic optimism in his diary in Basel: "Here I have created the Jewish State."

Herzl spent the remaining years of his

thedral in Vienna, where Europe's Jews could solve their problems once and for all. He soon became convinced, however, that anti-Semitism was not based on religious or even racial issues, but on something altogether irrational. Quite independently, he began to meet with leading Jewish philanthropists and thinkers to lobby them for support in finding a haven for the Jewish people. In 1896, finding little interest in the West for his cause, he published *The Jewish State*, a how-to guide to national independence remarkably similar in content to Pinsker's *Auto-emanzipation*.

He soon concluded that world leaders

short life in shuttle diplomacy. In an effort to pressure the Ottoman Empire to yield a portion of Palestine for Jewish settlers, he met with the Prussian Emperor Wilhelm II, the Russian Czar and his ministers, the Italian King and the Pope, ministers of the British and Turkish governments, and three times with the wily Sultan himself. In fact, his negotiations were a series of audacious bluffs: he never had enough money behind him to buy the Jews a home. His great hope was that he could convince the world's leaders that

**Above**, delegates at the Sixth Zionist Congress at Basel, Switzerland, in 1903.

the Jewish presence in all nations would be a source of social unrest, until the Jews had their own land. When it became clear that the Turks were in no hurry to strike a deal, he asked the British to help him obtain Cyprus, the Sinai Peninsula or Egyptian Palestine. Rebuffed again, Herzl took interest in 1903 in a British counter-proposal to settle Jews in modern-day Uganda. He brought the plan before the 6th Zionist Congress and provoked storms of protest, but won a vote that authorised a commission to review the proposed site. It was his last performance before the Congress; he died in July of 1904, aged 44.

**Fateful factionalism:** Political infighting very nearly tore the Zionist movement to shreds after he was gone. Zionist organisations had been founded all over the globe, and the ever-growing gaggle of delegates boasted religious zealots, socialists, nationalists, and unlikely combinations of the above. The Uganda proposal was dumped at the 7th Congress at Basel in 1905, and a group of delegates led by Israel Zangwill, a British writer and early supporter of Herzl, left in protest to form an independent group. Some who stayed on aligned themselves with Asher Ginzberg (Ahad Ha'am), a Russian intellectual who maintained that the Jews had no need of a nation, only a small religious community in Palestine that could act as a magnet for their faith. Chaim Weizmann, later to become the first president of modern Israel, maintained with others that Herzl's diplomatic or "political" efforts had been a failure. He called for the "practical" use of the Zionist movement's limited funds and time to promote gradual settlement in Palestine instead, and got his way after 1911.

World War I accomplished for the Zionists what pure diplomacy couldn't. The conflagration, which could have been ruinously divisive in that it pitted Jews from all nations against one another, was turned to advantage by the foresight of a Jewish leader who – like Herzl – ignored the conflicting directives of world Jewry. By appointing himself chief negotiator for the Zionist movement in London at the start of the war, Chaim Weizmann laid his bet with the Allies. At the same time, Weizmann's abilities as a chemical scientist were rapidly advancing British war efforts.

The turning point was the Balfour Declaration, approved by the British Cabinet on 2 November 1917, which endorsed the creation of a national home for the Jewish people in Palestine and promised support, as long as it would not prejudice the civil and religious rights of non-Jews in Palestine or of Jews in other nations. With the collapse of the central powers in 1918, control of Palestine fell into British hands, and the Promised Land seemed only a step away.

In truth, the worst was yet to come. In 1919, pogroms of unprecedented horror erupted in the Russian–Polish borderland. As close to 100,000 Jews were slaughtered by Ukranian and Russian counter-revolutionary army units within a three-year period, the first priority of the Jewish leaders became a declaration of universal rights for the Jewish people. Rioting became common in Palestine, as Arabs and Jews clashed over the growth of Jewish settlements, and it became increasingly clear that, despite the Declaration, the British government was at best indifferent to the Zionist cause.

Within the Congress, Weizmann came under increasing pressure from Vladimir Jabotinsky, a charismatic writer and orator from Russia with a militant streak. While Weizmann weighed his words about the Jewish homeland carefully, wary of provoking Arab hostility in Palestine, Jabotinsky and his "Revisionist" movement demanded an independent state with a Jewish majority population and an army to defend it. Weizmann was defeated at the 17th Congress in 1930. When the same congress failed to elect Jabotinsky president and avoided a firm resolution in favour of a Jewish state, Jabotinsky mounted a chair, tore up his delegate card and shouted out: "This is no longer a Zionist Congress!"

The feuding continued even as anti-Semitism was reborn in Western Europe in new and vicious form. The Zionist movement's internal strife was no help in negotiations with the British and the Arabs, and progress dragged under the presidency of Nahum Sokolow, who replaced Weizmann. The lull can only have encouraged the tragic apathy of European Jewry, whose final hour was near when the 21st Congress met in Geneva in 1939 on the eve of World War II. By the time the war had ended and the full dimensions of the Nazis' genocidal madness had been revealed, the Jewish people and the Zionist movement had learned their lesson: they would have to fight their own battles.

Deeply religious Jews had actually been living in the Holy Land since the Middle Ages, in ghettos similar to those from which 19th-century Europe's Jews had only recently emerged. Though they survived on the contributions of the European Jewish community, they had little sympathy for notions of national self-determination, and far less for the leftist ideologies that motivated the early Zionist thinkers. Jews of Sephardic origin who lived among the Arabs as merchants, artisans and professionals felt the same way: the last thing they wanted to do was endanger the position in society that they had so painstakingly attained.

The Jews who arrived in Palestine starting in the 1870s were a different breed. Mostly die-hard socialists from Eastern Europe and Russia, their faith in worker solidarity had been shattered by the increasingly frequent anti-Jewish riots or pogroms they had to endure in their native lands. With little or no training in agriculture or survival in a strange and different country, they formed small support groups and travelled to Palestine to found agricultural settlements.

Even by the standards of the Eastern European ghettos, life in Palestine in the 19th century was awful. Sheltered only by tents or hurriedly constructed huts, the early settlers faced plagues of malaria and other diseases, and hosts of snakes, scorpions and insects of remarkable variety. They found their Palestinian neighbours unfriendly, and the native Jewish population unwelcoming. Because of Turkish restrictions on Russian-Jewish immigration, Russian Jews trying to buy land had to bribe local Turkish authorities and register their plots in the names of European Jews instead. Worst of all, the settlers soon became aware that there was only a meagre living to be made from the crops they knew how to plant. Thus, eager as they were to lead the independent lives of pioneers, the new arrivals, too, quickly became reliant on the philanthropy of European Jews – or more accurately, of the Baron Edmond de Rothschild, a wealthy Jewish capitalist. Enlisted by members of the newly formed Lovers of Zion, Rothschild spent close to $5 million in the 1880s supporting new settlements such

as Rishon le Zion (First in Zion), Zikhron Ya'akov, Rosh Pina, Ekron, Metulla and others. While Rothschild's colonies survived, producing grapes, wheat, silkworms, rose oil and other products, they were kept under strict supervision by his representatives, and thus quickly lost their leftist flavour.

The second immigration wave or *aliya* was no better prepared for Palestine's hardships, but was larger and more determined. The continuing pogroms were not the only negative forces driving the new pioneers

from their homes; the Russo-Japanese War of 1904–05 was depleting Russia's scarce resources and the army's ranks, and conscription was being forced on Jews as young as 12. The new immigrants also had reason for hope: the World Zionist Congress had been established in 1897, and the Jewish National Fund had been created four years later to organise land purchases in Palestine.

The first group arrived in January 1904, and from then until the start of World War I, between 35,000 and 40,000 made their way to Palestine. (Another 50,000 took a look at their surroundings and set sail again.) Mostly teenagers from lower-middle class Russian,

Polish and Lithuanian families, the new immigrants were brimming with socialist zeal. They saw themselves as the vanguard of a new Jewish society; the slightest departure from their Utopian vision was sacrilege. They spoke Hebrew whenever possible. They regarded the already established landowners of the first *aliya* as the class enemy, and immediately set to work forming groups to protect workers' rights. They refused to run their own farms because they did not want to become exploiters. When they were over-

The second wave of immigration was also responsible for founding Israel's powerful labour movement, establishing two organisations to look after workers' welfare – Poale Zion and Hapoel Hatzair – in 1905.

Coordination of Palestinian settlement ironically only began with the death of Zionism's father, Theodore Herzl, in 1904. Deeply devoted to the Zionist cause, Herzl had nevertheless withheld money collected by the Jewish National Fund for Palestine for fear that it would be wasted on bribes for the

paid, they were insulted. They practised austerity as if it were a religion.

Although their convictions may seem naive today, the members of the second *aliya* were to become Israel's leaders. David Ben-Gurion, the future nation's first prime minister, was among them; so were Eliyahu Golomb, future leader of the Jewish Defence Force, the Hagana, and Dov Hos and Moshe Sharett, leading figures in Zionist diplomacy.

**Left**, Zionist Dov Ber Borochov and friends in Plonsk, Poland, *circa* 1920. **Above**, Jewish elders in Palestine strike a more conservative pose in this portrait by Mattson.

Turkish authorities. In 1908, under the influence of Zionists advocating an active settlement policy, the German lawyer Arthur Ruppin was chosen to represent the Zionist executive leadership in Palestine. Ruppin was a brilliant intellectual with great organizational skill, and quickly established an office in Jaffa and launched a systematic plan to acquire land in the lower Galilee and Judea. Between 1908 and 1911, over a dozen new settlements were founded, among them the city of Tel Aviv. The Palestine Land Development Company (PLDC) went to work in 1908 to train Jewish workers to cultivate the land.

The dramatic changes afoot were not to the liking of many Palestinian Arabs. They had lived with Palestine's Jews for centuries, but the new arrivals' communal living, radical political and social ideas, and insistence on the equality of the sexes were at odds with traditional Muslim and Christian Arab life. Far more important, most Arabs were too poor to refuse Jewish offers to buy their land, but greatly resented losing what had been theirs for generations. While Arab immigration to Palestine increased as Jewish labour brought life to the arid soil, fears spread that the Jews were building a majority population that would one day control Palestine.

The Arab mood changed from mostly mute gether for freedom from Turkish rule, but their voices were soon lost in the clamour of the approaching world war.

The Ottoman Empire's entrance into the war sent Palestine's economy spinning into turmoil. Money for construction disappeared, prices soared overnight, wages fell, and large-scale unemployment ensued. Seizing an opportunity, the Turkish leader Jamal Pasha arrested, persecuted and expelled many prominent Zionists, among them Ben-Gurion.

Only the great skill of Chaim Weizmann, the *de facto* leader of the Zionist movement during World War I and *de jure* leader after, and the intervention of American Jewry in the person of the American diplomat Henry

to militant with the fall of the Turkish ruler Abdul Hamid in 1908, and the rise of the liberal Young Turks. With new hope that their own nationalist dreams might someday be fulfilled, Arab leaders led armed attacks against Jewish settlements and spread anti-Zionist propaganda. Arthur Ruppin and other Zionist leaders made numerous efforts at rapprochement, but on the whole Arab leaders saw little benefit in negotiating. They pressed their case in the newly accessible Turkish parliament, as did the Jews, and the Young Turks responded by distributing promises liberally in both camps. Some Arab and Jewish leaders considered working to-

Morgenthau, prevented Pasha from expelling or massacring the entire immigrant Jewish population.

By April of 1917 the British Cabinet had decided to invade Palestine, and had promised British support for a Jewish homeland there through the Balfour Declaration. Jerusalem fell to the British General Allenby on 9 December 1917. The following January the British sent a Zionist Commission headed by Weizmann to collect information and seek agreements with the Arabs. Weizmann met with Emir Feisal, a son of the Grand Sharif of Mecca and the leader of Arab forces who were poised to attack the Turks. With the aid of the British Colonel T.E. Lawrence – better known as Lawrence of Arabia – Weizmann secured assurances of Feisal's sympathy for Zionist aims.

The Turkish surrender on 30 October 1918 did not mean peace for Palestine. When Syria proclaimed independence on March 1920 and Feisal was crowned king, Arab nationalist fervour in Palestine reached a peak. Riots broke out during a Muslim festival in Jerusalem on 4 April, and 250 people were killed, 90 percent of them Jewish. The British authorities rounded up Jews and Arabs alike. Eager to avoid angering the Arabs further, they gave the same 15-year sentence to the Russian Jewish militant Vladimir

Jabotinsky, who had tried to arm the Jews during the riots, as to two Arab men who had been caught raping Jewish women. The Jewish community – Yishuv – in Palestine was scandalised, and thrown into confusion about the depths of Britain's commitment to its cause. It was in such a political climate that, on 24 April 1920, the San Remo Peace Conference granted Great Britain a mandate to govern Palestine under the auspices of the year-old League of Nations.

**Left**, British soldiers in Jerusalem, 1917. **Above**, a young David Ben-Gurion, dressed in Turkish fez, reflects the era's conviction.

**Britannia waives the rules:** British leaders were hopelessly divided on the question of Palestine even in Herzl's day. Men like Lord Balfour, Winston Churchill, Sir Herbert Samuel and David Lloyd George saw the Jews as important allies, and viewed the ever-worsening pogroms in Europe as proof that they deserved a Palestinian refuge. Ernest Bevin, Anthony Eden, and many others saw Arab territorial claims as legitimate and viewed the Arabs as far more important friends in the Middle East. Unfortunately for the Jews of the Yishuv, the British authorities in Palestine were not so evenly split; Churchill, perhaps the most consistent friend the Zionists had through World War II told Weizmann bluntly at a meeting at Balfour's home in mid-1921 that 90 percent of the British contingent opposed the idea of a national home for the Jews. When new Arab-Jewish riots shook Palestine in 1922, British concessions to the Arabs followed in the form of a White Paper from London. It included restrictions on Jewish immigration.

Yet Jewish enthusiasm for immigration to Palestine after World War I only increased. From 1919 to 1923, 37,000 new settlers – the third *aliya* – gained entry to the Promised Land from Poland and Lithuania via Turkey and Japan. Thanks in part to Hehalutz, a Zionist organisation that, starting in the early 1920s, trained prospective pioneers for agricultural work, some arrived with rudimentary skills – but they were as Utopian as their predecessors. Many were outspoken leftists, like Golda Meyerson (later Golda Meir), and their views sparked turmoil in the Yishuv's labour movement.

In 1920 the Histadrut (the General Federation of Jewish Labour) brought most major labour groups together in a non-partisan coalition. Not only did the Histadrut come to operate a network of schools, libraries, cultural clubs, newspapers and publishing houses, banks, cooperative stores and medical care programmes, but it also became a pioneer in new forms of industry and agriculture, and became Palestine's largest employer. The settlers learned to swallow the conflict of interest as necessary medicine to maintain Labor's internal stability.

The Kibbutz movement, spearhead of the development of large-scale collective agriculture in Palestine, was another Utopian scheme of the third *aliya*. Nothing short of fanatical in their commitment to socialist principles, the kibbutzniks went so far as to raise children communally so as to purge them of bourgeois notions of parenthood. All property and earnings on the kibbutz were pooled, assuring that the communities – comprising anywhere from 60 to 300 members – would stand or fall as one. With 4,000 workers in 1927, the movement grew rapidly to 16,000 in 1930 and close to 25,000 by 1939, and by 1928 there were already three separate kibbutz associations at one another's ideological jugulars.

Prosperity in 1925 and 1926 drew a fourth *aliya* of some 60,000 lower-middle-class Jews from Eastern Europe to Tel Aviv and Haifa, but the combined weight of the newcomers led to widespread unemployment among Arabs and Jews alike. In the summer of 1929 a dispute over Jerusalem's holy sites led an Arab mob to attack the city's Jewish quarter, and violence spread quickly to other cities. Within four days 133 Jews and 87 Arabs were dead. The British responded with another White Paper that virtually negated the Balfour Declaration, and suggested severe restrictions on Jewish immigration. Both Arabs and Jews began to seek arms abroad, and in late September 1929, Musa Kazim Pasha, the President of the Arab Executive in Palestine, warned the British of an armed uprising unless the British policy in Palestine changed in the Arabs' favour.

An even more ominous spectre hung over Europe. The Nazi party had begun its drive to power in Germany, and quickly made the nation's 600,000 Jews the scapegoats for all the sufferings of the German people since World War I. Adolf Hitler was pronounced Chancellor on 30 January, 1933, and the brutal persecution of Jews that he directed unleashed a tidal wave of terrified European refugees on Palestine – 61,000 in 1935 alone. Arab leaders responded to the continuing Jewish influx by calling a general strike against Jewish concerns in April 1936, and in May Arab rioting began that lasted throughout the summer. The Jewish Agency succeeded in restraining the Yishuv from reprisals, but when rioting gave way to revolt in 1937 and 1938, the growing Jewish defence organisations – the Hagana, a largely leftist underground army, and Irgun Zvai Leumi, a rightist band led by future Israeli Prime Minister Menachem Begin – responded with force. The British, in turn, appointed another commission, which proposed that Palestine be partitioned into Arab, Jewish and British sectors.

Convinced that the situation in Europe and Palestine was more desperate than the British wanted to admit, Vladimir Jabotinsky directed his Revisionist party to organise a boatlift on a grand scale for European Jews seeking to reach the Promised Land: the British countered by sending back as many boats as they could. In May of 1939, well aware of Hitler's public promises to eradicate the Jewish people, the British issued a White Paper, limiting Jewish immigration to Palestine to 100,000 over the next five years.

Faced with the sadistic and systematic extermination of 6 million of their brothers and sisters, Jews all over the globe reached the same conclusion: a strong, independent Jewish state had to be established at any cost.

In January 1944, Menachem Begin's Irgun called on the Jews of Palestine to revolt and form a provisional Jewish government. Preserving British military installations and equipment that could serve the Allies against Hitler, the Irgun assaulted police stations and offices and seized weapons. Many Jews enlisted in the British army towards the end of 1944, fighting the Axis powers while acquiring important combat skills for the struggles ahead. David Ben-Gurion made a secret visit to the US within weeks of the Allied victory in Europe, to secure arms from sympathetic American suppliers for the coming Arab-Jewish conflict.

With Germany's surrender on 8 May 1945, many of the pitiful 150,000 Jewish survivors of Hitler's holocaust sought to return to their homes in Eastern Europe. They were horrified to discover that they were still unwelcome. Many returned to the Allied Displaced Persons (DP) camps in the West and sought passage to Palestine. From August 1945 to May 1946, 64 ships from European ports carrying over 73,000 refugees set sail for Palestine with the aid of the Hagana and

intransigence, the Irgun planted powerful explosives hidden in milk cans in the British administration HQ at Jerusalem's King David Hotel. Ignoring a warning to evacuate the hotel, the British were shocked as an entire wing exploded and collapsed, killing 91 people. Many Jews condemned the bombing, but there was no longer any denying the bitter hatred that had developed between the British forces and the Yishuv.

With the British public clamouring for a withdrawal, Great Britain's deadlocked postwar Cabinet decided in February of 1947 to let the United Nations sort out the Palestine problem. After nine months of debate the UN produced a plan to partition Pales-

other clandestine organisations.

Incredibly, the British clung to their 1939 immigration limits, turning back dangerously overcrowded refugee boats and throwing captured refugees into internment camps. The Hagana retaliated by simultaneously blowing up nine key bridges in Palestine, and the British in turn responded by arresting 3,000 Jews, including most key Zionist leaders. On 22 July 1946, incensed by British

**Left**, a young girl and her grandmother look out over the Promised Land. **Above**, crowds of illegal immigrants gather to achieve the same ambition, under the guard of the British.

tine, between a Jewish and an Arab state.

On 29 November, the UN General Assembly voted in favour of the plan. As Jews of the Yishuv celebrated, Arab rioting began throughout Palestine and the Arab world. In the first five months of 1948 every isolated Jewish village in Palestine was attacked, and Jerusalem's Jewish quarter was besieged by Arab troops. In less than half a year, 6,000 Jewish soldiers and civilians were killed – close to 1 percent of the Jewish population of Palestine. As 15 May – the scheduled date of the British pullout – drew near, the armies of Egypt, TransJordan, Syria and Lebanon massed on the future Jewish state's borders.

# THE DREAM BECOMES REALITY

On 14 May 1948, David Ben-Gurion pro-claimed independence for the new State of Israel. The people rejoiced as they danced the hora in the streets of Tel Aviv and Jerusalem. But the euphoria of statehood needed to be tempered by harsh reality. Along with independence, came an invasion of the fledgling nation by the combined forces of seven Arab states. The concerted Arab attack, designed to "throw the Israelis into the sea" was repelled by the 30,000 member Haganah (later becoming the Israel Defence Forces-IDF). Overcoming tremendous odds in a victorious War of Independence, the Israelis set the tone for a militarily strong and politically democratic nation.

The War of Independence lasted for seven months. Although Israel was victorious, the tiny country lost 6,000 lives in self-defence. In the battle over Jerusalem, the Jewish population resisted British-trained Jordanian troops exemplifying their military tenacity. However, the Jewish quarter of the Old City ultimately fell to Jordanian Legionnaires. In a desperate attempt to re-supply the 85,000 Jews of Jerusalem, a plan was designed which turned a small footpath into a major road providing an umbilical cord of support and supply to the besieged city.

The State of Israel, arising from the ashes of the Holocaust, was immediately thrust into the throes of an unsettled international community. In the post-World War II era, the major powers politically battled, vying to fill the vacuum created by the British withdrawal from the Middle East. The super-powers found themselves on the same side for a short period as both the US and USSR hurried to recognise the new state of Israel. The USSR seeking a foothold in the strategic Middle East, was the first major power officially to provide Israel with *de jure* (by right of law) recognition while the US initially granted only *de facto* recognition. During the War of Independence it was Soviet-bloc weaponry which enabled Israel to withstand the initial assault, while the US imposed an arms embargo in the region.

Left, woman settler becomes woman soldier during the 1948 War of Independence.

**Ideological struggle:** The newly formed government of Israel sought to make a home for itself in a hostile environment. Prime Minister Ben-Gurion was charged with the challenging task of turning Zionist ideological dreams into modern Israeli reality, absorbing large numbers of immigrants and developing the barren Israeli wilderness.

Wedded to a policy of non-identification with respect to the growing Cold War struggle, Israel's first Foreign Minister, Moshe Sharrett, attempted to walk his country on a tenuous tightrope between the two superpowers. But in the increasingly polarised political world, that policy proved unfeasible for the economically strapped nation. It was only natural that the democratic Jewish State turn towards another democracy, the US, for friendship and support.

From the outset, the natural allegiance between the US and Israel was clear. In 1949, Israel accepted a $100 million American loan, making its policy of non-identification suspect, especially to the USSR. Soviet-Israeli relations, strained from the start because of the Kremlin's refusal to allow free emigration of Soviet Jews, continued to deteriorate and were ultimately severed in 1953. Although relations were subsequently resumed, Israel by the mid-1950s had clearly become allied with the West. From inception, Israel received both the economic and moral support of American Jewry whose unyielding loyalty helped Israel grow.

**Period of maturation:** Immigrant absorption and resettlement was an immediate priority as the "ingathering of exiles" began. The task of absorbing Jews from all corners of the globe while trying to develop an economically viable state was indeed a staggering endeavor for the infant nation. In July 1950, the First Knesset passed a "Law of Return" investing all Jews with the right to Israeli citizenship. By 1953, only four-and-a-half years after independence, the Israeli population doubled in size as a result of immigration. The Jewish Agency, a non-governmental organisation established in the 1920s, was initially charged with aiding *olim* (immigrants) from their departure through resettlement in Israel. *Aliya* (immigration) was viewed by the government as a priority. Entire Jewish communities were transplanted to Israel as thousands expelled from the Arab world came in a massive wave of immigration. The Jewish communities of Yemen (about 45,000) and Iraq (about 123,000) were brought to Israel in dramatic airlifts known respectively as Operations Magic Carpet and Ali Baba.

The influx of Jews from different regions of the world severely tested Israel's tenacity. Housing, employment and language training posed immediate problems for both the *oleh* and the government. An innovative solution was designed as the government authorized

the construction of *ma'aborot* – transitional camps where immigrants were housed and trained. *Ulpanim* were established to provide Hebrew language instruction for all immigrants. Development towns were created and, along with *Kibbutzim* and private industry supplied jobs for many. Nonetheless, the financial burden of absorption strained the Israeli economy.

Considering the paucity of natural resources, the nation's economic growth over the next decade was remarkable. Void of even the most basic resource, water, Israel struggled to develop an agriculturally based economy. Production rose with the infusion of foreign capital, including to a large extent grants and loans from the US government and American Jewry. By the end of the 1950s, the standard of living had improved dramatically. Agricultural self-sufficiency and per capita income increased. Roads were built and electricity generated throughout the countryside. The policy of immigrant absorption and resettlement, although costly, proved successful. By 1960, most of the *ma'aborot* were closed as the population was housed and employed.

In perhaps the most remarkable of its achievements, Israel created a green oasis in a barren land. Innovatively developing modern farming and irrigation techniques, the desert was made to bloom with orchards and groves. In the years 1950 to 1957, in Northern Galilee, the muddy lake and marshes of the Hula Basin were reclaimed to add 15,000 fertile acres to Israel's usable land area. To compensate for the lack of water elsewhere, work was begun on a National Water Carrier, a concrete channel that would eventually siphon water from the Upper Jordan and Sea of Galilee to arid sands of the northern Negev Desert.

In the early 1950s Minister of Agriculture Levi Eshkol designed a plan to make the country agriculturally self-sufficient. *Kibbutzim*, communal dwellings, dotted the countryside, and served as a base for both agricultural and industrial development. The government's agriculture policy reaped quick rewards. By the beginning of the 1960s, agricultural export had provided the world with the sweet taste of Jaffa oranges, bananas, grapefruits and many other Israeli products. Israel's agricultural expertise was generously shared with the Third World. Throughout the 1960s agricultural specialists were dispatched to Africa, significantly adding to the food supply of that continent.

**A Nation on edge:** Israel has always been a nation on the edge – the edge of war. In 1956, Israel again found itself under Arab attack when the Egyptian President, Gamal Abdul Nasser, led a vitriolic anti-Israel front into battle. The USSR, seeing an opportunity to gain influence in the Middle East, sold Egypt $320 million worth of modern weaponry. Guerrilla attacks were repeatedly launched from both Egypt and Jordan in 1955 and 1956. On 29 October 1956 Israel began a campaign against Egyptian forces in the Sinai – Operation Kadesh, designed to secure control of the Suez Canal for the West. The governments of Britain and France supported Israel both before and during the war effort.

The campaign ended quickly when on 5 November, after Israeli occupation of the Sinai, a ceasefire was announced. All territories were quickly returned. In the wake of the Sinai War, alignments became clear: Israel with the West; Egypt and Syria with the USSR. The relationship between the US and Israel warmed considerably during the next decade. US-supplied weaponry to Israel counter-balanced increased Soviet supplies to the Arab world.

The clouds of war again filled the Israeli well as military strategy, Dayan was the major architect of the plan which led to swift victory. A pre-emptive strike was launched, completely surprising Israel's adversaries. As the Israeli airforce annihilated its Arab counterpart, IDF divisions routed the Syrians in the north taking control of the strategic Golan Heights. Nasser's Sinai troops cast off their shoes as they retreated in defeat. Meanwhile, in the old city of Jerusalem, after bloody hand-to-hand fighting with King Hussein's crack Jordanian troops, Israeli soldiers, with Uzi submachine guns slung over their shoulders, wept – bowing their heads in victorious reverence at the foot of the Wailing Wall. Their lightning-swift

horizon in June 1967, when the entire country was poised against attack. Nasser blockaded the Gulf of Aqaba as each of Israel's neighbours prepared for war. The Israelis, mobilised and ready for the impending Arab attack, grew restless in anticipation of the coming assault. Israel, utilising flawlessly bold battlefield strategy, was led into the fray by its battle-tested eye-patched general, Moshe Dayan. A student of archaeology as

**Left**, a wax museum tableau commemorates Chaim Weizmann's swearing in as the nation's first President. **Above**, Russian immigrants arriving at Lod Airport in the early 1960s.

victory in the Six Day War underlined Israeli military dominance in the Middle East. The country celebrated within what were thought to be secure boundaries.

The decisive Israeli victory proved not only a shocking defeat for the Arab world but for the Soviet Union as well. Following the war, the USSR again severed diplomatic ties with the Jewish State. As a result, Israel, to its great dismay, was completely cut off from the 3 million Jews still residing in the USSR. The Soviets resupplied their Arab allies with sophisticated modern weaponry.

**The new Israeli reality:** The people of Israel basked in a wave of euphoric brashness in the wake of the Six Day War. However, along with new territorial gains, including the Sinai peninsula, the West Bank, East Jerusalem, the Gaza Strip and the Golan Heights, came many problems. The occupation of new territories, along with over 1 million Palestinian Arabs on the West Bank (also known as Judea and Samaria) and the Gaza Strip meant that Israel would serve the administrative needs of an occupied people. To make matters worse, unwilling to admit defeat, Egypt launched a war of attrition against Israel. From the Egyptian side of the Suez Canal, artillery shells constantly bombarded Israeli positions through 1970. In addition Israel became heavily dependent on

the supply of highly sophisticated US weaponry. Spurred by increasing military expenditures, greater costs of defending newly expanded borders and the uneasiness of managing a large Palestinian population, the burden of victory began to weigh heavily.

UN Security Council Resolution 242, signed on 22 November 1967, remains as one of the only agreements recognised by each of the Arab States, Israel, the US, and USSR. It calls for the return of territory along with secure and recognised borders for all states in the region. Israel immediately adopted the position that it would withdraw from occupied territories only with Arab

recognition of its right to exist within secure boundaries. Airline hijackings, the murder of Israeli Olympic athletes in Munich in 1972 and suicide attacks sponsored by the Palestine Liberation Organisation (PLO) blossomed like poison fruit in the wake of the bitter Arab defeat in the Six Day War.

In October 1973, the Superman self-image was abruptly shattered. Pouring through the "impregnable" Bar-Lev Line (a series of tunnels and bunkers on the Israeli side of the Suez Canal), Egyptian troops attacked, crossing the Canal on the holiest day of the Jewish calendar. The traditional Yom Kippur prayers were interrupted by a frantic call for full military mobilisation. Caught unprepared, the country scrambled to defend itself. After the initial assault, which inflicted heavy losses on the Israeli defenders, the Israeli military command was able to redress the situation. Quickly resupplied with US weaponry, Israel recaptured all territories initially lost. General Ariel Sharon was summoned out of retirement to take command of a quickly mobilised unit of reserves in the Sinai. Sharon was able to implement a plan which he had designed in 1968: Israeli troops, using rafts and barges, crossed the Suez Canal. The Egyptian forces were caught in disarray as the Third Army, which constituted the bulk of Egyptian forces, was completely entrapped on the eastern bank of the Canal by the IDF. It was only as a result of US-sponsored diplomacy that Egypt was saved from a crushing defeat. The US Secretary of State, Henry Kissinger, shuttled between Jerusalem and Cairo, finally securing a negotiated settlement which allowed the Egyptian troops to return home.

The 1973 war stunned the nation. Although victorious on the battlefied, the political and personal scars of guilt and responsibility for military unpreparedness were clearly etched on the haggard visage of Israel's matriarch and Prime Minister, Golda Meir. She never truly recovered from the devastating losses inflicted upon Israel. Although Meir's Labour Party won re-election in 1973, with Yitzhak Rabin at its head, the Party was in decline for the first time since independence. Many of Labour's constituents defected from its ranks, joining Likud – Menachem Begin's right-wing party. In addition, Israel's economic position deteriorated dramatically in the aftermath of the

1973 war. Nonetheless, US-sponsored shuttle-diplomacy produced disengagement agreements between Israel, Egypt and Syria.

As a result of heavy war casualties and economic distress, the Superman image was destroyed. Israel's increasing reliance on American economic and military aid was made obvious by the 1973 war; increased taxes and inflation stifled economic growth. A series of monetary devaluations was imposed and the deficit increased. The electorate turned away from the Labour Party in 1977 in favour of the hard-nosed policies of Begin's Likud.

The Yom Kippur War underlined the popular theory that the Arab-Israeli conflict

Nixon placed US military forces on nuclear alert. Superpower interests in the Middle East continued to diverge, and the danger remained for a possible conflagration.

**A tenuous peace:** The burden of continuous war between Israel and its neighbours exacted a heavy toll on the people of Israel. In 1977, a glimpse of hope was seen when President Sadat of Egypt severed ties with the USSR and announced his fervent desire for peace. Prime Minister Begin extended an olive branch to the Egyptian leader who accepted an invitation to address the Israeli Knesset on 20 November 1977. When Sadat arrived at Ben-Gurion airport, he was greeted by crowds of Israelis waving both Egyptian

could prove to be the trigger for global nuclear disaster. The USSR was quick to resupply its Arab allies with military hardware and the US responded in kind, when on 19 October President Nixon asked Congress to authorise $2.2 billion in emergency aid for Israel. When the tide of war shifted in Israel's favour, the USSR threatened to send troops into battle if the encircled Egyptian Third Army was not released. In response,

**Left**, Israeli soldiers see the Western Wall for the first time in 1967's Six Day War. **Right**, Anwar Sadat is greeted by Menachem Begin on the Egyptian leader's arrival in Israel in 1977.

and Israeli flags. A sense of euphoric optimism spread through Israel as the people waited for a message of peace. They were not to be disappointed.

The peace process culminated in the signing of the Camp David Accords on 26 March 1979. Begin, who stubbornly resisted the British during the mandate period, proved his flexibility when he traded territory for peace. In a ceremony held on the White House lawn, Sadat and Begin clasped hands and signed the first peace treaty between Israel and one of its neighbours. The Israeli sacrifice was indeed great. After heated Knesset debate, Israel agreed to return the

Sinai to Egypt along with its productive oil fields and the newly developed settlement Yamit. In return, Israel received official recognition from its most powerful and populous enemy along with the promise of peace. The decision to dismantle Yamit met with much resistance and was personally a difficult decision for the brash Israeli Prime Minister, who had planned his future retirement on the coast of the Sinai.

The framework for peace established in the Camp David Accords envisioned an overall end to the Arab-Israeli conflict. Calling upon other Arab states to join in the peace process, Israel agreed to work on a framework for peace, including a provision for Palestinian autonomy. However, these initiatives were strained by the untimely assassination of President Sadat and then the War in Lebanon.

The bloody Lebanese Civil War, raging since the mid-1970s, allowed the PLO to move into strategic positions in southern Lebanon. From those areas, the PLO sporadically shelled Israel's northern frontier. Following increased shelling and the terrorist attack against Israel's Ambassador to Britain, on 6 June 1982, Israel launched Operation Peace for Galilee. At the outset, Begin stated that Israel's objective was to clear a 40-km (25-mile) *cordon sanitaire* in southern Lebanon in which the Palestinian military presence would be expelled, providing peace for Israel's northern settlements. Toward that goal, the IDF destroyed Syrian surface-to-air missiles located in the strategic Bekaa Valley and shot down 80 Syrian jet planes.

The decision to advance into Lebanon, initially supported by the Israeli populace, which was led to believe that the campaign would last only six weeks, became increasingly unpopular as the military campaign continued for almost three years. For the first time in history, Israel was not fighting a purely defensive war. Although provoked by shelling and terrorist attacks, Israel was not directly attacked by another state. Begin, allowed his controversial Defence Minister, Ariel Sharon, to plan the military strategy. But instead of just moving PLO forces out of southern Lebanon as planned, IDF troops pushed all the way to the outskirts of Beirut.

On 30 August 1982, Yassir Arafat and the remaining remnants of his PLO fighting forces left Beirut. The toll on the Israeli military forces and on the nation's morale was very high. Casualties climbed as the increasingly unpopular war continued. For the first time in Israeli history there were anti-war demonstrations outside the Knesset. The situation in Lebanon continued to deteriorate as no clear victory could be had. Israeli forces ultimately withdrew from Lebanon, without complete victory.

The war in Lebanon devastated Begin, who resigned in September 1983. The elections, of 23 July 1984, were forced by the breakup of the Likud Party's fragile coalition. As a result of the election, the Labour Party, led by Shimon Peres gained a slight advantage over Likud.

A national unity government was formed with Peres serving as Prime Minister for the first two years and Yitzhak Shamir succeeding him for a period of two years. By the summer of 1985 virtually all IDF troops were withdrawn from Lebanon. A minimal Israeli military presence was maintained in a security zone, set up north of the border to bolster the Israeli backed Southern Lebanese Army. The government also succeeded in reducing inflation from 400 percent annually to less than 20 percent during 1986. A new currency was introduced and an era of relative economic stability ensued.

The sense of accomplishment and national harmony that the national unity government engendered was rudely shattered in December 1987 by an uprising in the West Bank and Gaza. Characterised by stone-throwing and tyre-burning to block highways, the revolt became known as the Intifada, Arabic for brushing-off. Unable to contain riots, the IDF shot dead several hundred Palestinian protestors in the first years of the Intifada. This damaged Israel's image and reopened divisions between right and left, and the debate over whether the territories taken in 1967 should be annexed or returned in exchange for peace.

Despite these divisions, a second national unity government was formed following the elections of November 1988. Though neither the Likud nor Labour was able to set up a government, the balance of power had shifted to the right and Peres agreed to allow Shamir to serve as Prime Minister for the full four-year term.

Nevertheless, it was the Intifada that broke

up the coalition in January 1990. While Labour was eager to pursue peace talks with Palestinian representatives, the Likud was more circumspect. So Labour brought down the government in the Knesset and President Herzog charged Peres with the task of forming a new government. Peres failed and Shamir was able to put together a narrow right-wing government.

If the Intifada caused Israel problems in both the domestic and international arenas, the tumultuous events taking place in the Soviet Union acted greatly in Israel's favour. All the newly liberated nations of Eastern Europe renewed diplomatic relations with Israel. More signficantly, the Jews of the

civil defence authorities prepared for a chemical weapons attack. In the event, Israel was attacked by conventional missiles, wreaking havoc but claiming few lives. By not retaliating, Israel managed to repair much of the damage done to its international reputation by the Intifada, which had become increasingly violent with hundreds of Arab "collaborators" killed by Palestinians.

Diplomatic relations were established with numerous states, including China, India, most of the countries of the former Soviet Union, Nigeria and many other African nations. The UN resolution equating Zionism with racism was repealed. And, most dramatically of all, the Madrid peace talks in November 1991

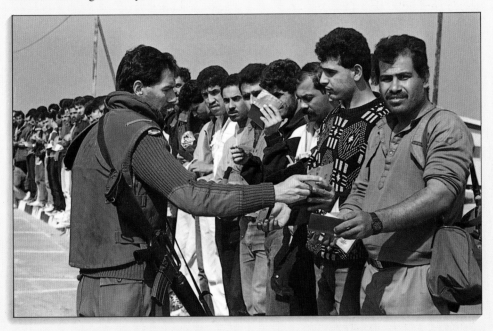

Soviet Union were allowed to emigrate freely. They flooded into Israel, with nearly 200,000 arriving in 1990 and a further 150,000 in 1991. Immigration was further boosted when 20,000 Ethiopian Jews were brought to Israel in 1991. Moreover, the rapidly disintegrating Soviet Union distanced itself from Syria and the PLO, drastically weakening the Arab rejectionist cause.

However, hopes of peace rapidly faded in the wake of Iraq's invasion of Kuwait. The PLO sided with Saddam Hussein as Israel's

saw Israel sitting face to face with the Syrians, Jordanians, Palestinians and Lebanese.

As the peace talks floundered by early 1992, Israel's relations with the United States became severely strained. The Israeli voters finally resolved the deadlock in June 1992 by electing the more dovish Labour Party led by Yitzhak Rabin. The new government forged ahead with the peace process, and the breakthrough came in September 1993 when Rabin shook Yasser Arafat's hand in Washington DC as President Bill Clinton looked on approvingly. It was an historic moment; but the real work of negotiating Palestinian self-rule in the still occupied territories lay ahead.

**Above**, an Israeli soldier checks work permits of Palestinians at Gaza's Erez checkpoint.

Israel confounds expectations. It is a nation rooted in religion, yet the majority of the people are brazenly secular, turning to religion for births, barmitzvahs, weddings and funerals. There are picturesque bastions of orthodoxy in Jerusalem, in Bnai Brak near Tel Aviv, and elsewhere a quaint mixture of medieval Poland and the Middle East, but for the most part long rabbinical beards are rare, many restaurants serve forbidden unkosher foods, the Sabbath is barely observed, and women dress anything but modestly.

Women, like their counterparts in the west, have cut the umbilical cord tying them to their homes but have not escaped from their traditional roles. Expected to pursue a career and raise a family, they have lost ground in some aspects of Israeli life. On the kibbutz, women once undertook all the same jobs as men. Today they tend to be found in the kitchen and the kindergarten. In the army, many women fought as front-line troops for Israel's independence. Today they rarely occupy combat positions.

**A people's army:** It is the army generals rather than the rabbis who have forged the nation's values. Modern Israel is a nation whose military has a peerless reputation for executing the swift, the precise and the dramatically unexpected. "Visit Israel before Israel visits you," goes the joke.

Yet the ubiquitous Israeli soldier, rifle slung casually over his shoulder, seems so slovenly and unregimented. Israel's famous informality extends even to the Israel Defence Forces (IDF) with long-haired paratroopers, unshaven officers and pot-bellied reservists. The soldier at the roadside hitchhiking post might be gay and may have refused an order to serve in Lebanon or the West Bank because of his political conscience. These are the unstereotypical heroes who undertook the Entebbe rescue, bombed the Iraqi nuclear reactor and triumphed in the Six Day War.

Israel's greatest achievements, however, have not been on the battlefield. A nation has been created out of immigrants from over 80 countries, who shared a religious heritage and a desire to return to their ancestral homeland, but little else – not even a language. In the street you will hear an astonishing Babel of languages: Russian, English, Arabic, Amharic, Hungarian, French, Persian, Spanish, Yiddish. But Hebrew, the language of the Bible, has been successfully resurrected and adapted to everyday life.

**Vigorous democracy:** Even more astonishingly, parliamentary democracy has flourished in Israel with no hint that the Knesset's sovereignty is likely to be overthrown. This though most Israelis originate in countries with no experience of parliamentary democracy. This despite the fact that almost a fifth of citizens are Arabs with inevitable sympathies for Israel's enemies. This despite the frictions between religious and secular, and right and left. This despite the centrality and power of the army in a nation under siege.

If a general seeks political power, he does not plan a *coup d'état* but resigns his commission and enters the political fray. Prime Minister Yitzhak Rabin is a former chief of staff of the IDF and half a dozen other former generals serve in the Knesset. Another political safety-valve is the system of proportional representation that allows all interest groups representation in parliament. This enables small parties to hold the balance of power between the major blocs, often granting them extortionate powers.

Civil rights, freedom of the press and an independent judiciary further reinforce democratic values in a country that takes an exuberant pride in flouting authority and disobeying regulations.

**Organised chaos:** The eye may initially see Levantine chaos and Mediterranean madness, but beneath the surface is a society that functions effectively. The wars have been won, the desert has bloomed, high-tech industries compete on world markets. From a socialist base, a dynamic capitalist economy has been built with sustained economic growth, enabling Israel, with the considerable help of military aid allocations from the United States, to enjoy living standards comparable to those of Spain or Italy.

Moreover, the diverse landscape and cli-

**Left**, a teenage Sephardic Israeli from one of the development settlements.

mate complements the heterogeneous nature of the people. The verdant, rolling Galilee hills in the north lead down to the stark and stunning canyons of the Dead Sea and Negev desert. The secular sun worshippers along Israel's heavily populated Mediterranean coast lead up to the more religious and conservative residents of Jerusalem, Judea and Samaria (West Bank).

The heat of the summer leaves the country looking parched and brown except for the ripening grape vines, cotton fields and well watered lawns. But, come November, the rains begin, driving forcefully down throughout the winter, and occasional snowfalls can cover the inland hills. Flash floods in the

Israel's population; it was the equivalent of Britain taking in 5½ million immigrants or the US 25 million.

The task has been tackled with relish, though inevitably problems abound. Housing shortages resulted in the establishment of caravan sites, especially for the more acquiescent Ethiopians, that many fear will become ghettoes for the weaker sectors of society. And unemployment plagues the newcomers, most of them professionals who, even if they find work, must usually take a drop in status. Many fall a long distance. Physicians sweep the streets with clinical meticulousness and former members of prestigious philharmonic orchestras in Moscow

desert destroy all in their path, uprooting trees and shifting boulders. By spring, the countryside is ablaze with wild flowers and fields are as emerald as Ireland itself. But then the rains cease and gradually the land becomes thirsty and faded. The land, like its people, is full of surprises and in a state of constant flux and renewal.

**Ingathering of the exiles:** The essence of this ongoing change is *aliyah*, Hebrew for immigration. Between the autumn of 1989 and 1992, 500,000 new immigrants poured into Israel, principally from the former Soviet Union, though some 25,000 were from Ethiopia. This figure represented 10 percent of

and Minsk, Kiev and Kharkhov serenade passers-by in pedestrian malls, with undoubtedly the best-quality busking in the world.

Angry with the attempts of the right-wing Likud administration to absorb them, these new immigrants used their votes to give Labour and the left a chance. It's ironic, considering that the average newcomer from the Commonwealth of Independent States has hawkish views.

**Mosaic or melting pot:** But Israel can draw from a lengthy experience of making enormous waves of newcomers blend into the overall society. They have come from Russia before the revolution, from Germany and

Austria fleeing the Nazis, from Poland, Hungary and Romania out of the ashes of the Holocaust, from Iraq, Syria, the Yemen and North Africa expelled by Arab anti-Zionism, from Latin America and Turkey fleeing cruel military juntas, from Iran escaping the ayatollahs, and most recently from the Soviet Union and Ethiopia.

There has also always been a steady flow of immigrants from North America, Britain, France, Benelux and Scandinavia, South Africa and Australasia – immigrants prepared to forgo a comfortable life to rebuild Zion. The late Prime Minister Golda Meir came from America, while President Chaim Herzog was born in Ireland. There are preju-

tions a melting pot. Contemporary Israeli music attests to the fusion between east and west. Middle Eastern music has retained its rhythms but been adapted to the demands of the electric guitar and three-minute radio slot. Food, too, produces interesting combinations: *felafel* and chips, goulash and *cous cous*, chicken soup and *kubbe*.

The children and grandchildren, whether the family is originally from Marrakesh or Minneapolis, Tunis or Tashkent, are endowed with the values of the Zionist founding fathers – though, to be sure, successive waves of immigrants from Arab-speaking countries have tempered the strident secularism and socialism of David Ben Gurion, the

dices against newcomers, but immigrants can eventually reach the top despite their heavily accented and awkward Hebrew. The young make affectionate fun of their grandparents' flawed Hebrew, while comedians find it easy to imitate Shamir's Polish accent or David Levy's Moroccan pronunciation.

Nurtured by determined government attempts towards social integration, the cultural mosaic becomes over several genera-

**Left**, an official in Jerusalem Post Office's dead letter department, which receives hundreds of sacks of mail addressed to God, Jesus, etc. **Above**, a Franciscan waters a garden in Galilee.

political and economic architect of modern Israel and its first prime minister. And, despite all government attempts, the nation's poorest are almost exclusively from the Arabic-speaking countries of the Middle East.

**A stable economy:** Ben Gurion built Israel's economy around the all powerful Histadrut Trade Union Movement. Onto this socialist base, which encompasses agricultural production through the kibbutz collectives and moshav cooperatives, much of the health service and industrial conglomerates that include the country's largest bank, a dynamic capitalist system has been grafted. In the 1980s, when three-digit inflation raged,

Israelis spoke of their "muddled" economy as opposed to the "mixed" economies of Western Europe. But since 1986 economic order has been restored, with manageable inflation and sustained economic growth.

Meanwhile, the Histadrut is in decline. Many of its unprofitable assets have been sold off. Even so, union membership today is remarkably universal, including not only the blue-collar industrial workforce but also senior management up to the highest echelons as well as white-collar professionals. Visitors may be surprised to find suddenly that all the banks are on strike, or that doctors are receiving only emergency cases. The high-status composition of its membership has seen the erals extracted from the Dead Sea. Through efficient automated and computerised mining techniques, the Dead Sea Works exports $500 million worth of goods a year.

Elsewhere, Israel must rely on know-how rather than nature. Nowhere epitomises Israel's prosperity more tangibly than the glistening, glass high-rises of the Diamond Exchange in Ramat Gan, adjacent to Tel Aviv. This is the nerve centre of a lucrative $4 billion-a-year export industry in polished diamonds, precious stones and jewellery.

**Exploiting free trade:** Other exports include high-tech machinery, computer software and electronics goods, agricultural produce and petrochemicals, with some 40 percent of

Histadrut retain much of its power and influence when union movements elsewhere in the world have lost their significance. All the same, although the Histadrut is still capable of calling a general strike, its power has been diluted by a combination of 15 years of Likud rule and the kind of competitive-edged capitalism needed to make commodities sell on overseas markets.

For the fact is that Israel must export to survive. The early 1990s saw the country selling overseas about $1 billion worth of goods each month. This has been accomplished with almost no natural resources save for the potash, bromine and other minerals goods sold to Western Europe and a further 30 percent purchased in North America. From developments as diverse as new strains of fruit, metal coils to remove the hair on women's legs, colour imaging systems for publishing and Uzi machine guns, Israeli manufacturers are best at improvising according to market needs. As an associate member of the EC and with a free trade pact with the US, Israel is the only country with tariff-free access to the world's two largest markets.

Israel also enjoys an income approaching $2 billion a year from tourism, and a similar sum from donations by world Jewry and other supporters of Israel. These are channelled through organisations such as the Jewish Agency, responsible for bringing immigrants to Israel, and the Jewish National Fund, which takes care of aforestation. World Jewry also gives generous support.

And then the country has received substantial aid from the United States, amounting to upwards of $3 billion a year. This aid was initiated in the 1970s because Israel was perceived as an important military ally of America in the confrontation with the Soviet Union. In the post-cold war era, such help cannot be taken for granted. American aid has always been viewed ambivalently by Israelis. It has allowed Israel to build a prosperous, affluent society, but the money also

want to attack Israel. For that reason, the peace accord with Egypt was a relatively simple treaty to negotiate. Much more fraught with difficulties were the negotiations begun in 1993 when Yitzhak Rabin met the chairman of the PLO, Yasser Arafat. The difficulties of setting up a Palestine council which would administer and legislate for all the territories occupied by Israel since 1967 (except for east Jerusalem) were a daunting test of diplomatic skills. On the right, the West Bank settlers did not wish to yield an inch of land. On the left, the doves of Peace Now sought to cede the territories unilaterally.

But what of the silent majority in Israel, whose opinions are seldom heard in the

makes Israel more dependent on the diplomatic desires of the United States.

**Yearning for peace:** The main anxiety caused by dependence on the US concerns peace and territorial compromise. Many Israelis fear that American pressure to hand back land to the Arabs will leave Israel vulnerable to a future Arab attack.

Giving up the Sinai for peace with Egypt was one thing. After all, the Sinai is now a vast, demilitarised desert providing an effective tell-tale trip-wire should Egypt ever

**Left, Russian immigrants go shopping. Above, children dress up to celebrate festival of Purim.**

international press? Most, tired of the constant prospect of conflict, were ripe to be persuaded by the PLO that the Palestinian leadership was serious about peace. They seemed prepared in principle to give up land but were cautious in practice about the implications. This caution was fuelled partly by a lingering mistrust of Arabs and partly by the knowledge that the most sincere negotiations can rapidly be wrecked by an assassin's bullet. Although the extremists could use such a weapon of sabotage at any time, the greatest thing going for the peace process was that the average Arab and the average Israeli no longer had any stomach for war.

If it's a cliché, it's no less true: Israel's greatest resource is its people. Under almost constant economic, social or military stress, they have created a strong, modern homeland from little more than sand and smarts.

How did they do it? It hasn't been easy. As part of an immigrant society whose citizens hail from over 80 countries across the globe, at times it seemed the only thing they had in common with each other was their religion, their lack of knowledge of the Hebrew language and their swarm of adversaries. Today, Israel remains an abundantly diverse society, but with over half its population native-born Sabras, the country has evolved a national identity all its own.

Roughly four out of five of six of Israel's 5.2 million residents are Jews. Conceived as the Jewish State, Israel always held the "in-gathering of the exiles" among its most basic tenets. Thus, pressed as it was economically, the Israeli government did all it could in its early years to reach out to world Jewry. Between the years 1948 and 1952 the Jewish population of the country doubled from 650,000 to over 1.4 million. Many of the newcomers were Ashkenazi Jews from Europe, refugees from the Nazi Holocaust or from behind the Iron Curtain. Sephardic Jews (a misnomer referring to Jews of Spanish origin) from North Africa and the Arab nations came by the hundreds of thousands, often in mass airlifts.

Of the remaining 950,000 Israelis, the vast majority are Arabs, mainly Muslims and a small group of Christians, who, though they don't serve in the armed forces, do serve on sports teams, university faculties and the like as Israeli citizens. Other minorities include notable populations of Druze and Bedouin and a wide variety of Christian representatives. In addition, Israel is the focus of unique religious communities such as the Bahai, who have their world HQ atop Mount Carmel, the Samaritans, who gather at Mount Gerezim in Samaria and today number less than 250, and other miscellaneous off-shoots such as the Black Hebrews.

Israel also serves as home for a small community of Circassians – Arabic-speaking Caucasians who trace their roots to Central Asia – and even several hundred Vietnamese "boat people", proving that its human kaleidoscope is practically unfathomable.

A final cliché holds Israelis as a whole to be brusque, self-confident, outspoken, full of life. Perhaps there is a seed of truth to this. But amid such astonishing diversity, it would be mindless to attach labels. They embrace every possible opinion and a range of customs and cultures from every continent but Antarctica. Just calling them Israelis is simplification enough.

**Preceding pages: Georgian Jews in traditional dress at Ashdod; and Orthodox Jews in Mea Shearim. Left, the rugged charm of the Sabra.**

Take immigrants from more than a hundred lands, mix and blend and the result is a Sabra, the native-born Israeli who is named for the cactus fruit – prickly on the outside, sweet on the inside. A cute oversimplification but surprisingly apt.

For millions of Jews around the world, the native-born Sabra – tall, invariably handsome, sunburnt, plough in one hand, gun in the other – is the symbol of renewed pride and Jewish renaissance.

Perhaps you guessed. The reality is a little more complicated and not quite so romantic. Young Israelis are more likely to be academics, bureaucrats or factory workers than pioneering farmers. And it's a long, long time since most of them danced the *hora* by firelight or wrote sentimental poetry about the Jewish homeland.

The Sabra scorns sentimentality of any sort. He prides himself on being straightforward and plain-talking – often to the point of downright rudeness. Argument – strong, loud and articulate – is a major-league sport, although physical violence, like drunkenness, is rare.

Ferociously critical of himself and his country, he is also quick to resent the interference of outsiders, particularly those who pass judgement from the safety and comfort of more tranquil lands.

Sabras display their fair share of contradictions. On the one hand, they are cynical and energetic in pursuit of the good life, with the ultimate ambition of attaining the "Two Vs" – Volvo and Villa. On the other hand, however, young Israelis act suspiciously like old-fashioned idealistic patriots. They willingly, if not uncomplainingly, pay some of the highest taxes in the world, devote much of their youth to the army and live with the knowledge that the next war, like the last five, might be just around the corner.

Sabras, who comprise the majority, are creating a society that is a blend of east and west. One-third of all marriages are "mixed" (Ashkenazi-Sephardi) and the resulting progeny not only look different from their forebears, they increasingly think and act

differently, too. Sabra self-confidence is no accident. The Israeli child grows up in a society that values its children above all else. He is simultaneously pampered and prodded toward independence and the heavy demands that will be made on him the moment childhood is over.

At 18, life begins in earnest when boys and girls are drafted into the army. By the time they are in a position to look for a job or go off to university they are in their early twenties, often already married and shouldering family-size responsibilities.

The state of the Sabras is relentlessly monitored by older Israelis anxious to know if the post-Holocaust generations, which have grown up in their own land untouched by anti-Semitism, are performing as planned.

The answer seems to be yes and no. The Sabras are maintaining proud Jewish traditions of scholarship, scientific research and excellence in fields like medicine and law. There is a whole new crop of home-grown musical prodigies and indigenous theatre, dance, film, poetry and literature are thriving. At the same time, young Israelis are perhaps the first generation of Jews in 2,000 years who have grown up as an unselfconscious majority. One irony is that many young Israelis scarcely think of themselves as being Jewish at all: they are Israelis, period. And Diaspora Jews who feel a passionate connection with Israel and its people are sometimes dismayed when they discover that their Israeli brothers and sisters do not always feel the same intense bond.

High-school teachers and army officers regularly express concern that so many young people are reaching maturity without a clear grasp of Jewish history and tradition and, therefore, no real concept of what their country represents and why they should sacrifice so much to defend it.

In contrast are the thousands of young Israelis who have returned to their Jewish roots with a vengeance. *Yeshivas* (academies of religious studies), which cater exclusively to this phenomenon, have mushroomed in recent years. Nothing could be further from the vision of Israel's secular and socialist founding fathers.

**Left, policewoman takes five in Jerusalem.**

Israel is the infant child of the Ashkenazim, those Jews from Eastern and Western Europe whose vitality, idealism and drive are largely responsible for shaping the dynamic, modern Jewish state.

It was in the Ashkenazi image that Israel's values and institutions were conceived, fashioned and given life. And for 30 years of statehood, they maintained a virtually unchallenged monopoly over the country's political, economic, military, cultural, legal and religious institutions.

For centuries before the modern philosophy of Zionism, small bands of religious Jews made the perilous journey from their homes in the *shtetls* of Eastern Europe to settle in the inhospitable Holy Land, where they came to await the arrival of the Messiah and if, God forbid, they died beforehand, to be buried in sacred soil. Wherever they settled – in the ancient cities of Tiberias, Safad, Hebron or Jerusalem – they endured terrible material privations. Their only certainty, the one which made it all worthwhile, was the knowledge that they were living in the ancient land of Divine Promise.

But the settlers who arrived in Ottoman-ruled Palestine from the late 1800s were an altogether different breed: young men and women fired by the intellectual and ideological "enlightenment" that soon set Russia on fire. They formed *kibbutzim* – collective agricultural settlements – and established a nascent government-in-waiting.

All the while their ranks were augmented by newcomers from Russia, Austria, Hungary, Czechoslovakia, Romania and Germany, some drawn by the excitement and challenge of building a Jewish homeland after 2,000 years of exile, others by necessity born of persecution.

In the 1920s, for example, a depression in Poland goaded many Jews toward Palestine. Unlike their pioneering predecessors, who were determined to create a "new Jew" through agricultural toil, they clustered in the towns and established a new petit bourgeoisie of merchants, teachers and other professionals.

The rise of Nazism in the 1930s spurred an influx of German and Austrian Jews – known as "Yekkes" – who made an immediate im-

pact on education, commerce, the arts and social life. With a highly developed sense of pomp and order, the Yekkes – a corruption of the word jacket (which they wore, with neckties, for all occasions and in all types of weather) – were appalled by the casual, irreverent, shirt-sleeved chaos of their new fellow-countrymen.

But while the Yekkes did not arrive with the same heavy ideological baggage as their Eastern European counterparts, they – together with Jews from Britain – brought

attitudes that were crucial to a young state-in-the-making. They made an indelible mark on the civil service and the legal code, and established a work ethic in Israel's commercial and industrial institutions as well as its diplomatic corps.

The ending of World War II brought with it a flood of impoverished refugees and traumatised survivors of the Nazi death camps. They came illegally at first, in wretched ships that ran the British naval blockade designed to keep them out.

Since the establishment of the state, Ashkenazi ranks were swelled by successive waves of Jews migrating from war-ravaged

Western Europe, from Czechoslovakia, Hungary, Romania and, most particularly, from the Soviet Union. Many of them were secular, but others were religious. They brought with them their unique customs and traditions. Some of the great Chassidic courts – savaged during Hitler's reign of destruction – have been transplanted from Eastern and Central Europe to Israel.

There is yet another, far larger, ultra Orthodox Ashkenazi movement – Agudat Yisrael – which is non-Zionist.

West – from the United States, Britain, South Africa, Canada, Australia and New Zealand (lumped together under the misnomer Anglo-Saxim), South America and Scandinavia.

These are the "de luxe" immigrants, most of whom arrive from the heartlands of the affluent world. They arrive with assets, education and highly marketable skills that give them a considerable headstart in adjusting and making good in their new homes.

One discernable phenomenon in recent years has been the growth in the proportion

A still larger movement of religious Zionists have their origins in the same religious pot as their ultra-Orthodox brethren. They are fiercely political and provide the ideological base of the Gush Emunim settler movement on the West Bank. Unlike the ultra-Orthodox, they engage in secular studies and willingly serve in the army, where they constitute some of the most highly motivated fighting men.

Added to the pot-pourri of Ashkenazi Jews are the more conventional migrants from the

**Left and right, Ashkenazi faces display a sunwashed, healthy diversity.**

of Western immigrants seeking religious fulfilment in the Holy Land. They come in spite of the political, military and economic crises and are highly visible in the religious nationalist movement.

But if the new Ashkenazim are not so much attracted to kibbutz life, they have much in common with their forefathers. They want to get things done, and quickly. They are no sooner settled than they are setting up lobby groups to change the electoral system, clean up the left litter, be kind to animals, monitor artificial food additives and protect the environment. *Nu*, as they say in Yiddish, so what's new?

If "Ashkenazi" is a catch-all for a polyglot collection of Jews from widely different backgrounds, how much more so is the identification "Sephardim".

Strictly speaking, Sephardi Jews are those who originate in, or follow the traditions of, the Jewish community that flourished in Spain (literally, *S'farad*) before its members were either forcibly converted or expelled during the Inquisition in the Middle Ages. Some found their way to Palestine, forming a religious and cultural elite that remains visible today.

But Sephardi has come to mean almost every Jew who is not Ashkenazi. Jews from Morocco, Kurdistan, Iran, Iraq, Tunisia, Algeria, Libya, Lebanon, Yemen and Egypt, Soviet Georgia and the Bukhara, Greece, Turkey and Afghanistan. Jews from dozens of countries speaking dozens of languages and practising totally different traditions find themselves, on arrival in Israel, lumped under the label "Sephardim", or "Edot Mizrach" (peoples of the East.)

Perhaps the only common denominator was a sense of their own disadvantage in the face of Ashkenazi dominance over almost everything that mattered.

The Sephardim were relative late-comers to the modern Holy Land, and most arrived destitute, illiterate and totally ill-equipped to cope with a Western-oriented, dynamic new country which had little time, patience or money to deal adequately with their special needs and problems.

Within two years of the founding of Israel, "Operation Magic Carpet" was underway as immigrants from North Africa and the Arab Middle East began flooding into the fledgling state. Most were simultaneously pushed by anti-Zionist riots and pulled by the age-old dream of "ascending to Zion".

In a few cases, like the Jews of Iraq, they came with their educated, cosmopolitan communal leaders who did much to ease the pains of transition into a new society. Others, like the Moroccans, came virtually leaderless, the educated and wealthy having opted to settle in France, with which they already had a strong cultural and linguistic affinity. Those who came to Israel were largely poor, unskilled and uneducated, and suffered from a lack of a powerful representative voice in their strange new home.

The Sephardim were wanted and needed. While they placed intolerable burden on the country's fragile services, the Israeli authorities encouraged their immigration.

This "ingathering of the exiles" was, after all, the realisation of the Zionist dream. But the arrival of 600,000 new-comers from the east between 1947 and 1952 also served to double the size of the population, immeasurably improving the state's ability to settle and defend the land.

Under the circumstances, the largely Ashkenazi establishment – socialist and secular – which was given the task of absorbing each successive wave of new immigrants made mistakes. The prevailing ethos was to transform the deeply traditional Sephardim into "Israelis" – into models of themselves.

Most traumatic was the effect on family life: traditional patriarchal authority was brutally undermined, religious devotion was scorned and children were alienated from the so-called "primitive" culture and traditions of their parents.

The results were not long in coming. By the 1960s, politicians and sociologists were beginning to worry out loud about the emergence of a "Second Israel" and to warn of terrible inter-communal strife if nothing was done to close the gap between the haves and the have-nots. An aggressive Black Panther movement which sprang out of the Sephardi slums of Jerusalem seemed a harbinger of things to come.

An across-the-board campaign was quickly mounted to upgrade opportunities and living standards. Pre-school enrichment programmes, vocational schools, scholarship, pre-entry university programmes, child-support benefits, community centres and a crash building program to rejuvenate the worst slums was a feature of the 1970s and early 1980s. It worked.

By the late 1970s, members of Israel's Sephardi community had found their feet

**Left, a young Yemenite bride looks regal in her traditional wedding costume.**

and their voice. No longer willing to be imitation Ashkenazi Jews, they were reviving old and beautiful traditions and insisting that their cultures and achievements find expression in the education system.

This upsurge in pride has led to a general awareness of the contribution through the ages by Sephardi Jews.

Ironically, the most dramatic consequence of all this social revolution was a political revolution against the very establishment that brought the Sephardim to their old/new home and, however inexpertly, absorbed them into Israeli society. In 1977 they turned in their masses away from the elitist paternalistic, Ashkenazi Labour Party, which had

compoop when he first came to national prominence in Menachem Begin's 1977 Likud administration.

David Levy has served as foreign minister, deputy prime minister and housing minister. He is a serious challenger for the leadership of his party and, ultimately, the leadership of the country. Nobody is telling "David Levy" jokes anymore.

Nor does one hear ethnic witticisms about the other Sephardi Members of the Knesset (parliament), who bustle through the corridors of power confident of their place in the political sun and representing almost the full spectrum of ideological opinion from the left (though rarely far-left) to the religious and

held power since independence, and swept the right-wing, populist Menachem Begin and his Likud bloc to power.

It seemed not to matter that Menachem Begin, himself a Pole of aristocratic bearing, was the quintessential Ashkenazi. While not religious, he was in tune with the profound Sephardi sense of tradition and his fiery oratory spoke to their hearts. The streets of Sephardi towns and quarters rang with chants of "Begin, King of Israel."

"Today, Sephardi leaders have entered the Israeli mainstream. The most visible example of their rising success is Moroccan-born David Levy, who was pilloried as a nin-

ultra-nationalist right.

Most Sephardi leaders earn their spurs at the grass-roots local-council level. Young, energetic Sephardi mayors – most of whom arrived in Israel as children – have quickly grasped the potential of the democratic system and have taken control of many development towns and regional councils.

And not a few have used their local power bases as a springboard into national politics. They have, in short, learned the Ashkenazi rules of the game. And fast.

One intriguing facet of the Sephardi surge towards power is the recent emergence of a strong, ultra-Orthodox religious party, Shas

– acronym for the Sephardi Torah Guardians – which has six seats in the Knesset and which enjoys the position of power-broker.

The Shas men are indubitably Sephardi, but are black-hatted and garbed as their Ashkenazi brethren in the ultra-Orthodox religious establishment. They represent a phenomenon that makes nonsense of any attempt to classify Israeli society according to a clear-cut Ashkenazi-Sephardi "tribal" division.

"Adopted" by the Orthodox non-Zionist Agudat Yisrael, which threw open its schools and *yeshivas* to Sephardi children, a new generation of Sephardi rabbis and politicians has emerged which hews proudly to its

look to Ashkenazim for role models: the glamorous singer on the television screen, the football hero, the high-tech entrepreneur is as likely to be a generation away from Morocco or Yemen as he is himself. But it is in the army – the ultimate melting pot of Israeli society – that the Sephardim have finally come of age and proved themselves. It is many years since Israel's first prime minister, David Ben-Gurion, said that a true new Israel would emerge when the first Sephardi chief of staff was appointed. General Moshe Levy, the country's top soldier in the 1980s, is of Iraqi origin.

As young Ashkenazim tend increasingly to shy away from army careers in favour of

Sephardi origins, declares itself primarily concerned with the welfare of the Sephardim, but also unabashedly turns for advice to the sages and mentors of the super-Ashkenazi Aguda rabbis of Bnei Brak.

Not all is political. Sephardim are making their mark in the bureaucracy, the trade union movement (whose powerful new leader, Yisrael Kessar, has his origins in Iraq), the arts, academia, sport and entertainment.

The Sephardi youngster no longer has to

**Left**, **Sephardic women in their traditional garb.**
**Above**, **a foreman in charge of one of Israel's many highway-building projects.**

more lucrative jobs in the private sector, Sephardim from dead-end development towns have stepped in to take their places. And those who feared that this new generation of Sephardi tank commanders, infantry officers and elite paratroopers would mean a deterioration in the army's performance have been proved quite wrong.

There is still a gap: a very high proportion of prison inmates, school dropouts, social-welfare cases and the unemployed are from the ranks of the "Second Israel."

But given the strides they have made in the past three decades the Sephardim are a spectacular success story.

It is one of those romantic stories that, with television's help, captures the world's imagination: an isolated community of Jews in the heart of Africa, threatened by famine, war and a hostile regime, carried to safety in the Promised Land. But whether the fairy tale will have a happy ending remains to be seen. Before arriving in Israel most of the 40,000-plus Ethiopian Jews had been illiterate subsistence farmers living in simple villages that have never known electricity or the motor car. Being thrust into a fast, technological society has been traumatic, especially for the older generation.

The sense of alienation felt by many Ethiopians has been exacerbated by the reluctance of Israel's rabbinical authorities to recognise the unequivocal Jewishness of the Ethiopians. Thus Ethiopian Jews are required to undergo a symbolic conversion to Judaism by being immersed in a ritual bath, and their religious leaders, called Kessim, are not permitted to officiate at marriages.

But while the change of lifestyle has been beyond many Ethiopians, the younger generation has shown an adept ability, with the enthusiastic encouragement of the secular establishment, to assimilate Israeli values. Indeed, the vigour with which they have protested their grievances through demonstrations, the media and political lobbying bodes well for the absorption of this exotic community. About half the community is aged under 18, and the Israeli authorities have invested enormous resources in education and vocational training programmes for them.

The Ethiopians began reaching Israel via the Sudan in the early 1980s and Operation Moses in late 1984 saw 7,000 airlifted to Israel. Most had trekked hundreds of miles northwards across desert to the Sudanese border and many had died en route. Even more dramatically, 14,000 Ethiopians were flown to Israel in Operation Solomon in a 24-hour period in May 1991. These Jews had

gathered in Addis Ababa over the course of a year but had not been allowed to leave by the ruling Marxist regime. In a daring operation aided by the Americans, the Israeli Air Force rescued them just as the regime was toppled by rebels. The reaction of the West was generally one of admiration. Here was a people from a pre-technological culture being welcomed with open arms by a sophisticated society.

The origins of Ethiopian Jewry are shrouded in mystery. Known in Ethiopia as *falashas* (invaders), they are believed by some scholars to be remnants of the tribe of Dan, one of the 10 lost tribes scattered when the Kingdom of Judah was conquered by Babylon in 586 BC. The Ethiopians themselves – who were generally known as *falashas* (strangers) in Ethiopia – claim to be the descendants of King Solomon and the Queen of Sheba.

Cut off from world Jewry for two millennia, the community has sustained traditions remarkably similar to the rites practised by mainstream Jewry. There are distinctions, though; for example, the Ethiopians took with them into exile the Five Books of Moses and the stories of the Prophets, but have no knowledge of the Oral Law, which was codified only after the fall of the Second Temple in AD 70.

In modern times, Ethiopian Jewry was located in two regions of Africa. Those Jews who emigrated to Israel in the early part of the 1980s came primarily from Tigre, while in the late 1980s and early 1990s Ethiopian newcomers have originated principally from Gondar. The two groups use the same Amharic alphabet but speak different Ethiopic languages.

All but several hundred Ethiopian Jews have now reached Israel. However, controversy continues over the status of the Falas Mura, Ethiopian Christians who are said to have converted from Judaism in recent centuries. The Israeli government ordered a check to be made into the legitimacy of the Falas Mura's claim to settle in Israel. So far, it is also unclear whether the Falas Mura number merely several thousand or many tens of thousands.

**Left, an Ethiopian Jewish soldier guards a tomb at Hebron. The Ethiopian Jews are said to be remnants of the Tribe of Dan, one of the 10 Lost Tribes scattered nearly six centuries BC.**

Not all the Arab inhabitants of Palestine heeded the call of the surrounding states (and "promptings" from the nascent Israeli army) to flee their homes when Israel was established, with the promise that they would return within weeks once the Jewish state had been snuffed out by the invading armies.

About 150,000 remained and have since grown to their present 950,000. Half of Israel's Arab population is urbanised in the towns and villages of the Galilee. There are large Arab communities in Nazareth, Haifa, Ramle, Jaffa and Jerusalem.

Israeli Arabs – 77 percent are Muslim, 13 percent Christian and 10 percent are Druze and Bedouin – present the real paradox of being at once Arab, with linguistic, historic, cultural, religious and familial ties to the Arab world, and also citizens of a state which, for 38 years, has been in conflict with that world. And yet, Israel's Arabs have managed to walk the tightrope.

The only legal discrimination against Israeli Arabs is that they are not liable to military conscription – although they may volunteer – because it is thought to be unreasonable to ask them to fight against their co-religionists and kinsmen (only the small Druze community is subject to the draft – and that at their own request).

But exemption from military service is a double-edged sword. The army is, after all, the great equaliser, the shared national experience, the common thread that unites Israelis from wildly different backgrounds. Exclusion from it inevitably involves social handicaps. In a more tangible form, it renders Israeli Arabs ineligible for certain jobs and state benefits.

In spite of this and other disabilities, the Arabs of Israel have flourished, making great strides in health, education and generally improved living standards.

One indicator of the process of change is education. Arab illiteracy has plunged from 95 percent in 1948 to just 5 percent today. While in 1948, only 32.5 percent attended grade school, by 1982, 92 percent had five to

eight years of education, and more than 30 percent nine to 12 years, reflecting the growing numbers of Arabs enrolling in Israeli institutes of higher learning.

Most Israeli Arab parents choose to send their children to Arabic-language schools, which combine instruction in Arab history and culture with that of the Jews.

Today around 6,000 Arabs are studying at Israeli universities. Others travel abroad to study, but not, like the Arabs from the West Bank and Gaza, to the Arab world because they carry Israeli passports.

The impact of education and involvement with Israel's vigorously open and democratic society has been profound. These days most young Arabs live with their own Western-style nuclear families and are economically independent of their elders. There is still, to be sure, strong attachment to traditional values and customs, but these are tinged with a clear preference for the comforts of the affluent West.

Israeli laws granting women equal rights have helped to liberalise attitudes towards women in Arab society. The changing aspirations of women (and their husbands) is reflected in the birthrate – down from an astonishing average of 8.5 children per family in 1968 to 5.5 in 1982 and expected to continue falling during the 1990s to the Jewish average of 3.2 children per family.

For all that, there is a strong trend toward polarisation of Jewish and Arab Israelis, though programmes to foster understanding between youngsters are arranged by Israel's Education Ministry.

A spiral of radicalism is not inevitable. A new breed of young Arab mayors and leaders – educated in Israel and at ease with the Israeli system – is emerging at a grass-roots level. They are demanding that facilities in their areas be brought up to the standard of their Jewish neighbours, and their style demonstrates a self-confidence that is at once proudly Arab and unequivocally Israeli.

The increasing Arab clout in the political arena is another significant development. At present, there are seven Arab Members of the Knesset out of a total of 120, representing a broad spectrum of opinion.

# PALESTINIANS

Who are the Palestinians? The word once meant all those – Muslims, Christians and Jews – who lived in the land of Palestine, that fiercely disputed piece of land which now encompasses Israel, the West Bank and the Hashemite Kingdom of Jordan.

In the super-heated Arab-Israeli conflict, the term "Palestinian" has been narrowed to mean exclusively Arabs and their descendants who originate in what was British-mandated Palestine, including the estimated 500,000 who fled their homes during Israel's

with sometimes contradictory pressures that are radically changing traditional ideas and life-styles.

On the surface, the major West Bank towns of Nablus, Ramallah and Hebron and the rural villages present a traditional face of large, extended patriarchal Muslim families or clans, to which individual members owe absolute fealty, where earnings are pooled, and women play a decidedly subservient role. Parallel to this, however, is a generation of educated young people adopting Western

1948 War of Independence. It was their interests that the chairman of the PLO, Yasser Arafat, was representing when, in 1993, he opened negotiations with Israel's prime minister, Yitzhak Rabin, over Palestine self-rule in the Israeli-occupied territories.

It is uncertain how many Palestinians there are. Estimates vary from 4 to 6 million. Most of them are scattered through the Middle East, but the main concentration of Palestinians today is the 1.7 million Muslim and Christian Arabs who live in the West Bank and Gaza, which since the Six Day War have been under Israeli occupation. These are, above all, societies in ferment, grappling

ways and attitudes while simultaneously demonstrating a fierce devotion to their Palestinian identity.

The five Palestinian universities on the West Bank, which were forbidden under Jordanian rule, were established after Israel conquered the area from Jordan in the Six Day War and have grown into the seed-bed of social change and political activism. They have a combined enrolment of some 5,000 students and are a constant source of irritation to the Israeli authorities.

**Change and contradictions:** One of the most visible indicators of change in the West Bank today is the role of women. While still less liberated than her Israeli Arab sisters, the Palestinian woman is gradually breaking out of the traditional moulds which limit her to organising the home and family and insist on a segregated social life.

Child-marriage and bigamy are still permitted in the territories, where Egyptian military and Jordanian civil law apply. Despite this, increasing numbers of Palestinian women are moving into education and today comprise 44 percent of West Bank universities' students.

In the vanguard of this social revolution is the small urban community of Christian Palestinians, which has had the advantage of being educated in church schools for several generations. This has given the Christian Palestinians a head start over the Muslims in many fields of life, and they are resented accordingly, both for their wealth and for their ability to adapt into the new social and technological realities.

However, many young Christian Palestinians are in the forefront of PLO support on the West Bank. This has presented some acute dilemmas for them, not least during Israel's 1982 invasion of Lebanon, when Israeli forces were supporting Lebanese Christian militias in their struggle against growing PLO domination.

Living standards for Palestinians in the West Bank and Gaza rose dramatically under Israeli rule, and this led directly to a 30 percent population increase since the Six Day War: while they have one of the highest birthrates in the world, there has been a dramatic decrease in infant mortality (one-fifth of the Egyptian rate and one-third of the Jordanian rate), and a big increase in life-expectancy (from 48 to 62 years.) Today, a remarkable 45 percent of the population is under the age of 14. Moreover, there has been a decline in emigration as a result of improved local employment opportunities, both in the occupied territories and in Israel itself, where the construction industry relies almost exclusively on Palestinian labour.

A boom in agriculture on the West Bank,

where local farmers have taken advantage of Israeli-developed technology, coupled with Israel's "open-bridges" policy between Jordan and the West Bank, meant prosperity for thousands who exported West Bank produce to Jordan and, from there, throughout the Arab world. The same "open-bridges" policy meant that West Bank residents – who continued to hold Jordanian passports – were not isolated from the Arab world or from their families in Jordan and elsewhere.

In terms of housing, ownership of house-

hold goods, and access to education, the Palestinians of the West Bank and Gaza became measurably better off than people in neighbouring Arab states. But Jewish nationalism gave birth to Palestinian nationalism and, however great the material benefits the Jewish state brought to the Palestinians in the West Bank and Gaza, these could not compensate for their overwhelming sense of being a dispossessed people. Indeed, if anything, the emergence of a burgeoning Palestinian middle-class that was both confident and articulate fuelled the fires of nationalism and increased the Palestinians' demand for self-determination.

**Left**, group portrait in an Old City café. **Above**, making a point outside Jerusalem.

Nowhere in the world is the observant traveller more aware of the rich and fascinating diversity of Christianity than in the Holy Land. On a morning's stroll through the Old City of Jerusalem, he might encounter Greek Orthodox or Syrian Orthodox monks, Ethiopian and Coptic clergymen, Armenian priests, Catholic priests and, without knowing it, clerics and scholars from virtually every Protestant church in Christendom.

There is no mystery to the extraordinary variety of Christian congregations in the Holy Land. From the time of the Byzantines (324–636 AD) through the era of the Crusader kingdoms (1099–1291) and 400 years of Ottoman rule (1517–1917) until today, churches sought to establish – then struggled to retain – a presence in the land where their faith was born.

The result is a plethora of denominations served by 2,500 clergy from almost every nation on earth. The Greek Orthodox, Russian Orthodox, Roman Catholics, Syrian Catholics, Maronites, Greek Catholics, Armenian Catholics, Chaldean Catholics, Armenian Orthodox, Syrian Orthodox (Jacobites), Copts, Ethiopian Orthodox – all have secured claims, sometimes competing claims, to revered holy sites.

The "younger" churches – the Anglicans, the Church of Scotland, the Seventh Day Adventists, the Pentacostals, the Church of Christ, the Baptists, the Brethren, the Menonnites and the Jehovah's Witnesses – maintain institutions and congregations.

The founding of Israel provoked unease among the Christians, who were uncertain what to expect from the new Jewish state and were deeply suspicious of Jewish intentions (the Vatican still does not recognise Israel). Nevertheless, Israel's Declaration of Independence spelt out the state's attitude to the diverse faiths within its borders, pledging to "guarantee the freedom of religion, conscience, education and culture (and) safeguard the holy places of all religions."

The Six Day War of 1967, which left Israeli forces in control of the old city of Jerusalem, revived religious misgivings. Yet, the Israeli government has been scrupulous in its attitude toward the rights and prerogatives of the churches, adhering to the intricate balance created by the Ottoman rulers and British Mandatory authority in apportioning responsibility for the holy places.

As a result, relations have been good – or at least correct – between the Jewish state and the churches. Indeed at times, the Israeli government has found itself a reluctant referee of intra-Christian rivalries.

A recent phenomenon that is having an impact on the face of the Holy Land and Christian-Jewish relations is the world-wide

growth of Christian Zionism, which regards the birth of the State of Israel as a fulfilment of biblical prophecy. Over the past decades, theological and ecumenical institutions have mushroomed to cater to this movement and enable young Christians to study in Israel.

The "Christian Embassy" in Jerusalem – the focus of much Christian-Zionist activity – has delighted and intrigued many Israelis. But it has dismayed others who fear that the real intention of their proclamations of friendship is the conversion of Jews.

This deeply held suspicion was given expression in vociferous opposition to a Mormon project on four acres of prime land overlooking the Old City – a likely precursor to other Christian groups which are seeking a toehold in the Holy Land. Among them, the Apostolic Church of Switzerland, Nigeria's Celestial Church of Christ, the Korean Evangelical Church and the Hope of Israel Church in California.

The work of Christian-Jewish reconciliation is, however, not the sole preserve of the "new" churches. The Roman Catholic order of the Sisters of Zion, established in Jerusalem in 1855 by French Jewish converts to

Christianity, has been working towards such understanding for many years.

Every year, some 250,000 pilgrims visit the order's Ecce Homo Convent next to the Second Station of the Cross on the Via Dolorosa and many stay to hear the sisters speak of Jesus the Jew and of Judaism as the wellspring of their faith. The sisters study Jewish history and the Talmud and sometimes celebrate Mass in Hebrew. They hold classes for Jews and Arabs wanting to learn each other's

**Above, Greek Orthodox Christians celebrate Christmas amid the rich surroundings of their church in Bethlehem.**

languages, and have set up a department of adult education at the Hebrew University with a convent sister as its administrator.

The Hebrew University boasts yet another Catholic of note: Father Marcel Dubois, a Dominican monk, is chairman of the university's philosophy department.

The grassroots language of Christianity in Israel is Arabic. The great majority of Israel's 100,000 Christians (including the 13,700 Christians of East Jerusalem) are Arabs and the parish clergy who serve them are either Arabs or Arabic-speaking.

The allegiances of Christian Arabs in Israel clearly favour the established Patriarchates: there are 35,000 Greek Catholics; 32,000 Greek Orthodox; and 20,000 Catholics. There are small communities of Anglicans and Lutherans (both churches are stronger on the West Bank than in Israel proper), and despite more than 100 years of missionary work by more than 50 organisations, there are no more than 1,000 local Arab adherents of evangelical churches. There are also about 2,000 Messianic Jews, mostly immigrants from Eastern Europe.

The Roman Catholic Church has established indigenous orders, such as the Rosary Sisters and the Sisters of St Joseph, and at its seminary in Jerusalem trains Arab priests from both Israel and Jordan.

Arab Christians, while growing in numbers and flourishing economically – particularly those living in areas that attract Christian tourism – have been hesitant about asserting themselves politically to press issues of specific Christian concern. As a group, the Christian community displays many of the characteristics of a marginal minority trying to maintain a balance between its Christian identity, Arab nationalism and its delicate relations with its Muslim neighbours – all within the context of a Jewish society.

Nonetheless, an Anglican Arab clergyman is prominent in the Arab-Jewish Progressive List for Peace, a political party which supports the establishment of a Palestinian state on the West Bank. Israel's Greek Orthodox community, on the other hand, traditionally supports the oddest political bedfellow: the Communist Party.

Although some of the first clashes between the Jewish pioneers in the 1880s and the local residents were with Druze villagers in Metulla and other parts of Galilee, Israel's Druze community has traditionally been loyal to the Israeli state. Young Druze are conscripted into the Israel Defence Forces, and many serve in the regular army in the paratroops, armoured corps and reconnaisance units and border police. Traditionally a warlike people, always ready to defend their interests, they have proved to be first-class soldiers and large numbers of Druze have been decorated for bravery.

In the Lebanon war of 1982–84, Israel's Druze found themselves in a delicate position, when the IDF was aligned with Christian forces in Lebanon fighting the Lebanese Druze. It is a tribute to the strength of the friendship between the Jewish and Druze that their alliance survived this period.

The Druze have been a persecuted minority in the Middle East since they broke off from mainstream Islam in the 11th century, accepting the claims to divinity of the Egyptian Caliph El-Hakim Abu Ali el-Mansur. For this reason they tend to inhabit inaccessible mountain ranges, where they can defend themselves against their enemies. Most Druze live today in the Mount Lebanon region of Lebanon, in Jebel Druze in Syria and some 70,000 of them in the hills of Galilee and on the Carmel range in Israel, with a further 15,000 in the Golan Heights.

There are records of Druze communities in Galilee as early as the 13th century, but the first Mount Carmel settlement was established in 1590 when Syrian Druze fled their homes after an abortive revolt against the Turkish sultan.

Their villages are not very different from Arab villages in Galilee and the coastal plain, although the elders do not wear a black headband with their *keffiye* head-dresses, as the Arabs do. The older Druze tend to cultivate impressive moustaches. The women dress in modern style, the younger ones in jeans and short-sleeved blouses. The young

**Left**, a Druze village elder in Pekiin looks dapper in his traditional clothing.

men are indistinguishable from Israeli Jews, and indeed many of them affect Hebrew names, such as Rafi or Ilan.

There are tendencies both to assimilate into the Jewish society, and to convert to Islam and assimilate into the local Arab society; but these are definitely minority movements, and most Druze are proud of their identity and culture and do not intermarry with other communities.

Some Israeli Druze live in mixed villages, notably Pekiin in Galilee, where they lived alongside their Christian Arab neighbours and some Jewish families, who have lived there since Second Temple times.

The Druze were recognised as a separate religious community with their own courts in 1957. Their religion is said to be similar to that of the Isma'ili Muslims. The sheikhs, the religious leaders of the community, guard its secrets, and the ordinary Druze are simply required to observe the basic moral laws prohibiting murder, adultery, and theft.

They have their interpretations of Jewish, Muslim and Christian prophets, believing their missions were revealed to a select group, first of whom was Jethro, the father-in-law of Moses. One of their religious festivals is an annual pilgrimage to the putative grave of Jethro, near the Horns of Hittim in Galilee.

Traditionally the Druze were successful hill farmers; but with the development of modern agriculture this declined. However, their traditional weaving, carpet-making, basketwork and other crafts are flourishing. Daliyat el-Carmel, south of Haifa, has the biggest market offering Druze wares, and is a popular spot for tourists. Most young Druze work today in industry and service.

Serving alongside the Druze in the minorities unit of the IDF are the Circassians, which in Israel number nearly 3,000. The Circassians are a Caucasian mountain people, originating in Russia; most of them are blond, and have blue or green eyes. Although many of the Russian Circassians are professing Christians, the Middle East branch of the people are Muslims. Almost all the Israeli Circassians live in the village of Kfar Kama, overlooking Lake Kinneret in Galilee, and Rechaniya.

# BEDOUIN

The Bedouin is the quintessential Arab, the nomad herdsman, dressed in flowing robes, riding his camel across the sands, pitching his tent under the palms before riding on to his next camping site. Like many romantic images, this one is false – or at least rather out of date.

Some 20 percent of Israel's 70,000 Bedouin live in Galilee and the coastal plain in settled villages, virtually indistinguishable from other Arab villages.

In the Negev traditions are stronger, and you can still be invited for coffee, reclining on cushions under the black goat's hair, but few Bedouin still live in the traditional manner. Some still live in tents; more possess camels and herd sheep and goats; but increasing numbers are moving into permanent housing, and work in construction, industry, services and transportation.

They farm the loess soil extensively, growing mostly barley and wheat, but also cucumbers, tomatoes, peppers, watermelons, and almonds, figs and vines. The latter is carried out using both dams, which they have built themselves, and former Nabatean structures, which they have restored. They also use ancient water cisterns, which they have excavated, and of course old wells.

While the Bedouin are not conscripted into the Israel Defence Forces, many serve in the army as scouts and trackers, and several have reached senior rank.

Scores of Bedouin fled from the Negev from 1947 to 1949, around the time of Israel's War of Independence; but later returned. The situation was stabilised in 1953, when a census was conducted, all those present at the time being accepted as citizens of Israel.

Formerly wandering freely between Transjordan, the Judean Desert, the Negev and Sinai, the Bedouin were forced to recognise the new international realities in the early 1950s. Israel's Bedouin are now confined to an area east of Beersheba going north as far as the former border with Jordan, and south as far as Dimona. This is only some 10 percent of the area over which they once wandered; but includes some excellent farming land. Today, there is no tribe that does not farm as well as herd.

The traditional life of the Bedouin shepherd, involving moving their herds from pasture to pasture, is a thing of the past and their camps have long been permanent in the Negev; but their nomadic tradition, and their tendency to live with their dwellings spread out all over the desert, have made it difficult to plan modern villages for them.

Today, most of the major tribal centres have their own elementary schools and there is now a modern high school at Kuseifa near Arad. Bedouin take education seriously, walking more than 10 miles to school where necessary. It is a common sight, when driving from Beersheba to Arad or Dimona, to see a Bedouin boy, walking through the desert, his nose buried in the pages of a book, or sitting on a rock, writing in a notebook.

Bedouin arts and crafts still exist, with a flourishing home industry, based on weaving, sewing and embroidery. These wares are on sale, notably, in the Beersheba market every Thursday, a popular tourist attraction.

**Left**, tending the fire in a Bedouin guest tent. **Right**, displaying touristic wares at Beersheba Bedouin market.

Over the centuries, pilgrims of all faiths found gratification journeying to the Holy Land, and today their shrines remain powerful magnets to individuals across the globe. Jews flock to the Western Wall; Christians to the Via Dolorosa and the Church of the Holy Sepulchre; Muslims worship at the magnificent Dome of the Rock. The Bahai have their world centre on Mount Carmel in Haifa.

In recent years, Israel has made great efforts to accommodate these visitors and hordes of lotion-toting pleasure-seekers. Perhaps, then, it is not pushing a point too far to recognise Israel's tourists as an all-embracing faith of their own, with Jerusalem's Jaffa Gate as their best-loved gathering point and the mighty tower-and-beach strip of Tel Aviv their cathedral.

With the flood of visitors exceeding 1½ million people a year, Israel's tourist population is nothing to shrug away. From their vital role in the economy of this resource-pressed nation to their impact on the look and style of the already teeming spectrum of faces here, Israel's demanding tourist population is aggressively making its presence felt from coast to coast.

In both motivation and point of origin, the tourists are a happily mixed lot. Approximately half of all tourists today hail from Europe. Close to that continent in terms of geography, airfare and living standards but a world away in terms of culture and mystique, Israel to these travellers means the Mediterranean sun, sand and antiquity.

The country's youth hostels are regularly crowded with German-, French-, Dutch- or English-speaking backpackers of all ages, and the popular kibbutz volunteer programme has routinely been composed in part by adventurous European teens out for a unique – and free – Israeli experience. (In recent years the programme has been curtailed somewhat, with the complaint that the visitors were introducing loose sexual *mores* and other disruptive habits among the younger generation of kibbutzniks.)

A third of all tourists come from the United States and the rest of North America, while the others come from all over.

Understandably, a large number of tourists are Jews, looking to re-acquaint themselves with their roots or to celebrate Passover, Channukah or other Jewish holidays in the place of their origin. Jewish youths descend on Israel by the tens of thousands each summer, to the *kibbutzim*, to *yeshivas*, to archaeological digs and to special programmes arranged by the Hebrew, Tel Aviv or other universities.

Yet over half the total number are Christians, including some 300,000 who come specifically as pilgrims, either individually or on Holy Land tours especially organised around a Christian itinerary.

**An ancient resort:** Historically, the Levant ranks among the earliest recreational retreats known to man and, if fabled Eden was indeed located here, served as the original inspiration for the entire concept. Abraham passed through, as did the Children of Israel during their quest for the Promised Land, and the two spies who described to Moses a "Land of Milk and Honey", carrying a giant cluster of grapes between them, have since become the official logo of the Israel Government Tourism Ministry.

Jewish pilgrimage dates back to the destruction of the Second Temple and found expression in the famous 12th-century travelogue of Benjamin of Tudela. Christian pilgrimage, spurred by the discoveries of St Helena in the 3rd century, further blossomed after the Christianisation of the Byzantine Empire under her son Constantine (and eventually reached a grim pinnacle with the bloody Crusades). The Ummayid Caliphs, who ruled from 651 to 750, deemed Jerusalem as holy as Mecca and Medina, and vacationed along the Jordan River close by, while ruins at the hot springs of Tiberius and Hammat Gader attest to Roman appreciation of the area's natural resources.

Today, the tourist industry brings in nearly $2 billion in much-needed foreign currency each year and, despite setbacks from time to time as a result of upsurges in Middle East violence, it enjoys continuing expansion, with enviably year-round business.

**Wish you were here; well-groomed models wave from a friendly camel. Next stop, Nazareth!**

Visitors to Israel notice them as soon as they arrive at Ben-Gurion Airport. They see them strolling in the streets of the cities, lounging at the outdoor cafés, hitchhiking on country roads, checking purses and parcels at the entrances to public buildings, supermarkets and cinemas. Soldiers – of all shapes and sizes, of all ages, and of both sexes.

Since they've never known peace, Israelis don't give a second thought to sitting on a bus next to a youth with a submachine gun, or to seeing uniforms among the audience at a concert (or even occasionally among the musicians). The time to worry, say the locals, is when you *don't* see soldiers around.

**The defence burden:** Israelis are reportedly the most heavily taxed people in the world, and the chief reason for that is the maintenance of defence. The nation is forced to expend 24 percent of its gross national product on the Israel Defence Force (IDF). By comparison, the United States devotes 7 percent of its GNP to defence, most other countries even less. But, because 5 million Israelis can never hope to have a quantitative edge against 250 million Arabs, their only hope is to maintain the qualitative balance.

The Israeli people feel the impact of the IDF very personally: by being part of this "people's army". Few are enthusiastic about devoting time to military service, but virtually everybody serves. At the age of 18, men are drafted for national service for three years, women for two. Men in the Navy and Air Force normally serve an extra year.

Married women are exempt from military service, as are women from religious backgrounds, although some of the latter do serve and many volunteer for alternate national service. Men devoting themselves full-time in religious academies may be exempted, although many participate in a special programme that combines army life with religious studies. Non-Jews are exempted, but many volunteer; Bedouin, for example, are famed as army trackers and scouts, and the Druze have long distinguished themselves in the army and the paramilitary Border Police.

**Service at will:** The vast majority of Israelis who do serve in the army do so freely. Applications for elite combat units always

outnumber available places, and there are always more young men eager to be pilots than there are planes. It is also not unusual for someone who is turned down for military service for health reasons, or because he has a prison record, to petition the Defence Ministry or even go to court to secure his right to serve in the army. Not doing army duty is something of a social stigma.

Interestingly, the country's active grassroots peace movement was started by reserve combat officers, who still serve as its

leaders; indeed, some reserve generals are in the forefront of the peace movement. "The peace camp in Israel doesn't include pacifists," says dovish one-time Knesset Member Mordechai Bar-On, a former IDF chief education officer. "We recognise the necessity of the army, and we believe in serving in it. Even as we urge every effort to make peace with our neighbours, we favour a strong army, and a good army."

The IDF has places for young people with just about every interest or inclination. The army, for example, maintains its own entertainment corps, where almost every major professional actor, singer or dancer in Israel gets a start. The army's lively radio station is widely listened to by the civilian population. IDF teachers and social workers serve in poor development towns and help in the absorption of new immigrants.

**A woman's place:** Although women fought alongside men in the 1948 War of Independence, no Israeli amazons – contrary to popular belief abroad – take part in combat today. They do get most of the desk jobs, so as to free the men for their battlefield roles, but more and more women have also been called

motion also comes early – and, in the upper echelons, so does retirement. Generals are usually put out to pasture at age 45. The result is that the IDF exudes youthfulness and an informality rarely found in an army.

The IDF does not publish manpower figures, but analysts abroad believe the standing army numbers around a modest 100,000. For proper defence, the nation relies on its reserve force, which foreign observers say consists of about 500,000. Women are generally not called for reserve duty, although

on to help prepare the men for combat units. So it's not unusual to find women training men on the rifle range, in field artillery units, or in the tank corps.

The presence of women throughout the IDF is hardly the only uncommon aspect of Israeli army life. Because the manpower pool is small and the defence needs large, young recruits are often given enormous responsibility quickly. It is not surprising to find an 18- or 19-year-old soldier in charge of a piece of equipment costing $500,000. Pro-

**Left**, a female tank instructor. **Above**, a playful tug-of-war provides training for the real thing.

they may be on tap for specialised technical tasks, administrative work or civil-defence jobs. Men are liable for about 35 days a year of reserve army duty and refresher courses. This obligation continues up to age 50, and for the next five years men must do an annual stint of civil defence service.

The Israel Defence Force serves as the society's greatest glue. It's where the new immigrant best learns his Hebrew, and where people from vastly different backgrounds learn about each other. Perhaps more than in any other sense, the Israeli army is where a multifaceted nation puts on a uniform and really becomes one people.

There's more than an even chance that day or night, someone, somewhere in Israel will be praying. Whether under a prayer shawl in a synagogue, beneath a cross in a church or on a mat facing Mecca, the faithful will be lauding the Creator of the Universe.

The sheer intensity of the religious ardour in this small country is overwhelming: in Jerusalem's Old City, Jews at the Western Wall, Muslims at the Dome of the Rock and Christians at the Church of the Holy Sepulchre may well be saying their prayers simultaneously, to say nothing of the myriad other synagogues, churches and mosques in the Old City alone. Likewise, the diversity of religious experience here is of a category all its own. Hassidim in 18th-century *kapotas* and *shteimels* (coats and hats) rub shoulders with robed monks and nuns from every Christian denomination East and West, while Muslim *imams* in *tarboosh* and *galabiyah* walk unnoticed among secular Israelis and pilgrims to the Holy Land. Many of the holiest sites from the Bible have alternately hosted synagogues, churches and mosques over the centuries, and today, still, visitors of one faith may well find themselves paying respects to a chapter of their own history in the house of worship of another.

**The Jewish presence:** Jewish spiritual life revolves around the home, house of study (*cheder* for youngsters, *yeshiva* for adolescents and adults) and synagogue – of which the latter is the most accessible to the visitor. Jerusalem's 500 synagogues range from the humblest *shtible* and Sefardi community synagogue to the gargantuan Belzer Center (seats 3,500) and the "Great" along downtown King George Street. The Great's massive edifice gives people the idea that it might be the third Temple. Other large synagogues in Jerusalem include the Central, Yeshrun and Italian.

The Orthodox pray three times a day, but it is on weekends and festivals that the liturgy is at its most elaborate. This is a good

time to catch the Hassidic services whose more modest premises are compensated for by the fervour of the prayers. Such groups exist in Safed, Bnei Brak and in Jerusalem's Mea Shearim and Geula districts.

Among the warmest and most approachable of the Hassidic groups is the Bratslav, whose Mea Shearim premises contain the renovated chair of their first and only rebbe Rabbi Nahman. He was famous for his delightful tales; one of his sayings, "the world is a narrow bridge; the main thing is not to be afraid at all," has endeared him to all Israelis.

At the other end of Mea Shearim is Karlin, whose devotees screech their prayers – unlike their Geula neighours, Ger, whose tightly-knit organisation is reflected in their operatic music and self-discipline: "A true Ger Hassid," says one, "never looks at his wife." A similar outlook is espoused by Toledot Aharon, opposite Bratslav, whose purity of purpose is matched by their animosity towards political Zionism, which they view as usurping the Divine process of Redemption. In this they follow the line of Neturei Karta (Guardians of the City), which boasts its own government-in-exile in its campaign for political autonomy. Both, too, campaign against the Conservative and Reform Movements, which have their own centres and desegregated houses of prayer in Jerusalem (on Agron and King David streets, respectively).

**The cycle of the Jewish year:** The framework of Jewish piety is determined by the lunar cycle beginning around September and October with Rosh Hashona (the New Year) and Yom Kippur, the Day of Atonement – a rigorous fast of 25 hours duration. Synagogues are packed; services are long but moving. If you're Jewish and you hail from Minsk, Marrakesh or Manhattan, you're sure to find at least one service meeting your liturgical needs. An unusual and controversial custom precedes Yom Kippur: Kaparot, which entails swinging a white chicken above the head of the would-be-repenter, after which the slaughtered fowl is sold and/or given to charity. The gruesome ceremony can be witnessed in most open marketplaces.

Succot, the Festival of Rejoicing, combines harvest gathering and prayers for winter rains and is celebrated on secular kibbutzim as well as by the Orthodox. The celebrants live in a temporary hut for seven days. During the evenings, the pious let down their sidelocks to dance, somersault and juggle to live, intoxicating music. Some Hassidic sects cap off the ceremonies with a candlelight procession by their children.

More lights burn during Channukah, usually in December, when eight-branched candelabra shine in most homes. This celebration of the Maccabean victory over the Greeks some 2,300 years ago was preceded by a couple of centuries by one over the upstart Haman, whose sad fate is recorded in the Scroll of Esther and read on Purim (usually

the Temples, culminating in the day-long fast on Tisha B' Av.

**New Jews and Messiahs:** Orthodoxy is fashionable, no less so among the Jews, and in the past 15 years a whole wave of "returnees" have passed through special yeshivot for the uninitiated, eventually to weave themselves into fabric of the local religious life. Their devotion takes expression in a variety of ways, from those Jews who integrate their Western careers or professions with a pious daily routine to such phenomena as the Selah Torah Rock Band, now located at the Israel Center on Jerusalem's Strauss Street, which blends Jewish and Western styles with consummate ease.

in March). Children and adults dress in costumes, shout, get drunk, and give each other presents of food or drink. In April, everyone spring-cleans for Passover, the annual feast celebrating the Exodus from Egypt. Seven weeks later is Shavuot, the Feast of Weeks, when thousands congregate at the Western Wall for dawn prayers, having spent the night studying Israel's national book, the Torah. Between Passover and Shavuot, the Orthodox invest Independence Day and Jerusalem Unity Day with spiritual significance, creating new festivals. The yearly cycle reaches full circle in high summer, with the three-week period of mourning for

**The Christian presence:** These Messianic messengers are not always Jewish, but include long, blond-haired types with pre-Raphaelite faces. They may be part of the growing Evangelical presence in Israel whose belief in the Redemption has made them enthusiastic supporters of Zionism. The Christian Embassy on Jerusalem's Brenner Street recently attracted over 5,000 people from 40 countries to participate in their Christian version of the Feast of the Tabernacles. Another sort of backing comes from Nes Ammim, a semi-collective village near Acco where Christians of various denominations work the land – in co-founder Christine

Pillon's words – "in returning to our sources and being subjected to a new kind of Reformation. Our principles include the rejection of proselytising and the call for respect for Judaism as a living, ongoing tradition."

Most of the traditional Christian communities in Israel – numbering in total roughly 120,000 souls – are more concerned with their own internal affairs. Many devote themselves to lives of prayer and meditation, and preserving the presence of their church in the Holy Land. Often the priests, monks or nuns watch over and maintain traditional shrines associated with figures in the New Testament: a cave where the Holy Family found refuge, or the site of one of Jesus's miracles. With the West Bank in its control, Israel holds practically all of what is commonly known as the "Holy Land", and the devoted visitor can follow in the footsteps of Jesus from Virgin Birth in Bethlehem to early life at Nazareth, to Crucifixion at Golgotha, in Jerusalem.

Complicated by their variety, the Christian groups celebrate some 240 feasts and holy days any one year, using two separate calendars, the Julian and the Gregorian. This provides three dates for Christmas: 25 December for Western Christians, 7 January for Greek Orthodox, Syrians and Copts, and 19 January for the Armenians – as well as two sets of Holy Week(s). Only genuine pilgrims are allowed into Bethlehem for Christmas, where the main events take place at the Church of the Nativity; just as, in Easter Week, there is a reenactment of Jesus's last days with readings and processions on the sites historically associated with the original events. These include walks from the Mount of Olives, complete with palm branches, and along the Via Dolorosa to the Church of the Holy Sepulchre. Here, two unique ceremonies take place: the Washing of the Feet (John 13; 1-18), on Maundy Thursday, and the Kindling of the Holy Fire (symbolising the coming world Redemption), by the Orthodox and Eastern Churches on Holy Saturday. The climactic carrying of the cross on Good Friday between the Praetorium and Calvary (Golgotha), along the Via Dolorosa, is repeated weekly by the oldest resident group of priests, the Franciscans. One of the

**Left, study and pastel hues at a Safed yeshiva. Right, a latter-day prophet spreads his word.**

most unique Christian sites is the place of Jesus's baptism on the Jordan River. For a long time neglected, the site has been newly marked and is now commemorated in work and deed by more and more devotees.

**Interfaith, the dialogue of hope:** The existence of modern Israel has brought together Christian, Muslim and Jew in a once-in-a-thousand-years opportunity for interfaith dialogue. When they do occur, such encounters provide a means of transcending the most intransigent problems with new understanding. As Dr Abu Ghosh of Israel's Sharya Muslim Court says: "Islam is extraneous to the present political strife. Islam, Christianity and Judaism can live peacefully side by

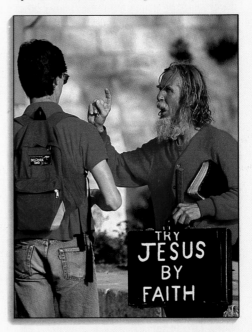

side, as is the case in Israel." Mary Carse, a Carmelite from Vermont, winters every year in Israel where she studies "at the feet of the rabbis." In Israel, she found that "everything began to fall into place." French Dominican priest Marcel Dubois also believes that "we are witnessing a Christian rediscovery of the continuity in the design of God." Sent to East Jerusalem in 1962, he became an Israeli citizen on Christmas Day, 1974. Appointed head of Hebrew University's Philosophy Department, he is fully aware of the tensions that exist around him, but speaks of more than just himself when he observes that "Jerusalem is the capital of contradictions."

"The experiment that worked" is how philosopher Martin Buber described what is Israel's best known institution – the kibbutz. Since the first one was established on the banks of the Jordan River in 1909, 260 of these uniquely Israeli communes have sprung up all over the country. Though today they account for less than 3 percent of the population, the influence these communal farms have had on Israeli society is vastly disproportionate to their modest numbers.

In this way, kibbutzim (plural of kibbutz) differ radically from communes in any other country. Rather than founded as an alternative to society, Israel's communes were meant to be – and to some extent, still are – the very core of society.

**Ideology and Irrigation:** The founders of the kibbutz movement were Jewish pioneers who, stirred by the revolutionary spirit brewing in turn-of-the-century Russia, became intent upon establishing the ideal socialist society. With an almost religious fervour, these secular Jews of Eastern Europe set out to build an egalitarian Jewish society that would be rooted in the soil.

If once it was the learned rabbis who were the role models of the Jewish community, these secular societies acquired a whole new set of heroes; men like Yehoshuah Henkin, who bought up hundreds of thousands of acres of land for Jewish settlement; or Benzion Yisraeli of Kibbutz Kinneret who, on a clandestine mission to the Persian Gulf, managed to smuggle 60,000 choice date tree shoots into Israel.

However, the first attempts to reclaim the land in the 1880s through what were essentially private farming ventures, proved nearly disastrous. The settlers in places like Rosh Pina, Petach Tikva and Rishon Le Zion were up against malaria, locusts and bands of Bedouin; it is doubtful they would have held on at all if not for the continuous financial support of Jewish philanthropist Baron Edmond de Rothchild. In these circumstances, the kibbutz model had a built-in practical advantage; by working together the settlers could effectively pool their sparse resources – and perhaps beat the odds.

The first effort at communal living in 1909

began with no more than a dozen men and women. But when they ended their first year with a surplus, what had been only an experiment was made into a permanent institution, "Deganya" (The Cornflower) became the mother of kibbutzim. A decade later, another 40 had joined her.

**First fruits:** Israeli fruit is usually the first to reach European countertops in winter; Israeli cows produce more milk, and Israeli chickens more eggs than any of their counterparts in the world. The country's farm

equipment brings in even more money than the bulk of food it exports. Kibbutzniks are sent to the Third World countries to share their expertise with other struggling farmers.

Yet when they began, everything south of Tel Aviv was a desert, and much of the Hula, Jordan and Jezreel Valleys, a wasteland. The overwhelming transformation of this land was aided by one development in particular which has since become synonymous with Israeli agriculture: drip irrigation.

Conventional methods of irrigating – via trenches in the ground or sprinkler systems – mean a lot of water never reaches the plants. Through drip irrigation, a series of plastic pipes with "drippers" attached to them brings water and nutrients directly to the roots of the plants. Considerably less water is wasted; crop yields are increased substantially; and the system enables saline water to be used for irrigation – turning areas by the Dead Sea into oases of palm trees and fertile fields.

Later on, necessity sparked another Israeli improvement on the system. In the late 1960s, terrorists from Jordan began to infiltrate into the Beit Shean and Jordan valleys; Kibbutzniks who went to tend their fields

**Backbone of society:** While they supply the country with 50 percent of its food needs the kibbutzim's contribution to Israeli society does not end there. For years these settlements provided the backbone of political and defence leadership in the country. The Palmach, Israel's elite fighting force in pre-state days and the predecessor of its army, drew most of its members from kibbutzim. Since then, kibbutzniks have traditionally continued to volunteer for the commando units of the army with the result that they

were killed by land mines. Automated irrigation systems were invented; from the safety of a computer room farmers could control the whole process.

Such innovations were not the kibbutzim's doing alone. Israeli scientists and industrialists were often behind them. But the kibbutzniks were always deeply involved, often improving on what industry came up with, and eventually setting up factories to manufacture their own farm equipment.

**Left**, women are protected from the sun but not hard work in the early days of the kibbutz experiment. **Above**, kibbutz children at play.

have accounted for a quarter of all Israeli war casualties even though they make up only 3 percent of the population.

From their beginning, these highly ideological institutions tended to band together in groups, each one aligned with a different political party (all falling within the general leftist framework of the Labour movement). From their ranks came a whole generation of leaders, including a few prime ministers. At one point, kibbutzniks were estimated to hold seven times as many positions of power as their numbers warranted.

The kibbutzim's direct influence over the political system – through the Labour Party

– has diminished considerably in the last decade with the rise of the opposition Likud Party. However, many of the values of the kibbutz movement have filtered through society. The casual style of the kibbutznik and his irreverent attitude towards rank have left their mark, and it is not unusual for members of Israel's parliament to saunter into a meeting wearing jeans and a T-shirt.

**New challenges:** If the typical kibbutz was once a fenced-in strip of swampland with clusters of makeshift shacks, today's communal farm looks more like a holiday village. Consummately landscaped, containing two-and three-storey apartment buildings, the contemporary kibbutz is equipped with

were shared; identical khaki-coloured work outfits – and even clean underwear – were distributed to every member once a week. Privacy was spurned. So was higher education; university was thought to be a needless for people whose lives were to be devoted to working the land. On more radical kibbutzim, even marriage was considered a contemptuous institution of the bourgeois.

Much of this is now history. The average kibbutznik today is married, has his or her own radio, television, and often, stereo system and video as well, and certainly his own clothes. Apartments are built with kitchenettes; there is no longer a stigma attached to eating a meal in the privacy of one's home.

at least one swimming pool, basketball court, library, and often, concert hall, enjoying a much higher standard of living than most of the nation's urban centres.

How has success affected the strong ideological foundations of the kibbutz? Certainly the dogmatism of the early days has died down. Differences over ideological matters have provoked bitter splits in a kibbutz. In the worst of cases, two kibbutzim would be set up side by side and their populations divided along ideological lines – which frequently took precedence over family ties.

The ban on private property used to mean that even a transistor radio was taboo. Clothes

One substantial change has been in the manner of raising children. Many first generation kibbutzniks, who were themselves brought up in communal children's houses, have decided they want their own children to be at their side – and on many kibbutzim today, the children sleep at home.

Like the oh-so-conventional parents they used to scoff at, kibbutzniks have come to hope their kids go on to university. The kibbutz, which foots the cost, is well aware of the more sophisticated skills required of its members nowadays as their energies switch from milking cows to marketing. This is perhaps the most substantial change to affect the kibbutz in recent years and also the one that presents the most serious practical – and ideological – challenge.

Having exploited their agricultural potential, kibbutzim have been undergoing rapid industrialisation. Their limited manpower, however, has forced many of them to hire outside labour – a practice that is anathema to their egalitarian principles. The result has been a souring of morale and drop in production. What the kibbutzim are now pinning their hopes on is high technology, a field which requires specialised know-how and capital, but not a heavy labour force. In the last decade the number of research and development projects initiated by kibbutzim

has jumped from 10 to 100. The projects range from steel tools moulded to the thousandth of an inch with a computerised laser to plastic egg collectors moulded with almost equal precision to the derrière of a hen.

The differences that characterise kibbutzim today include the extent to which they've welcomed the advent of high technology (with some boasting as many as five new industries); but also include size, which can range from 60 to 600 members; location, anywhere from a mountaintop to a desert

**Above**, Kibbutznik, tractor and irrigated fields still define the basic kibbutz aesthetic.

and, of course, as always – the ideology.

But what is common to all kibbutzim is that the means of production, as well as housing and community facilities are all jointly owned by the members; decisions are jointly taken through democratically elected boards; and while members don't receive salaries for working on the kibbutz, all their basic needs are met; housing, food, medical care and education are provided – even vacations and travel allowances are allocated and laundry taken care of. "From each according to his ability; to each according to his need" remains the guiding principle.

**Other options:** The kibbutz may be the most renowned of Israel's agricultural institutions, but it's by no means the only one. A much less communal venture called the *moshav* sprung up about a decade after the first kibbutz and has gone on to become the most popular form of agricultural settlement today. Only the costs of equipment and marketing are shared on a moshav; each member is allowed to own his own house and work his own plot of land. The *moshavim* (plural) have not, however, fared as well as kibbutzim on the whole, and many of them are now teetering on the point of bankruptcy.

A slight variation of the conventional kibbutz is the religious one, founded in reaction to the often stridently anti-religious tone that characterised the country's early kibbutzim. Members of religious kibbutzim are committed to living according to Jewish law: work is not performed on the Sabbath, food is kosher and Jewish holidays are strictly observed. Such settlements are still a minority among what are largely secular societies.

If you have the energy and time to spare you could offer to volunteer on a kibbutz. In return for picking fruit, dishing up dinner or chaperoning chickens, you get room and board, a bit of pocket money and a chance to see first hand what kibbutz life is like. You won't be alone: each year, thousands of young Scandinavians and Europeans, and Jewish-American teens take the plunge to live for free and make new friends in the Promised Land.

If you'd rather not get your hands dirty, you might prefer a kibbutz guesthouse. Across the country, from Ein Gedi on the Dead Sea to Nasholim on the Tel Dor coast, these hostelries afford comfortable rooming in an authentic kibbutz atmosphere.

Had one to name the single most fundamental contribution made by Israel and the Jewish people to mankind, obviously the immediate answer is the Bible. The Book of Books is the underlying philosophical and moral web which unites most of civilisation as the core of human values. And that book, for all its five millennia or so, remains the most important source and inspiration for much of Israel's cultural creativity.

It is, of course, only one of the strands, but it is the most pervasive. Other distinct strands are the great literary creations of the Jewish exile – the Mishna and the Talmud – the accumulated wisdom of 2,000 years of Jewish thought. No less important is the cumulative experience of a mere blink in the history of the Jewish people: the 38 years of modern statehood, and the reflection of the pressures of a society whose population has multiplied more than sixfold in those years and, through force of circumstances, had no alternative but to develop a siege mentality which has often produced a siege culture.

Israel, like the United States before it, has often been described as a "melting pot" as it has struggled with the absorption of one-and-a-half million immigrants from 100 nations speaking 70 tongues. But a melting pot – in which the id melts into a normative unity – is the wrong image. The cliché does not hold true. A better image, for all its disregard of *kashrut* (Jewish dietary laws), would be a *bouillabaisse*, the classic Mediterranean fish stew in which all the elements come together into a homogeneous whole, each retaining its own character, distinct identity and flavour.

**Literature:** If the heartbeat of a nation's culture lies in its written word, then here, already, is Israel's single most basic problem: its language. Hebrew, the language of the Prophets and of the Old Testament, ceased to exist as a vehicle for everyday speech during the exile and was replaced by the tongues of the nations among whom the Jews found refuge in their dispersion, and by a handful of composite Jewish languages such as Judeo-German (Yiddish), Judeo-Spanish (Ladino), and others.

The revival of modern Hebrew was the work of one man, Eliezer Ben-Yehuda. He determined, when he came to Palestine in 1881, that he and his family would utter no word in anything but Hebrew. His efforts and those of his followers created a whole new vocabulary, and in a scant decade or two helped one of the most ancient of tongues to become, at the same time, one of the newest.

Nevertheless, for all its revival, there are no more than 4 or 5 million people worldwide who can speak and understand Hebrew. If one speaks of those who can comfortably *read* Hebrew, the figure is certainly no more than 3 million. Hebrew can be considered an arcane, rather exotic language; one where those who choose to write in it must inevitably be faced with the frustrations of writing for an intrinsically minuscule audience. But a lively, articulate and robust body of literature has evolved. While the giants of modern Hebrew – Bialik, Tchernikhovsky, Brenner, Agnon (who won Israel's only Nobel Prize, that for literature, in 1966) – and others, are still required reading in schools, they are supplemented by indigenous, increasingly local-born writers whose work can stand comparison with the best of the world's contemporary authors.

One of Israel's best writers (and certainly best-known abroad) is Amos Oz. A former member of Kibbutz Hulda who now lives in Arad, Oz is heavily influenced by the Return to the Soil labour-Zionist *mores* espoused by the founding fathers of the kibbutz movement. Many writers who maintain a prolific literary output belong to the "Palmach Generation" (the Palmach was the pre-state élite fighting force drawn from the kibbutzim). Among them are Haim Guri, Moshe Shamir, S. Yizhar, Benjamin Tammuz and Hanoch Bar Tov. An important phenomenon of the last 15 years or so has been the maturation of a group of writers of Sephardic origin for whom Arabic, rather than Yiddish, was a formative influence. Such writers include A.B. Yehoshua, Samy Michael and Amnon Shamosh, whose *Esra Safra and Sons* became a popular television series.

**Left,** a Hebrew University student improves his mind in the shade of a sculpture by Menashe Kadishman, at Mount Scopus campus.

A one-man literary phenomenon is Ephraim Kishon. Israel's best-known humorist and a prophet somewhat without honour in his own country, his books have sold literally millions of copies overseas, especially in Scandinavia and Germany.

Literature, too, cannot evade the influence of the decimation of European Jewry in the Holocaust. It is that theme which is the all-pervasive *leitmotif* in the writings of Aharon Appelfeld, whose books have been widely translated, Abba Kovner, "Ka-Tsetnik" (the pseudonym of Benzion Dinur) and others, all of whom experienced that period themselves. A younger generation of writers is exploring more universal literary themes. The Lebanon war, increased political polarisation, the appearance of anti-democratic trends in Israeli society, the threat of racism, are rightly the concern of these intellectuals.

The centre ground in Israeli writing is held today by those who came to literary maturity after the Palmach days and whose literary vision was tempered through the fires of austerity, of absorption of immigrants and four wars of survival. Such writers include Yitzhak Ben Ner, Shulamit Hareven, the late Ya'akov Shabtai, Yoram Kaniuk and others.

Poetry holds a special place in Israel's literary life. According to a calculation based on books and the literary magazines, 10,000 new poems are published in Israel every year. New works by Yehuda Amichai, Dan Pagis, Natan Zach, or T. Carmi are as avidly awaited as any by Michener or Le Carré.

**Music:** The musical life of Israel is a quintessential example of bipolarity. There is a constant inflow of immigrant musicians and an outflow of performers who have reached the highest international peaks. Yitzhak Perlman, Pinhas Zuckerman, Shlomo Mintz, Daniel Barenboim, all received their training in Israel and went on to glittering careers on the world's concert platforms. Israel's orchestras, including the Israel Philharmonic, the Jerusalem Symphony, the Beersheba Sinfonietta and many chamber groupings, have provided a home for hundreds of players. Rehearsals are a Babel of Russian, German, Romanian, French and English – united by a lot of music and a little Hebrew.

Israelis are a concert-going people: Subscription series to the major orchestras are sold out and a subscription to the IPO is jealously handed down from parents to chil-dren. The music-loving tourist would have many opportunities to hear his best loved pieces being played by some of the world's greatest talents. Placido Domingo, incidentally, got his first job at the (late-lamented) Israel Opera, with whom he spent a year. Opera lovers, however, should leave their opera going for other climes. Choral singing, too, is on a very high level, especially with the United Kibbutz Choir, the Rinat National Choir and the Camaran Singers.

Israel hosts a series of international musical events including the Artur Rubinstein piano competition, the Pablo Casals cello competition, a triennial international harp contest, the Zimriya choirs festival, and an-

nual music festivals in Jerusalem, Kibbutz Ein Hashofet and, notably, at Kibbutz Ein Gev on the shores of the Sea of Galilee.

For all this wealth of musical life, it is not only the highbrow that is catered to. In Tel Aviv (Jerusalem from this point of view hardly counts!), there is a great deal of popular music around. While jazz aficionados will do better elsewhere, rockers, popsters and balladiers are out in force. Moshe Wilensky, Yoram Taharlev, Nurit Hirsch, Sasha Argov and, above all, Naomi Shemer, write music that is played on radio, television, in kindergartens and sunshine-home singsongs from Metulla to Eilat. Locals still remember Israel's two consecutive Eurovision Song Contest victories with *Abani-bi* sung by Yizhar Cohen and *Halleluia* sung by Gali Atari? Pop superstars in Israel include Ofra Haza, Ilanit, Yehoram Gaon, Arik Einstein, Shalom Hanoch, and many more. A new generation of ethnic singers such as Boaz Shar'abi, Chaim Moshe, Moshe Giat and the Breira Hativ'it group have given a new sense of ethnic pride to young Israelis of Sephardic background.

**Dance:** Israel owes its place in the world of dance to three women. The first was a Russian-trained ballerina, Rina Nikova, who came to Palestine in the 1920s and determined to create a local art form incorporating

themes from the Bible, (remember Salome?), Middle East dance tradition, folk dance and Russian classical ballet. The second, Sarah Levi-Tanai harnessed the Yemenite dance tradition, one of the richest and most exotic dance cultures of the Middle East, into a modern framework and created the Inbal Dance Theater, the forerunner of several other successful ethnic dance groups. The third, Baroness Bethsabée de Rothschild founded the Batsheva and Bat Dor dance companies. Both remain leading exponents

**Left**, Israeli novelist Amos Oz burns elbow grease.
**Above**, conductor Zubin Mehta takes a bow.

of modern dance in Israel, the latter also has three thriving ballet schools. The formative influence on modern dance in Israel was undoubtedly that of Martha Graham, but the companies have since grown and expanded their horizons with a series of overseas tours. In recent years, the two companies have been joined by the Kibbutz Dance Company and the Israel Ballet, the country's only classical ballet company.

Another company unique in concept and achievement is Kol Demama ("Voice of Silence"). This group is composed of deaf and hearing-impaired dancers and their performances are electrifying, it being impossible to distinguish which dancers are deaf and which are not. The training method developed by director Moshe Efrati is based on vibrations through the floor transmitted by the dancer's feet.

Folk-dance groups abound throughout the country and there is not a kibbutz or town that does not have its own troupe. Outstanding among them is Hora Yerushalayim, a Jerusalem-based group, whose four companies, divided by age, perform to a very high standard at home and overseas.

Israelis take to dance happily and with easy élan, and any occasion is likely to end up with an exuberant and exhausting round of *horas*, *krakoviaks*, *debkas*, Hassidic dances and other European and Arabic dance forms, now part of the Israeli dance heritage.

**Theatre:** Israeli theatre owes its origins to the histrionic, melodramatic tradition exemplified in the first Hebrew theatre in the world, Habimah, founded in Moscow in 1917 (which moved to Palestine in 1931). Since then, theatre has come a long way in style, presentation method, especially, in content. Of all the arts in Israel, theatre is perhaps the most socially involved, with a new generation of playwrights breaking taboos, tackling controversial topics, and attempting to act as the mirror and conscience of society.

Concerns of the past, the Jewish experience in pre-war Europe, the Holocaust, all these still manifest themselves on the Israeli stage but, increasingly, dramatists are addressing themselves to contemporary issues, problems of daily life in Israel, the Arab-Jewish conflict, alienation between ethnic, religious and other social groups. A new play by Hanoch Levin, Yehoshua Sobol or Hillel Mittlepunkt is a major event which will be dissected, analyzed and discussed as energetically as the Camp David Accords. Hanoch Levine, especially, is a defiant, iconoclastic writer whose works inevitably cause controversy and sometimes even attempted censorship. But his irreverent, nihilistic, often obscene satire makes him Israel's most interesting and original theatrical talent.

The major repertory theatres, most of whom enjoy substantial official support, such as the Habimah, Cameri, Ohel, Haifa Municipal Theater, Beersheba Municipal Theater and the Jerusalem Khan have subscription series which are usually heavily attended. Naturally, the language barrier prevents the visitor from sharing in the rich offerings. Efforts

outlying areas which do not generally get the chance to see live performances. For thousands of new immigrants and youngsters, Omanut La'am performances are their first introduction to the world of theatre.

**Cinema:** Film as an art form in Israel still has a long way to go. Most of its productions are strictly for local consumption and are based on stale ethnic sitcoms, sexcoms, and in-joke situations such as teenage affairs, marital conflicts and army life. Such products are loosely known as "Burekas" films (named after a kind of flaky pastry pie popular in Israel).

Serious filmmaking in Israel began in the early 1920s and 1930s, mainly with docu-

are being made, however, to bridge the gap. Several theatres have experimented in translations through earphones and others have attempted to mount versions of their works in English.

Great popular success has attended a recent annual theatrical innovation: the festival of Alternative Theater in Acre. It has become a hoopla occasion of theatrical dynamics, innovative performances and indoor and open-air attractions.

A programme enjoying substantial support is Omanut La'am ("Arts for the People"). This state-run enterprise brings theatre to settlements and development towns in

mentaries as a fundraising device aimed at demonstrating the Zionist pioneering effort to audiences abroad. These films, with their images of muscle-rippling pioneers making the desert bloom and bringing water to the arid wastes against a background of stirring music and an exhortatory sound track, became known as "Keren Kayemet films" after the Hebrew name of the Jewish National Fund which sponsored most of them.

Some Israel films made in the 1960s managed to rise above mediocrity and brought actors like Haim Topol, Uri Zohar, Gila Almagor, Oded Kotler and Arik Einstein to the fore. Kotler's *Three Days and a Child* won the best actor's prize at the Cannes Film Festival in 1967. A film which made a lasting impression was *Sallah Shabtai*, written by Ephraim Kishon and starring a young Topol, which told the story in a whimsical and ironic manner of the recent North African immigration to Israel and their culture clash with the hidebound kibbutzim.

Israeli cinema-goers have been ill served in the past by cinema owners. This situation has recently changed in a radical way. Tel Aviv boasts a sybaritic cinema complex, the Rav Chen, which incorporates five halls, while Jerusalem has the Cinemathèque, which not only shows the best films in town, but is also the place where the capital's

beautiful people go to see and be seen. The one international superstar in Israel's cinematographic life is mogul Menahem Golan, who became one of the movers and shakers in Hollywood, together with his cousin, Yoram Globus. They were originally two small-town boys from Tiberias.

**The plastic arts:** Israeli art owes its fundamental quality to a combination of two factors. In the first place, a classical European tradition brought here by the country's early painters and art teachers, and second, the

**Mordechai Ardon's stained-glass windows at Givat Ram are the artist's best-known work.**

influences of the special quality of the light, and the natural attributes of the country.

In the space of about 80 years (since the establishment of the Bezalel School of Art in Jerusalem in 1906), an Israeli visual art has been created, possessing its own individual character. Israeli artists have experimented with all the movements and trends of the contemporary art world from expressionism to cubism, from Russian social realism to environment and performance art. However, not many Israeli artists have managed to make the quantum leap from local to universal recognition. Among contemporary artists who have are Ya'akov Agam (his kinetic room at the Pompidou Centre in Paris is a seminal work), Menashe Kadishman, Avigdor Arikha, Mordechai Ardon, Joseph Zaritsky and Avigdor Stematsky.

Two sculptors, Dany Karavan and Ygael Tumarkin, are well-known abroad, and their work can be seen all over Israel. Marcel Janco, (1895–1984) founder of the Dadaist Movement, Reuven Rubin (1893–1974) with his lyrical large-scale canvases, and Anna Ticho (1894–1980) with her exquisite line drawings of her beloved Jerusalem hills have also gained a considerable following.

At the end of the 1970s, Israeli art made its entry into the Post Modernist era, following in the footsteps of the US and Europe. This art is energetic and forceful, often containing violent images which are, perhaps, part of the post-Lebanon War reality in Israeli life.

Museums and galleries all over the country cater to the art lover. The main galleries are concentrated in two areas, Gordon Street in central Tel Aviv and in Old Jaffa. Others are in Jerusalem, Haifa, Ein Hod (an artist's village south of Haifa), Safed and elsewhere.

Tel Aviv Museum has a large and representative collection of Israeli modern art on permanent display along with temporary exhibitions. The Israel Museum, which has impressive collections of classic, impressionist and foreign modern art (as well as its vast collection of archaeology, Judaica and Jewish art, ethnography *et al*), has, until recently, not been noted for its diligence in showing and acquiring Israeli art. This has now changed with the opening in 1985 of the new Ayala Zacks-Abramov Pavilion of Modern Art, which should eventually become the nation's main repository of contemporary Israeli painting and sculpture.

# HEBREW: A LANGUAGE REBORN

One of the most remarkable facets of the rebirth of the Hebrew nation was the revival of the Hebrew language. Not that the language had been forgotten, but through the 2,000 years of dispersion it had become almost solely a language of worship and expression of the yearnings for Zion.

Some small communities of Sephardic Jews in Jerusalem used Hebrew for everyday speech but the lingua franca of the Jews in exile had become either the language of the country in which they found refuge, or special Jewish dialects that developed as an amalgam of the local language with an admixture of Hebrew. In such a way there evolved Yiddish as a combination of Hebrew with medieval German, Ladino—Hebrew with Spanish, Mughrabi—a North-African blend of Hebrew, Arabic and French, and others. The first pioneers who arrived in 19th-century Palestine brought with them their own languages, usually Yiddish or Russian, but they insisted on using Hebrew in conversation in the early agricultural communities and the recreation of Hebrew became a cornerstone of Zionist ideology.

In fact, the rebirth of Hebrew was virtually the work of one man, the Zionist thinker and leader, Eliezer Ben-Yehuda. Born in Lithuania in 1858, he immigrated to Palestine in 1881. He saw the revival of the language as an indispensable aspect of the political and cultural rebirth of the Jewish people and with single-minded, almost fanatic, determination embarked upon a lone campaign to restore the Hebrew tongue as a vibrant, living vehicle for everyday expression not just in the synagogue but in the street, in the market-place and in the home. When he and his new wife Dvora arrived in Jaffa he informed her that henceforth they would converse only in Hebrew and their son Itamar became the first modern child with Hebrew as his mother tongue. His efforts horrified the Orthodox population of Jerusalem who, when they realised that Ben-Yehuda proposed using the Holy Tongue to further secular, nationalist and political causes, pronounced a *herem* (religious excommunication) against him. To this day, the Ashkenazi ultra-Orthodox Jewish community condemns

the secular use of Hebrew and the defilement of the "holy" language, and confine themselves to Yiddish for everyday speech.

Yet the introduction of Hebrew for secular communication was not greeted with universal acclamation even by the non-Orthodox, or the supporting Zionist bodies and organisations abroad. Bitter battles were fought over the language of instruction to be used at, for example, the Bezalel School of Art in Jerusalem (founded in 1906), and the Technion (founded in 1913). The latter was

opened with German as its official language and it took a strike by both faculty and students to compel the supporting institution, the *Hilfsverein*, to give way on the issue. Only a few years after that, the language of teaching in all Jewish schools in the country (except for those of the ultra-Orthodox, of course) was established as Hebrew.

The crowning achievement of Ben-Yehuda's life was the publication of his *Dictionary of Ancient and Modern Hebrew*, which was completed after his death by his son Ehud and his second wife, Hemda (Dvora's younger sister). This dictionary, and the Academy of the Hebrew Language, which Ben-Yehuda established in 1890, were the main vehicles through which a new and modern vocabulary was disseminated. He wrote in the introduction to his dictionary: "In those days it was as if the heavens had suddenly opened, and a clear, incandescent light flashed before my eyes, and a mighty inner voice sounded in my ears: the renascence of Israel on its ancestral soil." Through his dictionary, the Academy and several periodicals that he founded and edited, Ben-Yehuda coined literally thousands of new *makushit* ("something that is tapped upon") take the place of "piano".

No one has yet successfully coined Hebrew words to replace the ubiquitous "automati", "mekhani", "democratia," etc., although the existence of such words in the language seriously disturbs Hebrew purists, just as *le weekend*, *le piquenique* and *le football* disturb Franceophone purists. Some post-Ben-Yehuda slang neologisms would undoubtedly make him turn in his grave as they have become soundly embedded in the

words and terms relating to every field of life and every discipline.

Not all of Ben-Yehuda's neologisms took root. Modern Hebrew, which is today the all-purpose language of the country from mathematics, physics, medicine, agriculture to the most arcane fields of scientific learning, still borrows a great number of words from other languages which sound familiar to the non-Hebrew-speaking ear. Ben-Yehuda's *sah rahok* ("long-distance speech"), for instance, never displaced "telephone", nor did

**Left**, a Torah scribe preserves the sacred script. **Above**, the secular script.

language. "Tremp" (clearly from "to tramp") is the Hebrew for "hitchhiking", a sweatshirt is a "svetcher", over which you might pull a "sveder" if it gets cold. When your "breks" fail, the garage might find something wrong with your "beck-ex," or even, God forbid, with your "front-beck-ex". Most of these words do have Hebrew equivalents, but they have often been pushed aside in common usage.

Despite these contemporary dilutions, there's no denying that Hebrew is once more a thriving, and still-evolving, vehicle of daily discourse employed in great works of literature and the backs of postcards alike.

From the artists' quarter in old Safed to the seaside boutiques in Eilat, on every major city avenue and in the oriental markets, the visitor to Israel has a choice of an almost endless array of local handicrafts. Simple straw baskets and sleek stone sculptor, ceramic and textile arts, glassware and jewellery, mass produced religious mementos and one-of-a-kind ritual items are available everywhere. Not surprisingly, Israel has become the international centre of Judaica production, and tourists – whether they are looking for something "just like grandma had" or something just a bit more sophisticated – find what is undoubtedly the world's best selection of Jewish ritual arts concentrated in the shops and studios of Jerusalem.

Jewish art and craft, like almost everything else in 20th-century Israel, has its roots in the Bible Bezalel Ben-Uri Ben-Hur, specially blessed "with the spirit of God, in wisdom, in understanding, and in knowledge..." appears in the Book of Exodus to produce a Divine-commissioned work of art, the Tabernacle for the wandering Children of Israel. The order came down loud and clear: "To work in gold, and silver, and in brass, and in cutting of stones for setting, and in carving of wood, to work in all manner of skillful workmanship." Bezalel clearly proved worthy of the task; under his direction the desert Tabernacle was successfuly completed, and from it emerged the *Menorah*, the magnificent seven-branched candlestick which became the eternal symbol of the Jewish people.

When the wanderings in the desert were over and ancient Jerusalem established as the capital of the Jewish nation, the tourist industry was born. Three times a year – at the festivals of *Succot* (autumn), *Pesach* (spring), and *Shavuot* (early summer) – pilgrims came from outlying areas of the country to worship at the Temple. On the slopes of the city beyond the Temple mount, they found Jerusalem's earliest art centres – special quarters for weavers, dyers, leather workers, glass-

makers, potters and goldsmiths, all turning out functional and artistic wears for visitors to use during their Jerusalem sojourn and to take home as keepsakes.

The destruction of the Second Temple in 70 AD and consequent dispersion of the Jewish people left few opportunities for the artistic Jewish soul to express itself visually in the Holy Land for almost two millennia. But with the birth of the Zionist movement in the 20th century came a revival of interest in "Jewish art". Alongside the pioneers who set out to rebuild the land physically came a tiny group of artists, intellectuals and craftspeople dedicated to creating a new Jewish culture. Bezalel reappeared in the name of a fledging art academy, and its founder, a Lithuanian Jew named Boris Schatz, came from Bulgaria to prove that art and craft could become the touchstone of economic well-being and national pride in the Zionist settlement.

"Eretz Israel," wrote Schatz, "is sacred to all nations... and is a land which tourists visit by the thousands... all of whom wish to purchase souvenirs from the Holy Land, objects made in good taste bearing the mark of Eretz Israel, and who are prepared to pay for them."

Today Jerusalem is again the undisputed centre of Israel's tourism and, not coincidentally, of its arts industry. As in ancient times, many of the city's craftspeople are to be found in their own centrally located artists' quarters. A unique feature of Jerusalem's art scene, in fact, is the immediate accessibility of its artists. Serious collectors, particularly of Judaica, are advised to take advantage of the opportunity to buy directly from the studio-shops.

**Ritual and tradition:** Jewish ritual art, which forms the bulk of what is called Judaica, is divided into two categories: holy vessels, directly associated with the Torah itself, and ritual utensils, used for fulfilling ritual arts in the home and synagogue. While not considered holy themselves, these objects acquire a certain sanctity by virtue of their presence or use in the performance of religious duties (*mitzvot*). When a ritual object adds as an aesthetic dimension to the observance of a ritual, its users have the benefit of fulfilling

**Left**, a gouache-on-paper *mizrach* (wall-hanging) by Yoram and Jane Korman depicts one of the most traditional Jewish themes: Jerusalem.

an additional commandment, *hiddur mitzvah* – glorification of the commandment. Thus, special value is attributed to lighting a beautiful pair of candlesticks for the Sabbath rather than two simple oil wicks, though the latter would fulfil the requirement.

*Halacha*, Jewish law, guides the craftsperson with only a few rules for creating specific ritual objects. The Hanukkah lamp is perhaps the most clearly defined. It must have eight separate lights of the same height, and a distinguishable ninth light for kindling the others; and they must burn, in a publicly visible spot, for at least 30 minutes past sundown. The rest is left to the artist.

Wine cups, candlesticks, and spice boxes which they were produced. We have Hanukkah lamps, dating from the 12th century on, with French Gothic windows, Moorish arches, or Italian garlands; wine cups and candlesticks reminiscent of the Renaissance and baroque periods, and so forth. A single Hebrew letter or inscription is sometimes the only sign that these were used by Jews.

Symbols of the artists' surrounding cultures – architectural details, national, and even political motifs – were given new significance in Judaica when combined with classic Jewish symbols. Long-standing favourites included (Torah) crowns and double columns invoking the Temple; biblical

used for Sabbath and holiday blessings; cases for *mezuzot* (tiny parchment scrolls hung on every Jewish doorpost); charity boxes, festive plates, decanters, hanging – these and many other objects long ago became associated in the Jewish ritual and are accepted today as Judaica. For most of them, there are no design restrictions, or even descriptions, in the *halacha*. Individual artisans throughout the centuries in the Diaspora picked the artistic style and material of their choice, created items to suit the religious need of the moment, and tradition was established.

In most cases, form and decoration closely followed the fashions of the time and place in scenes and signs of the Zodiac; lions of Judah, grape vines and pomegranates, griffins and fish and a wealth of other flora and fauna; and of course the seven-branched *menorah*. Representations of the human figure and face were generally avoided in deference to the Second Commandment ("Thou shalt have no graven images..."); but they do appear from time to time.

Materials were usually the best the community or individual patron could afford: lavish textiles, parchment and gold leaf, semi-

**Above**, a silversmith crafts *menorahs* and other ceremonial objects in his studio.

precious and precious stones and metals were the ideal. When these were not available, almost any other material would suffice: charming examples of Jewish folk art in wood, tin, paper, and other modest media have been preserved. (A magnificent collection of these is displayed in the Judaica/Heritage Galleries of the Israel Museum, where replicas are also on sale.)

**Contemporary artists:** Israel's contemporary Judaica artists, like their ancestors, favour semi-precious and precious metals for their work, but some items can be found in almost every other material, ranging from rare woods to Lucite. In the past decade two distinct schools in Judaica have emerged. One is highly traditional, basing its shapes and decorations on patterns from the Baroque period or earlier. Many of these works are uncamouflaged imitations or "adaptions" of well-known museum pieces; others are brought up to date by ingeniously incorporating the lines of modern Jerusalem or devices such as whimsical moving parts. The second school is strictly, sometimes aggressively contemporary. Here form prevails over function: the artist strives to create art works which may be used in Jewish ritual.

Proponents of both styles are usually highly proficient in their techniques, and many of them are world leaders in their field.

There are four or five major areas in the capital of note to Jewish art/craft hunters, all located at relatively short distances from each other. They are, according to general geographic proximity: the Old City's Jewish Quarter; Khutzot HaYotzer/Art & Crafts Lane (beneath Jaffa Gate); the House of Quality (12 Hebron Rd., near the railroad station); Yohanan MiGush Halav and Shivtei Israel streets (which both meet Jaffa Rd. at Zahal Square, facing the Old City); and the neighbourhoods of Geula/Mea Shearim.

An informal arts-and-crafts tour should begin at one of the two non-profit galleries which offer an instant overview of Israel's craft scene. Neither "gallery" sells anything but refers visitors directly to its selected artists. At the House of Quality, this means just going upstairs to the studios where several Judaica silversmiths, including famous veterans Arie Ofir and Menachem Berman, work full-time. At the Alix de Rothschild Crafts Center (4 Or HaHaim St.), recently set up in a renovated Jewish Quarter home, the Director may be on hand for tea and a chat about his latest crafts discoveries. Nearby, the Courtyard Gallery (16 Tiferet Israel St.) is the place for fibre-art fans seeking chic handmade baskets, fabrics and wall hangings. Those who prefer a strictly ethnic look can go across town to Kuzari (10 David St., in the Bukharan Quarter), where local women embroider everything from tea cosies to Torah covers, based largely on traditional Near Eastern patterns.

Khutzot HaYotzer/Art & Crafts Lane boasts top craftspeople like Uri Ramot (ancient glass and beads in modern settings); the Alsbergs (ancient coins in custom-made jewellery); and Georges Goldstein (hand-woven tapestries and *tallitot* – prayer shawls). But the Lane's greatest distinction is its concentration of outstanding silversmiths. Yaakov Greenvurcel, Zelig Segal and Emil Shenfeld rank among the world's top designers of contemporary Judaica, and Michael Ende is one of the founders and chief purveyors of the "nouveau antique" school.

Anyone seriously interested in the latter must also stop in at Yossi's Masters' Workshop (10 King David St.) and The Brothers Reichman (3 Ezer Yoldot St., just off Shabbat Square in Geula): both offer extraordinary workmanship and classic designs in fine metal. Similiar style and quality characterise the ceremonial pieces by Catriel (17 Yohanan MiGush Halav), a carver of rare woods. Catriel's neighbours are also worth visiting: silversmiths Davidson and Amiel, calligraphic artist Korman, and jeweler Sarah Einstein, who transforms antique Mideastern beads into high-fashion baubles.

Around the corner and down the block at 18 Shivtei Israel St. is a brand-new co-op featuring ceramic *hanukkiot* by Shulamit Noy and the works of seven other Jerusalem potters. From here, it is a short walk either to the centre of town or the Old City, where for under $10, inveterate *chachka*-hunters can find happiness with "ivory" amulets, mother-of-pearl miniatures, carved stone mezuzot and crocheted *kepot* (skullcaps), olivewood camels or jangling goats' bells.

And finally, for the traveller who wants a trip in time as well as space, a mere $30 or so can buy a genuine ceramic lamp made when the Second Temple was still standing – and the earliest tourists came in search of Israeli arts and crafts.

"A land flowing with milk and honey" Israel is not. Despite biblical pronouncements to the contrary, no abundance of natural resources is to be found here. No oil, coal, gold – not even water.

Sand is about the only thing in abundance – and ingenuity. The latter has catapulted this tiny nation into the top league of nations competing in high technology. "We can't drill the ground for wealth like the Arabs do, so we have to drill our heads," is how one Israeli scientist put it.

With this philosophy in mind, Israel has mobilised more scientists in research and development than any other country (on a per capita basis). The portion of the gross national product that goes to R&D is also one of the highest of any industrialised nation. And Israel, on a per capita basis, publishes more scientific papers and graduates more Masters and Doctoral students annually than anywhere else in the world.

From the central processing unit, or brain, of the IBM personal computer to the automated page layout system used by *Time* and *Newsweek*; from the remote control pilotless planes recently purchased by the US navy to the world's largest solar pond in San Bernadino County, California, Israeli innovations have made their mark far beyond the small country's borders, and today account for a third of the country's overseas sales.

A lucrative export market, however, is only a fringe benefit of technologies which were originally designed for Israeli use and often sparked by dire necessity.

A classic example is defence. When France suddenly cut off Israel's supply of Mirage fighter planes in 1967, the country became painfully aware of the need to begin developing its own aircraft and weaponry. Israel's defence industry, led by Israel Aviation Industries (IAI), has since then been setting milestones in the sophistication and effectiveness of its systems from the Kfir dog fighter to the Gabriel sea-to-sea missile. The IAI's remote pilotless planes, or drones, were largely responsible for wiping out the entire Syrian airforce within two days of the start of the Lebanon war.

The resources Israel has been forced to invest in defence have, fortunately, had spinoffs in civilian fields as well. Israeli robots designed to defuse bombs and foil terrorists have been adapted to help prevent industrial accidents in chemical plants and nuclear reactors. Nowhere, however, does the adage of "beating swords into ploughshares" seem more appropriate than in the case of the Merhava tractor. The state-of-the-art computerised tractor is indebted to Israel's Merhava battle tank for much of its makeup, particularly its frame and suspension engineering. (The high-tech tractor also draws on the US lunar probe vehicle for its hydrostatic computer-controlled wheels.)

It is in farming that high technology has had perhaps its most far-reaching effects, making Israel, for many years, the world's leader in agriculture. Here, again, innovation had to compensate for a dismal lack of resources. Working together, the country's farmers and scientists – notably the team at Haifa's Technion University which boasts the largest agricultural engineering faculty in the world – were able to overcome adversity. A lack of fossil fuels spurred them to develop solar and other alternative energies.

Nor did a lack of water faze scientists, who, using crop dusting planes, learned to inject clouds with silver iodide so that they produced up to 15 percent more rain than they normally would. The most fruitful marriage of technology and tillage has been the advent of drip irrigation which turned thousands of acres of desert into arable land.

The wish of nearly every Jewish mother to have a son who's a doctor comes close to fruition in Israel which claims the highest number of physicians per capita of any coun-

bloodless scalpel to open up blocked arteries, restore fertility, treat "blue babies", and cure myriad eye problems.

Israel is also a world leader in medical-imaging equipment, with a Haifa-based company, Elscint, supplying many of the world's CAT (computer assisted tomography) scanners which provide depth images of the body's organs and are particularly effective at locating brain tumours.

War, too, has had an effect on inspiring new technologies of treatment. For example,

try – 277 per 10,000 people compared to 177, for instance, in the United States. This abundance of doctors, working in close conjunction with engineers and scientists, has been responsible for a number of breakthroughs in medical technology. In the field of laser surgery, for instance, the Israeli company Sharplan, founded by an Israeli doctor and engineer, now supplies close to 30 percent of the US market for surgical lasers. Israeli doctors are also at the vanguard of pioneering new ways to use what is known as the

**New frontiers in high-tech include computer graphics, left, and bio-genetic research, above.**

Israeli doctors were able to save hundreds of victims of Mexico's 1985 earthquake, employing techniques improvised in the wake of the collapse of Israel's army HQ in Tyre, Lebanon, three years before.

The institutions behind Israel include the Hebrew University and Hadassah Medical School, Haifa's Technion, the Weizmann Institute in Rehovot, the Volcani Institute of Agriculture, private companies such as Elscint and Scitex, a world leader in computerised graphics systems, and several US firms, including IBM, Motorola, and Elbit.

Jaffa oranges were once Israel's major export. Today, its harvest consists of ideas.

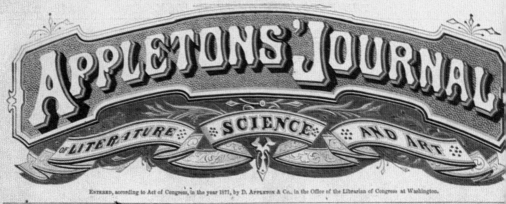

# APPLETONS' JOURNAL

## of LITERATURE · SCIENCE · AND ART

ENTERED, according to Act of Congress, in the year 1871, by D. APPLETON & Co., in the Office of the Librarian of Congress at Washington.

No. 99.—Vol. V.]     SATURDAY, FEBRUARY 18, 1871.     { PRICE TEN CENTS. { WITH SUPPLEMENT

## THE RECOVERY OF JERUSALEM.*

THIS is the somewhat pretentious title of the narrative of recent English explorations of Jerusalem, by means of excavations conducted by Captain Wilson, of the Royal Engineers, under the auspices and at the expense of the Committee of the Palestine Exploration Fund. Without, perhaps, fulfilling the meaning of the old crusading war-cry, exact knowledge of the scenes and localities in which their re first appeared on earth. The explorations have solved many di problems, and settled many fierce and protracted controversies. have been sunk and tunnels made in the most secluded and myst parts of the sacred city, and structures brought to light that ha

WILSON'S ARCH, DISCOVERED AT JERUSALEM IN 1867.

the "Recovery of Jerusalem," it is undoubtedly a record of researches and discoveries of the highest value, and of the greatest interest to scholars, antiquarians, and, above all, to Christians who desire an

been seen by mortal eyes since the days of Titus, or perhaps of mon.

The beginning of this great work was the Ordnance Surv Jerusalem, made by Captain Wilson, of the English Royal Eng in 1864–'65. Early in the year 1864 the sanitary state of Jeru attracted considerable attention; that city, which the Psalmi described as "beautiful for situation, the joy of the whole earth

---

* The Recovery of Jerusalem. A Narrative of Exploration and Discovery in the City and the Holy Land. By Captain Wilson, R. E., and Captain Warren, R. E. With an Introduction by Arthur Penrhyn Stanley, D. D., Dean of Westminster. D. Appleton & Co.

Archaeology is Israel's national hobby – from school child to senior citizen, from the curious to the serious scholar, tourists and natives alike are all encouraged to "dig in" to the land of the Bible.

With 3,500 sites in an area about the size of the state of Maryland and finds dating as far back as 150,000 BC, Israel boasts 22 archaeological museums in addition to numerous private collections. Yet only a small proportion of Israel's potential sites have been thoroughly explored: time, money, manpower – these have all placed limits on the scope but not the devotion to the exploration of Israel's past.

**A gentlemanly hobby:** Adherents past and present to what one scholar called the "study of durable rubbish" have been drawn to biblical archaeology for a range of reasons: greed, adventure, religion and scholarship. During the Victorian period it was something of a gentlemanly hobby.

The first known "archaeologist" to work in Israel was religiously inspired. In 325 CE St Helena, mother of Constantine, the emperor who declared Christianity the official religion of his empire, ordered the removal of a Hadrianic temple to Venus on a site she had determined was the hill of Golgotha. Constantine erected the Church of the Holy Sepulchre to commemorate the alleged site of the crucifixion and entombment of Jesus.

Over the next 16 centuries the territory, sometimes referred to as Palestine, the Levant, Syro-Lebanon, the Holy Land or Israel, exchanged hands almost as many times. Explorers of all religions crossed its borders, armed with little more than a compass, pick, shovel and curiosity. Stories of bribery, untimely deaths and mystical reunions with sages and prophets from time past pepper their accounts. Medieval adventurers report that those who dared to enter the burial cavern of the patriarchs and their wives at Hebron were struck blind or senseless or worse. Such tales did not always deter.

For Western explorers, interest in the Holy Land intensified after the Napoleonic conquest of Egypt in 1798 and the subsequent discovery of the Rosetta Stone. Scholars, amateurs and snake-oil salesmen descended on Palestine, then a backwater country that was sparsely populated. Some of these adventurers became the victims of this archaeological fever. For example, when the British Museum rejected as fake certain "ancient" parchments that Moses Wilhelm Shapira had bought from a Bedouin, the amateur archaeologist disappeared.

In 1911, Captain Montague Parker and his crew of treasure hunters barely escaped with their lives when they were discovered conducting an excavation under the Mosque of Omar on the Temple Mount. The British mission had been following the hunch of a Swedish clairvoyant who insisted that this was where they would find a cache of golden objects from King Solomon's temple. Offended Jerusalemites rioted in the streets.

**Method in the madness:** The foundations of modern archaeology as we know it were not laid until the late 19th century, and were marked by the establishment of major academic institutions sponsoring field trips and

**Left**, an 1871 journal recounts the discovery of Wilson's Arch. **Right**, Theo Seibenberg examines a newly found artifact.

publication societies. The Palestine Exploration Fund, founded in London in 1865, is the grandfather of these groups, which include such venerable institutions as the American Schools of Oriental Research and the Ecôle Biblique et Archaeologique Française. The work during this period of Edward Robinson, Claude R. Conder, Sir Flinders Petrie and other giants continues to cast a long shadow on modern archaeology.

It was Petrie who first recognised the importance of stratigraphy, that is, the examination layer by layer of a tel, the artificial mound formed by successive settlements. He was also among the first to recognise the importance of using pottery to date each of these layers or strata. He realised that in different periods, particular types of pottery would be associated with particular strata.

After World War I, Mortimer Wheeler and Dame Kathleen Kenyon refined the debris analysis method of pottery dating. At about the same time a separate methodology arose, emphasising the importance of uncovering large areas to expose the architecture of a settlement. Devotees of the so-called architectural method accused the debris analysis subscribers of overlooking the "big picture." The latter in turn accused their colleagues of ignoring the importance of stratigraphy.

Today an eclectic approach to excavating a tel prevails. Technological advances have altered archaeology to the degree that surveyors can provide archaeologists with considerable information before a single shovelful of earth has been removed. Carbon-14 dating has further improved the archaeologist's ability to fix an artifact in time. Archaeologists can now dig underwater, cross-reference finds on computers and learn more quickly what their colleagues have discovered. They can call on a host of specialists, including paleo-botanists, osteologists, ethnologists, philologists and biblical exegetes, whose talents can help interpret their finds.

Most important, archaeologists have come to emphasise that once a locus, that is, a three-dimensional area designated for excavation, is dug and artifacts removed, the site will have been ineluctably altered. By the very nature of their work, archaeologists destroy irreplaceable evidence in their search for remnants of the past.

**Politics and pioneers:** But for many archaeology is a field whose study bolsters or

threatens religious and political beliefs – as well as pet scholarly theories. In the late 1970s, for example, a small but vocal ultra-religious minority tried to stop a dig at the City of David, saying the archaeologists were desecrating ancient graves. But, the archaeologists countered, no evidence pointed to the existence of any graves at the original site of King David's Jerusalem.

For political reasons, Jordan has filed formal complaints with UNESCO against Israeli digs in East Jerusalem – even though the Israeli government has done much to preserve important archaeological sites there.

And among secular, apolitical scholars the real value of the Bible in their archaeological

work is hotly debated. Many have reason to doubt its utility as a historical document and a source of verifiable reference. Others cling firmly to the Bible's documentary importance and infallibility.

The careers of Israel's greatest archaeologists were hewn from this complex web of scholarly debate, political instability, plus a national passion to unearth the Jewish past. Eliezer Sukenik, his son Yigael Yadin, Moshe Dayan, Benjamin Mazar – who can think of these archaeologists apart from Israel's struggle for independence?

In an interview, Mazar, director of the excavations next to the Western Wall in

Jerusalem, remembers his 1936 dig at Beth She'arim in northern Israel: "Everyone had a keen interest in the excavation, because finding Jewish antiquities reinforced the meaning of Zionism and strengthened the reason for creating a Jewish state. We were interested in building a homeland, and Jewish antiquities were part of its foundation."

Of Sukenik's discovery in 1947 of the Dead Sea Scrolls, Yadin writes: "(My father) found something symbolic in the thought that this was happening at the very moment when Jewish sovereignty in Palestine was about to be restored after almost 2,000 years – the very age of the parchment he had seen." That parchment is now part of the collection

television mini-series in which millions learned about the heroic, suicidal stand of a handful of Jews against the Romans.

Today, digs at Tel Dan on the Israeli border with Lebanon, Tel Dor, south of Haifa and nearby Caesarea, where digs are conducted on land and underwater, attract a stream of volunteers from across the globe.

Despite difficulties, Israelis and scholars who come to dig in Israel from all over the world have produced an impressive amount of literature further illuminating the pages of the Bible. And, perhaps, in many ways archaeology is the perfect pasttime for the inhabitants of the Middle East, who have a penchant for argument and disputation.

at the Shrine of the Book, the Israel Museum's home for the Dead Sea Scrolls.

Yadin's own digs and subsequent books on Masada, Hazor and the Dead Sea Scrolls have dramatised the history of the "people of the book." In addition, much of his work has been popularised by others. Hazor, a site in northern Israel with an impressive underground water system, is the subject of James Michener's novel *The Source*. Yadin's dig at Masada – where he discovered a ritual bath and synagogue – became the focus of a

Whether wandering the Arab markets of Jerusalem, visiting a kibbutz school house, or sipping coffee on Dizengoff Street in Tel Aviv, one of your neighbours will doubtless have an opinion on just who is buried in David's Tomb. Or, you may stumble on to the multi-million dollar excavation of Theo and Miriam Siebenberg, amateur archaeologists who determined that their home in Jerusalem's Jewish Quarter was planted on top of important remains.

Indeed, for the average Israeli, the tumbling walls of Jericho are as vivid as the Gulf War. And, in Israel, everyone is welcome to rebuild its ancient past.

**Left**, the underground city at Amatzia, a new attraction. **Above**, archaeologists in action.

Wine, the Good Book says, "maketh glad the heart of man." (Psalms; 104, 15). In Israel, where that Book was written, winemaking keeps the birds happy too. That's because Israeli wine is kosher, and ancient Jewish dietary laws require all fields – including vineyards – to lie fallow every seventh year.

Each year, one-seventh of Israel's viticulture production hangs unharvested: a glorious banquet for the birds. As a bonus, these grapes usually ripen just in time for fall migrations, and songbirds flitting from Eurasia to warm wintering grounds in Africa enjoy a sweet and nutritious Israeli stopover.

The kosher-wine migratory-bird connection is but one of the many unique advantages nature enjoys in the Land of Milk and Honey. The establishment of the modern State of Israel in recent decades has proved an extraordinary benefit to nature. Israeli programmes have devoted much energy and talent toward the revival of the land, and the restoration of its ecological integrity. As a result, Israel today is a cornucopia of nature, abundant and diverse with many species of wild fauna and flora.

**Redeeming the land:** Early in the 20th century, when the Zionist ideal was little more than a philosophical debate, the Land of Israel was a desolate backwater of the crumbling Ottoman Empire. Its ecological dynamics had suffered catastrophy. Nature had been ravished. The hand of havoc had reached into the Garden of Eden.

The introduction of modern firearms was an enormous tragedy for wildlife. Within a few decades, the gazelles and ibex which had graced the landscape since the days of the prophets, were ruthlessly decimated. A monstrous hunting binge literally shot several species into extinction.

The local race of ostrich, which so perplexed Job, was blasted to nothingness. Israel's native race of Asiatic wild ass, a creature which several religious scholars identify as the animal Jesus rode on Palm Sunday, was mercilessly annihilated. The spectacular

white oryx antelope, the re'em of the Hebrew Bible, translated in the King James Version as "unicorn" suffered a similar fate. Fortunately for this species, however, a few specimens were captured for breeding before the last of the wild population was exterminated.

Flora also sustained great hardship. As far back as the Crusades, Christian pilgrims were scouring the countryside for biblical wildflowers. These were picked, pressed and sent back to Europe to serve as bookmarks in

family Bibles. Generations of Europeans could "consider the lilies" of the Holy Land – but these lilies were lifeless, dried, and incapable of reproduction. Today, Israel's native Madonna lily is a very rare plant.

The big disaster came a century ago, when the Ottoman Turks built a railway into the Arabian Desert. Israel's forests were levelled. The heavy timbers were used to bridge ravines; middle-sized logs became rail ties, and the smaller pieces were burned as fuel. By the time the fabled Col. T. E. Lawrence (Lawrence of Arabia) got around to attacking those Ottoman trains, the Land of Israel had less than 3 percent tree cover.

**Left**, sunset at the HaMasrek Nature Reserve outside Jerusalem. **Right**, ibex have existed in Israel since the days of the prophets.

With the loss of vegetation, the soil dried out, turned to dust, and was swept out to the desert by the wind. The scant winter rains had no absorbent material to hold them, and water ran quickly to the sea. Wells dried out.

Jews determined to recreate the State of Israel were confronted by severe problems. The land was exhausted, and literally could not support either a human population or its own natural processes. The ecological integrity of Israel had to be restored. The land itself had to be "redeemed."

**Tu B'Shevat:** The 15th day of the Jewish month of Shevat, Tu B'Shevat is an Israeli Arbor Day; it is celebrated by planting trees in any of the scores of special planting zones

of millions of trees, each planted individually. With the return of the trees – winter rains could be captured and funnelled to the aquifer. Wells again became productive.

With the return of the trees – and particularly the fast-growing Jerusalem pine, (Pinus halepensis) – soil was regenerated. In many places, once the soil was adequate, the pine trees were cut away and immediately replaced with apricot, almond and other fruit and nut trees.

With the return of trees, soil and water, Israeli agriculture prospered. Israel is one of the very few arid lands which grows enough food to feed itself, and also has enough to spare to count agricultural exports as its

in the nation's forests. Israelis plant trees on other days, too – to mark birthdays and weddings, for example. Children honour their parents by planting trees – and parents honour their children the same way. In one forest about 20 km (12 miles) west of Jerusalem, 6 million trees have been planted as a memorial to the Jews who perished in the Holocaust. Entire classes of Israeli youngsters go each year to the forest to plant saplings, and to visit the ones they planted in former years.

Since the founding of the State of Israel in 1948, planted forests have grown to cover 2,000 sq km (770 sq miles) – 10 percent of the total land area of the country – hundreds

major foreign exchange product. With the return of the trees, Nature also flourished. The ecological integrity of the land began to recover. Life processes dependent upon a good vegetative cover reappeared. Some are hardly noticed – the sprouting of orenit mushrooms in the Jerusalem forest after the first winter rains, or the growth of colourful mosaics of lichen upon fallen logs. And some life processes are so dramatic it is quite impossible not to notice them.

The majestic golden eagles have returned to Israeli skies, and one pair even builds its nest each year in the branches of a planted pine forest just south of Jerusalem.

**Nature reserves:** There are 280 established nature reserves in Israel, and together they cover more than 4,000 sq km (1,540 sq miles) – better than one-fifth of the country's total land area.

Israel's nature reserves are considered "strict" by international conservation standards. Visitors are forbidden to interfere with life processes in any way. There is no flower picking, camping or picnicking allowed. The reserves are maintained in as pristine a state as possible.

Administered by the Nature Reserves Authority, these reserves serve a variety of functions. Generally, they reflect the need for humanity and nature to coexist. An ex-

ample of this can be seen at Banias, a beautiful nature reserve at the foot of Mount Hermon, on Israel's northern border.

The name Banias is a corruption of the Greek "Panaeus"; and here, one finds the remains of an ancient Greek temple dedicated to the god of the forests. Other archaeological treasures found in the area include the remains of the ancient Nimrod Fortress, and the Crusader town of Belinas.

The lush and colourful growths of wild

**Left**, a pair of scimitar-horned oryx at Hai Bar.
**Above**, wild-flowers form a carpet of lavender at Nimrod Castle in the Golan.

oleander, the thick groves of myrtle, plane and willow trees appeal to the naturalist's eye. The reserve is a haven for a great variety of birds and mammals. The rare stone marten and wild cat live here. Playful otters splash with carefree abandon in the chill waters flowing from the slopes of Mount Hermon.

These waters give a human dimension to this nature reserve, for they are the headwaters of the Jordan River. Much of this water eventually enters Israel's national water carrier system, and flows from taps in Tel Aviv and Haifa. It helps irrigate the productive fields of the Galilee, and brim the fish ponds of the Bet Shean Valley.

Not every nature reserve had a direct human-interest purpose. Many are established solely for the preservation of particular natural values: a seasonal pond, a secluded valley where rare wildflowers blossom, a sunny cliff with several good nesting ledges. Some of these nature reserves are off-limits to human visitors, and kept protected simply because of their importance to nature and the ecological equilibrium of the region.

An underlying philosophy of Israeli nature reserves recognises that all nature protection ultimately benefits humanity as well. Sustained human use of the environment requires sustained protection of the environment – an obvious requirement too frequently ignored around the world.

**Hai-Bar:** One of the more compelling projects aimed at the restoration of natural ecological processes in Israel is the Hai-Bar programme. Hai Bar is a Hebrew term which simply means "wildlife." But to Israeli conservationists, it also identifies an international effort to "return the animals of the Bible to the land of the Bible."

Under the auspices of this project, Israeli conservationists have searched the world to find remnants of those species which once inhabited Israel. Some of the discoveries were prosaic: addax antelope were found in a Chicago zoo, and a few Asiatic wild ass were acquired from the Copenhagen zoo.

A few of the discoveries have involved some spectacular rescue work. Mesopotamian fallow dear, for example, were spirited out of revolutionary Iran during a howling storm and on false export papers. White oryx – those "unicorns" of the King James Version – reached their ancestral home in the Negev Desert after a globe-trotting journey of tens of thousands of kilometres. Their source: a few hundred kilometres southeast of the Negev – in the personal zoo of the late Saudi King Faisal. And a flock of ostrich chicks was air-lifted out of Ethiopia's Danakil Desert when the Israeli Air Force was ordered on a "special mission" to fetch a few new immigrants to Israel.

All the animals, regardless of their origin, are first brought to special nature reserves in Israel which are set up to readapt them to life in Israel's wild areas. One Hai-Bar reserve is deep in the Negev, about 40 km north of Eilat; it specialises in desert animals. Another is on top of Mount Carmel, on the Mediterranean coast near Haifa; it specialises in wildlife of the Mediterranean oak-forest region. A third Hai-Bar reserve is in the process of being organised on the Golan, to handle animals indigenous to the Galilean plains and Golan Heights.

The restoration process is comprehensive and involves years of painstaking work. Indeed, 14 years passed between the acquisition of those Asiatic wild ass from the Copenhagen Zoo, and the day when their offspring were judged tough and experienced enough to live freely in the wild. Those offspring were released and today they are repopulating remote areas of the Negev and giving birth to their own wildborn foals.

**Ecological diversity:** Despite its small size, Israel is one of the most ecologically diverse countries in the world. Two factors contribute to this remarkable diversity: geography and topography.

Geographically, Israel is located at the confluence of the great Eurasian and African landmasses. Any land traffic between these landmasses must pass through Israel. Many life forms have migrated through this keystone country; the evolutionary spread of the equines from Asia into Africa, and the migration of humanity itself from African origins through the rest of the world, filtered through what is now Israel.

Migration is still an extremely important phenomenon in Israel, and, twice yearly, millions of migratory birds pass through on their way to and from northern nesting grounds and southern wintering areas. More than 150 species of migratory birds are seen in the town of Eilat alone.

Topography in Israel is a matter of spectacular contrasts. Mount Hermon, on the northern border, towers at a snow-capped 2,814 metres (9,223 ft); the Dead Sea, at 400 metres (1,300 ft) below sea level, is the lowest point on the face of the earth. Broad plains stretch across parts of the Galilee, and fringe the northern Negev with expanses of steppe grasslands. Makhtesh Ramon, a natural crater 40 km (25 miles) across, is carved from the central Negev highlands. The north-south range of the Judean Mountains forms a continuous ridge nearly 1,000 metres (3,280 ft) high, an hour's drive east of the Mediterranean coast.

The great geographical and topographical diversity is responsible for tremendous biological diversity. In Israel, one finds subalpine meadows on the slopes of Mount Hermon, and a mere 25 km (16 miles) south, at the Hula Nature Reserve, there is a lush tropical jungle: the world's northernmost papyrus swamp. Israel is a land of Eurasian oaks and African acacias, Eurasian foxes and wolves and African dorcas gazelles and rock hyrax. It is a land of blending continents, flora, fauna and geology.

**Nature protection:** The fabric of nature in Israel is a complex matrix responding to an unusual array of influences. This is further complicated by human activity: modern agriculture, new cities, military necessities. Nature protection, then, requires extraordinary vigilance and activism – tasks which are shared by both government agencies and non-government associations.

But education is the keystone to conservation, and the Society for the Protection of Nature in Israel (SPNI) is the undisputed giant in this field. Operating a network of 24 field schools – each capable of housing 150 to 250 overnight guests – SPNI conducts an active programme of conservation education and nature protection.

For those who want a bit of soil beneath their fingernails, visitors are encouraged to join their Israeli nature-loving counterparts at any of the Jewish National Fund's tree-planting centres located throughout the country. There, they will find a forester and a bit of on-the-job instruction on how to take a tender sapling, set it into the earth, and start its task of growing, forming soil, conserving water, sheltering wildlife and restoring the ecological integrity of the land.

**Right, poster kids do their bit for conservation.**

# PLACES

The beauty in visiting Israel is that within a territory less than 125 km (75 miles) wide and 445 km (275 miles) long lies a diversity of sights and places equalled in few other parts of the world. Israel's roster of environs sweeps expansively from the spiritual to the sensual – from the luxury hotels of Tel Aviv to the steeples of Jerusalem, from the coral reefs of the Red Sea to the timeless shores of the Jordan River and the Sea of Galilee.

Although Israel is still a new nation, civilisations have swept across this land with the regularity of the Mediterranean tide. History is everywhere, and the layers of interest – religious, technological, architectural, cultural and natural – overlap liberally.

Our first "Places" chapter focuses on Tel Aviv, Israel's Mediterranean metropolis. A cosmopolitan city of beachfronts, boulevards, cafés and modern architecture, it serves as the hub of the nation's cultural life, and holds close to a quarter of Israel's population.

The fertile coastal plain is Israel's summer playground, the site of some of the country's first settlements and the centre of its thriving citrus and diamond industries. The modern city of Haifa, rich in technology and spirit, sits atop Mount Carmel further north, sharing the coastline with ancient Crusader forts.

The Galilee is Israel's lush reclaimed bread-basket, and its green valleys hold communities of Arabs, Druze and Jews alike. The land of Jesus's youth, it cradles the biblical town of Nazareth as well as the ancient Jewish holy cities of Tiberius and Safed. The Sea of Galilee, Israel's placid northern lake, channels the twisting Jordan River southward from its mountainous headwaters.

To the northeast, the Golan Heights: wrested from Syria in 1967, a looming natural fortress crowned by snow-capped Mount Hermon.

The Central Crossroads serve as the historic corridor between the coast and Jerusalem, while Jerusalem itself glitters, golden at the centre of the country. This city of cities is the capital of modern Israel. Sacred to three religions, its sites include the Western Wall, the Dome of the Rock and the Holy Sepulchre.

The West Bank, including the hills of Samaria in the north and Judea in the south, remains both the hub of the Holy Land and a political hot potato: in Israel's hands since 1967, it holds the cities of Bethlehem, Hebron and Jericho. The Gaza Strip along the coast remains in a similar state of limbo.

The Dead Sea and Judean Desert, along Israel's southeastern rim, once the realm of ancient ascetics, is the site of the famed citadel of Masada, oases, mineral spas and spectacular geology.

The Negev Desert, the vast and rugged southern badlands, is receiving new life with a variety of agriculture and its boom-town capital, Beersheba. Eilat is Israel's strategic Red Sea playland.

They all await you in the pages that follow.

<u>Preceding pages</u>: Mount Hermon; Banias; Judean Desert at Neot Hakikar. <u>Left</u>, tour bus in Timna Valley, Negev.

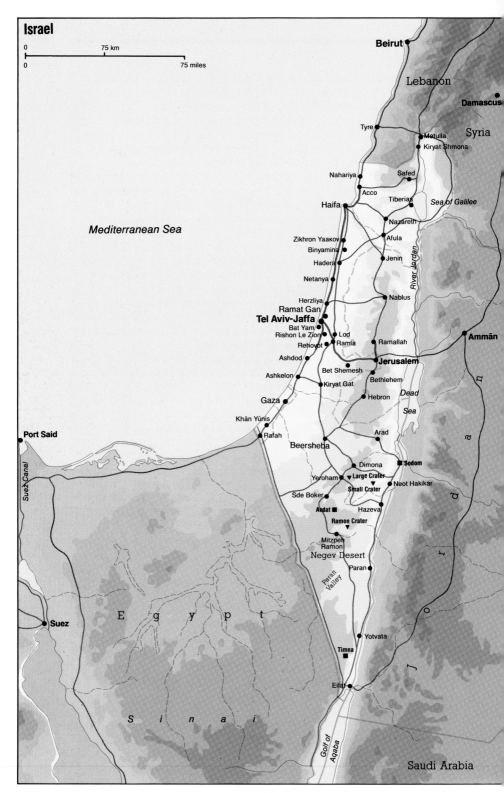

# Israel

Mediterranean Sea

Beirut

Lebanon

Damascus

Syria

Tyre
Metulla
Kiryat Shmona

Nahariya
Safed

Acco
Tiberias
Sea of Galilee

Haifa

Nazareth

Zikhron Yaakov
Afula

Binyamina
Jenin

Hadera

Netanya
Nablus

Herzliya
Ramat Gan
Tel Aviv-Jaffa
Bat Yam
Rishon Le Zion
Lod
Rehovot
Ramla
Ramallah
Amman

Ashdod
Jerusalem

Ashkelon
Bet Shemesh
Bethlehem

Kiryat Gat
Hebron
Dead
Sea

Gaza

Khān Yūnis
Arad

Rafah
Port Said
Beersheba

Suez Canal

Dimona
Sodom
Yeroham
Large Crater
Sde Boker
Small Crater
Neot Hakikar

Avdat
Hazeva

Ramon Crater

Mitzpeh
Ramon

Negev Desert
Paran

Paran
Valley

Suez

E g y p t

Yotvata

Timna

S i n a i

Eilat

Gulf of
Aqaba

River Jordan

Saudi Arabia

0    75 km

0    75 miles

# Northern Israel

0       25 km

0       25 miles

Tyre

Metulla   Tel Dan

**Lebanon**

Kiryat Shmona

Merom Golan

Rosh Hanikra

Hula Valley

Achziv

Kuneitra

Nahariya

Mt. Meron ▲

Golan Heights

Acco

Safed ●

Katzrin

Capernahum

Gamla

**Haifa**

G a l i l e e

**Syria**

Kiryat Ata

Sea of Galilee

Atlit ■

Tiberius

'En Gev

Nazareth

Mt. Tabor ▲

Hammat Gader

Nasholim Beach ●

J e z r e e l  V a l l e y

Afula

Belvoir

Tel Dor ●

Megiddo

Zikhron Yaakov

Bet Shean

Caesarea ■

Binyamina

Mt. Gilboa ▲

Hadera ●

Jenin

**Mediterranean Sea**

Mikhmoret Beach ●

Yamma

Zababida

Netanya ●

Mehola

S a m a r i a

Tulkarm

Sebastia

Mt. Ebal ▲

Herzliya ●

Kfar Sava

Nablus

Azzun

Mt. Gerezim ▲

Mekhora

Bene Brak

**Tel Aviv-Jaffa**

Petach Tikva

Sawiya

Ramat Gan

Shiloh

Bat Yam

Gilgal

Rishon Le Zion

Lydda

Palmachim Beach ●

Ramla

Ramallah

Jericho

**Ammān** ●

Modiin

Rehovot

Jericho

Yavne

Ashdod ●

Jerusalem

Nizzanim Beach ●

Bet Shemesh

Qumran

Ashkelon ●

Betlehem   Mar Saba

Kfar Etzian

**D e a d**

Kiryat Gat

Beit Guvrin

Lachish

J u d e a n  D e s e r t

Gaza ●

Hebron

**S e a**

Bureij

Bet Qama

En Gedi

Shibbolim

J u d e a

Khan Yunis

Tel Arad

Masada

Beersheba

Nevatim

Arad

Neve Zohar

N e g e v  D e s e r t

Sodom

Dead Sea Works

To Sde Boker

Dimona

141

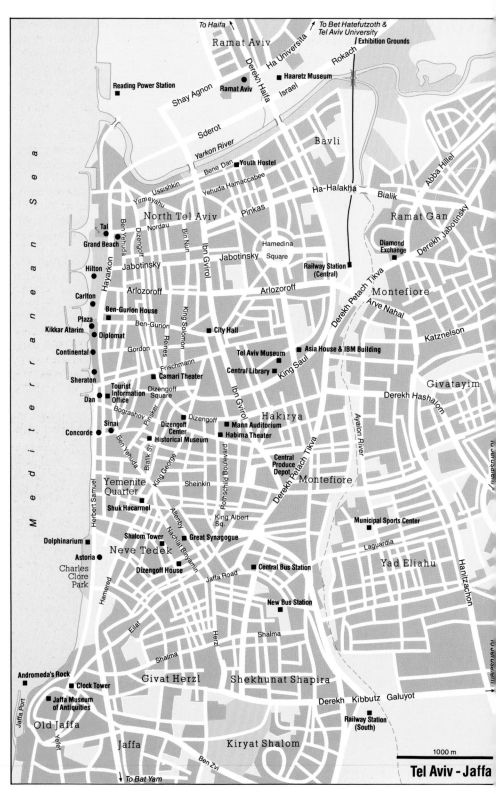

Tel Aviv - Jaffa

1000 m

# TEL AVIV

A hundred years ago, who could have predicted Tel Aviv? The stretch of coastline north of Jaffa was a bleak collection of dunes, devoid of life and impoverished of resources. By the mid-1900s, the fledgling metropolis had blossomed with tree-lined boulevards and spanking-new International-style apartment homes, and had already overtaken its ancient mother city in population and vitality.

Today, Tel Aviv has grown to be the centre of culture, business, *haute couture* and nightlife in Israel, its white beaches, sunny weather and posh hotels making it a year-round tourist resort. While the city itself holds only some 350,000 residents, Tel Aviv's sizeable metropolitan district contains nearly 2 million people – close to 40 percent of the population of the entire country. With its celebrated cafés and sleek new office towers, the world's first modern Jewish city is as contemporary as it is boisterous, combining the *joie de vivre* of a Mediterranean people with the style and sophistication of Europe's most fashionable cities.

Ruins? Cathedrals? Red-brick manors? No, not many. But Tel Aviv has a debonair charm all its own, which, if sometimes out of reach to the casual tourist, is as much a part of the fabric of modern Israel as the Bible itself.

Tel Aviv is actually just part of the greater city of Tel Aviv-Jaffa: the two being combined officially in 1950 after years of merging into one another. While Tel Aviv was born with the 20th century, **Jaffa** (or "Yafo" according to the strict transliteration) is ancient and today still harbours its own rich history.

**Jaffa, where it all began:** When God got fed up with his creatures, he brought the "Great Flood" on the world to wipe the slate clean and start afresh. After the flood subsided and Noah's Ark landed upon Mount Ararat, Noah's youngest son Japheth found a pleasant hill overlooking a bay and settled down, naming the site "Jaffa", Hebrew for beautiful.

One of the oldest cities in the world, Jaffa has retained its biblical flavour, spiced by historical events and myths throughout the ages. It was from here that Jonah the prophet boarded the ship for Tarshish, in his attempt to flee God's injunction to warn the evil city of Ninveh (Jonah; 1, 34). The famous cedars of Lebanon were shipped to Jaffa – early on an important Mediterranean trading port – to be used by King Solomon in building the Temple in Jerusalem.

The miracle of Tabitha was performed by the Apostle Peter when he stayed at the Jaffa house of Simon the Tanner (Acts; 9, 36-42). And Greek mythology holds that the beautiful Andromeda, daughter of the King of Jaffa, was chained to a rock just off Jaffa's port, to appease the wrath of a sea monster (subsequently being rescued by Perseus on his winged white horse).

Some 3,400 years ago Jaffa was conquered by the Egyptians. The Philistines, Israelites, Persians, Alexander the Great, Syrians, Maccabees (Israelite Warriors), Romans, Herod the Great, Muslims,

Crusaders, Richard the Lionhearted, Mamelukes, Napoleon and the Turks all passed through, alternately destroying and building. The British eventually took over from the Ottomans at the end of World War I, and Jaffa returned to Israeli hands during the War of Independence in 1948.

Jewish residence was resumed in Jaffa long before that, in 1820, when a Jewish traveller from Constantinople settled here. Soon after came a larger community of Jewish residents, mainly North African merchants and craftsmen, who merged with the local Arab community. By the time of Israel's independence, the city had close to 100,000 residents, over 30,000 of them Jewish. Modern Jaffa has retained its Eastern flavour, and today holds a colourful medley of immigrants from North African and Central European countries.

**Old Jaffa today:** Old Jaffa was reconstructed and renovated in 1963, with cobbled paths and winding alleys twisting through the massive stone fortifications surrounding the city. Today it sports an artists' colony, art galleries, craft shops, tourist shops, seafood restaurants and nightclubs. The old Jaffa harbour, destined for demolition (and eventual reconstruction as an exclusive marina) is still the home port of the local fishermen, who haul in their catch every dawn. Their potluck findings end up in the cauldrons of the town's many restaurants, three of which are located right in the old port, overlooking the pier and bobbing boats.

Looking seawards from the port, one can make out a cluster of rocks, the largest of which is believed to be Andromeda's. However, recent renovation of the pier, which included the bombing of some of the formation, may have blown the fabled **Andromeda's Rock** out of existence.

For the rest, time seems to have stood still. Primitive ovens still churn out an infinite variety of oriental-spice pita breads, and the ancient streets hum as of yore with aggressive shopkeepers, pastry vendors and meandering passers-by.

Old Jaffa "begins at the **Clock Tower**

Left, doorwa in Old Jaffa. Below, suns: sihouettes minaret.

144

on **Yefet Street**, built in 1906. Facing the local police station, the tower's stained-glass windows each portray a different chapter in the town's history. Opposite the tower, past an arched entranceway, is a large inner courtyard, once the **Armenian Hostel** which served as a "central station" for travellers and convoys going to and from Jewish settlements throughout the country. Beyond the police station, a large entrance leads to the **Mahmoudia Mosque** (the actual entrance is around the back), built in 1812 and named after the city's Turkish governor.

Turning right from Yefet Street, towards the renovated section, one passes the **Jaffa Museum of Antiquities**, where archaeological exhibits from more than 20 years of excavations trace the city's development. Erected in the 18th century, the building was once the Turkish governor's headquarters and the local prison. In a later reincarnation, it won acclaim throughout the Middle East as the soap factory of the Greek Orthodox Damiani family.

The Franciscan **Saint Peter's Church** is next door. The **Saint Louis Monastery** in the courtyard was named after the French king, who arrived at the head of a Crusade, and stayed here in 1147. The monastery later served as a hostel for pilgrims to Jerusalem and was known in the 17th century as "The Europeans' House." Napoleon also relaxed here after conquering Jaffa.

A little way towards the sea is the minaret of the **Jama El-Baher Mosque**, located next door to the first Jewish house in Jaffa. Built in 1820, the house was also a hostel, for Jerusalemites who came to swim off Jaffa's beach. The **Armenian Convent** and church here mark the site of a large Armenian pilgrims' inn from the 17th century. A magnificent, renovated Turkish mansion behind the museum, once a Turkish bath house, has been converted into a nightclub and restaurant called **El-Hamam**.

At the top of the hill, past the **Pisgah Park**, **Horoscope Path** begins to wend its way through the Jaffa wall. It goes all

the way to the lighthouse at the wall's southern entrance. At the centre of the renovated section is a square called **Kikar Kedumin**, in which the Jaffa excavations present a reconstruction of the city's multi-faceted history; this is also one of Tel Aviv's most popular evening spots.

On the southern side of the wall, along Pasteur Street, a modern structure mars the beauty of the ancient (renovated) walls. This is the **Israel Experience**, a new tourist centre comprising an auditorium for a multimedia show, a shopping area and a restaurant. The main show combines computerised projection systems on giant screens by means of 40 slide projectors, accompanied by special light and sound effects, for those who like that sort of thing.

Back on Yefet Street, and facing Tel Aviv to the north, the road passes two famous pitta-bread establishments, which reputedly do their best business on Passover and Yom Kippur, when droves of bread-craving Israelis queue outside them. Jaffa's famous **flea mar-**ket lies in the next complex of alleys just east of here. The market specialises in antiques, copperware ("antique" specimen made while you watch), jewellery and second-hand junk.

**A city on sand:** Tel Aviv sprang out of the desolate sand dunes north of Jaffa almost overnight, when a group of Jewish Jaffa residents purchased some land and raffled it off among themselves in 1909. They intended to build a garden suburb in which they could find respite after a day's work in noisy, crowded Jaffa. But they also had hopes to create the first new Jewish city in 2,000 years.

They named it Tel Aviv – Hill of Spring – a name symbolising hope for a new future to be built on the ruins of the past. A *tel* in Hebrew is an artificial hill, created on the accumulated debris of past, abandoned cities; *aviv* means spring, connoting new life. First mentioned in the book of Ezekial, Tel Aviv was the name of a town in the exile in Babylon where the prophet went for his dry bones prophecy. Tel Aviv was also the name given the Hebrew translation

**Panorama of Tel Aviv shows its urban sprawl**

of Herzl's book *Alteneuland* (Old-New Land), in which he predicted and conceived of the Jewish State.

The first houses were completed before the year was out. By the eve of World War I, the suburb had grown to 20 times its original size, and Jaffa's Jewish institutions began draining one by one into the new city to the north. When World War II began, the Turkish rulers expelled the Jewish population of Jaffa and Tel Aviv to other parts of the region, but with the advent of British occupation in 1917, the settlers drifted back into their homes. They continued laying out their city, and by 1984 there were already some 230,000 Tel Avivians.

**Architecture and navigation:** In the city's early days, people built their own dwellings infusing their own vision and hope into the city they were moulding. The first residents built houses to remind them of their home back in Europe, inspired by neo-classical buildings in Vienna, Odessa or Warsaw. Local architects tried to conform the European styles to their new Middle Eastern abode by softening the symmetrical corners with rounded balconies, or adding domes, arched entranceways, and wall decorations depicting Biblical motifs. In the 1920s and '30s, Tel Aviv became an eclectic collection of styles and influences. Its staid neoclassical structures were jazzed up with a spectrum of Art Nouveau, Middle Eastern and kitsch elements.

In the 1930s, the new or International building style, inspired by the Bauhaus in Germany and such architects as Le-Corbusier and Erich Mendelsohn, took over. The symmetry and colonnades made way for clean, minimalistic lines and severe functionality became the name of the game. Tel Aviv became the only city in the world to be dominated by the International style. In later years, the "White City", as Tel Aviv was dubbed by poet Nathan Alterman, was peeling and its buildings were repainted in various colours, partly in reaction to the severe style. But city streets are still characterised today by apartment blocks

raised up on columns and the roof gardens introduced by that school of architecture, and many of the newer apartment complexes going up are once more indeed white.

The most important streets to get to know are Ben Yehuda Street, which goes parallel to the shoreline and serves the various hotels along that strip, and Dizengoff Street, which runs from the Mann Auditorium complex and the famous café hub of Dizengoff Circle down to the intersection with Ben Yehuda at the northern tip of the city. These routes are both conveniently serviced by the number 4 and 5 buses, respectively, which in turn run all the way to the **Central Bus Station**, a crazy open-air terminal, near the southern end of Allenby Street. Allenby is the final important connecting street, passing through most of the downtown area, to Ben Yehuda, where it turns left for two blocks before terminating at the beachfront.

**Near the Shalom Tower:** The tallest building in the Middle East, the **Shalom Tower** on Herzl Street soars 35 floors above the city, an austere white rectangle. Its main significance to the city is in its location. For on these premises stood one of the very first buildings to be erected in Tel Aviv – the Herzliya Gymnasium (High School). Built in 1909 on the new town's first thoroughfare, the school was a symbol of pioneering and became the cultural and economic nucleus of the embryonic town. The school building was torn down in 1959. Only a huge fresco on the wall of the tower, created by artist Nahum Gutman, remains of the old building.

The tower consists of a 4-storey department store area and some 30 office floors. Its top floor is open to the public and presents a magnificent view of the area, reaching on a clear day from Mount Carmel in the north to the Negev in the south, with Jerusalem visible to the east.

The **Wax Museum** on the third floor displays figures from a century of Jewish history (1867 to 1967). There are wax likenesses of former prime ministers David Ben-Gurion and Golda Meir, and even Nazi war criminal Adolph Eichman. A chamber, "The Enchanted World", intermixes Neil Armstrong on the Moon, Hansel and Gretel, the Manson Murders and Michael Jackson (next to Israeli pop star Ofra Haza).

Right behind the Shalom Tower's sharp modernism is an entirely different world. The **Yemenite Quarter's** exotic winding streets are a jolt back in time, preserving the look and feel of the Yemenite community which settled here some 100 years ago. This is the best place you'll find to sample the spicy, pungent Yemenite cuisine, in authentic, Arab-style stone houses. **Pundak Shaul**, **Zion**, **Pninat Hakerem** and **Maganda** are among the best Yemenite restaurants in the country.

One of the most impressive old buildings remaining in Tel Aviv, although in a sorry state of disrepair, is the **Pagoda House** in **King Albert Square**. The square, once destined for the site of city hall, had the town's prettiest buildings erected around it. Located across Allenby Street, at the intersection of Nahmani, Montefiore and Melchet streets, the

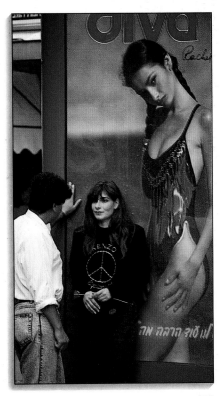

**ft, Shalom wer looms er the city. ght, odern style.**

Pagoda House was built in 1925 for American Joseph Bloch, who lived in it six months a year. The house had a pagoda-like structure at the top of its three floors, and boasted the first passenger elevator in Tel Aviv.

**Rothschild:** Built in 1910 over a dried river bed, **Rothschild Boulevard** was once Tel Aviv's most elegant address. It's still lovely, its central promenade dotted by trees, benches and refreshment kiosks, and its buildings, embrace a jumble of styles. At number 13 is the Bezalel style (named after the Bezalel Art School in Jerusalem), combining European and Oriental design. The public museum **Independence Hall** is at number 16, the former residence of Tel Aviv's first mayor Meir Dizengoff. Israel's Declaration of Independence was signed in this building on 15 May 1948. The second and third floor comprise the **Bible Museum**. Across the road is the **Israel Defense Force Museum**, located in the former residence of Hagana commander Eliahu Golumb.

**Breuer House** at number 46 was built in 1922; it has tiny, decorative balconies, a slanting, pagoda-like wooden roof, a minaret, and a large, enclosed garden. On the verge of demolition in 1948, the building was saved when the Soviet ambassador requested it for his headquarters. It served as the Soviet Embassy until 1953, when diplomatic relations between Israel and the USSR were severed.

Typical Bauhaus buildings may be observed at numbers 89, 91 and 140, and on nearby Engel Street, recently converted into a pedestrian mall.

**A walk on Bialik Street:** Further west along Allenby, **Bialik Street** is another pleasant street left over from the city's early days. At number 14 is the **Rubin House**, the former residence of noted Israeli artist Reuvin Rubin; a short walk from here is the **Bialik House**, once the home of Israel's national poet Haim Nahman Bialik. Built in 1925, it has a little tower and dome, a prominent pink balcony and arched columns, like those of the Doge Palace in Venice.

At the end of the street is **Skura House**, today housing the **Museum for**

the **History of Tel Aviv-Jaffa**. Built in 1925, this house never became the hotel it was supposed to be, instead housing the Tel Aviv municipality from 1928 to 1968, when the City Hall moved north to Ibn Gvirol Street.

Next to the building, stairs lead down to Idelson Street, near **Gan Meir** (Meir Garden), one of the prettiest in town. Across the park, and a little way up King George Street one reaches Tel Aviv's shortest street. This is **Anonymous Alley** (Simta Almonit), sister to the nearby **Unknown Alley** (Simta Palmonit). These two tiny alleys were built as academics' residences in American Colonial style for American and British immigrants in the 1920s. Inside the buildings' curved facade stands the faded, peeling statue of a lion. Its eyes, destroyed long ago, were once glowing electric torches which shone at night.

**Neve Tzedek:** The oldest quarter in the city, **Neve Tzedek** was founded in 1887 as a suburb of Jaffa, and is a picturesque maze of narrow streets flanked by low-built Arab style houses. At the time, the

**Allenby Stre** **in mid-193C**

quarter was considered a luxury suburb, despite the crowded housing and less-than-sanitary conditions. In recent years, the quarter's quaint old dwellings have taken the fancy of artists and well-to-do families, who restored them and re-planted the inner courtyards.

The **Neve Tzedek Theater**, which specialises in *avant-garde* drama, opened in the building of the city's first girls' school, which was also the first all-Hebrew school in Israel. With the theatre's opening, several colourful restaurants and nightclubs popped up, lending new ambience and vitality to the century-old streets.

On the border of Neve Tzedek and Tel Aviv, at the intersection of Lillienblum and Pines streets, stands Israel's first cinema hall. The **Eden Cinema** was built in 1914, seating 600 wide-eyed movie viewers who marvelled at the silent movies accompanied by a not-always-synchronised orchestra. When talking movies were invented at the end of the 1920s, the cinema management was pressurised by the powerful Labour Federation to continue paying the un-employed orchestra members' wages for a year and a half.

Between Neve Tzedek and the sea, on the fast road to Jaffa, is the **Hassan Bek Mosque**, contrasting sharply with the contemporary high-rise near it. Built in 1916 by Jaffa's Turkish-Arab governor of the same name, the mosque was in-tended to block development of Tel Aviv towards the sea. Supposedly, Hassan Bek had robbers pilfer building materials from Tel Aviv in order to construct the mosque. During the War of Independence, the Mosque served as an outpost for Arab snipers who would shoot at the Jewish population.

**Levantine markets:** If Tel Aviv is often noted for its European air and lifestyle, its marketplaces are an inseparable part of the Levant. The biggest and best known of these is the **Carmel Market**, on and around Hacarmel Street, off Allenby. Always crowded with shoppers and hagglers, the market is a medley of colours, smells and sounds. A large variety of fruits, vegetables and herbs

quiet
moment at
Carmel
Market.

can be found here, as well as underwear, fashion items, clothes, shoes, pickled foods and pitta bread at bargain prices. Exotic anonas, fijoyas, persimmons and star fruit are piled along more prosaic fruits like bananas and oranges.

The nearby **Bezalel Market**, off King George Street, is reputed to have the best felafel in Israel, as well as the usual discount quality fashion items and second-hand bric-a-brac.

Tourists have not yet discovered **Sheinkin Street**, the local equivalent of New York's Village, tinged with Lower East Side. Stretching from Allenby all the way east to Yehuda HaLevi Street, Sheinkin is one street that has it all. Only on Sheinkin can you buy wallpaper, furniture and home appliances, discover a second-hand Georgian fakefur coat, bind a book, buy eggs in a shop which sells only farm-fresh produce, have your hair done, and wind up over coffee in a Bohemian café that has trees growing in it. This, by the way, is **Café Tamar**, a veteran establishment facing the editorial offices of Davar – the Labor Party newspaper. Nobody remembers exactly how old the café is; old-timers affirm it has always been there.

**Gateway by the beach:** Most tourists spend at least their first and last nights at one of Tel Aviv's hotels. These establishments, concentrated along the beach promenade, have inevitably become the gateway to Israel.

From the north of the city to its south, the coastline is dominated by an imposing row of hotels, lined up like dominoes, their number including the Hilton, north of Arlozorov Street, and working down through the Carlton, Moriah, Holiday Inn, Ramada, Sheraton and Dan. The **seaside promenade** is dotted with cafés, restaurants, ice-cream parlors and the like all offering free sea air and costly refreshments. On summer nights the promenade is clogged with people on foot and in cars, manoeuvring for some sea breeze after the day's humid, oppressive heat.

In front of the Carlton, Penta and Marina hotels is Tel Aviv's large seawater **swimming pool**, maintained

Sun-bronzed Israelis at beachside.

at 24°C (70°F) year-round. Aerobic exercise sessions are held on the beach in the summer, and, if this is passé, a rollerskating rink operates at evening hours near the pool. The **marina** next door, largest in the Middle East, rents out sailing and motor-boats, and equipment for windsurfing, seasurfing, waterskiing and other water sports.

You can't get away from Kikar Namir (still known locally by its former name, **Kikar Atarim**), a concrete monstrosity squatting over the marina, at the end of Ben-Gurion Boulevard. This is an open-air square and mall, offering concrete mushroom sunshades, tourist items and a chance to lose one's way. Its cafés, pizzerias and restaurants, tolerable in the sunlight, turn seedy at night.

Each hotel has its own beach strip (the beaches are all public), most of them quite civilised, with showers, easy chairs and refreshment facilities.

Marking the end of the hotel line to the south, across from the Dan Panorama, is the **Dolphinarium**, a white elephant, now unused, obscuring the magnificent view of Old Jaffa from Tel Aviv's coast.

**Dizengoff's cafés:** Café-going is a major part of any self-respecting Tel Avivian's way of life. Some people go to cafés for their first coffee of the day; others conduct business meetings or entertain guests; senior citizens spend their mornings over cappuccino and croissants at their regular haunts. On a sunny day, a newcomer may get the impression that the entire city is on holiday, sipping coffee at sidewalk cafés.

The bulk of Israeli café activity takes place along the city's main drag, **Dizengoff Street**, an indigenous cross between the Via Venetio and Fifth Avenue. Young, upbeat and action-packed, this street is a never-ending parade of beautiful people, window shoppers, tourists, famous actors or models or in-vogue popstars, vagabonds, soldiers and business people. A seat in a Dizengoff café is an excellent vantage point for observing the multifaceted human panorama moving by.

At no time is Dizengoff more glamor-

**Kar Atarim dusk.**

ous or crowded than on Friday afternoons, when groups of Tel Avivians congregate to unwind from the long work week with friends, try to chat up girls, catch up on gossip, and learn of the night's best parties.

The café scene begins in the north of Dizengoff with "respectable" veteran establishments like **Café Afarsemon** and **Batya**. Eminent literary figures and the Austro-Hungarian set used to favor the former Café Stern a little way down, today the **Stern-Dolphin Fish Restaurant**. On the corner of Ben-Gurion Boulevard is **Café Cherry**, particularly crowded on Fridays when singles come to meet and greet. A short walk west on Ben-Gurion brings you to the former **David Ben-Gurion House**, today a public museum housing his personal mementoes and 20,000-volume library.

The next street to cut across Dizengoff is **Gordon**, known as Gallery Street. Works of the great masters, such as Picasso and Chagall, are displayed here beside paintings by leading Israeli artists like Agam, Gutman and Kadishman.

Those who like to combine sightseeing with food can then eat their way down Dizengoff, which, as it proceeds southwards, gets crowded with snack bars and restaurants, offering everything from fruit juice, pizza and hamburgers to Hungarian blintzes and *shwarma*.

The raised piazza with the sculpture-fountain spouting in its centre is **Dizengoff Circle**, named after the first mayor's wife, Zina. Originally a traffic circle for streets converging on Dizengoff the pedestrian level since has been lifted above the street, creating a peculiar urban hub, but allowing for the free flow of people and traffic. A block further south is **Dizengoff Center**, a modern multi-level shopping complex, offering everything from offbeat pets to carpets, complete with cinemas, restaurants, sport shops and banks.

**Bring on the night:** Tel Aviv is one of the few large cities of its kind to be relatively safe at night, and its main streets throng with activity at least until midnight. Pubs and nightclubs, which according to municipal law should close

People-watching from the Dizengoff Street café.

154

down by 1am, usually stay open much longer, although they invariably look shut from the street.

In recent years, the evening action has gravitated to **North Tel Aviv**, at the converging point of Dizengoff Ben Yehuda and Hayarkon streets, where a night-time eating and entertainment centre has blossomed. Dozens of Chinese, French, Japanese, Hungarian and Oriental restaurants illuminate the streets. **Yirmiyahu Street**, which cuts across the three north-south streets, leads from the Peer Cinema to countless eating establishments, adding to the general atmosphere of culinary well-being.

Apart from the many nightclubs, discotheques and bars dispersed throughout the city, the remaining nightlife focuses on **Old Jaffa**. Popular clubs here include El Hamam and The Cave, specialising in Israeli folklore, and Ariana for Greek music and dancing.

**Independence Park** hides among its shrubbery various archaeological finds, but in the evenings the park is the gathering spot of the city's gay community.

From here they may go on to Divine, a gay-oriented nightclub on Dizengoff Street, or another (mixed) club.

**The modern city:** During the Russian Revolution, a group of young Jewish Russian actors formed a collective and dreamed of a Hebrew theatre. The dream came true in Tel Aviv, dozens of years later. The **Habima Theater**, built for the company in **Habima Square** (*habima* means 'the stage' in Hebrew) originally had creaking wooden chairs and lousy acoustics: today it has two theatre halls (one seating 1,000 and a smaller seating 300), revolving stages, orchestra seats and simultaneous translation into a number of languages during the hot seasons. The square itself fronted by Dizengoff Street in the north, Huberman Street in the east, and Tarsat Boulevard in the west, also holds a large abstract sculpture by Menashe Kadishman and has become synonymous with Tel Aviv's performance prowess.

Just next to the Habima Theater is the **Mann Auditorium**, the home of the Israel Philharmonic Orchestra. Tickets

Asia House and the IBM Building.

here are always highly prized. The third building in this complex is the **Helena Rubinstein Pavilion**, a branch of the Tel Aviv Museum, which specialises in modern art exhibitions. The little park in the middle of the complex hides the chic, brass and chrome **Apropos Café**.

From here, the new part of the city splays out northwards, along a network of tree-lined residential boulevards, bisected by the main strip of **Ibn Gvirol Street**, and featuring the luxuriously wide circle of **Kikar Hamedina**.

At the corner of **Shaul Hamelech Street** (King Saul) and **Weizmann Street**, are the most striking modern edifices in the city. The most unusual of these is **Asia House,** created by architect Mordechai Ben-Horin in gleaming white to resemble a horizontal series of giant, rolling waves, taking a morphological cue, perhaps, from the amoeba. Its entrance holds a permanent exhibit of sculpture under a pastel-coloured mosaic ceiling. The building houses embassies, offices and restaurants.

The **IBM Building** next door towers above, a three-sided cylinder supported on a mushroom-like shaft. Designed by Israeli architects Yasky, Gil & Silvan, it creates a handsome profile for the city skyline. Across the street, the red slated roofs of the **German Templar colony** (1870–1939) provide one more architectural contrast in a city of contrasts.

Located at Golda Meir Square further in on King Saul Boulevard, the **Tel Aviv Museum** has four central galleries, an auditorium which often features film retrospectives, numerous other halls, a statue garden, a cafeteria and a museum shop. The museum has exhibitions of 17th-century Dutch and Flemish masters, 18th-century Italian paintings, Impressionists, post-Impressionists, and a good selection of 20th-century art from the US and Europe, in addition to a collection of modern Israeli work.

**North of the Yarkon:** Defining the northernmost limit of the city proper is the **Yarkon River** which at one time marked the border between the tribes of Dan and Ephraim. Today, it is lined with rambling parkland and serves to accommodate scullers who row quietly up and down its length in the cooler hours of the day. Near the western rim, across the river, can be seen the dome and chimneys of the **Reading Power Station**, while the greenery of the city's **exhibition grounds** mark the river's eastern limit.

Across the river in Ramat Aviv, the sprawling **Ha'aretz Museum** comprises the most comprehensive storehouse of archaeological, anthropological and historical findings in the region. The museum's spiritual backbone is **Tel Quasile**, an excavation site in which 12 distinct layers of civilisation have been uncovered, its finds including an ancient Philistine temple and Hebrew inscriptions from 800 BC. The museum complex consists of 11 pavilions, including glassware, ceramics, copper, coins, folklore and ethnography museums, and a planetarium. In the section entitled "Man and his Toil," staff members demonstrate ancient methods of weaving, jewellery and pottery making, grain grinding and bread baking.

No visit to Israel would be complete

**Yarkon River at dawn.**

without calling at least once at the **Beth Hatefutsoth**, on the **Tel Aviv University** campus. Founded only in 1979, the **Museum of the Jewish Diaspora** is known throughout the Jewish world; it is also, in concept and methodology, a radical departure from the accepted notion of a museum. For apart from a few sacramental objects, Beth Hatefutsoth contains no preserved artifacts. Its principal aim is reconstruction.

The body of the main exhibit is handled thematically, focusing on general themes of Jewish Life in the Diaspora: Family Life, Community, Religious Life, Culture, Interrelations with the Gentile Environment and the Return to Zion. Its striking displays include a collection of beautifully intricate models of synagogue buildings from across the globe. A memorial column in the central atrium commemorates Jewish martyrdom through the ages.

An audio-visual depiction of the migrations of Jews in relation to world history is presented in the hall known as the "Chronosphere". Four video "study-areas" enable visitors to view documentary films selected from a catalogue, while a computer system allows visitors to trace their own lineage. Special exhibitions highlight topics related to Jewish communities around the world.

On north, east and south Tel Aviv is surrounded by what Tel Avivians refer to as the "bedroom suburbs", whose residents commute to the city for work, shopping and social activities. On Tel Aviv's southern border are Holon and Bat Yam (literally, Daughter of the Sea); in the north a disparate sprawl. To the east as well as Ramat Gan and its diamond exchange, which handles around $3 billion worth of stones a year, is Giv'atayim, and a **Safari Park**.

Still further east: the religious town of **Bnei Brak**, established in 1924 by Orthodox Jews from Poland; and **Petach Tikva** (meaning Gate of Hope, from Hosea; 2,17). Petach Tikva was known as the "Mother of Settlements", for it was founded in 1878, the first Jewish settlement of modern times. The town's emblem is an orange tree and a plough.

Model of Florentine synagogue at Beth Hatefutsoth.

# THE SOUTH COAST

The Mediterranean coast means many things to the Israelis. It is, foremost, the spine of the country, in terms of population as well as geography, with over half of all Israelis living along its vital and accommodating lowlands. The coastal plain is the site of the country's most luxurious hotels, as well as some of its most important ruins. It is a prime transportation corridor and is the location of the fertile "Sharon Plain", the source of Israel's renowned citrus industry. Its harbours service industry, military and tourist needs alike.

But for the average Israeli, the Mediterranean coast really means one thing: recreation. From April to October, from Yad Mordechai to Rosh HaNikra, thousands of bronzed Sabras flock in droves, day after day, to the glimmering sands at the western rim of their country, to bake in the sun, play paddle-ball along the water's edge, swim, wade, run, sail, tan, and then in turn watch everyone else do the same. While many of the best-known beaches are a kaleidoscope of human activity in the summer, there are quite a few lesser known beaches as well, which offer fewer facilities, but equally pleasant access to sun and sand. Similarly, because of the density of resources, it's not unusual to take a dip against a backdrop of an ancient aqueduct, or the looming gray silhouette of a power plant.

With so much vitality in unlikely co-existence – orange groves and vacation villages, minimal bikinis and Philistine *tels* – the Israeli coastal plain is as unexpected as it is inviting. And with all the various civilisations whose pillars and monuments have crumbled into the waves here, one can't help wondering if even the sand underfoot is a uniquely Israeli blend.

**Israel's beginnings:** Israel's southern coast begins just north of the Gaza Strip, with the kibbutz of **Yad Mordechai**. Named after Mordechai Anilewitz, a Jewish leader who died in the Warsaw Ghetto Uprising in 1943, the kibbutz was founded the same year by Polish immigrants, and played a pivotal role during the Israeli War of Independence. Attacked by the Egyptian army on its way northward in May 1948, the settlement managed to hold out against vastly superior forces for six days, thereby allowing for the adequate defences of Tel Aviv. Several structures commemorate this event. The morbid but effective **battlefield reconstruction** includes cut-out figures of advancing Egyptian soldiers, and a taped narration of the course of events. Close by, the imposing museum houses displays about the fighting, the four *kibbutzim* that stood together here, and a memorial to the Polish-Jewish community which was annihilated during the Holocaust. On a ridge nearby are the graves of those who fell defending the young settlement.

Overlooking today's community, the **statue of Anilewitz** stands in defiant protection, grenade in hand, while behind him rests the fallen watertower, its rutted surface preserved in commemoration of all it withstood. The overall effect of Yad Mordechai is unquestion-

ably sobering rather than joyful, yet it does provide a potent insight into the mentality of this small nation, time and again besieged by hostile forces. Slightly eastward of Yad Mordechai lies the sister kibbutz of **Negba**, which was not taken by the Egyptians, and which throughout 1948 served as Israel's main supply line to the Negev, and the south.

**Philistine cities:** Some 16 km (10 miles) to the north of the kibbutzim sit the time-washed stones of **Ashkelon**, one of the oldest cities in the world. Situated on a crest of dunes above the sea, Ashkelon is an amalgam of industrial plants, contemporary apartment towers and lovely beaches. But it is the archaeological part that makes Ashkelon special, and thoughtful preservation has made this erstwhile Philistine city quite accessible to visitors.

The multi-layered ruins of this strategic harbour city attest to the diversity of peoples that have made their habitation here over the centuries. Lying along the famous Via Maris, the roadway linking Egypt and Syria, the city was a trading centre from its earliest days, its exports including wine, grain, and a variety of local onion now known as "scallion" after its place of origin. In the early 12th century BC, the town was conquered by the Philistines, in their sweep of the southern coast, and in the following years grew to become one of the five great Philistine cities – the others being Ashdod, Gaza, Gath and Ekron. The next two centuries witnessed bitter rivalry between the Philistines and the Israelites, and although the Jews never took the city, it filtered into Jewish history in the story of Samson, whose exploits included his victory with the jawbone of an ass, the episode in which he set fire to the Philistine fields by tying torches to foxes' tails, and his famed ill-fated romance with the Philistine barber-girl, Delilah. When King Saul died at the hands of the Philistines, it prompted David's oft-quoted lament: "Tell it not in Gath, publish it not in the streets of Ashkelon, lest the daughters of the Philistines rejoice," (II Sam; 1, 20). Three centuries later, Ashkelon was

**Left**, fallen Roman pillar in surf at Ashkelon. **Below**, brilliant blooms add colour to a kibbutz.

still a Philistine stronghold, provoking the wrath of the prophet Zephaniah, who, in the final pages of the Old Testament, proclaims "For Gaza shall be forsaken, and Ashkelon a desolation: they shall drive out Ashdod at the noonday, and Ekron shall be rooted up," (Zeph; 2, 4).

Eventually, of course, all were. Taken in the ensuing centuries by Assyrians, Babylonians, and the like, Ashkelon once more realised growth in the years of Greek and Roman rule. Herod the Great was supposedly born here, and contributed by adding greatly to the city. Ashkelon fell to the Arabs in the 7th century, and briefly to the Crusaders in 1153, and, in the process, was pillaged amply of its monuments and stones. In 1270 it was destroyed completely by the Sultan Baibars, from which time on it remained largely ignored by all.

Today, most of the city's antiquities are encompassed within the **National Park**. Here, one can ramble by the ruins of Herodian colonnades and ancient synagogues, a Roman avenue presided over by the headless statue of Nike, goddess of victory, and a long-abandoned Roman amphitheatre. The site is surrounded by a grass-covered Crusader wall, while on the beach below, fallen pillars rest forlorn against the pressing of the tides. Nearby are a camping area and holiday village.

The modern city consists of two distinct residential areas: **Midgal**, a former Arab town, to the east, and **Afridar**, a newer suburb along the shore, founded in 1955 by Jews from South Africa. Locatable by its tall, fenestrated clock-tower, Afridar holds Ashkelon's pleasant downtown, where one can find the commercial centre and information office, and two preserved Roman sarcophagi. There are a number of hotels here as well, including the fancier King Saul and Swissotel, and the affordable self-contained Dagon, which means "mermaid." The beaches are fine for bathing, and enjoy such biblical sobriquets as **Samson Beach, Delilah Beach, Bar-Kochba Beach**, etc. Other notable sights include the Roman-era **Painted**

**Tomb**, and, in **Barnea** to the north, the remains of a Byzantine church and 5th-century mosaic. Continuing up the coastal highway, leaving Ashkelon behind, one passes an access road to **Nizzanim**, a settlement founded by South American immigrants, which boasts a fine strip of beach.

Some 40 km (25 miles) north of Ashkelon, the concrete skyline of **Ashdod** comes into view. Its Philistine history now long behind it, Ashdod is a burgeoning man-made harbour, Israel's most important port, and, if not much of a gift to tourism, a striking example of commercial success.

Founded only in 1957, Ashdod has grown in three decades to a city of over 85,000 people, and is virtually bursting at its seams with rugged vitality. With its prospering economy based on the new deep-water port, Ashdod is a major immigrant absorption centre. Its populace includes Arabic-speaking Jews, Indian Jews, Sabras, and Soviet Jews, among them a large community from Soviet Georgia, "Gruzinim". From **Me**-morial Hill**, just below the lighthouse, is a clear view of the port, with great ships lined up to carry away exports such as potash and phosphates.

Outside the city, to the southeast, lies the grave of the ancient metropolis, **Tel Ishdud**. The site is quite literally a *tel*, or "mound", as little remains of its previous incarnation other than a hillock and the scattered shards of Philistine pottery. Returning towards the highway, keep an eye out for the sycamore trees which dot the environs, and which, outside of their biblical mentions, bear a sometimes edible fruit.

Ashdod marked the official northernmost advance of the Egyptian army in 1948, and supposedly hosted Nasser himself, at the time a young officer. At the point where the roadway crosses the streambed, just east of the city, two relics of that period can be found. The first, the **railroad bridge** parallel to the road, is a reconstruction of the original: blown up by the commandos of the Israeli Givati Brigade, whose nickname – The Foxes of Samson – recalls earlier

**Tetrapods lend support in Ashdod port.**

history. To the west of the bridges, a small white **pillbox**, built by the British in World War II, stands by in lonely vigil, a bullet shot and an echo away.

**First in Zion:** To the north of Ashdod, the quiet town of **Yavne** proffers a rich history. The legend goes that in 70 AD, when the fall of Jerusalem seemed imminent in the war against Rome, the renowned Rabbi Yohanon Ben Zakkai appeared before the Roman general Vespasian, to request permission to found an academy here, predicting that one day the general would become emperor. The prophesy came true shortly after, and the request was granted. Regardless of the tale, Yavne did become the site of a great academy in the years following, and is known as the site where the Mishnah, the great commentary on the Bible which adapted Judaism to a modern framework, was started.

The tel of Yavne today consists of a lone Mameluke tower, built on Crusader ruins on top of a ridge. More recently, Yavne is notable as the site of a small atomic research reactor, Israel's

**Mameluke tower at Yavne.**

first, built in 1960 by architect Philip Johnson. Just north of here, where the **Sorek River** winds into the sea, is the site of the ancient port of Yavne, **Yavne-Yam**, and the swimming beach of **Palmakhim**, said to offer Israel's finest surfing as well as the site where Judas Maccabeus marked a victory over Greek forces in the 2nd century BC.

The whole area from Ashdod to Tel Aviv is historically known as "Darom" (the South) in ancient times a seat of wisdom, thanks to Yavne, and in this century the location of some of Israeli's earliest, and southernmost, communities. Continuing towards Tel Aviv, the road passes through two of these. **Nes Ziona**, founded in 1884, is said to have been the first place where the now familiar blue-and-white flag of Zion was unfurled; **Rishon LeZion**, meaning "First in Zion," was founded in 1882 by Polish and Russian Zionists.

After struggling for five years, the community was given new life in 1887 by the Baron Edmond de Rothschild, who in one of his first acts as Israel's benefactor, established a wine cellar here. Using shoots of grape vines from Beaujolais, Burgundy and Bordeaux, the vineyards flourished, producing mainly sweet wines for Jewish ceremonial occasions. After years of Rothschild ownership, the company reverted to cooperative ownership in 1957 and today the **Carmel Oriental vineyards** produce a variety of lovely dry whites and table wines as well. After touring the wine cellars and the old Rothschild offices, the visitor can enjoy a free wine-tasting, courtesy of Carmel.

Another bonus is the small garden, which contains all seven of the trees mentioned in the Bible – fig, date, grape, pomegranite, olive, palm and carob. Also to Rishon LeZion's credit are the first synagogue built in Israel in modern times (1885), the first kindergarten to teach in Hebrew, and the first Hebrew cultural centre, where the Israel National anthem *HaTikva* ("the Hope") was composed and sung for the first time.

From Rishon LeZion, it is only 10 km (6 miles) to the resort-suburb of **Bat Yam** and the outskirts of Tel Aviv.

# THE CENTRAL COAST: CITRUS AND RESORTS

From Ashkelon in the south to around Caesarea in the north, Israel's central coast is citrus country–the fertile **Sharon Plain**. In Hebrew, the word for citrus, "hadar," is the same as the word for "splendour," and in the proper season both meanings are equally appropriate as the entire strip from seashore to foothills becomes lush with orchards and ripe, hanging fruit.

It is one of Tel Aviv's greatest ironies that its development as a city came at the expense of its initial drawing point – its fine, sandy soil, perfect for growing citrus – and today the metropolitan area continues to sprawl out over thousands of acres of prime citrus land. Yet the crop was never indigenous to the area, and, in fact, well into the 19th century the central coast was generally regarded as a miasma of swamps and malaria, avoided even by the roadway, which twisted northward along higher ground further inland.

By the turn of the century, however, the development of pumps which could raise the buried groundwater to the soil surface suddenly harnessed the land to the desires of its pioneer settlers, who set about draining the marshes and cultivating new orchards.

Exporting their crop to Europe via the central port of Jaffa (hence Jaffa oranges), the industry hit a high in the 1930s; World War II and the ensuing struggle for independence seriously hindered its development in the decade following. But in the 1950s and 1960s the industry once again was brought to bloom, and the 1970s witnessed another doubling of exports.

Today, citrus is Israel's most valuable agricultural export, making up a large share of the nearly half-billion dollar-a-year market. The variety of citrus under cultivation runs the spectrum, including all sorts of offshoots and varieties, with the sweet "Jaffa" oranges and their kin dominating along the coast, and the grapefruits mainly thriving in the thicker, riverwashed soil closer inland. The citrus gathering season is in the winter, from roughly mid-December to April, and this is when the fruits are at their most intoxicating, swinging ripely off their evergreen branches, their scent wafting gently out over the road, to the Mediterranean.

**Cities of wealth and taste:** From Tel Aviv and Ramat Aviv, the coastal highway wends past a number of modest **memorials** on its route northward. On the shore side of the highway, approaching Herzliya, is a metallic rectangle standing upright atop a layered curve of a pedestal: this commemorates the 34 people killed in the 1978 sea-launched terrorist attack, whose victims included American nature photographer Gail Rubin. A short way further, a faded ship's hull commemorates those would-be immigrants who died attempting to gain refuge in Palestine in the final years of the British mandate.

A fascinating monument lies a short distance to the east in Ramat HaSharon, the Memorial to the Fallen Members of Israel's Intelligence Community, inaugurated in 1985.

The city of **Herzliya**, boasting a population of some 70,000, includes among its inhabitants the elite of Israeli society, and, for that matter, just about anyone else who has money to play with: from wealthy real estate developers to industrial moguls to intelligentsia savants such as Abba Eban. It is a favourite stomping ground of diplomats and ambassadors, who are only too happy to take advantage of the stylish beaches and company, and whose posh villas stud the slopes above the shore amid such ritzy five-star hotels as the Sharon, Accadia and Daniel.

Reflecting the general atmosphere of opulence, some of the nicer beaches charge a fee for admittance. This is the scheme in **Herzliya-by-the-Sea**, at the town centre. Along the highway, the city puts on a different face: a haven for high-tech entrepreneurs. Numerous well-known company names – Scitex, Elbit, Digital – glow brightly with futuristic logos here, their office complexes beneath complementing the city's repu-

*Planting a seedling at coastal kibbutz.*

tation as the base of Israel's fledgling communications industry.

Just north of the seaside resort city, the ruins of a Crusader fortress and ancient Hellenistic city – **Apollonia** – overlook the water, and it is said the beach still contains visible remnants of the ancient coloured glass that was once produced here. All but disappeared are traces of the battle fought in this area between Richard the Lionheart and Saladin during the mid-twilight years of the Crusader kingdom.

Approaching Netanya, we pass over the **Nahal Poleg**, or Poleg River, at one time an unpleasant morass, since tamed as a nature reserve. Close by stands the **Wingate Institute**, Israel's premier centre for sports and physical training instruction. It is named after Charles Orde Wingate, a British Officer who served in Palestine from 1936 to 1939, and who helped instruct the Jewish policemen in defensive fighting techniques that would later prove invaluable during the War of Independence. Wingate reputedly carried a Bible with him frequently, reinforcing the Jews' knowledge of their land through appropriately quoted passage.

Some 20 km (12½ miles) north of Herzliya, lies **Netanya** itself, the capital city of the Sharon region. Founded as a citrus colony in 1929, the settlement was named after American millionaire Nathan Strauss, as a potential encouragement for him to contribute to the town's development (supposedly he was unmoved). Netanya has proved to be just as well off without, boasting a charming beach and promenade, a population upwards of 100,000 and a galaxy of expensive and not-quite-so-expensive hotels, often filled to capacity with vacationing Europeans and in-the-know Israelis. Most of the hotels are clustered along King David and Machnes streets, by the beachfront, while the bus station is situated on the main drag, Herzl Street, a few blocks walk away. All three avenues come together at Independence Square (Kikar Ha'Atzmaut), where a kiosk at the southeast corner houses the Tourist Information Office. Their offerings in-

clude regular performances of Israeli folk dancing, information about horseback riding and various recreational sports, visits to a citrus packing plant (in season, of course) and a "Meet the Israeli" programme in which the tourist can drop by the home of a native Netanyan for an informal cup of coffee and exchange of views. All in all, the boldly modernistic concrete beach facilities and pleasantly landscaped greenery make Netanya a fine place to spend a lazy afternoon.

Netanya also happens to be the hub of Israel's formidable diamond industry, the country's second most important export next to the ubiquitous citruses. Inaugurated by immigrants from Belgium and the Netherlands in the early years of the state, the business has grown to the extent that, since 1974, Israel has held the title of world's number-one exporter of polished diamonds (the raw stones being imported from Asia and Africa). Unsurprisingly, several companies offer opportunities for the gem-stricken tourist. Taub & Company, the

Upholding citrus fruit, the No. 1 coast export.

largest, selling over $20 million worth of stones from their Netanya offices each year, operates an expansive showroom of precious stones. Female guides take visitors on a tour of their facilities which includes a brief video presentation, a chance to see workmen in action and a stop-off in their showroom. There is also a modest museum on the history of diamonds.

The region just north of Netanya is the **Valley of Hefer** (Emek Hefer, in Hebrew), and although there isn't really a valley the area gets a mention in the Old Testament. This marshy plain is inextricably linked to the efforts of the pioneers of the 1930s, whose sweat and foresight restored the land to the productivity it bears today. **Kfar Witkin** was among the first of these new settlements and today it is among the largest *moshavim* (collective farming settlements) in the country.

A little way further on, less than 10 km (6 miles) from Netanya, is **Mikhmoret** beach, as lovely as its city cousin, but a lot less crowded. **Hadera**, the city inland of the beach, derives its name from the Arabic word for green (nothing to do with the Hebrew word for citrus), and serves as transfer point for visitors to the northern Sharon.

**Crusaders at their best:** Although its greatest historical importance was as a Roman colony, it is the Crusader ruins at **Caesarea** that tourists flock to by the busloads today, and truly, they are as impressive as any in Israel. It takes a good half a day just to take in the site, while the visual cacophony of Crusader arches, crumpling walls and smashed Roman pillars is constantly disarming, and attests to the layered history of habitation here. Despite its being one of Israel's most lauded archaeological sites, Caesarea is still difficult to reach via public transportation, which means the single tourists must either rent a car, stay overnight nearby, or join a tour.

While settlements in the region date back as far as Phoenician times, the history of the city only really begins with the Romans in 22 BC, when royal master-builder Herod the Great founded

it, naming it in honour of the emperor Augustus. Around the year 6 BC it was designated the official residence of the governors of Judea, and for some 500 years Caesarea was to remain the capital of Roman administration in Palestine. At the time of Jesus, Pontius Pilate lived here, and St Paul was imprisoned here for two years before being sent to Rome from this port.

The great Jewish Revolt in 66 AD was set off in Caesarea initially, and in the struggle that followed the city's prisons saw the torture and execution of many captive Jewish zealots. In 70 AD, the Roman general Vespasian was crowned emperor here. With the Bar Kochba uprising, many notable Jews once again met their deaths here, among them the great sage and spiritual leader Rabbi Akiva, in 135 AD (who is commemorated in the nearby community of Or Akiva).

During the periods of Pax Romana, the city was a centre of Hellenistic, and, later, Christian culture. Among the most notable of the early Christians was Eusebius, one of the Founding Fathers of the Christian Church, who became the first bishop of Caesarea in the 4th century, and who was responsible for codifying Christian religious law, and outlining the geography of the Bible in his book *Onomastikon*.

The Crusaders, under Baldwin I, captured the city in 1101, and during the next 200 years Caesarea changed hands so often it could make a camel cross-eyed. King Baldwin treasured the city, believing it to hold the Holy Grail sipped from by Jesus at the Last Supper, but the massive fortifications that so commend it today were only added after 1254, with the reconquest of the city by Louis IX, "the Holy". Muslim forces captured the city in 1265 (and again in 1291), and Caesarea never again regained importance, its fine marble pillars and carvings being pillaged over the centuries by successive rulers.

The contemporary visitor to Caesarea enters the city through a vaulted Crusader gatehouse, after passing over a bridge across a wide moat. The walls

**Crusader ruins, Roman pillars at Caesarea.**

around the city, which slope down precipitously from an imposing height, are perhaps the most awe-inspiring monument here; walking the breadth of this imposing redoubt the imaginative tourist can easily sicken himself picturing the spectacle of hand-to-hand combat that took place here time and again. Inside the city are numerous ruins of Crusaders' homes and streets. Along the waterfront, Roman pillars used as foundation stones by the Crusaders jut out among the waves. If the postcard shops and eateries within the Crusader city limits jar your sense of decorum, you may want to remind yourself that the Israeli economy is always in need of spirited help.

Outside the entrance to the Crusader city, a Byzantine Street of Statues represents the far larger Byzantine city that preceded the Crusaders, its headless figures (Roman dignitaries) pondering, like Ozymandius, the passing of their power. A half-km south of the city walls is the restored **Roman amphitheatre**. This arena witnessed mass executions in Roman times; in modern years it has served to host popular summer concerts by the likes of virtuosi such as Pablo Casals and Issac Stern.

The handsome Roman **aqueducts** stretching north from the city once conducted fresh spring water; today they provide shade for lounging bathers.

Inland from the ruins is the only golf links in Israel, on the grounds of the elegant and pricey Dan Caesarea hotel.

**Martyrs and benefactors:** Kibbutz **Sdot Yam**, just south of Caesarea, is worth special note as the former home of Jewish poetess-martyr Hannah Sennesh. Joining the young kibbutz after escaping Hungary for Palestine at the outbreak of World War II, she parachuted back behind Axis lines in 1944 to fight the Nazis; soon after, she was caught and summarily tortured and executed at the age of 23. The modest **archaeological museum** here is named in her honour.

Heading north from Caesarea, one immediately enters the area of the Kabara marshes, which hosted some of the early Zionist settlements at the turn of the

Caesarea's amphitheatre still impressive.

century. The Crocodile River bears testimony to the once intimidating nature of the terrain; the last croc, however, bid sweet life adieu in 1910. A short distance inland, is the town of **Binyamina**, named after the great benefactor of Israel's first settlers, Baron Edmond (Benjamin) de Rothschild. (This lower portion of the Carmel Range bears the title Ramat HaNadiv – Benefactor's Heights).

Two km (just over 1 mile) further is **Rothschild's Tomb**, built in the 1950s to house the remains of the Parisian banker and his wife Adelaide. Situated amid a fragrant garden of date trees, sage, roses and all varieties of flowers, this sensuously designed landscape opens up to a magnificent panorama of the upper Sharon, while a concrete map indicates the locations of the many settlements made possible by Rothschild (whose generosity lingers today in the barroom phrase "put it on the Baron's account"). The crypt itself is contemporary and tasteful; the site all told is one of the most significant in Israel.

A minute's drive further, the town of

**Zichron Yaakov** was established in 1882 in memory of Rothschild's father James (Jacob). The Aaronson House and Museum, just off the main street, describes the lives of Aaron and Sarah Aaronson. Aaron was the botanist who in the early 1900s isolated durable strains of wheat for cultivation in Palestine; he and his sister are enshrined in legend because of their role in organizing the pro-British "Nili" spy ring during their front against the oppressive Turkish regime. Caught by the Turks, and afraid she'd give up information, Sarah shot herself in her home in 1917.

Like Rishon LeZion further south, Zichron Yaacok is one of the original homes of the Carmel Oriental wine-cellars, and grape-happy tourists are welcome to take a free tour of the facilities, capped off by a complimentary wine-tasting break.

Heading back toward the coast, a road passes the gentle, slope-hugging Arab town of **Faradis** (Paradise).

**The Carmel coast:** One of Israel's most active on-going archaeological sites is

Striking a classical pose in vineyard, in Zichron Yaakov's early days.

**Tel Dor**. The excavations as yet have only unearthed a fraction of this sprawling ancient city, but the ruins on display, dating from Canaanite to Israelite to Hellenistic times, give indications of a vast ancient metropolis of tens of thousands of inhabitants. Archaeology aside, this is a site of enormous natural beauty, the lagoons and water washing against the cliffs, complementing the rolling hills of Mount Carmel inland.

Abutting the *tel* just to the south is a lovely beach, **Nasholim** (Breakers) and a kibbutz of the same name which offers a roomy guest house and friendly mien. On the grounds of the kibbutz you will find an illuminating **Maritime Museum**, housed in a turn-of-the-century building that had been a glass factory under Rothschild. This rocky portion of the Carmel coast just south of Haifa, along a major ancient shipping lane, is the site of hundreds of **undersea wrecks**, which were the focus of a major underwater excavation in 1985. The museum holds a selection of these treasures culled from the depths, and their exhibits range from Phoenician catapult balls to ancient bronze anchors and coins to relics dating from Napoleon's naval misadventures off this shore in 1799.

Along the length of the northern coast, rows of vegetables sheathed in white plastic dot the roadsides, often under the stately presence of towering cypress or eucalyptus trees. Towards evening when the hues in the sky drift into violet and lilac and pale orange, the landscape seems to have been painted by Claude Monet, an unreal, curvaceous Impressionist silhouette.

Continuing past the beach of **Neve Yam** is the imposing Crusader fortress of **Atlit** perched wearily on the rocks above the Mediterranean. At the time of writing the ruins are off-limits to the general public, although a modern-day fortress, the prison in which Israel held Shi'ite prisoners during its War in Lebanon, is visible in the shadow of the highway.

Heading upwards and eastwards into the twisting greenery of Mt. Carmel, the wildness of the scenery is echoed by the primal nature of the site: prehistoric caves, inhabited by Neanderthal Man some 50,000 years ago. Discovered in 1929, the three cliffside caves were found to contain flint tools and dozens of skeletons that provided anthropologists with revelations about the lifestyle of these early hunters, and their place in the chain that led to the proficient homo sapiens we know today.

Ensconced introspectively amid gnarled olive trees and Moorish arches, the artists' colony of **Ein Hod** was conceived of in 1953 as a rugged oasis of creativity, and today holds the living and working space for some 200 artisans. The gallery and restaurant in the town centre warmly welcome company.

Winding deeper into the mountainside, the road arcs through gorges and a severe, often astonishingly attractive landscape: the region known as **Little Switzerland**. (Kibbutz **Bet Oren** tucked between the pines here operates a guest house.) At the crest of the ridge lies the ultimate view of the Carmel coast, and the gateway to Israel's ebullient third-largest city.

e Tel Dor
ast.

# HAIFA AND MOUNT CARMEL

In a fit of pique, a Bedouin sheik destroyed a squalid coastal village because its inhabitants neglected to pay homage. The town lay in ruins for eight years, until 1758, when having made his point Sheik Dahr Al-Omar rebuilt it, and improved its natural harbour. **Haifa** grew from that unpropitious beginning, and, in the years since its rebirth, has evolved into a bustling port city and maritime centre.

Today Haifa is Israel's third-largest city, and the centre of the nation's renowned high-technology industries. From its original cradle on the narrow coastal strip between the Mediterranean and the biblical Carmel Range, Haifa has marched up the mountainside, settling itself lazily among the gentle slopes. The city is essentially built on three levels, rising from its first location along the waterfront. The second level, in the Carmel foothills, is **Hadar**, the central business district and the oldest residential area. The newest neighbourhoods have climbed all the way to the crests of the peak, and cling to its sides, connected by a network of excellent roads. At the very apex is the **Carmel Center**, where some of the city's most attractive homes and classiest hotels and shops are located

**Historic port:** Since the 2nd century, Haifa had been known as a safe haven for passing ships, situated as it was along one of the Mediterranean's oldest sea-lanes. But the village itself was little more than an assemblage of wretched huts, at the time of its premature destruction in the mid-18th century having less than 250 inhabitants. Reborn, it thrived, and by 1890 Haifa had some 8,000 people living within its limits. Yet it took a combination of railroads and war to catapult the city into significance and the 20th century.

The two causes, in fact, were interlinked: under the impending pressures of World War I, the Ottoman Turks built the Hejaz Railroad connecting Haifa to Damascus in the north, while at the same time the British started the Sinai Military Railroad, which was later to link Haifa to Qantara on the Suez Canal. Haifa was now, by land as well as sea, a prime stopover. At the end of the war the British controlled all of Palestine under a League of Nations mandate, and they gradually began to modernise Haifa's port. With a steady increase in maritime traffic, and a continuing stream of Jewish immigrants, the population had reached some 25,000 by 1918. By 1923 it had more than doubled, and by 1931 it had doubled again to exceed 100,000.

Although it was now a city, Haifa was still a modest enclave, clinging to the shore, and extending only as far as the Carmel foothills. When the nation achieved independence in 1948, however, further development of Haifa's port became essential. At war with the surrounding Arab countries, Israel's land borders were suddenly sealed, and Haifa's port became the Jewish state's only opening to the world.

**Blue-collar city:** Today the port, monitored by a centralised computer system, bristles with massive electronically operated cargo-handling equipment, berths the world's seagoing mammoths, and is Israel's premier maritime centre. But Haifa has grown beyond the limitations of a port city to become a versatile industrial centre as well. Known affectionately as the "Red City" because of its long-standing identification with the nation's labour movement, Haifa is a blue-collar city, and Haifites proudly explain that, while Tel Aviv plays and Jerusalem prays, Haifa works.

The evidence is everywhere. At the northern edge of the city, an industrial zone accommodates an extensive petrochemical industry, oil refineries, and many small manufacturing units. Israel's high-technology companies are centered in a new science-based industrial district at the southern entrance to the city. According to the Haifa labour council, 70 percent of the area's 120,000 wage-earners are employed in industrial enterprises, excluding civil service and tourist-related jobs.

Haifa's blue-collar character is mitigated by the presence of two major academic institutions, the Technion and the University of Haifa, whose faculties and students total about 40,000.

Now covering 15,000 acres, with a population of over 250,000, Haifa is known as the city that works and where everything can be worked out. The amiable atmosphere is due in part to the sensible implementation of a policy promulgated in 1947 by David Ben-Gurion. Known as the Status Quo Agreement, the policy guarantees the preservation of the status quo on religious issues as it was at the time the state was established in 1948. In other municipalities, the amorphous agreement has become a platform for squabbling, but prosaic Haifa transformed it into a political instrument which assures that everybody gets something.

**Religious communities:** Haifa's religious population lives in distinct communities contiguous with secular neighbourhoods in the heart of the city, near Hadar. The atmosphere around **Yosef Street**, near the municipal theatre, around **Geula Street**, near the Glory of Israel religious school or in **Ramot Wishnitz**, just below Rupin Road, is as rich in intensity and devotion to tradition as comparable communities elsewhere in Israel. But in Haifa they never throw stones.

For tourists, the amicability between Haifa's secular and religious communities means that although movies are closed Friday evenings, theatres, discos, restaurants and night clubs operate as usual. Haifa's zoo and most museums are open during the Sabbath, but are not allowed to charge admission fees, and hotels request that their departing guests pay their bills before Friday evening.

**Arab communities:** Haifa's Saturday bus service is unusual in Israel. It reflects the formative influence of its Arab citizens on the city's social patterns. There has always been a significant Arab presence in Haifa, and Jews and Arabs here have a long history of mutual give-and-take. The buses ran on Saturdays to accommodate Haifa's Arabs in pre-state days, and they still do. Today Israeli

Turkish bath house dominates view of Haifa

Arabs constitute about 10 percent of Haifa's population, and the city attracts thousands more every day from the surrounding villages, coming to take advantage of the work opportunities and to share the amenities of the city with their Jewish fellow-citizens.

Although there are some mixed areas in Haifa, most Arabs have preferred to remain in their own homogeneous neighbourhoods, in many cases in the same place where their families have lived for generations. There are two distinctive, venerable and easily accessible Arab communities in Haifa.

**Wadi Nisnas** is among the area's oldest neighbourhoods, and is adjacent to Hadar, near **Bet Hageffen**, Haifa's Arab-Jewish community centre. A visit to the community centre, with a phone call in advance to assure the availability of an English-speaking staff member to answer questions, is a useful prelude to touring here.

The Wadi Nisnas, with its buildings of massive sandstone blocks, its window grilles and arched door-ways, its prevalence of Arabic and Middle-Eastern music, and the gamut of exotic food and clothing for sale in the shops, gives graphic reminder that Haifa – microchips aside – still stands with one foot firmly planted in the Levant.

In sharp contrast to Wadi Nisnas, **Kababir**, perched high on a ridge overlooking the Mediterranean, is an Arab neighbourhood of sumptuous dwellings and lush gardens. Established as an independent village in 1830, the community opted for annexation to Haifa when the state was established in 1948 anticipating the benefits of schools, health, water and sewage systems.

The majority of residents are Ahmdya Muslims, a small Islamic sect ditinct from the larger Shiite and Sunni groups in Wadi Nisnas. Although fully integrated into the Haifa municipality, Kababir is administered locally by a committee of six elders elected annually by the men of the community. The committee deals with everything from bloc-voting in national elections to problems of interpersonal relations. A

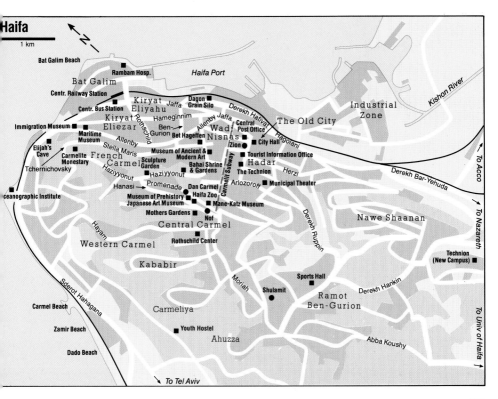

new mosque, completed in 1984, is the only one of its kind in the Middle East.

**The Carmel Center:** The Carmel Center is where most of Haifa's hotels are located. Here, atop towering Mt. Carmel, panoramic scenes of the city, sea and mountains burst into view at every turn. Modern shops line **Hanassi Street** along with sidewalk cafés and restaurants specialising in kosher – Chinese, Italian and Middle Eastern foods. Israel's only museum of Japanese art, the **Tikotin Museum**, is in the heart of the Carmel Center, at 89 Hanassi Street.

A few blocks from Hanassi Street, a half-mile long **Promenade** at the edge of the precipice reveals the city scrambling across the side of the mountain all the way down to the sea. The view from the Promenade is dominated by the **Bahai Shrine and Gardens** halfway down the slope. Founded in Persia by Mirza Ali Mohammed, the sect was proscribed and its leader publicly executed there in 1850. Claiming over 3 million adherents throughout the world, the Bahai faith is based on brotherhood,

love and charity. Its followers view Moses, Christ, Buddha and Mohammed as messengers sent by God to different parts of the world in different eras, but all preaching more or less one philosophy, and they advocate a common world language and religion. With its unusual dome and Corinthian-style columns, the shrine is probably Haifa's best-recognised landmark, and the world centre of the Bahai faith. Both the building and the lovely gardens are open to the public. From above the shrine, **Panorama Road** now leads either outward towards the sea and the Promenade view, or back in towards the city centre.

**Carmel slope retreats:** Tucked within the mountainous folds of upper Haifa are a number of hidden treasures. Hugging the slope near the Promenade, the **Mané-Katz Museum** is housed in the building where the Jewish-French Expressionist lived and worked in his later years. Besides his paintings and sculptures, the display also includes his personal collection of Judaica and antique furniture. A short distance away is the

Haifa University's Eshkol Tower crowns Mt Carmel.

Edenic **Mothers' Garden**, the biggest of Haifa's nearly 400 parks. Among curving paths, flowers, and picnicking families, is the city's **Museum of Prehistory**, displaying finds of the Carmel area, which way back then was home to Neanderthal Man. A little farther is the pleasant and well-maintained **Haifa Zoo**, and in the far corner of the park, an open-air restaurant specialising in Middle Eastern foods.

Atop the crest of Mt. Carmel, marking the end of one's ascent, loom the contemporary features of the **University of Haifa**, its distinctive tower thrust up resolutely against the sky. Founded only in 1972, the university serves the entire northern district, and operates branches in some of the region's more remote areas. The 25-storey **Eshkol Tower**, designed by Brazilian architect Oscar Niemeyer, is said to straddle a mild fault and offers an unparalleled view of northern Israel. To the east, one can make out the fertile valleys of the Galilee and the brooding outline of the Golan Heights beyond, while down below

miles of yellow-sand beaches stretch like satin ribbon along the Mediterranean shore. To the north, are Haifa Bay, Acco, and the white cliffs of Rosh HaNikra. On a clear day it's all visible: a living map, sparkling with sun and sea. At night, harbour lights vie with the stars and the city marks its place with a million glinting shadows.

Returning back down the slope, continuing past the Promenade, you reach that part of the city known as **French Carmel**, an expensive but cozy residential district. At the end of this area, Mt. Carmel levels off into a promontory, and this is the site of the **Carmelite Church**, the world centre of the Carmelite Order. Situated at the end of the mountain, along **Stella Maris Road**, the church commands one of the most spectacular views of the city. The site was selected in the 12th century by a small band of Crusaders who settled there to devote themselves to ascetism, solitude and prayer. The Order which grew from that beginning was officially founded by St Brocard in the 13th cen-

tury. The church edifice was built in the 18th century, over a grotto associated in the Christian tradition with the prophet Elijah and his disciple Elisha. The interior dome depicts events in their lives and a small museum displays local archaeological discoveries.

**Along the seaside:** Opposite the church entrance, a sinuous platform marks the upper terminal of Haifa's **cable car** system. Delayed for more than a year due to controversy surrounding its intended operation on the Sabbath, the system ferries passengers from the Carmel heights down to the seaside **Bat Galim Promenade**. It is an easy walk to the **National Maritime Museum** and the **Clandestine Immigration Museum**. The immigration museum includes the tiny ship in which Jewish immigrants sought to evade the British Mandatory government's blockade in the years before the state of Israel was declared.

A little way up the hill from the museums is **Elijah's Cave**, where the prophet is said to have rested and medi-

tated in the 9th century BC, before his momentous encounter with the Baalists on one of the peaks of the Carmel Range. After leaving the cave, Elijah is said to have climbed to the top of Mount Carmel, where an altar had been erected by the worshippers of Melkart and other Phoenician deities. Elijah challenged their priests to light a flame under a sacrifice by means of their religious rites. According to tradition the pagan priests failed; Elijah called upon the Lord and the flames were instantly ignited. Ahab, the Jewish king who had angered the Lord by worshipping Baal, was witness to the event. Rejecting paganism, he ordered the massacre at the **Kishon River** of all the Baalists. The event is recorded in detail in I Kings; 18, 17-46. Christians believe the cave to have sheltered the Holy Family on their way back from Egypt, and know it also as the Grotto of the Madonna.

Adjacent to the port area, a short bus ride from the prophet's retreat, is the **Dagon Grain Silo** – probably one of the only architecturally pleasing silos in the

**Left**, altar at Carmelite Church. **Below**, Dagon Silo.

world. Besides its commercial use for receiving and storing grain from ships anchored in the port, the silo houses a museum depicting the history of bread and beer making. Ancient implements are displayed with explanatory photographs, murals and mosaics, and there is a working model of the silo's own mechanised operation system.

Hugging the waterfront, the **Railroad Museum** opposite 40 Hativat Golani Street is a tribute to the importance of the railway in Haifa's history. Steam engines that hauled freight from the hinterlands to Haifa's port are preserved there along with luxury passenger cars, ornate bedroom cars, and wood-paneled dining cars. Visitors are encouraged to climb aboard, try out the accommodations, and toot the engine's whistle.

**Hadar:** In Hadar, the level above the waterfront, the original edifice of Israel's preeminent Institute of Technology, **The Technion**, has been preserved as an architectural landmark and is now the home of the unique touch-and-feel **Museum of Science and Technology**.

The magnificent old building, constructed in 1924, was designed by Alexander Baerwald, and combines European lines with an eastern dome, crenelated roofs and intricate mosaics. The Technion recently expanded into a large new campus in the Neve Shannon neighbourhood; free tours are offered daily. The city's **Museum of Ancient and Modern Art**, at the southern edge of Hadar, on 26 Shabtai Levy Street, is crammed with displays. Comfortable viewing from vantage points is not always possible, but the variety and quality of the collections make a visit well worth the effort. Special exhibitions are infrequent but excellent.

**Food and fun:** Sidewalk cafés are everywhere in Haifa. They range from a couple of tiny tables crowded against a storefront on a sidestreet where excellent coffee *afuk* can be purchased, to the umbrella-shaded elegance near the Cinematique at the **Rothschild Center** on Hanassi Street in the Carmel Center. Haifa also boasts a wide variety of other dining facilities, ranging from dinner-

laying with ...sers at the echnion.

and-dancing in the Rondo Grill of the **Dan Carmel Hotel** to a Middle Eastern evening of folkdancing at **Al-Pasha** on Hamman-al-Pasha Street.

More local flavour can be sampled at **The Pleasant Brothers**, an unassuming place on the corner of Moriah and Pica streets in the Ahuza neighbourhood, and is a long-time local favourite: its shish kebab, shishlik and salads are a Middle Eastern version of down-home cooking. After dinner, have a cup of coffee with German or Middle Eastern pastries in the coffee houses around the corner on **Pica Stree**t.

For informal dining, the favourite of Jewish and Arab Haifaites alike are the felafels bought at any of the kiosks lining **Hehalutz Street** in Hadar. Standing up alongside the kiosk, diners help themselves to hot peppers, fiery sauces, olives, pickles and eggplant as space and palate permit. At night, unpretentious Hehalutz Street, with its strolling crowds munching felafels under the glare of unshaded light bulbs, is a typical Haifa scene.

Evening entertainment in Haifa is often a matter of luck. There are the usual discos, pubs and bars but the most popular places depend on their patrons to join in the singing and dancing. When that happens, the evening takes on a special Haifa quality. An evening stroll along Panorama, also known as Yefe Nof, Street, in the Carmel Center, or along Balfour and Herzliya streets in Hadar, will reveal where the fun is.

**Israel's only subway:** One block up the hill from the felafel stands of Hehalutz Street is the Hadar entrance to the **Carmelit**, Israel's only subway. While most visitors are accustomed to traveling in subways, the Carmelit is truly one-of-a-kind. Its tunnel hacked through the interior rock of the mountain, it operates on the same principle as San Francisco's cable cars: one train hurtling down from the Carmel Center at the top of the mountain, hauls the other train up the steep incline from sea level. Even the cars themselves are designed at an angle. From top to bottom, the trip takes seven minutes.

**Portside view shows city hugging slope.**

184

**The Carmel Range:** The Carmel Range, which runs about 25 km (16 miles) northwest-southeast along the coast, rises to some 500 metres (1,650 feet) and falls steeply to the Mediterranean. The Kishon River, known since biblical times, flows at its feet. Its name is taken from the words "Kerem-El," meaning "Vineyard of God." Carmel's traditional association is with ripeness. Today, at the southern limit of the city, it contains **Mount Carmel National Park**, Israel's largest national forest preserve, which is lush with hilly woodlands, well-marked hiking trails, picnic facilities and breathtaking vistas. The 21,000-acre park includes a 2,000-acre **Nature Preserve** where deer and gazelle roam freely.

Just beyond the park, tucked among the slopes and valleys of the Carmel Range are the Druze villages of **Daliyat el-Carmel** and **Isfiya**. The Druze, a distinctive Islamic sect, are a well-respected and integral part of the state. Surrounded by tawny precipices plunging to verdant valleys carpeted with tangled foliage, the villages are easily accessible by car or bus. The market places offer traditional handicrafts and pleasant cafés where Turkish coffee and succulent pastries can be enjoyed under the trees.

The Carmelite monastery at **Muhraka**, nearby, stands over the site where Elijah defeated the Baalists.

The aura of sanctity of the Carmel Range has been recognised since ancient times. Successive waves of conquerors set up their altars on its wooded peaks and hillsides. Tutmoses III mentions it as holy. The Greeks dedicated a temple to Zeus here. The prophet Elijah wandered its slopes, honing his faith. Jewish, Christian, Muslim and Druze tradition revere the region. King Solomon sang of it in the Song of Songs (7:5) and Isaiah extols its glory (33:9).

For modern Haifaites, the gentle slopes and softly rounded ridges of the Carmel Range hold their neighbourhoods, define their lifestyles, and establish an enduring link between them and their ancient roots.

rmel slope, ore wild, rther south.

# THE NORTH COAST: FROM ACCO TO THE BORDER

If Israel were ever to name a capital for sheer atmospheric charm, it would have to be Acco. The Old City of Jerusalem, of course, is in a class all its own, but, between the purchasing, piety and politics, can be more intense than charming; Old Jaffa, itself a venerable walled city, has since been integrated into the fabric of Tel Aviv, as a museum city and crafts centre. Only Acco, battered time and again over the centuries by successive invaders, has held its own against the flow of time and tourist.

The old sea wall, originally built by the Crusaders, still wearily overlooks the expanse of the Mediterranean, on the northern tip of Haifa Bay, while Gothic archways and minarets mingle within. The ancient stone piers still give port to fishermen bringing in the catch-of-the-day; the markets and cafés still overflow with warm service and mysterious faces. Made the key port of the Crusader Kingdom by Baldwin I in 1104, and successfully defended against such diverse notables as Simon Maccabeus and Napoleon Bonaparte, Acco has today left behind the glorious fury of its past. Yet if Acco is a backwater, it is a dramatic backwater, and the visitor wandering through its streets today will encounter stones and views as richly eloquent in their silence as any in the Holy Land.

**Crusader capital:** Mentioned as far back as 3,500 years by the Pharaoh Tutmoses III, Acco is among the world's oldest known seaports. It was already a major population centre during the time of the Phoenicians' dominance over the northern coast, and thwarted attempts at conquest by the tribe of Asher, to whom the city was assigned by Joshua. Its ancient industries included its glassware (the Roman historian Pliny credits Acco with the discovery of the art of glassmaking), and its purple dyes – an extract from a local variety of snail, which in time gave the colour its name. Around 333 BC,

Alexander the Great passed through the city, which was by then a flourishing Greek colony; Julius Caesar, travelling with his soldiers, followed suit some 300 years later, in the process laying the first stones of the first paved road in Roman Judea – from Acco to Antioch.

The Arabs took the city in 636, holding it to 1104, in which time fortifying and rebuilding much of it. Yet Acco only hit its zenith during the era of the Crusaders.

The First Crusade was launched with a bang with the capture of Jerusalem in 1099. Five years later, Acco fell too, and the victorious Crusaders immediately realised the value of their conquest as a Mediterranean lifeline. Developed into a major trading centre by Genovese and other port city merchants, the city was redubbed St Jean d'Acre, and in short time became the principal port on the eastern rim of the Mediterranean. Many of the most powerful and colourful Crusaders orders – the Knights Templars, the Teutonic Order, the Order of St Lazarus, and the Hospitaller Order of St

John – established centres here. In 1187 Saladin defeated the Europeans at the Horns of Hittim, and many Crusader cities fell into Saracen hands. Led by Phillip Augustus of Spain and Richard the Lionheart of England, the knights of the Third Crusade recaptured Acco, and, failing to do the same for Jerusalem, made it the capital of the Crusader Kingdom in 1192. Jews as well as Christians returned to Acco, and the remains left from the ensuing century of Crusader rule testify that this was the city's "finest hour" – in 1291, it fell once more into obscurity.

In the mid-1700s, the port was revived by the Bedouin sheik Dahar el-Omar, who was followed by Acco's most notorious prime builder, the Ottoman Pasha Ahmad, affectionately labeled "al-Jazzar" – the butcher – on account of his penchant for cruelty. His architectural legacies include Acco's best known landmarks. Also of note was his financial advisor, a flamascene Jew named Ham Farhi, who was later killed by Suleiman. In 1799, aided by a fleet of British warships, Jazzar accomplished what much of Europe could not; he defeated the adventuring Napoleon in a two-month siege. Turkish rule and the advent of the steam ship tolled the demise of Acco's importance as a port, and the town only regained prominence in the last years of the British mandate, when its prison held hundreds of underground Jewish freedom fighters, including such top Zionist leaders as Ze'ev Jabotinsky, and was the scene of a remarkable jailbreak in 1947. In the years since independence, the city has retained its portside character while developing its industry, and today holds close to 40,000 residents, some two-thirds of them Jewish immigrants.

**Many cities in one:** Like so much of Israel, Acco is divided into old and new sections, and it is the old city that is of particular interest to the tourist. Yet even the old city is actually many cities in one. To enter the old city from the new, one follows either the coastal strip, or, better, the parallel **Weizmann Street**, with its **Tourist Information Office**.

Arched exit
Subterranea
Crusader Cit

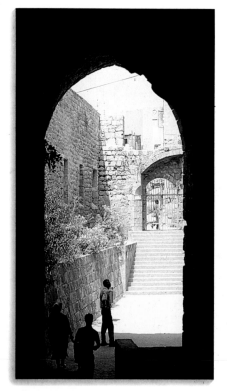

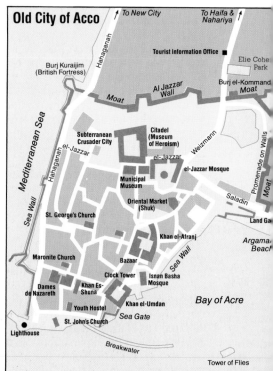

Old City of Acco

Either takes you through the dry moat and city walls, originally built by the Crusaders and subsequently refortified. It is now possible to climb the wall here, and visit the northeastern command post – the **Burj el-Kommandar**, which boasts a strategic view, as well as a restored promenade which continues on to **Land Gate**, at the bay.

As one passes through into the city, the first prominent structure is the elegant **al-Jazzar Mosque**, built in 1781–82 by al-Jazzar, and today the site of his, and his adopted son's and successor Suleiman's tombs. Ringed with domed arcades and swaying palms, the mosque is considered the finest in Israel, and serves as a primary spiritual centre for Israel's Muslim community (take note of the modest dress code before entering). Except for a shrine containing a single hair from the beard of the prophet, the interior is as stark as it is magnificent. In fact, the courtyard is built over a Crusader cellar, while the building also covers other Crusader structures. Across the street is the entrance to the most interesting site of all, the dank and dramatic **Subterranean Crusader City**.

While not yet excavated in their entirety, the halls of the sprawling complex contain such unusual historical testimony as carved *fleur-de-lis* insignia; today reclaimed, they serve as annual host to the autumn Acco Theatre Festival, which brings together the best of the country's experimental companies.

Emerging from the subterranean city, one turns off a small lane into a restored Turkish bathhouse, which is now the **Municipal Museum**. The museum contains exhibits on archaeology, Islamic culture, folklore and weaponry. Abutting both museum and Crusader city, the towering **Citadel** dominates the old city skyline. Built by al-Jazzar on Crusader ruins, the fortress was used variously as an arsenal and a barracks and, since Turkish times, as a prison. During the British mandate, it became a centre for the incarceration and execution of Jewish underground fighters; the Museum of Heroism within the citadel documents this unsettling period.

*mu'ezzin calls the faithful to prayer in Acco sunset.*

Wandering deeper into the maze-like streets of Acco, you may stumble across he **Sand Mosque**, off the main marke. It bears an inscription beseeching the reader to pray for the soul of its builder. Further in is the Greek Orthodox **St George's Church**, dedicated to two British officers who fell at Acco in 1799 and 1840. Of special interest are the *khans* – or inns – that grace the portside area of the city. These include the imposing **Khan el-Afranj**, or Inn of the Franks, near the **Bazaar**, and the unequalled **Khan el-Umdan**, or Inn of the Pillars. A handsome *caravanserai*, the *khan*'s lower storeys were used as stables as its upper were used as lodgings. Its geometric courtyard is memorable, and its **clock-tower** (minus the clock in recent years) offers a glimmering view of the port.

Beneath the tower, wander by the fishing port, and up along the sea wall, which houses one or two lovely cafés among its layered arches. The youth hostel is here, and, further on, the lighthouse, and from this corner you can take in the sunset view of the sea wall heading north to the new city, the old stone houses huddled safely within its tired embrace.

**North to the border:** Arching north from Acco along the coast lies the final architectural gift from al-Jazzar, the austere, self-contained spine of the **Turkish aqueduct**, which when new ran 15 km (9 miles) to the spring at **Kabri**, now a picnic and camping site. Further on, the **Bahai Tomb and Gardens** marks the burial site and villa of Mirza Hussein Ali, an early leader of the Bahai faith, known also as Baha Ulla – Glory to God. Surrounding the tomb is a lovely formal Persian garden. From the east, stretching down to Acco, lies a string of Crusader fortresses – the most important of which, **Montfort**, is located 15 km (9 miles) east of the coast, atop a steep ridge, accessible only by footpaths.

Just north of the gardens is **Nahariya**. A clean and modest resort community, founded in 1934 by German Jews, Nahariya offers a wide variety of amenities for water sports, and the per-

fect coastline on which to enjoy them. Its most noticeable landmark is the quiet stream, the **Ga'aton**, which flows down the centre of the main street, and in the winter occasionally rises to a more threatening posture. Nahariya has cultivated an image as the national honeymoon hideaway, and in the spring offers special discounts to newlyweds, and occasionally other couples. Its reputation is rooted in its association with a Caananite fertility goddess.

The honeymooning really gets into high gear during the celebration of Lag b'Omer – the one day in the six weeks following Passover that Jewish law allows couples to wed. Some 5 km (3 miles) northward along the coastal road are the ruins of **Achziv**, once a thriving Phoenician port, now a thriving **Club Med** resort. For non-members, there is also a holiday village, a campground, and a sparkling beach, equipped with shower facilities. The site is excellent for underwater fishing, and contains small tidal pools to explore.

From here continue northwards passing the **Achziv Bridge**, or Gesher Haziv – Bridge of Glory – where 14 young Hagannah men perished in a freak accident. The tragedy is memorialised in the name of both the local kibbutz and youth hostel.

Some 9 km (5 miles) north of Nahariya, towers the rocky border point of **Rosh HaNikra**, Israel's dynamic coastal limit and northernmost seaside tourist spot. While the view from the chalk-white cliffs set off against the crashing azure waves below is itself entrancing, it is Rosh HaNikra's unique grottos that are her prime attraction. Formed by millennia of erosion, the grottoes offer a dim, damp, splashing and surprisingly placid sojourn in an underground labyrinth of stone; a new cable car takes you down over the pounding tide, and a footpath is also there for the determined.

Atop the cliff, the southern-most edge of the range known as the "Ladder of Tyre" is a welcome cafeteria, and a view out over the now walled-up railway tunnel that in the days before Independence led to Lebanon.

White cliffs of Rosh HaNikra mark end of Israel coast.

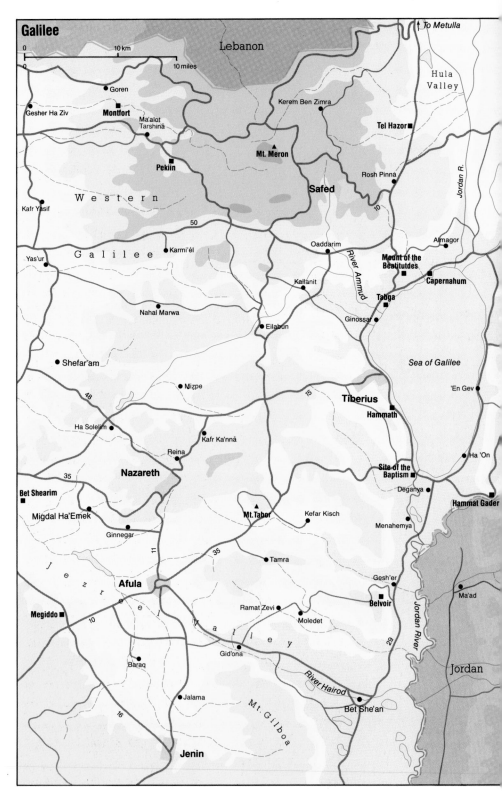

# Galilee

0 ____ 10 km

0 ____ 10 miles

Lebanon

↑ To Metulla

Hula
Valley

Goren

Kerem Ben Zimra

Gesher Ha Ziv

**Montfort**

Ma'alot
Tarshihā

Tel Hazor■

Mt. Meron

**Pekiin**

Rosh Pinna

Jordan R.

**Safed**

Kafr Yasif

W e s t e r n

10

50

G a l i l e e

Karmi'él

Oaddarim

Almagor

Yas'ur

**Mount of the
Beatitutdes**

River Ammud

**Capernahum**

Kallánit

Nahal Marwa

Tabga

Ginossar

Eilabün

Sea of Galilee

Shefar'am

Mizpe

48

15

**Tiberius**

'En Gev

Hammath

Ha Solelim

Kafr Ka'nnā

Reina

Ha 'On

35

**Nazareth**

**Site of the
Baptism**

Bet Shearim
■

Deganya

**Hammat Gader**

Migdal Ha'Emek

Mt. Tabor

Kefar Kisch

Ginnegar

Menahemya

11

35

J
e
z
r
e

Tamra

Gesh'er

**Afula**

Ma'ad

**Belvoir**

Ramat Zevi

**Megiddo** ■

10

e
l

Moledet

29

Jordan River

Gid'ona

Jordan

Baraq

River Hairod

Jalama

Mt. Gilboa

Bet She'an

**Jenin**

# GALILEE

A white-robed Druze puffing away on his pipe in a mountain top village; a bikini-clad bather soaking in sulphuric springs at a Roman bathhouse. These are the stark contrasts typical of Israel's dynamically diverse north – the Galilee.

Extending from the lush Jezreel Valley to the border of Lebanon, this relatively compact region, at one moment a desolate expanse of bare rock, can suddenly explode into a blaze of blood-red buttercups and purple irises. Here, Christians can retrace the steps of Jesus, while Jews can reflect on the place that produced their greatest mystics.

Lying on the main artery that linked the ancient empires, the Galilee has been a battleground for Egyptian pharoahs, biblical kings, Romans and Jews, Christians and Muslims.

More recently, Jewish pioneers established the country's first *kibbutzim* here. They have since mushroomed to

cover much of this region where tribes of Bedouin still roam and Arab and Druze villages lie nestled in the hills.

**The Valley:** The Jezreel Valley stretches from the Samarian foothills in the south to the slopes of the Galilee in the north, it is Israel's largest valley. Because of its strategic location on the ancient Via Maris route, the list of great battle scenes that have scoured this seemingly tranquil stretch is long and colourful. But the greatest battle of all has yet to be fought here. It is the one that the Book of Revelations says will pit the forces of good against the forces of evil for the final battle of mankind at Armageddon. The site referred to is Har Megiddo (Mount Megiddo), a 4,000-year-old city in the centre of the valley

Even the first written mention of **Megiddo** – in Egyptian hieroglypics – describes how war was waged on the city by a mighty Pharaoh some 3,500 years ago. Since then, many a great figure has met his downfall on this ancient battleground. It is said of the Israelite King Josiah, who went down to defeat at the hands of the Egyptians around 600 BC: "And his servants carried him in a chariot dead from Megiddo..." (I Kings; 10, 26). More recently, in World War I, the British waged a critical battle against the Turks at Megiddo Pass, with the victorious British general walking away with the title "Lord Allenby of Megiddo".

In the heap of ruins that make up the mound – or tel – of Megiddo, archaeologists have uncovered 20 cities. At the visitors' centre, a miniature model of the site gives definition to what the untrained eye could see as just a pile of stones. Once oriented, you will see in front of you a 4,000-year-old Canaanite temple, King Solomon's stables (built to accommodate 500 horses), and an **underground water system** built by King Ahab some 2,800 years ago to protect the city's water source in times of seige. Steps and lighting have been installed to facilitate exploration of the 390-ft tunnel, along with the almost 200-ft-high shaft which once served as the system's well.

The capital and largest city in the

Jezreel Valley, **Afula** is the antithesis of Megiddo. There are no epic dramas to be acted out in this sleepy backwater town. Much more in keeping with the larger-than-life dimensions of the valley is **Nazareth**. A strange blend of the timeless and topical, the sacred town where Jesus spent much of his life is today a bustling city of 40,000 Muslim and Christian Arabs – with a Communist mayor at its helm.

A water system that's not quite as historic as Megiddo's, but is impressive in its own way can be found at **Gan HaShelosha** (The Garden of Three). Modern developers have managed to recreate a tiny piece of Eden in this stunning park. It is also known as **Sachne**, meaning warm in Arabic, because of the warm waters of **Ein Harod** (The Spring of Harod) that bubble up from under the earth to fill a huge natural swimming pool. Around it, exotic flowers and lush forests are interspersed with wide open grassy spaces.

The Spring of Harod actually starts at the foot of the Gilboa mountains, just east of Afula, and flows all the way to the Jordan. But for most of the way, the warm waters are kept underground and diverted for use in local settlements. The only other spot where they surface is at **Gidona**. The site is named after the Israelite warrior Gideon, who supposedly assembled his forces at this gentle spring 3,000 years ago. In more recent times, it served as the meeting and training spot for the forces of the Palmach, the elite fighting unit of the Jews in pre-state Palestine. There is also a memorial here to Yehoshuah Henkin, a Zionist leader, who purchased hundreds of thousands of acres of land – including this piece – for Jewish settlement.

The Jezreel Valley was, in fact, the first and largest tract of land in what was then Palestine, to be purchased by Zionist leaders close to a century ago. The Arab landowners were only too pleased to rid themselves of what was at the time uninhabitable swampland. In draining the swamps, Jewish pioneers have planted some 125 million trees over the years. The act of planting a tree came to **Jezreel Valley view.**

symbolise the redemption of the Jewish homeland and has since become a quasi-religious ritual. Today tree-planting centres in Israel abound, with the largest one located in the Jezreel Valley. The **Balfour Forest**, named after Lord Arthur Balfour (the British foreign minister whose 1917 speech in favour of a Jewish homeland became known as the Balfour Declaration), has trees. Lord Balfour's nephew recently added his own sapling to the sprawling forest located 3 km (2 miles) southwest of Nazareth. Royal connections are not essential however; for a few dollars anyone can plant a tree. The centres are usually open weekdays from 8:30am to 3:30pm, earlier on Fridays.

For an idea of the considerably more gruelling conditions which confronted the original tree-planters a visit to the **Museum of Early Agricultural Settlers** at nearby **Kibbutz Yifat** is recommended.

To get an overview of the whole Jezreel Valley – a splendid patchwork of gold and green farmland – head up to **Mount Tabor**. This strangely symmetrical hill, shaped not unlike a skullcap, dominates much of the valley. It was here that the biblical prophetess Deborah was said to have led an army of 10,000 Israelites to defeat their idol-worshipping enemies. The two churches you see commemorate the transfiguration of Jesus Christ, also said to have taken place here.

About a mile west of Gan Hashelosha is **Kibbutz Beit Alpha** where you'll find the country's best-preserved ancient synagogue floor. Discovered when kibbutz members were digging an irrigation channel, the 6th-century floor consists of a striking zodiac mosaic and a rendition of the sacrifice of Isaac.

A particularly remarkable, if eerie, site can be found in the chalky slopes of **Beit Shearim** about 11 km (7 miles) northwest of the Balfour Forest. This is Israel's version of a necropolis. The limestone hills have been hollowed out to form a series of catacombs. Inside the dark labyrinths, vaulted chambers are lined with hundreds of marble or stone

sarcophagi (depending on the social rank of the deceased). Each of the often elaborately engraved coffins weighs nearly 5 tonnes. Since the Romans did not allow Jews to settle in Jerusalem, the centre of Jewish national and spiritual life moved to Beit Shearim. This 2nd-century burial ground became a favourite not only for local residents but for Jews all over the world.

Overlooking the whole length of the Jezreel Valley are the **Gilboa Mountains**. Here King Saul met his untimely fate at the hands of the Philistines, causing David to curse the spot forever: "Ye mountains of Gilboa, let there be no dew, nor rain upon you, neither fields of choice fruit…" (II Sam 20; 21-23).

**The Jordan Rift:** East of the Gilboa mountain range is one of the lowest points in Israel: the Jordan Rift. Encompassing the Jordan Valley and the Beit Shean Valley, it is part of the same 6,500-km (4,000-mile) rift that stretches from Syria to Africa and is responsible for the lowest point on earth – the Dead Sea. Even here at 120 metres (390 ft)

below sea level (it gets to 390 metres/ 1,280 ft further south), it's like a kiln baking under an unrelenting sun in summertime. By way of comparison, Death Valley, California, the lowest point in the United States, is only 87 metres (285 ft) below sea level. But nourished by the Jordan River, the Yarmuk River, and a network of underground springs (including the Spring of Harod), this remains a lush region, bursting with bananas, dates and other fruit. It is home to some of Israel's most prosperous *kibbutzim* including **Afikim**, **Gesher** and **Ashdot Ya'akov**.

The ancient *tel* of **Beit Shean** has revealed 6,000 years of civilisation. Near it sits Israel's best preserved Roman amphitheatre which once seated 8,000.

Easily accessible from the highway north of Beit Shean is the impressive Crusader fortress of **Belvoir**. Perched on the highest hill in the region, it offers a superb view of the valleys below and of neighbouring Jordan.

**Jewel of the Galilee:** Glowing like an emerald, its tranquil surface framed in a

Left, stalks asphodel grace Jezree Valley. Rigl netload of S Peter's fish.

purplish-brown halo of mountains, the **Sea of Galilee** is probably the most breathtaking and certainly the largest lake in the country. At 21 km (13 miles) long and 11 km (7 miles) wide, it may not be enormous by global standards, but it has, through some romantically inspired hyperbole, come to be known as a "sea". The Sea of Galilee, the Sea of Tiberias, the Sea of Ginossar are its most popular names. In Hebrew, it's called the "Kinneret" because it's shaped like a *kinnor* or harp.

Not surprisingly, these bountiful shores have been inhabited for millennia, with the earliest evidence of habitation dating back 5,000 years to a moon-worshipping cult that sprouted in the south. Some 3,000 years later, the same lake witnessed the birth and spread of Christianity on its shores, while high up on the cliffs above, Jewish rebels sought refuge from Roman soldiers. The dramas of the past, however, have since faded into the idyllic landscape. Today, it is new water sports, not new religions, that are hatched on these azure shores.

Nowhere is this "fun in the sun" spirit felt more than at the lake's capital, **Tiberias**. A sprawling city of 40,000, halfway down the west coast, it has become one of the country's most popular resorts. On its new boardwalk, lined with seafood restaurants, you can dig into scrumptious St Peter's fish, while enjoying a stunning view of the lake. On the marina you can have your pick of waterskiing or windsurfing, or go for a dip at any of the beaches along the outskirts of the city. (If you're visiting during a typically balmy summer you'll need to dunk yourself in the water one way or another.)

With all the distractions available in this popular playground, it's easy to forget that Tiberias is considered one of the four holy Jewish cities. To remind you, are the **tombs** of several famous Jewish sages buried here, including the great 12th-century philosopher Moses Maimonides and the self-taught scholar and martyr Rabbi Akiva.

When it was founded by Herod around 20 AD, Tiberias failed to attract devout

Where the Jordan River leaves the Sea of Galilee.

Jews and Christians because it was thought to be built over an ancient Jewish cemetery and considered impure. But eventually, economic incentives, as well as a symbolic "purification" of the city by a well-respected rabbi cleared the way for settlement. During the 2nd and 3rd centuries it reached its zenith. Boasting a population of 40,000, it became the focus of Jewish academic life. It was at Tiberias that scholars codified the sounds of the Hebrew script and wrote the great commentary on the Bible, the Mishnah.

By the eve of the Arab conquest of 636, Tiberias was the most important Christian centre outside Jerusalem. A 12th-century battle between the Muslims and Crusaders destroyed the city. After being resettled, it was again reduced to rubble in 1837, this time by an earthquake. A few devout Jews arrived to rebuild the town and lived there alongside their Arab neighbours until 1948 when the Arabs of the town fled during the War of Independence.

The repeated destruction of the city has, unfortunately, left only meagre souvenirs of its vibrant past. A few remains of Crusader towers dot the shoreline; an 18th-century mosque is crammed in between ice cream stands in the main square.

For historians and hedonists alike, Tiberias's main drawing card is its **hot springs** situated at the southern outskirts of the city. Legends abound as to the cause of this wonder of nature. In fact, the same cataclysmic convulsions that millions of years ago carved the Jordan Rift, also created these 17 springs that gush from a depth of 6,500 ft to spew up hot (60°C) streams of mineral-rich water. The therapeutic properties of the springs have been known – and exploited – for centuries.

For some contemporary healing go to **Hamei Tiberias**. This hotel-spa offers a range of treatments from whirlpools to "electrohydrotherapy" that are reputed to cure everything from skin ailments to respiratory problems and, claim some, sterility. In the winter, a soak in these mineral-rich jacuzzis can be a soothing respite from the damp Galilee air.

You can see the original Roman baths across the street at **The National Park** in a fascinating little museum devoted to the springs. Next to it, at the site of the ancient city **Hammath**, archaeologists have uncovered a 2nd-century mosaic synagogue floor–undoubtedly, the most exquisite ruins you'll find in Tiberias.

Just outside the city are the **Horns of Hittim** where in 1187 the Muslim forces of Saladin defeated the Crusaders in the decisive battle that brought an end to the Crusader Kingdom.

**Around the lake:** One of the best ways to see the many sites around the lake (provided you don't have access to a car) is to obtain a 1 or 2-day bus pass on Egged's Minus 200 Line (available at most major hotels) which enables you to get on and off at any of 23 stops. There are also ferry boats that go back and forth regularly from Tiberas to Ein Gev, on the east coast; for the more ambitious, swimming the same route has become a popular competitive sport.

Moving north from Tiberias, you will first come to the towering cliffs of **Arbel**.

**eft, hotels nd ancient
ᴊas dot ʜoreline at ᴉberius.
ᴉght, rare ᴉlboa Iris.**

Today, a rock climbers' haven, during Roman times they served as a hideout for Jewish rebels. Next is **Ginossar**, an especially beautiful kibbutz with a luxurious guesthouse (be sure to ask about the perfectly intact 2,000 year-old boat recently uncovered on the shores of the kibbutz). **Vered HaGalil** is a bit of an anomaly in these parts with its Wild West-style guesthouse-restaurant and horseback tours. At the northern tip of the lake you come to the ruins of **Capernahum**, one of the most important Jewish and Christian sites in the Roman period.

Hovering over the black pebbly beaches on the east coast of the lake are the **Golan Heights**, which until 1967, were in Syrian hands. The few settlements on this side of the lake used to be bombarded regularly by the Syrians making much of the lake inaccessible. Since the Israeli takeover, the area has undergone rapid development and tourism has burgeoned.

Several settlements have guesthouses and camping facilities including **Moshav Ramot**; **Kibbutz Ein Gev**, site of a gala music festival every spring; **Kibbutz Ha'on**, which boasts one of the few ostrich farms in the world outside South Africa; and **Kibbutz Ma' Agan**. Also on the east coast is the **Golan Beach** and its water wonderland, the **Luna Gal**. At **Beit Yerah** on the southern tip of the lake are the ruins from the ancient moon-worshipping cult.

Around the point where the lake merges with the Jordan River are three *kibbutzim*: **Deganya Aleph**, **Deganya Beth**, and **Kinneret**. Not having guesthouses, they attract fewer tourists than other *kibbutzim* around the lake, but it is these that are most worth noting because they were the first. From their ranks sprang many of Israel's legendary leaders, including Moshe Dayan.

At the entrance to **Deganya Aleph** is a Syrian tank, stopped in its tracks in the 1948 War of Independence.

**Cradle of Christianity:** It was, of course, on the waters of the Sea of Galilee that Jesus was said to have walked. The coast of the lake is dotted with churches marking the miracles Jesus reputedly performed in this region that was to become the cradle of Christianity.

"Can anything good come out of Nazareth," (John; 1,46). This rhetorical question might seem puzzling today, particularly to millions of Christians for whom **Nazareth** is equated with Christianity itself. But when it was posed two millennia ago, the one feature that most distinguished this village in the lower Galilee was its very obscurity.

Since then, the quaint town where Jesus Christ grew up has, of course, become renowned. Today, of almost two dozen churches commemorating Nazareth's most esteemed resident, the grandest of all is the monumental **Basilica of the Annunciation**. The largest church in the Middle East, it was built 20 years ago, but encompasses the remains of previous Byzantine churches. It marks the spot where the Archangel Gabriel is supposed to have informed the virgin Mary that God had chosen her to bear his son. The event is depicted inside in a series of elaborate murals, each from a different country. In one,

**An ostrich roams the grounds at Kibbutz Ha'on.**

Mary appears kimono-clad and with slanted eyes; in another, she's wearing a turban and bright African garb. Not to be outdone, the Americans have produced a highly modernistic cubist version of the virgin.

Some of the simpler churches, however, capture an air of intimacy and sanctity that the colossal Basilica lacks. This is especially so in the Greek Orthodox **Church of St Gabriel**. Upon entering the small dark shrine you hear nothing but the faint rush of water. Lapping up against the sides of the old well inside the church is the same underground spring that provided Nazareth with its water 2,000 years ago. It takes only a little imagination to envision the scene described in the Gospels in which, "Mary took the pitcher and went forth to fill it with water…" at which point the angel Gabriel is said to have descended and informed her of the surprising news.

In the basement of the **Church of St Joseph** (next to the Basilica) is a cavern said to have been the carpentry workshop of Joseph.

Shortly after Jesus left Nazareth at age 28, he met John the Baptist preaching near the waters of the Jordan. In the river that the Bible so often describes as a boundary – and more figuratively, as a point of transition – Jesus was baptised. Once thus "cleansed", he set out on his mission. Tradition holds that the baptism took place at the point where the Sea of Galilee merges with the Jordan River near what is today **Kibbutz Kinneret**.

A bathing area has been established just outside the kibbutz in order to accommodate the many pilgrims who still converge on the site. (There is a rival **"site of the Baptism"** further south near Jericho.)

A few miles outside Nazareth, nestled among pomegranate and olive groves, is the Arab village of **Cana**. Shortly after being baptised, Jesus attended the wedding of a poor family in this town. Here, say the Gospels, he used his new-found powers for the first time, making the meagre pitchers of water overflow with wine. Two small

Nazareth,
pastoral in
early
evening.

churches in the village commemorate the feat.

It was in the numerous fishing villages around the Sea of Galilee that Jesus found his first followers. The village of **Capernahum** on the northern tip of the lake, became a second home for him. Here he is said to have preached more sermons and performed more miracles than anywhere else.

It was a metropolis of sorts in its heyday, and at least five of the disciples came from this Jewish town. (It is after one of them, a simple fisherman named Peter, that the Galilee's most renowned fish gets its name). Today the site houses the elaborate remains of a 2nd-century synagogue – said to be built over the original one where Jesus used to preach. There is also a recently completed church shaped like a ship.

It was standing on a hilltop overlooking the Sea of Galilee that Jesus proclaimed to the masses that had gathered below: "Blessed are the meek for they shall inherit the earth." This, but one line of the now famous Sermon of the Mount, is immortalised by the majestic **Church of the Beatitudes** also near Capernahum.

In the neighbouring town of **Tabga**, he is said to have multiplied a few loaves of bread and fish into enough food to feed the 5,000 hungry people who had come to hear him speak. The new **Church of the Multiplication**, built over the colourful mosaic floor of a Byzantine shrine, stands there today.

When his sermons began to provoke the Romans, Jesus took three of his disciples and ascended **Mount Tabor**. There, the Gospels say he "was transfigured before them… his face shone like the sun and his garments became white as light." The Franciscan **Basilica of the Transfiguration** commemorates the event which Christians believe was a prelude to his resurrection.

**Atmospheric Safed:** A few miles northeast of the lake loom the two highest peaks in the Galilee. They are said to exude an air of something eternal and inexplicable that makes them seem even higher than their 1,170 metres (3,840 ft). Known as the **Mountains of Meron**, their mystique is attributed to the legendary town that faces them: **Safed**.

When one of the great 16th-century poets of Safed was returning to his town after a long absence, he was met along the way by a band of robbers who threatened to kill him. When granted a last request, he picked up his flute and began to play a haunting prayer. The melody so enchanted the robbers' camels that they began to dance, sending their bewildered owners fleeing.

Sheltered by the highest peaks in the Galilee, Safed seems also to be sheltered from time itself. Its narrow, cobblestoned streets wind their way through stone archways and overlook the domed rooftops of 16th-century homes. Devout men, clad in black, congregate in medieval synagogues, the echo of their chants filling the streets.

A modern area of Safed, with some 18,000 residents, has sprung up around the original city core.

When the Spanish Inquisition sent thousands of Jews fleeing, many ended up in Safed, bringing with them the

A mosaic recalls the miracle of fishes and loaves at Tabga.

golden age they'd left behind in Spain. The rabbinical scholars of Safed were so prolific that in 1563 the city was prompted to set up the first printing press in Israel (or Asia for that matter).

The Shulchan Aroch, the basic set of daily rituals for Jews was compiled here. But the real focus of Safed's sages was not the mundane, but the mystical. Many had been drawn to the city in the first place because of its proximity to the tomb of Rabbi Shimon Bar-Yochai, the 2nd-century sage who is believed to have written the core of the Cabala, Judaism's foremost mystical text.

The efforts of Safed's sages to narrow the gap between heaven and earth left not only great scholarly work and poignant poetry, but also a legacy of legends about their mysterious powers.

At one synagogue (Abohav), an earthquake apparently destroyed almost the entire building but left the one wall facing Jerusalem unscathed.

Every synagogue here is wrapped in its own comparable set of legends which the shamash (deacon) is usually de-

lighted to share. Not all the synagogues are medieval, many of the original ones having been destroyed and replaced by more modern structures. But the spirit of old still lingers in these few lanes off **Kikar Meginim**.

The special atmosphere that permeates Safed has captured the imagination of dozens of artists who've made it their home. Like the rest of the old city, the **artists' quarter** of Safed remains untouched. Nothing has been added for "the benefit of the tourist" – nothing has to be. Winding your way through the labyrinth of lanes, you'll find over 50 studios and galleries as well as a general art gallery and a printing museum.

Towering above the centre of Safed, littered with Crusader ruins, is **Citadel Hill**, an excellent lookout point taking in a panorama that extends from the slopes of Lebanon to the Sea of Galilee.

Like the ripples that form around a stone tossed in a lake, the hills surrounding Safed reverberate with the sacredness the city inspires. Starting at the **cemetery** at the base of Safed, where

n ancient
ewish grave
Safed.

the biblical prophet Hosea is said to be buried, the whole area to Mount Meron is dotted with the tombs of rabbis and scholars.

At the base of Meron, in the village of the same name, is the **tomb of Shinion Bar-Yochai**, the revered rabbi who drew Jews to Safed in the first place. On the feast of Lag Ba'Omer, you can still see thousands of his devout followers gather outside Safed's synagogues and make their way in a joyous procession to his grave at the foot of Mount Meron.

A tomb at nearby **Amuka** is the site of a pilgrimage of another sort. When Rabbi Jonathon Ben Uziel died in the 1st century, legend has it that he confided to his disciples that his greatest regret in life was not having married early enough in life to be fruitful and multiply. "Anyone who truly wishes to marry should pray at my tomb," said the dying rabbi, "And their wish shall be granted within a year." Thousands of marriage-minded singles have since taken the rabbi up on his promise.

Also in this region is the mountainside town of **Pekiin**, a quaint Arab village that's noted for being the only place in Israel where Jews have resided continuously since Roman times.

At the outskirts of Safed, flows **Nahal Ammud**. This river, which brings images of Eden to mind, leads down to the Sea of Galilee. In the summer you can wade through it, plucking pomegranates and figs along the way.

**Havens in the hills:** The mountains of Meron are but the two highest peaks in the steep slope-ridden region known as the **Western Galilee**. This is rough mountainous country – stretches of bare rock interspersed with patches of pine trees, olive groves and eucalyptus. Canyons, caves and gorges abound. A number of small rivers (*nahals*) cut through this rugged region, flowing from east to west and emptying into the Mediterranean. To get a real taste of this terrain follow one of them for a stretch. **Nahal Kziv** which runs parallel to the ancient seaside ruins at **Achziv**, takes you through natural pools and springs to **Montfort**, an immense Crusader fortress that makes a great lookout point.

(In touring less accessible spots in Israel you'd be advised to contact the Society for the Protection of Nature in Jerusalem or Tel Aviv. They provide invaluable information, tips and maps as well as English language tours.)

For all its raw beauty – perhaps, because of it – the Western Galilee's most fascinating natural resource may be its people. Each of the hundreds of small settlements scattered throughout this region is a world unto itself. At **Beit Jann**, the highest village in Israel, you'll find elderly men clad in turbans and white flowing robes – the clothes worn by the scholars in this Druze community of 5,000.

Sporting long sideburns and clad in black, Hassidim, a particularly religious sect of Jews, have their own village at **Kfar Hassidim** (and are not especially appreciative of visitors). A few miles away at **Bosmat Tivon** is an urban settlement of Bedouin. The difficulties these nomadic people face in making the transition to urban life create some poignant pictures. You'll find the

younger generation living comfortably in new suburban homes, while their stubborn parents continue to camp out – in the back yard.

The wide open space of the Western Galilee acts as a haven, attracting various idealists seeking to carve their own small utopias on its slopes. So, in addition to the more common settlements like *kibbutzim*, Bedouin encampments and Arab and Druze villages, you'll find a community of transcendental meditationists at Hararit who've found their nirvana on these secluded slopes. Or a colony of vegetarians at **Amirim** who have set up an organic farm as well as a guesthouse where visitors can indulge in gourmet vegetarian meals.

What has burgeoned into the largest town in the Western Galilee, **Karmiel**, is itself an unconventional experiment in urban planning – and by all accounts, a successful one. Established in 1964, its population of 20,000 includes native-born Israelis as well as Jewish immigrants from 34 different countries (including many Americans, and recently, Ethiopians and Russians). Clean, pretty and prosperous, Karmiel is considered to be a model development town. Near its centre, against a back-drop of desolate mountains, are a series of larger-than-life sculptures depicting the history of Israel's Jewish people.

Karmiel is set in the **Beit HaKerem Valley**, the dividing line between what is considered the Upper Galilee (to the north) with peaks jutting up to almost 4,000 ft, and the Lower Galilee (to the south), a decidedly gentler expanse of rolling hills, none of which are more than 2,000 ft high.

The latest social experiment to be undertaken in this region is perhaps the boldest and broadest one yet. In the midst of these isolated slopes, young Israelis are busy polishing synthetic diamonds, making sophisticated electronic components and designing computer software. They have set up schools and stores, clinics and community centres in what they hope will become Israel's own modest version of Silicon Valley. The single-minded ambition that

**Karmiel nestles in western Galilee hills**

drives California's whiz kids is not found in abundance here. Infused with idealism, the young settlers of these hi-tech havens are not just out to make a buck, or so they say. It's a question of lifestyle, of commitment to shared values that holds their enterprises together.

On some, like **Moresha** (which means Heritage), this takes the form of strictly observing Jewish law. Others, such as **Shoreshim**, share the socialistic principles of a kibbutz, with all members jointly owning the community's means of production and all receiving equal shares of the profits.

Both Moresha and Shoreshim are part of the largest group of new settlements here called the **Segev Bloc**. Set up in 1978 in the hills south of Karmiel, it has several thousand families spread out in 18 communities. One of them, **Manof**, which is made up of mostly English-speaking immigrants from South Africa, offers guest facilities.

Weaving across the northern extremity of the Western Galilee is a highway suitably called the **Northern Road**. In addition to providing spectacular lookout points, this route hugs the Lebanese border for over 100 km (60 miles), sometimes running as little as a few yards from Lebanese farmers nonchalantly tending their orchards. While for many years the Israeli settlements along this route were frequently the target of brutal terrorist attacks, the area is today considered extremely safe for residents and tourists alike. A worthwhile stop is **Baram** where the exquisite columns of a 2nd-century synagogue still stand.

**The road to Metulla:** The land extending north of the Sea of Galilee gradually narrows into what is known as the finger of the Galilee with Metulla at its tip. This is particularly pretty countryside. The east opens up into the sprawling Valley of Hula, beyond which hover the Golan Heights. Towering over the valley to the west are the Naphtali Mountains, beyond which loom the even higher – and often ominous – mountains of Lebanon. These picturesque peaks were in the past a source of frequent Katyusha rocket attacks on the Israeli towns below.

Aside from the beauty it offers, the road to Metulla is an odyssey through the making of modern Israel.

The first stop on this trek is **Rosh Pina**. On the rock-strewn barren terrain they found here a century ago, East European pioneers set up the first Jewish settlement in the Galilee since Roman times. They called it Rosh Pina, meaning the "cornerstone" after the Biblical passage: "The stone which the builders rejected has become the cornerstone." The original 30 families who settled here were part of the first wave of Jewish immigration that began in the 1880s and was partly triggered by the pogroms in Eastern Europe.

Rosh Pina, a quaint town of about 1,000, has maintained something of its original rural character. Cobblestoned streets line the old section of town and 19th-century homes, though badly neglected, still stand.

Continuing towards Metulla, the next stop takes one off the road of modern history, exposing instead the much more ancient foundations of the country. **Tel**

statue at rmiel lebrates e.

**Hazor** is one of the oldest archaeological sites in Israel – and by far, the largest. With its 23 layers of civilisation spanning approximately 3,000 years, it was the inspiration for *The Source*, James Michener's epic history of Israel. Across the street at **Kibbutz Ayelet HaShachar** there is a museum housing many of the finds. The kibbutz also runs a very popular guesthouse.

This is the region of the **Hula Valley**, a stretch of lush land dotted with farming villages and little fish ponds that would seem like a mirage to someone who stood on the same spot 35 years ago. Then you would have seen some 10,000 acres of malaria infested swampland – home to snakes, water buffalo and wild boar.

The draining of the valley was one of the most monumental tasks undertaken by the State of Israel in its early days. It took six years – during which the site's workers were often fired upon by neighbouring Syrian forces in the Golan Heights. But by 1957, the lake had been emptied, leaving a verdant valley in its place. You can get an idea of what the area was like before by visiting the 1,000 acres of swampland that have been set aside as a reserve. There is also a museum devoted to the natural history of the region at **Kibbutz Hulata** and a guesthouse in the northern part of the valley at **Kfar Blum**, a kibbutz with a distinctly Anglo Saxon tone.

North of the Hula Valley, you begin to enter the narrow tip of Israel known as the "finger" or "panhandle" of the Galilee. When the end of World War I left the status of this area unclear, gangs of Arabs attacked the Jews here, forcing them to abandon their settlements. The settlers at **Tel Hai** and **Kfar Giladi**, though vastly outnumbered, held out under siege for months until their leader, Joseph Trumpeldor, was shot and killed. The incident made the Jews painfully aware of the need to beef up their self-defence and triggered the formation of the Haganah, the predecessor of the Israel Defence Forces.

The building from which the settlers defended themselves is now a museum devoted to the Haganah. Nearby is a memorial to Trumpeldor and seven fellow fighters, including two women, who died in the attack. Thousands of Israeli youths converge on the Tel Hai site on the anniversary of Trumpeldor's death. There is also a youth hostel here and a guesthouse at neighbouring Kfar Giladi, today a flourishing kibbutz.

Just before Metulla, in the **Iyun Nature Reserve**, is a picturesque waterfall that flows impressively in the winter months (from October–May), but is completely dry the rest of the year. This is due to a longstanding arrangement in which Israel permits Lebanese farmers to divert the water for agricultural use.

The nearby town of **Kiryat Shmona**, "Town of Eight," is named after the heroes of Tel Hai and is, in fact, built on the site from where the Arabs used to launch their attacks. It is one of scores of development towns founded shortly after Israel became a state in order to absorb some of the 700,000 Jews who poured into the new country. Kiryat Shmona, like many "development towns," was hardly a town at all; it

Outdoor education in the early 1900s.

began as a series of corrugated iron huts known as *ma'abarot*. Situated close to the border, it was for years the target of rocket attacks from the Lebanese mountains that overlook it. Today, the mountains serve as a scenic backdrop for what is now a peaceful and, if not prosperous, at least developing town of over 20,000 inhabitants.

Some 10 km (6 miles) east of Kiryat Shmona, on the edge of the Golan Heights (and what used to be the Syrian border) is the archaeolgical site of **Tel Dan**. In Biblical times, as now, at the northern tip of Israel, it was founded by members of the tribe of Dan, after quarrels with the Philistines forced them to relocate from the southern coast. It is also notorious as one of two cities where Jeroboam permitted worship of the idolatrous golden calf.

Today the site includes various Israelite ruins, a Roman fountain and a triple-arched Canaanite gateway. In the summer, volunteers help excavate this active scenic *tel* where the source waters for the Jordan River emerge. The museum at **Kibbutz Dan** nearby describes the geology of the region and the reclamation of the Hula Valley below.

Until the Hermon was captured from Syria in 1967, **Metulla** was the target of rocket attacks from the most northern point in Israel, surrounded on three sides by Lebanese territory. Founded in 1896 by the same wave of immigrants that settled in Rosh Pina, for two decades it remained the only settlement in the area. Even today, the nearest shopping centre is 10 km (6 miles) away in Kiryat Shmona.

Aside from the fresh mountain air, abundant apple orchards (most of the country's supply comes from here), and charming pensions, what draws tourists to this secluded town of 600 is its now famous border with Lebanon. Every day (except Saturday) hundreds of Lebanese stream through what has come to be known as "**The Good Fence.**" Some, victims of the turmoil in Lebanon, come for medical care, but most are simply labourers commuting to their jobs – in Israel.

**ple harvest arks rebirth the land.**

# GOLAN HEIGHTS

The Golan is a brooding and sombre massif doomed by history to be bloodied by nearly ceaseless war. It is a great block of dark gray rock lifted high above the Upper Jordan Valley, and those who have the Golan have the power to rain misery upon their neighbours.

The Golan is a mighty fortress created by the hand of nature. During the Tertiary Age, geological folding lifted its hard basalt stone from the crust of the earth. Today it is a sloped plateau, rising in the north to heights greater than a full kilometre above sea level. It is 67 km (40 miles) from north to south and 25 km (15 miles) from east to west.

Today, the Golan Heights are considered by Israel to be part of Israel, although few other countries seem willing to accept this *fait accompli*. However, in 1981 Israeli military occupation of this former Syrian territory was replaced with civil law and administration, and for practical purposes, the Golan today is as much a part of Israel as the Negev.

Israeli justification for absorbing the Golan focuses on Syria's implacable belligerence, and the fact that it was used as a base for frequent artillery shelling of the Israeli settlements below when it was in Syrian hands. Since the start of the peace process with Syria there has been much talk of territorial compromise over the Golan. Many in Israel vehemently oppose such an eventuality

**Historic redoubt:** The Golan has been disputed throughout history. In remote antiquity, it was the greatest natural barrier traversed by the Via Maris, the "Sea Highway" that led from Egypt and the coastal plain across Galilee and Golan to the kingdom of Mesopotamia.

Genesis 14 relates Abraham's struggles against the four Mesopotamian kings, led by Kedarlaomer of Elam, who had been pillaging the land. Gathering 318 of his best trained soldiers, Abraham pursued the raiders and surprised them at Dan, on the northwest

limit of the Golan. In the ensuing rout, the partriarch chased the brigands out to the gates of Damascus. The Golan was allocated to the tribe of Menasseh during the biblical era, but was frequently lost and recaptured by the Israelites over the centuries.

Under Roman rule, Jewish settlement in the Golan increased, and a few generations later, during the Jewish Revolt against Rome, many of the descendants of those settlers met cruel deaths during the epic battle for the fortress of Gamla.

The range changed hands frequently during the following centuries, though archaeological evidence indicates a substantial Jewish population until the time of the Crusades; for the next eight centuries, the area was largely desolate.

Toward the end of the 19th century the ruling Ottoman Turks tried to repopulate the Golan with anyone who wasn't Jewish, to serve as a buffer against invasion from the south. Among those who did set roots here were some Druze, Circassians fleeing the Russian invasion of the Caucasus Mountains, in 1878, and Turkemans who migrated in from Central Asia. A village of Nusseiris (North Syrian Alaouites) also was established here.

After World War I, when British General Edmund Allenby drove the Ottomans off the Golan, the region was included in the British Mandate of Palestine, but in the San Remo conference in 1923 it was traded off to the French sphere of influence.

From 1948 to 1967 the Syrians used the Golan Heights as a forward base of operations against Israel. Jewish villages in Israel's Hula Valley were shelled by Syrian artillery mounted here. Syria continued to install fortifications in the Golan throughout the 1960s, converting the region into a military zone.

War finally broke out on 6 June 1967 with Syrian Army attacks on Kibbutz Dan, Ashmura and She'ar Yashuv. The attack was blunted the following day, and on 9 June Israeli troops counterattacked and swung behind the Syrian defence emplacements. Within 48 hours, all Syrian units on the Golan had either retreated or surrendered.

**The aftermath:** Only six inhabited villages, with a total population of 6,400 people, remained on the Golan at the time of the Israeli victory, these including five Druze communities and one Nusseiri village at Ghajar. Within weeks, Israeli *kibbutzim* began establishing daughter communities in the unpopulated hills, the first being Meron Golan in July of that year.

In the following years, the region received schools, medical clinics, old age programmes, and the like. Modern Israeli agricultural methods vastly increased productivity of many crops, particularly apples, pears, peaches, almonds, plums and cherries, and all residents of the Golan were integrated into Israel's wage scale system.

Syria attacked again on 6 October 1973, the Jewish Day of Atonement, when most Israeli troops were on leave with their families. The next day, Syrian troops occupied nearly half the Golan. Israel responded on 8 October in what was to become the greatest tank battle in history. Within a week, Syria had lost some 1,200 of an estimated 1,500 Soviet-built tanks. By 24 October, Israeli units were within sight of Damascus when the United Nations called for peace, and Israel complied. Today, minefields still remain as dangerous mementoes from this era.

In recent years, the Golan has gained a new, more peaceful distinction – as the source and soil of a new Israeli vineyard; the wine, called "Yarden", is said to be the best yet produced for export, comparable to some of France's finest.

**Tourism:** The Golan is not a popular tourist attraction in Israel. Most Israelis see it as a vital buffer zone between their country and Syria, an enormous bunker filling its ancient role of blocking invasion. Visitors to the Golan usually tour old Syrian battlements. **Nimrod Fortress** on the northern Golan is one of these. From this 13th-century Crusader fortress, one has a spectacular view of the northern Galilee and the Naphtali Hills beyond.

Another often-visited site is **Gamla**, but there is little joy attached to this

A destroyed Syrian tank decorates the roadside in Golan.

ruined bastion. Gamla was the "Massada of the North", a fortified town of the south-central Golan which, in the year 66 AD, was the focus of one of the early battles in the Jewish revolt against Rome. Initially, the rebels put Vespasian and three full Roman legions to shame. The over-confident Roman threw his legions recklessly against the Jewish bastion only to have them humbled by a much smaller and less professional Jewish force. Recovering, the embarrassed Romans besieged the Jewish town in one of the most bitter battles of the war. Vespasian vowed no mercy would be shown the defenders.

The Romans gradually pushed the Jews to a precipice on which this mountain top city was built and, when Roman victory appeared imminent, many defenders committed suicide rather than surrender. Four thousand Jews were killed in battle; another 5,000 either committed suicide or were slaughtered by the Romans after Gamla had fallen to them. "The sole survivors were two women," historian Josephus Flavius wrote. "They survived because when the town fell they eluded the fury of the Romans, who spared not even babes in arms, but seized all they found and flung them from the citadel."

The site, reduced to rubble by the Romans, was lost to history for precisely 1902 years. In 1968, Gamla was rediscovered during a systematic Israeli survey of the region. Today it is possible for the visitor to stroll the ancient streets of this community, view the remains of many ancient homes, and even a synagogue, all built of the Golan's sombre black basalt stone.

The ruins of Gamla are clustered on a steep ridge and, if the visitor tours the area between late winter and early summer, there is a very good likelihood of seeing magnificent griffon vultures soaring overhead on their 2-metre (7-ft) wingspans.

In the fields east of Gamla it is possible to find several prehistoric **dolmens**. These are stone-age structures which look something like crude tables, with a large, flat stone bridging several sup-

ncient
olmen near
amla.

porting stones. They are generally considered to be burial monuments, and most are dated to about 4,000 BC. Dolmens are found at several other sites around the Golan and the Galilee.

About 6 km (10 miles) northwest of Gamla, **Katzrin** is the modern "capital" of the Golan and the region's only municipal centre.tourists however, usually prefer to shop in Druze villages, particularly **Majdal Shams** and **Mas'sada** because of the several shops which specialise in local handicrafts.

Ancient baths dating from the Roman period are found on the southern Golan at **Hammat Gader**, near the Yarmuk River. These hot baths were built over springs warmed by volcanic activity deep within the earth; when the waters emerge to the surface, they're steamy hot and rich in minerals. The baths were internationally famous during Roman times, and people came from all over the empire to relax here. Israeli archaeologists have done a marvellous job at excavating and restoring them. Visitors are now invited to take a dip, and to inspect the fine Roman theatre, pools, plazas, mosaics and sundry inscriptions.

Epiphanius, a 4th-century monk, complained about them, noting: "a festive gathering took place at Hammat Gader annually. For several days people from all over came to bathe and wash away their afflictions. But there too the Devil set his snares... since men and women bathe together." They still do – but properly attired, of course.

**Mount Hermon:** Towering above the north end of the Golan is **Mount Hermon**, (2,814 metres/9,230 ft) with several ranges radiating from it. It occupies an area roughly 40 by 20 km (25 by 12 miles) and is divided between Lebanon, Syria, Israel and several demilitarised zones under UN jurisdiction. About 20 percent of the Golan lies under Israeli control, including the southeast ridge Ketef HaHermon (The Hermon Shoulder), whose highest point rises to 2,200 metres (7,200 ft).

The higher areas of Mount Hermon are snow-covered through most years, and each winter brings snows to all

Skiing on Mount Hermon.

elevations over 1,200 metres (3,900 ft).

Israeli ski enthusiasts have opened a modest **ski resort** on these slopes, with a chair-lift, equipment rental shop for skis, boots, poles and toboggans. The slopes are often compared to those found in New England – not particularly lofty, but nevertheless a challenge.

Nature on the Hermon is of particular interest to Israelis because it's the only sub-alpine habitat in the country. Several birds, such as the rock nuthatch and the redstart, are at the southernmost extremity of their range here, while others, such as the Hermon horned lark, are found nowhere else.

Many *dolinas* are scattered around the Hermon. These are cavities in the surface of the rock formed by karstic action on the mountain's limestone. In the winter, the dolinas fill with snow, and they are the last areas to melt in the spring. Thus supporting lush green vegetation long after the rest of the slope has dried out under the intense sun.

The spring at **Banias** is among the most popular natural attractions in the country – and has been for many thousands of years. "Banias" is a corruption of the Greek *Panaeas*, and in a cave near the spring a visitor may find the remains of an ancient temple built in honour of Pan, the Greek god of the forests.

Old Crusader ruins may also be visited in this nature reserve, but the real attractions are the waterfalls and inviting pools.

Before 1967, Banias was located in Syrian territory, but a mere 4 km (2½ miles) to the west, in Israeli territory, a number of other springs gurgled from the foot of Mount Hermon. The most important of these is the **Dan River**, which provides the greatest single source of the **Jordan River** – in fact, "Jordan" is but a contraction of the Hebrew *Yored Dan* – descending from Dan – and that's precisely what this biblical river does. For its 265-km (165-mile) length, the Jordan flows from the snowy peak of Mount Hermon to the catch basin of the Dead Sea, 400 metres (1,300 ft) below sea level, and the lowest point on the face of the earth.

**papyrus**
**ramp is a**
**ntrast to**
**e snow-cap**
**Mount**
**ermon.**

# CENTRAL CROSSROADS

It is not the most acclaimed tourist area in the Holy Land, nor is it the most famous for its ruins. Odds are, in fact, the average visitor to Israel will pass through this region, from Tel Aviv to Jerusalem and back, never bothering to venture from the main roads.

He won't be the first – the main historical routes between the ancient empires of Egypt and Mesopotamia passed through this region thousands of years ago, and the centuries following continued the pattern. In more recent years, this area – spanning from the fringes of Samaria above Tel Aviv in the north to the uppermost sands of the Negev to the south, and to the besieged citadel of Jerusalem in the east – became a strategic wedge of supplies and habitation during the war of Independence, connecting the coastal plain and the state's new capital city. Yet the consistent flow of conquerors, immigrants, wayfarers and settlers have left its mark on the landscape, and today the area – still the central crossroads of the nation – is rich in history.

Rising from the flat coastal plain into the gently rolling **Judean Foothills**, this area has always been one of the most densely populated in the country. Controlled by Egypt until the 13th century BC, it was the scene of some of Joshua's toughest battles during the conquest of Canaan. It became a flourishing community of villages during the time of the Israelite kingdom, but was decimated with the fall of Jerusalem at the end of the 6th century BC. Alexander the Great swept through in the 4th century BC and it was from here that the Hasmoneans launched their revolt against the Syrian-Greek empire. Some of the first modern Jewish settlements in the 1880s and 1890s were established here. Today several of these villages have grown into small towns; others, with their lush vegetation and smell of cow dung, convey an air of tranquillity at odds with the hectic pace of so much of modern Israel.

**Antiquity, technology:** Some 60 km (35 miles) south of Tel Aviv, at the edge of the Judean Foothills, is the development town of **Kiryat Gat**. Founded in 1954 as the centre of the Lachish Region, the city marked Israel's first attempt to deal in an organised way with the masses of immigrants who poured into the country in the late 1940s and early 1950s from war-torn Europe and the Middle East.

Earlier settlement had been realised haphazardly; for Lachish, planner Lova Eliav assembled a team of experts who created a whole area of coordinated settlement. The new immigrant villages were integrated with existing *kibbutzim*, grouped around four regional centres providing various facilities and services. In the centre: Kiryat Gat, with cotton mills, sugar refineries and other industries based on the local agriculture.

Southeast, near the moshav (farming village) of Lachish, is the ancient mound of **Tel Lachish**, which was a fortified city throughout the Bronze Age (4000 to 1200 BC). Captured by Joshua, it became a city in the tribe of Judah until destroyed by the king of Assyria in 701 BC. Rebuilt, it was destroyed again by Nebuchadnezzar of Babylon in 598 BC and never regained prominence. The most important find at the site were 21 Hebrew ostrocons (ink inscriptions on pottery fragments) dating to the period between the two destructions of the city.

About 35 km (20 miles) north of Kiryat Gat, just inland of Yavne, is the town of **Rehovot**, home of the **Weizmann Institute of Science**, Israel's well-known research and development centre, named after Chaim Weizmann, Israel's first president. Weizmann was also an organic chemist of international renown, and for many years the leader of the Zionist movement. His scientific research assisted the British war effort during World War I, toward the end of which he was instrumental in securing the Balfour Declaration. Founded in 1934, the Weizmann Institute originally concentrated on local agriculture and medicine, but in 1949, following the establishment of the state, it was transformed into a world-class research in-

receding
ages, young
ine trees dot
ne Judean
oothills.
eft, the rail-
oad winds
through Sorek
alley from
el Aviv to
erusalem.

stitute. Today it has a staff of 1,500 researchers and graduate students, with over 400 research projects in the pipeline, in such fields as cancer cures, hormones, immunology, ageing, cell structure, computer science, geophysics, lasers, atomic particles and astrophysics.

The moving spirit behind the centre in its early years was Meyer Weisgal, an American showbiz impresario who, in addition to raising millions of dollars towards the institute, used to pace the grounds picking up discarded cartons, plastic bags, even matchsticks. The institute is still one of the tidiest places in Israel. Guided tours of the grounds are conducted daily.

Apart from the laboratories, other sites worth seeing include the view from the top of the futuristic atomic particle accelerator, and **Weizmann's house**, designed by Erich Mendelsohn in 1936–37. Weizmann's Tomb is in the gardens of his former home.

North and inland from Rehovot, are the towns of **Ramla** and **Lydda**. They were originally Arab communities, but many of their inhabitants fled in the War of Independence of 1948; today they are two of the few mixed Jewish-Arab communities in Israel. Ramla has three important mosques: the **White Mosque**, dating to the 8th century, the **Mosque of the Forty**, built by the Mamelukes in 1318 and the **Great Mosque**, built on the site of the Crusader Cathedral of St John. The **Vaulted Pool**, an underground water cistern in the centre of town, dates from the 9th century.

North of Lydda (Lod in Hebrew) is **Ben-Gurion Airport**, the country's busy international terminal, named after Israel's first prime minister. Lydda, today in the shadow of soaring jetliners, was an important town during the Biblical and Second Temple periods. Visit the ancient **Sheikh's Tomb** built over the ruins of a 12th-century Crusader church, in the basement of which is the legendary **Tomb of St George**.

**The Judean foothills:** East of Ramla, in the Jerusalem foothills, is the site of **Modiin**, birthplace of the Hasmonean family, leaders of the great 2nd century BC revolt against the Syrian-Greek empire which controlled Judea. The revolt actually started in Modiin, when an official of the empire came to the village to order the people to sacrifice a cockerel on a pagan altar, in accordance with the policy of fostering Hellenisation and repressing Judaism.

Mattitiahu, a local priest, and his five sons killed the imperial official and his military escort, thus triggering the conflict. The revolt, led by Judas Maccabeus, the third son, rapidly expanded all over Judea, resulting in the recapture of the Temple and the restoration of Jewish worship in Jerusalem.

Not much remains of ancient Modiin, but an attractive park has been laid out, with a model of a village of the period of the revolt. If they like, visitors can bake pitta bread in the ancient-style ovens, handle replicas of ancient agricultural implements and spin yarn.

At Channukah, the festival commemorating the revolt, a torch is lit at Modiin and carried in relays to Jerusalem to light candles at the Western Wall.

Some 15 km (8 miles) southwest of

Chaim Weizmann (left) at his home at Rehovot in 1937 with a US diplomat, Henry Morgenthau.

Modiin is **Neve Shalom**, a unique experiment in Jewish-Arab coexistence. The only settlement founded specifically for people of the two groups to live together, it runs special courses, where Jewish and Arab schoolchildren learn about each other's cultures. Nearby is the French Trappist **Monastery of Latrun** (just across the old border with Jordan). Nearby are the remains of a 12th-century Crusader fortress called **Le Toron des Chevaliers** and an almost perfectly preserved Roman villa and bath house.

A little to the north is the **Canada Park**, a recreation centre with vineyards, almond orchards, ancient fig trees and adventure playgrounds. In the park are the ruins of a village thought to be the **Emmaus** of the New Testament, where the risen Jesus was seen, according to St Luke's gospel. Emmaus was also the site of one of the greatest victories of the Hasmoneans.

Less than 30 km (16 miles) further south is the ancient site of **Beit Guvrin**, opposite a modern kibbutz of the same name. There are ruins of many historic periods, notably the Crusader ruins on either side of the road, but it is the caves of Beit Guvrin that are of special note. There are hundreds of caves in the area, visibly bell-shaped, caused by ancient Roman quarrying operations. Some of them are even earlier, dating to Greek and even Phoenician times.

**The Jerusalem corridor:** Roughly 20 km (13 miles) west of Jerusalem, on a secondary road between the town of Beit Shemesh and Moshav Ness Harim, is a different type of cavern: the spectacular **Sorek Cave**, which extends across over 15 acres of the **Avshalom Nature Reserve**. Discovered by chance during a routine quarrying operation, it is by far the largest cave in Israel and contains stalactites and stalagmites of breathtaking beauty.

Just to the south is the **Valley of Elah**, where David killed Goliath, the Philistine from Gath. According to the Book, David rejected the armour given to him by King Saul, "and chose him five smooth stones out of the brook," one of

which he slung at the giant warrior, killing him. The battle is described in I Samuel; 17. The actual site of the encounter is not marked; today a kibbutz and a television satellite receiving station instead stand in the valley.

The main road to Jerusalem enters the gorge of **Shaar Hagai** west of Latrun, then climbs steeply through the wooded hills. They weren't always so green; when the first Jewish pioneers arrived to make their settlements they saw a hilly desert, stripped of its natural afforestation by centuries of abuse. Since then, over 200 million trees have been planted all over the country, and the Jewish National Fund continues to plant at the rate of 4 million trees a year.

Initially, the motivation was arresting the soil erosion, but improving the landscape, changing the microclimate, and creating recreation areas are more important reasons today. Picnickers in one of the groves can enjoy a temperature as much as 3 degrees cooler than in the surrounding area during the summer.

The early forests were made up almost entirely of indigenous Jerusalem pine – and this tree still dominates – but modern planters are diversifying for both ecological and aesthetic reasons. Among the newcomers are cypress, acacia, eucalyptus, pistachio, carob, and many varieties of the local scrub oak.

Visitors may be surprised to see dozens of ruined vehicles by the roadside, painted brown to prevent them from rusting. They are the remains of burnt-out armoured vans and buses which carried supplies to besieged Jerusalem in the 1948 war, and which sit permanently at the spots where they were destroyed as monuments to those who tried to run the siege. Jutting out from a hilltop farther ahead is the more formal **Monument to the Road Builders**, its aluminium spars pointing compellingly to the capital beyond.

The nearby settlements of **Shoresh**, **Neve Ilan**, **Kiryat Anavim** and **Maale Hahamisha** offer guest houses with stunning views of the Judean hills; all of them have attractive swimming pools and comfortable accommodations.

Stalactites form veils a Sorek Cave.

Also in this area are three Arab villages, each of them with features of interest. The largest, **Abu Gosh**, is named after the Arab family which still comprises the majority of its inhabitants. It has two fine churches and a French Benedictine monastery. A sacred spring, where Jesus is said to have drank, is situated in a garden of towering pines and old palm trees.

Nearby **Ein Nekuba** is the only Arab village built by the State of Israel from scratch; it was constructed for villagers whose homes were taken over by new immigrants, after they fled from their village of Beit Nekuba in the 1948 war.

Although most of its fruit trees and vegetable plots are watered by modern methods, neighbouring **Ein Rafa** has an irrigation system that dates back to biblical times. Some 10 acres of village land are watered by a natural spring, which is allowed to flow into the individual plots according to a traditional eight-day rota system, stringently observed by the villagers.

Between the two villages and the main road is **Ein Hemed** (or **Aqua Bella**), a landscaped camping site and nature reserve, with a stream flowing through it and a restored Crusader farm. Up the hill is the settlement of Mevasseret Zion, formerly **Kastel**, an important Arab town and the site for one of the key battles for Jerusalem in 1948. Part of the village has been preserved as a memorial to soldiers who died here, and some of the bunkers and pillboxes have likewise been restored. From Kastel, one gets a magnificent view of the surrounding Judean hills, and gleaming expanse of Jerusalem, to the southwest.

One last stop on the road to the capitol is the village of Motza, and the stump of **Herzl's Cypress**. Planted by the founder of modern Zionism on his visit to the Holy Land in 1898, the tree became a place of pilgrimage, and was later cut down as an anti-Zionist gesture. A glass case has been built around the stump, and it has become traditional for presidents of Israel to plant a tree in the surrounding garden as a symbol of the continuing growth of Zionism.

atellite
h marks
 spot
ere David
ght Goliath
the Valley
Elah.

# JERUSALEM: THE GOLDEN CITY

The Golden City. The Eternal City. The City of David. The City of Peace. Jerusalem. At one time considered the centre of the world, it has been ravaged by century after century of war, and is sacred to the three great monotheistic religions. To Jews, it is the incarnation of ancient Israel, where Abraham went to sacrifice Isaac, the site of David's glory and Solomon's Temple, the eternal capital of the Jewish people.

To Christians, it is the city where Jesus spent his last days on earth, the site of the Last Supper, the Crucifixion and Resurrecton. To Muslims, it is Al Quds, "The Holy", the place where Mohammed is said to have ascended to Heaven on his steed; indeed, it is Islam's third holiest city after Mecca and Medina. From its enduring power as a symbol to the quality of its daylight, Jerusalem is unique; and today, some 3,000 years after David made the city his capital, Jerusalem still has the ability to stir emotion and fire imagination like no other city on earth.

**Visiting Jerusalem:** Still the centrepiece of many a journey to Israel, as it has been over the centuries, Jerusalem continues richly to reward the traveller. The market places, shrines, ruins, hotels, temples, churches and mosques are all readily accessible and the city's tourist board is more than willing to provide directions. Yet the soul of the city is more elusive. The rhythm of daily life here is governed by prayer, usually channelled through tightly knit religious communities, and the visitor who merely barters for *chachkas* in the Old City between hops to famous churches or museums is missing the source and substance of the city's daily being.

Similarly, as the seat of government for the state and an important academic centre, Jerusalem also has an important secular profile, which shouldn't be overlooked.

Physically, Jerusalem is actually three cities in one, totalling over 500,000 residents. The modern part of the city spreading out to the west, northwest and south is West Jerusalem, a Jewish enclave since its inception in the late 1800s, and since 1950 the capital of the State of Israel. East Jerusalem describes the new part of the city east of the old "green line" that divided it from 1948 to 1967, during which time it was Jordanian; the section is still largely Arab in population and culture. In the centre of it all is the Old City, wrapped in its ancient golden walls, containing so much of historic Jerusalem and its shrines. It, too, was in Jordanian hands up to the Six Day War of 1967.

The Israeli victory that week effectively rolled away the barbed wire and roadblocks. Jerusalem is once more a united city with open flow of traffic. Israel officially annexed the Old City and East Jerusalem in 1967. The Arab states still look upon these as occupied territory and press for their return. But it seems highly unlikely that Israel will ever voluntarily part with the Old City with its thriving Jewish Quarter and the Western Wall.

**David's capital:** In ancient times it was said that the world has 10 measures of beauty, of which nine belong to Jerusalem. If the city's acclaim (or immodesty) made it that much more attractive to conquerors, so be it: since its greatest hour of glory as the capital of the Israelite kingdom the city has been the object of repeated siege and conquest. In part this was due to its strategic situation on a vital trade route, at the crossroads between East and West. Ironically, however, it later became the very holiness of the city that inspired its would-be champions' relentless ferocity.

Jerusalem first crops up in biblical narrative during Abraham's migrations from Ur to Canaan. Here, he was greeted warmly by Melchizedek, King of Salem, "priest of the most high God". The Israelites were already well-ensconced in the hills of Judea when David captured the city from the Jebusites in 1000 BC. Building an altar for the Ark of the Covenant on the crown of Mt Moriah, he made the city his capital, rechristening it Jerusalem – "Dwelling of Peace".

eceding
ıges,
owds gather
Western
all to
lebrate
rusalem
ay. **Left,**
ılden sunset
ɔm the
ount of
ives.

The 35 years under David's rule, and the ensuing 40 under Solomon brought splendour to the once modest fortress town. The site of David's altar saw the rise of Solomon's magnificent Temple, incorporating the much sought-after cedarwood from Lebanon, copper from the mines at Timna, and a wide variety of rich metals and carved figures. The city was embellished with the wealth of an expansive empire, its walls reaching in an oblong shape to include David's city on the slopes of the Ophel to the Pool of Siloam below.

Around 926 BC King Solomon died, and in the absence of his authority the kingdom was split in two by his successors. Jerusalem remained the capital of the southern Kingdom of Judah, as the following centuries saw the city and its kingdom succumb to the expanding control of the Assyrians. In 586 BC Nebuchadnezzar of Babylonia plundered the city, sending its inhabitants into exile. They returned in 539 BC under the policy of the new king, Cyrus the Great of Persia, and set once more to

the task of building a "Second Temple".

Alexander the Great's conquest of Jerusalem in 332 BC initiated a brief Hellenisation of Jewish culture in the city; in 198 BC the Seleucids took control. Deprived of religious rights, the Maccabees spearheaded a Jewish uprising, leading to the reconsecration of the destroyed Temple in 165 BC.

The Hasmonean rule gave way in 63 BC to Roman, with the conquering armies of the Roman general Pompey. In 40 BC the Roman Senate conferred rule on Herod the Great (Jewish on his father's side) and sent him to Judea; during his reign up to 4 BC his horrific, psychopathic acts towards his family and others were matched only by his extensive architectural endeavours. Jerusalem was still a Jewish city under Roman rule when Jesus was ordered crucified by the procurator Pontius Pilate around 30 AD.

The increasingly insensitive Roman administration was challenged by the Jewish Revolt of 66 AD, which was crushed four years later by Titus, who in the process razed Jerusalem and plundered the Temple. A second rebellion was instigated by the Emperor Hadrian's decree to lay the city out anew on a Roman plan and call it Aelia Capitolina; but the Bar Kochba revolt of 132 AD was stamped out and in 135 AD Hadrian initiated the reconstruction of the city making it illegal for any Jew to enter its boundaries.

The great Christianisation of Jerusalem was inaugurated in the 4th century by the Byzantine Emperor Constantine; in the 7th century it fell to Muslim rule, and in 1099 to the bloody grip of the Crusaders for some 80 years. The city once more came into its own under the Ottoman Emperor Suleiman, who rebuilt its walls from 1537 to 1541. From his death until modern times it fell into ignominious decline.

To this day, Suleiman's walls remain the most impressive monument to the city's multi-layered history. From stone stairways at various points in its span you can mount the restored **Ramparts Walk**, which follows every circuit but that by the Temple Mount. A "greenbelt"

**An Orthodox Jew protests against the building of a new road through a Jewish area of Jerusalem**

of lawns now surrounds much of the circumference, adding to the aesthetics of the view.

The seven gates of the city are often a source of fascination in themselves. Clockwise from the Western Wall, they are: the **Dung Gate**, the **Zion Gate**, pockmarked by gunfire from 1948; the **Jaffa Gate**; the **New Gate**; the **Damascus Gate**, the grandest of all the entrances, opening to East Jerusalem; **Herod's Gate**; and **St Stephen's (or Lion's) Gate**, at the Via Dolorosa. The **Golden Gate**, facing the Mount of Olives from Mt Moriah, has been sealed since 1530, and is said to be the one through which the Messiah will one day enter Jerusalem.

Just inside the Jaffa Gate, which serves as the main entrance to the Old City from West Jerusalem, is the famous **Citadel**, or **Tower of David**. In reality, the structure has little to do with David; it was built by Herod who named its three towers after his wife Mariamne, his brother Phaesal and his friend Hippicus and was so impressive that

Titus let it stand after burning the city. The Mamelukes and later Suleiman reinforced it, adding its familiar minaret.

For practical purposes we have divided the rest of the city into two chapters. The Old City describes not only the sites within the city walls but also those religious shrines of age-old devotion just outside its bounds. Both East and West Jerusalem are discussed in the chapter on the New City.

You shouldn't hesitate to follow your own instincts in exploring this city or to examine the possibilites of taking special daytrips or detours to the less obvious sites. For us to attempt to describe all of Jerusalem in 40 pages is like asking a rabbi to describe the entire Talmud while standing on one foot. Probably this is just as well, for no amount of historical recitation can ever hope to capture the spirit of this revered and complex place: the tired patina of gold on the Mount of Olives at sunset, the shifting moods of its houses and hills, the combination of thoughtfulness and pride in the eyes of its citizens.

# THE OLD CITY: CRADLE TO RELIGION

It's a museum, a bazaar, a collection of sacred shrines. It also happens to be home for 27,000 residents crammed within the 4-km (2½-mile) circumference of its old battlements. And its gates never close, night or day, for the 1 million visitors who are drawn to the Old City of Jerusalem each year.

The Jewish, Christian, Armenian and Muslim Quarters of the Old City each have their own special significance. We'll look at each, as well as those shrines and monuments immediately outside the walls of the city.

**The Jewish Quarter:** Inhabited by Jews as far back as the First Temple Period 3,000 years ago, the Jewish Quarter today is a modern neighbourhood housing nearly 700 families, with numerous synagogues and *yeshivas* (academies for Jewish studies).

This thriving little community was literally rebuilt out of the rubble following the reunification of Jerusalem in the 1967 Six Day War. Families who had lived in the Quarter prior to their expulsion by the Jordanians in 1948 were the first allowed to move back in. Religious Jews revived many of the old study houses and congregations. Artists, attracted by the picturesque lanes, soon took up residence. Today the Jewish Quarter is one of the city's most desirable (and expensive) areas.

Nowhere is the old-new character of the quarter more evident than in the **Cardo**. With its modern lamps and smart shopfronts, this submerged pedestrian byway at first looks like a trendy shopping mall incongruously set next to the old bazaar.

The Cardo was the north-south axis of the garrison town that the Romans built after they destroyed Jerusalem in 70 AD. Called Aelia Capitolina, the town was laid out geometrically like an army camp, with the Cardo (from Latin: cardinal, or principal) as its main thoroughfare. In the Byzantine period this colonnaded avenue ran for 180 metres

(600 ft) to a looming church called the Nea, built by the Emperor Justinian in 543 AD and destroyed in an earthquake in the 8th century. Later the Crusaders used the Cardo as a main market street. After they were expelled by the Muslims, Jerusalem reverted to a backwater and the Cardo was eventually buried beneath four metres (13 ft) of rubble, to be excavated and brought to life again only in the 1980s.

Signs and diagrams along either side of the "new" Cardo show the remains of the various civilisations that conducted their daily commerce here. A large excavation reveals the outer wall of the city of the Judean King Hezekiah. At another point Byzantine Corinthian-style columns have been restored, along with roofing beams, to illustrate how shops lined the thoroughfare.

The southern end of the Cardo is open to the sky. Here the big paving stones lie bright in the sunlight, the columns exposed in all their classic beauty. It's also from this point outdoors that visitors can best appreciate the reconciliation of

**Preceding pages, Orthodox children take seats at the Wall.**

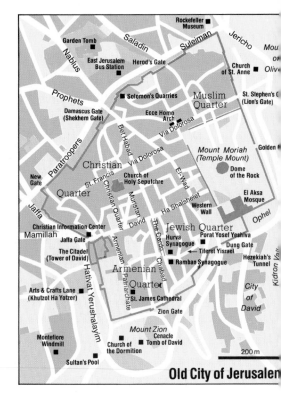

**Old City of Jerusalem**

demands for museum and neighbourhood. City planners had wanted apartments along the route, while archaeologists insisted that the historical heart of the city be exposed. The compromise: apartments standing on stilts above the ancient avenue.

Running parallel to the Cardo is Jewish Quarter Road, site of the **Jewish Quarter Museum**, which offers a 15-minute multi-media presentation on the history of the area from the Israelite Period to the present. The emphasis is on how the Jewish Quarter was lost to the Arab Legion in Israel's war of Independence in 1948, how it was subsequently regained in the Six Day War of 1967, and how it has since been reconstructed. The museum also has an unusual collection of pictures taken by *Life* magazine photographer John Phillips during the battle in 1948, and again in 1975 when Phillips returned to find and photograph the survivors.

A few steps away from the museum is a **memorial** to the fighters who fell defending the quarter. An electronic map recreates the battle, house by house.

Between the museum and the memorial is the **Ashkenazi Court**, a synagogue and residential complex established in 1400 by European Jews. The great **Hurvah Synagogue** was burned by angry creditors in 1720 (hence its name, which means ruin). In 1856 it was rebuilt, but in May of 1948 it was blown up by the Arab legion; today only the dynamic span of its front archway rises over the site.

Beneath the Hurvah is the **Ramban Synagogue**, built shortly after the noted Bible commentator Rabbi Moses Ben Nahman emigrated from Spain in 1267, and possibly the oldest of the many houses of worship in the Jewish Quarter. Now it's used every day.

The most enchanting of the Quarter's venerable houses of worship are on Hakehuna Street in the complex known as the **Four Sephardi Synagogues**. Destroyed during the 1948 battle and used as stables during the 19-year Jordanian rule of the Old City, these synagogues have been lovingly restored to

*e-afternoon light hes the vish arter.*

serve as both houses of worship and as a museum documenting their destruction and rebirth. Of particular interest are the Italian hand-carved Arks of the Law in the **Stambouli** and **Prophet Elijah Synagogues**, and the early 17th-century **Yochanan Ben-Zakkai Synagogue** with its cheery folk-character.

A short walk up Or Ha-Haim Street, the **Yishuv Court Museum** illustrates the lifestyles of the Jewish community of the Old City in bygone days.

At the end of Tiferet Israel Street is perhaps the most remarkable archaeological site in the Jewish Quarter: the **Burnt House**. This, apparently, was the residence of the priestly Bar-Kathros clan at the time of the Jewish revolt against Rome. Among other clues, ashes from a great conflagration indicate that the house was destroyed when Titus razed the city. The numerous finds within the house include a measuring weight bearing the name Kathros, and the skeletal arm of a woman in the kitchen who apparently was struggling to escape the fire.

**The Western Wall:** The wide stone steps at the end of Tiferet Israel lead down to the most important site – not only within the quarter, but in all of Jewish civilisation. This of course is the **Kotel Ha-Ma'aravi**, or the **Western Wall**.

Clambering up and down these steps at all hours of the day and night like so many angels ascending and descending Jacob's ladder is a stream of worshippers, pilgrims and tourists. The hum from the right comes from the students of the rebuilt **Porat Yosef Yeshiva**, the largest in the quarter and the work of noted Israeli architect Moshe Safdie.

Midway down the steps is an observation platform, a good place to take in the famous postcard panorama. Below and to the left is the Western Wall **plaza** and the Wall itself. Above the Wall: the **Temple Mount**, the biblical Mt Moriah where Abraham nearly sacrificed Isaac, where the First and Second Temples once loomed, and where the golden Dome of the Rock and the silvery Al-Aksa Mosque now stand. To the right of the Temple Mount is a vast maze of **archaeological excavations** which lead

to the Old City wall and to **Dung Gate**.

The Jewish Quarter area was known in Temple times as the Upper City. The plaza below occupies the lower end of what was called the Tyropoeon Valley, the rift that cuts through the entire length of the Old City. Because this was the lowest point in the Old City, rubble and trash were dumped here over the centuries, filling in much of the space between the upper level and the Temple Mount (and giving Dung Gate its inglorious name).

Rising to a height of 15 metres (50 ft), the Western Wall consists chiefly of massive carved stone blocks from the Herodian era, topped by masonry from the Mameluke and Turkish periods. Contrary to popular belief, it was not a part of the Temple itself, but merely the retaining wall for the western side of the Temple Mount. Nevertheless, because it was the only remnant of the Temple complex to survive the Romans' sack of the city, it has inspired the reverence of Jews for 1,900 years. Because Jews also gathered here to bemoan the loss of the

**t, showing e for the ll; the es in the hes convey yers. ht, ebrating a Mitzvah he Wall.**

Temple, the place earned the sobriquet "Wailing Wall".

The tunnel-like enclosure at the nothern end of the Wall is the site of continuing excavations. The main arch, named for the 19th-century British explorer Captain Charles Wilson, may have supported a huge pedestrian bridge between the Temple Mount and the Upper City. Below this arch is the deep shaft dug by Wilson's contemporary, Sir Charles Warren. Archaeologists have since determined that the Wall extends another 15 metres below ground level. Plans call for lowering the present plaza to reveal the Wall in all its grandeur, a delicate and complex task that would take as much as 20 years of work.

The **southern excavations** at the opposite end of the Wall contain a broad stairway where prophets harangued the crowds on their way to the Temple, the abutment called **Robinson's arch** (after its 19th-century American discoverer Dr Edward Robinson), and the remains of palatial buildings and purification baths from Temple times. From the walkway above the excavations the site is a jigsaw puzzle of incomprehensible stone. A licensed guide with Bible in hand makes the area come alive.

**Above the Kidron Valley:** More major sites of Jewish interest remain just outside the Old City walls. These include the City of David, the Kidron Valley and Mount Zion.

The **City of David** excavations are on the steep hillside outside of Dung Gate. This hill is called the **Ophel**, and the archaeological dig here, which is still going on, has been the scene of violent protests by religious zealots claiming that ancient Jewish graves have been violated. The diggers dispute this, and say that in any case the site is too important to leave buried. That's because the Ophel is where the earliest incarnation of Jerusalem stood: the Jebusite city of more than 3,000 years ago.

Around 1,000 BC, King David captured the city and made it his capital. Although his son Solomon was to build the Temple above it on the high ground, the main residential portion of the city

**City of David excavations at the Ophel.**

itself remained clinging to this slope above the Kidron Valley. It did so because at the foot of the slope is the **Gihon spring**, at the time the sole water supply for Jerusalem.

Since the spring was located in a cave on the floor of the Kidron, Jerusalemites were in danger of being cut off from their water when the city was attacked. But the stunning engineering project known as **Hezekiah's tunnel,** carried out by King Hezekiah about 300 years after King David, managed to connect the Gihon spring to the **Siloam pool** inside the city some 533 metres (more than a quarter-mile) farther down the valley. The intrepid 19th-century archaeologist Charles Warren not only explored the tunnel, but also discovered a shaft reaching up through the Ophel to an underground passage from where city residents could draw water in buckets.

In 1867 Warren had to crawl on his belly through the stream bed to explore the water system. Today visitors can study the schematics in comfort in the City of David **archaeological park**, and then stroll through the illuminated passageway to the top of **Warren's shaft** to peek at the water rushing below. In the Kidron Valley itself visitors with candles can tramp along the knee-deep stream in Hezekiah's tunnel from the Gihon Spring and through the Ophel hill until it emerges at the Siloam pool.

The upper end of the **Kidron Valley**, the portion also known as the **Vale of Jehosaphat,** contains several Jerusalem landmarks. The slope off to the northeast is the **Mount of Olives**, containing a Jewish cemetery dating back thousands of years.

In the valley itself are the **Pillar of Absalom** and the **Tomb of Zachariah**. Despite their traditional names, these stately tombs are not thought to be the resting places of David's rebellious son or of the angry prophet. Rather, archaeologists believe these tombs were part of the vast 1st-century necropolis that encircles Jerusalem, and probably served wealthy citizens or notables of the Herodian court. Take special note of the graceful pillars and elaborately carved friezes. The handsome **Tomb of Hezir** nearby bears an inscription identifying it as the burial cave of a noted priestly family. Isolated, silent and still, the tombs at this end of the hot and dusty Kidron Valley evoke something of the mood of Egypt's Valley of the Kings.

Occupying the promontory outside the Old City's **Zion Gate**, solemn and aloof, is **Mount Zion**. For ages symbolic of Jewish aspirations for a homeland, it bestowed its name to the national liberation movement. Suleiman supposedly executed the architects of his great wall for neglecting to include Mount Zion within the Old City's circumference. After 1948, the Old City fell to Jordanian hands but Israel retained Mount Zion and from 1948 to 1967 the historic ridge was a vital lookout point for the young country, as well as its closest approach to the shrines of the Old City and Western Wall. Today's Mount Zion is less controversial, if no less beloved. Churches and *yeshivas* huddle side by side amid the landmark's gardens and wind-bent pipes.

Within the Diaspora Yeshiva com-

e Tomb of chariah.

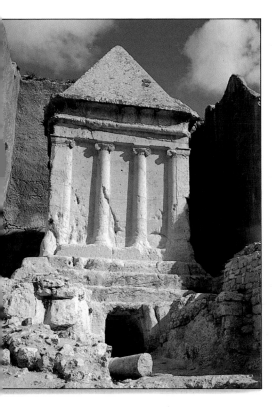

plex is the site of **King David's Tomb**. Archaeologists maintain that this is another example of a site not corresponding to historical truth, but that hasn't prevented the tomb from being venerated. The adjacent **Chamber of the Holocaust** is a memorial to the destroyed Jewish communities of Europe.

From here, the new stone pedestrian walk between Zion Gate and the church complex leads to a fine vista of the new Jerusalem.

**The road to Calvary:** Rome likes to think of itself as the centre of the Christian world, and St Peter's Basilica is certainly grander than anything Jerusalem has to offer. Yet within the worn walls of Jerusalem are sites that stir the most casual Christian: the **Via Dolorosa** and Calvary. Indeed, these names reside in the consciousness and reverberate in the vocabulary of all western civilisation.

Archaeologists, as they are wont to do, maintain that neither the way of Sorrows nor any of the other major sites that we identify today with the Crucifixion correspond to historical reality. But if the Via Dolorosa that we traverse was not walked upon 2,000 years ago, some ancient road at least is indeed buried underneath the present ground level.

In the same vein, pilgrims should not be unduly distressed that today's Via Dolorosa is a commercial street, complete with a Jesus Prison Souvenirs shop and a Ninth Station Boutique. They should bear in mind that the lane was a bustling city steet at the time of Jesus.

The Via Dolorosa begins at **St Stephen's Gate** (also called the Lions' Gate) which, despite the surrounding churches, is actually in the **Muslim Quarter**. The municipality's East Jerusalem Development Corporation recently opened a **Pilgrim's Reception Plaza** here, about 30 metres (100 ft) inside the St Stephen's Gate. This plaza was the finishing touch to an elaborate and delicate project of repairing the Via Dolorosa that included restoration of collapsing buildings and overhead arches, replacement of the 400-year-old sewage system, and proper demarcation of the Stations of the Cross. When the plaza was cleared of rubble, huge paving stones of the Roman period were exposed. These stones, which have been revealed at a few points elsewhere along the route, may very well have been walked on by Jesus and his followers.

Guided tours generally begin at the reception plaza, and are recommended, especially as some of the Stations of the Cross are difficult to locate in the hustle and maze of the Old City.

Directly opposite the plaza is the **Church of St Anne**, considered to be the best-preserved Crusader church in the entire Holy Land. In addition to a crypt designated as **Mary's Birthplace**, the church compound contains the **Bethesda Pool** where Jesus performed a miraculous cure.

The **First Station of the Cross**, where Jesus was sentenced, is tucked away inside the courtyard of the Umariyah school, a Muslim boys' institution. The **second Station**, where Jesus received the Cross, is opposite on the street outside the **Chapel of Condemnation** and the **Church of the Flagellation**. It was here that Jesus was scourged and had

A 1898 Bonfils photograph St Stephen's Gate.

the crown of thorns placed on his head. The latter church also has a graceful courtyard and quiet garden.

The events associated with the first two Stations are believed to have taken place in Herod's **Antonia Fortress**, remains of which are found today beneath the churches along both sides of the Via Dolorosa. In the nearby **Church of the Sisters of Zion**, for example, is a huge underground chamber called the Lithostrotos, often said to be the place where Pilate judged Jesus; on the paving stones are signs of "broad games" played by Roman soldiers.

Outside is the **Ecce Homo Arch**, which some maintain was constructed by the Emperor Hadrian in the 2nd century and which takes its name from Pilate's jeer "Behold the man!" At the end of 1985, the Sisters of Zion dedicated a Roman arch inside the church which they contend is the Ecce Homo.

Almost all of the ensuing Stations on the Via Dolorosa are marked by plaques bearing the appropriate quotations from the Bible, and many are accompanied by a fan-like design in cobblestone on the street.

The **Third Station**, where Jesus fell with the Cross, is commemorated by a column in a wall on El-Wad Street, which the Via Dolorosa traverses. Just beyond is the **Fourth Station**, where Jesus encountered Mary. On this site is the Armenian **Catholic Church of Our Lady of the Spasm**, which has a notable Byzantine mosaic within its crypt.

The Via Dolorosa at this point becomes a fairly steep and crowded commercial lane ascending to the right off of El-Wad. The **Fifth Station**, just at the juncture of El-Wad and the Via Dolorosa, is where Simon the Cyrenian helped Jesus carry the Cross. A bit farther on is the **Sixth Station**, at the **House of St Veronica**, where Veronica cleansed the face of Jesus with her veil.

Where the Via Dolorosa bisects the Souk Kahn ez-Zeit bazaar is the **Seventh Station**, where Jesus fell again. This is also believed to be the site of the Gate of Judgment from which Jesus was led out of the city to the place of crucifixion,

and the location where his death sentence was pubicly posted.

The Via Dolorosa at this point unaccountably disappears; buildings in fact cover the rest of the route to the **Church of the Holy Sepulchre**. But the church and the last Stations of the Cross are very close by.

The **Eighth Station** is outside the Greek Orthodox **Chapel of St Charalampos**, which is constructed on the site where Jesus addressed the women with the words, "Weep not for me, but weep for Jerusalem." At the Ethiopian Coptic Church compound off the Khan ez-Zeit bazaar, a pillar marks the **Ninth Station**, where Jesus stumbled the third time. The final Stations of the Cross are all encompassed within the vast Church of the Holy Sepulchre.

**The Holy Sepulchre:** Experienced travellers are probably aware that the more venerated the shrine in the mind of the pilgrim, the more disconcerting the reality upon pilgrimage's end.

In this case the church is rather bewildering in its size and complexity.

Here, at the highest point in the Old City, the Romans had a temple dedicated to Venus. Constantine erected a church here in the 4th century, after his mother, Helena, identified the tomb of Jesus. Constantine's church was later destroyed, and the present church was built by the Crusaders in the 12th century. Much more has been added since the Crusaders left.

Several Christian communities currently share the church, each maintaining its own chapels and altars and conducting services according to its own schedule. Each is responsible for the sanctity and maintenance of a scrupulously specified area. Church fathers have battled in the past over such issues as who cleans which steps.

With its gloomy light, its bustle of construction work, its competing chants and multiple aromas of incense, the church of the Holy Sepulchre on initial encounter can be intimidating. Freelance "guides" cluster about the doorway, offering to show visitors around for an unspecified fee. While some are

**Left, exterior of Church of the Holy Sepulchre. Below, 1683 floorplan of the Church.**

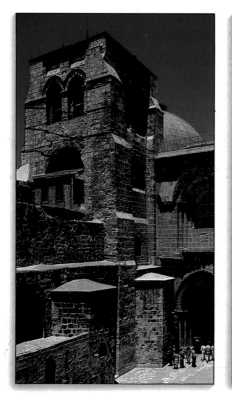

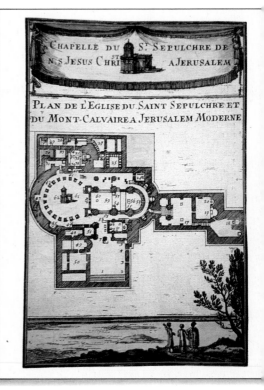

competent and sincere, many have a routine in Engish limited to the order of: "Here chapel, very holy. There picture, famous, famous."

Despite all this, the church maintains its unique magnificence. The focal points, of course, are the section built over the hillock where the Crucifixion took place (called **Golgotha**, from the Hebrew, or **Calvary**, from the Latin), and the tomb where Jesus was laid. These sites encompass the continuation of the Via Dolorosa and the final Stations of the Cross.

Stairs to the right just inside the door to the church lead up to Golgotha. The **Tenth Station** where Jesus was stripped of his garments, is marked by a floor mosaic. The next three stations are located at Latin and Greek altars on this same level and within a few paces of each other. They mark the nailing of Jesus to the Cross, the setting of the Cross in place, and the removal of his body. The **Fourteenth Station** is below, the **Holy Sepulchre** itself.

The tomb is located downstairs under the church's main rotunda. Within the Holy Sepulchre are the **Angel's Chapel**, the rock that was miraculously rolled away from the tomb entrance, the chapel containing the burial site, and the adjacent **tomb of Joseph of Arimathea**.

Other notable sites within the church complex include the **Catholicon**, the Greek cathedral close to the main rotunda, with its stone chalice on the floor marking the centre of the world; chapels dedicated to St Helena, to Adam, and to the Raising of the Cross, and **tombs of the Crusader Kings** of Jerusalem.

It is these side chapels and cavern-like tombs that offer the contemplative visitors respite from the troops of tour groups that forever pour through the church. In a chapel beneath the main floor of the church one can sit in relative silence, listening to an Eastern Orthodox mass being chanted in a distant nave, or perhaps watching a solitary monk polish a candlestick.

Outside the church of the Holy Sepulchre are churches of almost every denomination. Immediately to the left of

iest lights
ndles over
e Holy
epulchre.

the Holy Sepulchre plaza is the Lutheran **Church of the Redeemer**, a tall, graceful edifice whose tower – open to the public – offers a magnificent view of the Old City. Most unusual is the **Ethiopian Coptic Compound** mentioned above, at the Ninth Station of the Cross. The monastery is a replica of an African mud-hut village, and the nearby Coptic chapel is actually located on the roof of the Holy Sepulchre.

The main entrance to the **Christian Quarter** is **New Gate** – so named because it was punched through the Old City walls in 1887. It remains the newest of the city's entrances. Winding into the city from the gate are Greek Orthodox Patriarchate Road, Greek Catholic Patriarchate Road and Latin Patriarchate Road. All of these. logically enough, lead their respective compounds, with churches often containing interesting libraries and museums.

Armenian Orthodox Patriarchate Road is the street leading around the Citadel up from the David Street bazaar. Along this road, just between the **Chris-**tian Information Center** and the post office, stand **Christ Church** and the **Anglican Hospice**, home base in the 19th century to many of the British diplomats and clergymen who encouraged the exploration and modernisation of slumbering Ottoman Jerusalem.

The road next passes through a brief tunnel and then into the **Armenian Quarter**. A modest doorway leads to the Armenians' **St James Cathedral**, one of the most impressive churches in the Old City after Church of the Holy Sepulchre. A little further on is the **Armenian Museum**, a graceful cloister housing a fascinating collection of manuscripts and artifacts.

Jerusalem's 2,000 or so Armenians live in a tightly knit community behind the Cathedral-museum complex. As one of the city's smallest ethnic groups, the Armenians have a reputation for keeping to themselves. But in fact they are generally quite outgoing, proud of being descendents of the first nation to adopt Christianity, usually fluent in English and most hospitable to visitors.

**Left**, the ornate interior of St James' Cathedral. **Below**, Armenian choir boy at Easter.

This openness applies to the Armenian clergy (identifiable by their tall, pointed headgear), who train at the modern seminary on the opposite side of the road from the museum. Just around the bend, Armenian Orthodox Patriarchate Road leads past Zion Gate, with Mount Zion outside.

Primary among the Christian sites here is the **Cenacle**, believed to be the Room of the Last Supper (although the Syrian Orthodox Church's **St Mark's House** on Ararat Street in the Armenian Quarter makes the same claim). Today, the Cenacle is basically an elegant but bare room, empty but for the flow of daylight, and it requires considerable imagination to fill it as Leonardo did in his classic fresco.

It's located on the second floor of the large, rambling complex that contains David's Tomb.

Adjacent to this building is **Dormition Abbey**, a handsome Benedictine edifice commemorating the place where Mary fell into eternal sleep. The abbey has a noteworthy mosaic floor and crypt, and

its basilica is frequently the site for concerts of liturgical and classical music. The Armenians, meanwhile, are constructing a church nearby that promises to be equally splendid.

Also on Mt Zion is the **Old Protestant Cemetery**, where lie many of the British subjects who figured in the religious, cultural, archaeological and diplomatic life of 19th and early 20th-century Jerusalem. These Britons were instrumental in the initial expansion of Jerusalem outside the walls of the Old City, especially by establishing Anglican Church institutions and, not incidentally, by promoting a site to rival the Holy Sepulchre.

The **Garden Tomb** is on Nablus Road, leading from Damascus Gate into East Jerusalem. Within a landscape reminiscent of a sumptuous English garden is a dual-chambered cave that Anglicans and other Protestants revere as the authentic tomb of Jesus. The Garden Tomb is situated on a hill that, viewed from the East Jerusalem bus station, suggests to many the shape of a skull,

aceful but
pty arches
an the
nacle.

which is the meaning of Golgotha.

**Mount of Olives:** Wherever the historical Golgotha is located, it's agreed that Jesus made his triumphal entry into Jerusalem from the Mount of Olives. This hill, with its breathtaking view of the Old City, is mainly a Jewish cemetery dating back to the biblical period and still in use today. Round about the cemetery, the Mount of Olives has numerous sites of significance to Christians, for in a conjunction of faith, many Jews and Christians believe that the Messiah will lead the resurrected from here into Jerusalem via the Old City's Golden Gate, which faces the mount.

Tradition has it that it was through this big double gate that Jesus marched into Jerusalem, just as an earlier Jewish tradition says that this is how the Messiah will enter the city in the End of Days. The gate, however, is tightly sealed. It is said that either Saladin or Suleiman decided to have it bricked up to prevent any Messiah from arriving in Jerusalem and wresting the city from Muslim hands.

The mutual reverence for this most sacred of mountains is generally reflected in a spirit of mutual tolerance and understanding. In recent years, however, some ultra-Orthodox Jews have protested against any expansion of Christian presence in the area. Their attention lately has focused on a branch of the Mormons' Brigham Young University, which is being built between the Mount of Olives and the neighbouring Mount Scopus, and zealots periodically post notices around Jerusalem warning of "foreigners encroaching on our time-honoured cemetery."

And as to why the Mount of Olives is so bare and rocky: tradition has it that the Romans cut down all the olive trees to build the siege machines used in the destruction of Jerusalem in 70 AD – but that with the resurrection the trees will flourish again.

On the far side of the mount, with a view of the Judean Desert and the red hills of Edom across the Jordan, is the **Bethpage Chapel**, from where the Palm Sunday processions to Jerusalem begin. At the crest of the hill is the Russian Orthodox **Church of the Ascension** with its landmark bell tower. Nearby, the small octagonal **Dome of the Ascension** marks the traditional site of Jesus's ascent to heaven. Converted to a mosque with the Muslim conquest of the city in 1187, the structure is said to have been the architectural model for the Dome of the Rock. From this area, several paths lead down to the city. Walks, especially at dawn or sunset, are some of the loveliest experiences Jerusalem offers.

Among the most notable churches on the way down are the **Pater Noster Carmelite Convent**, with the Lord's Prayer in numerous languages on its interior walls, and the **Church of the Eleona**, on the site where Jesus revealed the mysteries to his followers. The small but entrancing Franciscan **Basilica of Dominus Flevit** marks the site where Jesus paused to weep over Jerusalem; built over Canaanite burial caves and a ruined Crusader church, the lovely, tear-shaped chapel was designed by Franciscan architect Antonio Barluzzi in 1953. The Russian Orthodox Mary Magdalene Church further down, easily identifiable by its golden onion-domes, was built by Czar Alexander III in 1873.

At the foot of the mount is the handsome **Church of All Nations**, noted for its fine Byzantine-style mosaic facade. Also known as the Basilica of the Agony, it, too was designed by Barluzzi; its 12 cupolas represent the 12 nations that contributed towards its construction. Its adjoining garden is the largest of several identified as **Gethsemane**, where Jesus was betrayed. The olive grove here has been verified as being 2,000 years old – not remarkable for olive trees. It has been suggested that Judas hanged himself from one of these trees.

Next to the garden is **Mary's Tomb**, deep within the earth and illuminated by candles of a number of Orthodox Christian churches. Midway down the stairs to the 5th-century chapel are niches that are said to hold the remains of Mary's parents, Joachim and Anne, and her husband Joseph.

**Muslim monuments:** The Muslim impact on Jerusalem came essentially in

e Mount of
lves, with
e Church of
Nations at
ttom and
rden of
thsemane
joining; the
ion domes
long to the
iry
igdalene
urch.

three stages. The first was shortly after the death of Mohammed, when his successors spread the faith out of Arabia and wrested Jerusalem from the crumbling Byzantine Empire in AD 638. In this period the Caliph Omar built a mosque on the Temple Mount which was later expanded to the Dome of the Rock, and in the 8th century the Al-Aksa mosque was constructed nearby.

The second Muslim phase followed the brief Crusader occupation of the Holy Land. The Europeans were defeated by Saladin, and with the recovery of Jerusalem in 1187 the Muslims began a major reconstruction of the city and especially of the mosques. As of AD 1249, the dominant Muslims were the Mamelukes, former slaves from Asia Minor who were highly accomplished architects and artisans. Much of the beauty of Islamic Jerusalem today is attributable to the Mamelukes.

But corruption and dissolution marked the Mameluke regime, and by 1516 they were easy prey for the invading Ottoman Turks. For the next 400 years, Jerusalem was ruled from Constantinople. Early in this period (1520–66), Suleiman I built the city ramparts that we see today, the Damascus Gate and the greatest water system in the city from the time of Herod to the present.

After Suleiman, however, the city simply festered until the collapse of the Ottoman Empire in World War I.

Today mosques and shrines dot the various quarters of the Old City, and most of the gates exhibit Islamic calligraphy. But the glories of Islamic Jerusalem are on the **Temple Mount**, which Muslims refer to as **Haram esh-Sharif**, the Venerable Sanctuary.

The mount is also the most disputed portion of contentious Jerusalem. The Arab nations are determined that an Islamic flag must fly over the site. In deference to the local Muslim authorities, Israel leaves the administration of Haram esh-Sharif entirely to Muslim officials. Israeli Border Police provide security in the area, but in cooperation with Arab policemen.

Israel's Chief Rabbinate, meanwhile, has banned Jews from visiting the Temple Mount. The reason is that somewhere on the hill is the site of the ancient Temple's Holy of Holies, the inner sanctuary which only the High Priest was allowed to enter, and even then only on one day of the year, Yom Kippur. Nevertheless, certain ultra-nationalist Israelis calling themselves the "Temple Faithful" periodically attempt to hold prayer services on the mount, an act that invariably incenses both the Arab community and other Jews.

The most eye-catching structure on Haram esh-Sharif is the **Dome of the Rock**. The outside of the mosque is a fantasia of marble, mosiacs and stained glass, painted tiles and quotations from the Koran, all capped by the gold-plated aluminium dome. Notable, too, are the curved pillars at the top of the steps, from which, according to tradition, scales will be hung on Judgement Day to weigh the souls of mankind.

The inside of the Dome of the Rock focuses on the huge boulder called the **Kubbet es-Sakhra**. This is the sacred rock on which Abraham was said to

**t, Dome of Rock at madan.
ht, meluke ntain near mple unt still ieves gance.**

have prepared the sacrifice of Isaac. It is also the rock from which, during his mystical journey to Jerusalem, Mohammed is said to have mounted his steed and ascended to heaven.

Appropriately enough, the heavenly interior of the famous golden dome shines down from above, a truly joyous achievement in goldleaf and mosaic and stained glass. Beneath the rock, meanwhile, is a crypt where the spirits of the dead are said to gather.

The silver-capped mosque at the southern end of the mount is **Al-Aksa**, a vast complex that can accommodate as many as 5,000 worshippers. Serving essentially as a prayer hall, Al-Aksa is more functional in design than the Dome of the Rock. Probably built on the remains of a Byzantine basilica, Al-Aksa also straddles vast underground chambers known as **Solomon's Stables**.

Al-Aksa features prominently in the modern history of the region. It was on the doorstep of this mosque in 1951 that a Muslim fanatic murdered Jordan's King Abdullah in sight of his little grandson, the current King Hussein. In 1969 a deranged Australian set fire to the building, causing extensive damage (reconstruction is still under way) and inflaming calls throughout the Muslim nations for *jihad*, or holy war, against Israel. It was at Al-Aksa, too, that Egypt's president, Anwar Sadat, prayed during his peace mission to Jerusalem in November 1977.

The **Islamic Museum** adjoining Al-Aksa has worthy exhibits covering the centuries of Muslim life in Jerusalem. Also noteworthy are the mount's elaborately carved fountains, intricate wrought-iron gates, the miniature **Dome of the Chain** and the marble-and-stone **minbar**, or preaching pulpit, outside of Al-Aksa.

Finally, it should not go unremarked that this area, which can ignite so much political passion throughout the Middle East, is marked by placid, sunny plazas and quiet gardens where the wind sighs through the trees.

**Old City atmospherics:** For those who thrive on crowds, people-watching in the Old City offers the enthusiast wave after perfect wave. The tradition that Jerusalem is the centre of the world certainly seems borne out by the variety of humanity that daily passes through its portals. Best spots for observing this continental drift are at the outdoor cafés at Jaffa Gate, on the steps leading to Damascus Gate, or at the Western Wall.

The diversity of Jerusalem's humanity is nearly matched by its wide variety of architecture. Indeed, history lurks amid the hurly-burly of the shopkeepers' displays. A butcher shop has Roman columns in its corners; a café where Arab and Jewish kids play video games has Byzantine arches; a furniture workshop is obviously part of a Crusader palace. Roman numerals incised on that lintel? Probably by one of Titus's legionaries. A wavelet cornice on a house? Definitely Mameluke work. One needn't be expert to spot these things, just alert.

When buying souvenirs, shoppers should take time to distinguish the quality from the trash, because both forms abound. Palestinian pottery and Armenian tiles are attractive and popular items,

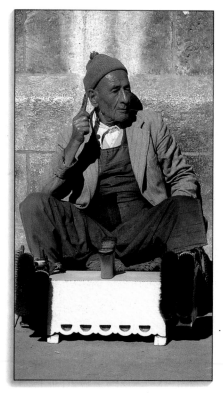

Shoe-shine man near Jaffa Gate waits for customer.

but the cheaper varieties have little or no glazing and will fade. Brass items such as coffee servers and tables should be judged by their weight: too light and it's probably plated tin. Too shiny is also suspect; a little tarnish suggests authenticity. Sheepskin jackets, gloves and slippers are popular, but bear in mind that in time these often smell too much like sheep.

Bargaining is the accepted practice, but not for trinkets costing a dollar or two. If the quoted price for a piece of carved olivewood or a *keffiyah* (Arab head-dress) sounds high, the shopper should walk on; 50 other shops are offering identical items. Arguing about prices should be saved for more expensive things such as carpets or hand-embroidered garments.

The authorised antiquities dealers are the address for old coins, glass, pottery and so on. Antiquities the street urchins offer for sale are rarely counterfeit; so many real artifacts are unearthed every day that forgery is unnecessary. But the kids' items are hardly museum quality –

and, in any event, such trade is illegal.

Similarly, the authorised money changers are generally reputable, and all give about the same exchange rate. None of this applies to the pointed-shoe types hissing *psst* from the alleys.

The most popular places to eat are at the cafés on David Street and at the funky sweet shops along Souk Khan ez-Zeit. Wildly popular with Israelis are pastry shops on Souk Khan ez-Zeit offering *kanaffi*, a hot cheese and honey dessert, and the *houmous* at Abu-Shukri's on El-Wad Street, right near the Fourth Station of the Cross. Yet another favourite treat is *sachleb*, a pudding made of essence of orchids and sold by street vendors.

Amid the crowds and the noise, the Old City affords some pleasant corners for rest and reflection. Among these are the gardens on Mt Zion, the park-like area between the mosques on the Temple Mount, the sunny Batei Machasei plaza in front of the Rothschild House in the Jewish Quarter, and of course in many of the church courtyards.

# Jerusalem

500 m

To Nablus, Ramallah

Hadassah Hospital

Mount Scope

Sderot Eshkol

Ammunition Hill

Derekh Shekhem

Tombs of the Sanhedrin

Sanhedria

Shmuel Hanavi

Sheikh Jarrah

Hebrew Univers

Biblical Zoo

Yirmeyahu

Bukharian Quarter

Tomb of Simon the Just

American Colony

American Colony Hotel

Tombs of the Kings

Wadi El Joz

Bet Yisrael

Geulla

Mandelbaum Gate

St. George

Saladin

Rockefeller Museum

Mount of Oliv

Romema

Malkhe Yisrael

Mea Shearim

Garden Tomb

Tourjeman Post

East Jerusalem Bus Station

Suleiman

Church of the Assumption

To Tel Aviv

Central Bus Station

Jaffa

Nathan Strauss

Mea Shearim

Shivte Yisrael

Nablus

Prophets

Church of All Nations

Derekh Jericho

Binyene HaUmma

Agrippas

Mahane Yehuda

Anna Ticho House

Russian Cathedral

Notre Dame de France

Paratroopers

Mary Magdale Chu

Hilton

Jerusalem Tower

Zion Square

Jaffa

Queen Shlomzion

Absalom's Pillar

Tom Zachar

Yad LaBanim (Soldiers Memorial)

Bezalel

Ben Yehuda

Italian Synagogue

Hillel

Central Post Office

The Old City

Tomb of Hezir

Intercontinental

Sacker Park

Bet Agron

Indepedence Park

Mamillah

City of David

Rose Park

Kiryat Ben-Gurion

Ruppin

Bezalel Academy of Art

Mamillah Pool

Plaza

Gershon Agron

Arts & Crafts Lane

King David Hotel

Gihon Spring

Hezekiah's Tunnel

The Knesset

Hechal Shlomo & Great Synagogue

Kings

YMCA

Herods Family Tomb

Yemin Moshe

Pool of Siloam

Silwa

King David

Moriah

Terra Sancta College

Keren Hayessod

Mount Zion

Montefiore Windmill

Shrine of the Book

Ramban

Azza

Sheraton King Solomon

Plumer Square

Cinemateque

Valley of Hinnom

Kidron Va

Sderot Shazar

Rehavia

Van Leer Foundation

Jabotinsky

German Colony

Church of St. Andrew

Liberty Bell Park

Khan Theater

Israel Museum

Monestary of the Cross

President's House

Jerusalem Theater

Railroad Station

Chopin

Neve Granot

L.A. Mayer Museum of Islamic Art

Natural History Museum

Peace Forest

Hebrew University

Hapalmach

Katamon

Emek Refaim

Emek Refaim

UN Headquarte

Sderot Herzog

Gonen

Derekh Bethlehem

Derekh Hebron

Haas Promenade

Talpiot

To Mount Herzle, Yad Vashem, Ein Kerem

Holyland

Model of Ancient Jerusalem

Pierre Konig

Yad Harutzim

Diplomat

256

# THE NEW CITY: A MODERN CAPITAL

*If I forget thee, O Jerusalem,
Let my right hand forget her cunning,
Let my tongue cleave to the roof of my
mouth, if I remember not thee;
If I set not Jerusalem above my chiefest
joy.* —137th Psalm

*Next year in Jerusalem!*
—traditional Jewish prayer

Throughout the ages Jews have wept over, sang and prayed for Jerusalem. Above all, they prayed that one day they might return to their holy city. Yet the Jerusalem that confronted the first waves of Jews who did return to start new lives here in the mid-1800s was a dismal rejoinder to the ideal spiritual capital they had dreamt of for so long. A backwater of the Turkish Ottoman Empire for 400 years, the city by 1917 had been left behind by time. It was filthy, decrepit and unsanitary, cramped within the confines of its great protective wall.

Even the founder of Zionism, Theodor Herzl, during his 10-day sojourn in Palestine in 1898, noted his disgust for its squalid conditions, writing: "When I remember thee in days to come, O Jerusalem, it will not be with delight. The musty deposits of 2,000 years of inhumanity, intolerance and foulness lie in your reeking alleys. If Jerusalem is ever ours... I would begin by cleaning it up. I would... tear down the filthy rat-holes, burn all the non-sacred ruins, and put the bazaars elsewhere. Then, retaining as much of the old architectural style as possible, I would build an airy, comfortable, properly sewered, brand new city around the holy places."

No visitor today would doubt the prophesy of Herzl's words. The capital of the Jewish State since 1950, and one united city since the Six Day War of 1967, Jerusalem is today every bit as sophisticated as its 19th-century predecessor was provincial. Bold geometric architecture erupts from every hillside; sleek thoroughfares lead into tree-lined boulevards; high-rises tower over church steeples and elegant city parks. There are bars, theatres and luxury hotels.

Yet the city that inspired so much Jewish yearning and Christian passion over the centuries is no less reverent for its modernity; the Christian visitor today will be struck by the vast array of churches and hospices of every conceivable denomination spread across the streets and hilltops of the city. But it is the tremendous blossoming of Jewish spirituality here that is most amazing. *Yeshivas*, synagogues and cultural institutions abound, the places of worship each reflecting the specific religious or ethnic colouring of congregants.

Shabbat is observed scrupulously; from midday Friday to midday Saturday all stores and buses cease their service, the streets empty, and unprepared visitors may well find themselves without food or transport, save that provided by their hotel, as Jerusalemites go to join their families for the holiday.

Yet as the capital of the State of Israel, Jerusalem – "Yerushalayim" in Hebrew

ceding
es, snow
nkets the
el slope.
ow,
norah
rns
dow at
hal
omo.

– holds special meaning even to its secular residents, who gripe that city is far less cosmopolitan and lively than far-off Tel Aviv.

The new city is still not exceptionally wealthy or grand, and many of her structures exude a symbolic significance that outstrips their otherwise modest aesthetic merits. The domineering presence of a few undistinguished highrises over the skyline, in particular, is jarring – if nonetheless useful for navigating one's way around. But from other perspectives, the new city can be magical: old and new merge seamlessly and Jerusalem seems as unearthly and splendid as any image its name evokes.

Another integration of old and new, considered by many to be the most lasting legacy of the British Mandate era, is the 1918 declaration forbidding all new construction to employ any material but the city's famous sandy-gold Jerusalem stone. While this has partially tied architects' hands creatively, the result has been a unique sense of visual harmony in the physical surface of the city, enhancing its unity while at the same time moderating the damage of its less successful architecture.

No event has had more influence on the shape of the city in recent years than its unification under Israeli hands in the 1967 war. Not only did this event clear away the barbed wire and concrete that separated east and west, it also, at least for a time, took Jerusalem off the front line of the Arab-Israeli conflict. As a result, the past 25 years or so have witnessed an explosion of unprecedented development. Presiding over this process has been one man, Teddy Kollek, Mayor of Jerusalem since 1965. The attraction of new institutions into the city and conservation of Old City landmarks, the colourful sweeps of new public art and hideous behemoths of rapidly erected housing are all in the end attributable to his office.

Today, the limits of Jerusalem enclose over 420,000 residents, and the city continues to grow, balancing, with mixed grace and awkwardness, the calls of the past and future.

**Knesset and high-rises glow at dusk**

258

**Navigating the city:** Cleft by the undulating crests and valleys of the Judean Hills and equally deep political boundaries, Jerusalem is united but disparate, and not always the easiest place to get around in.

Downtown **West Jerusalem**, however, is compact and easily navigable. The heart of this area is defined by the triangle of Jaffa Road, King George V Street and Ben Yehuda Street; Jaffa Road then continues to the northwest and the **Central Bus Station**, at the gateway to the city, while King George arcs southwards, eventually becoming Keren Hayesod Street and curving back towards the Old City and Mount Zion.

**Around Jaffa Gate:** As the main portal between the Old City and West Jerusalem, the **Jaffa Gate** acts as a pivot to the new city grid. The site offers a number of contemporary attractions. These include the **Museum of the City of Jerusalem** inside the body of the **Citadel**, which contains displays describing the tumultuous history of the city, figurines of Jerusalem characters, and the multilayered ruins of the structure itself. A **multi-media show** with a separate entrance describes the various moods of Jerusalem via numerous slide projectors. The walls themselves are the palette of the *son et lumière* (sound and light show) presented here in a host of languages, evenings from April to October. The **Government Tourist Office** just within the gate serves as a popular starting point for walking tours.

**Old new Jerusalem:** Twisting away from the Old City walls to the left of Jaffa Road, **Mamillah Road** was at one time the big commercial strip of the Jewish city. An expensive residential, tourist and shopping complex is under construction.

During his brief visit to Jerusalem at the turn of the century, Theodor Herzl stayed in a room at 18 Mamillah, the **Stern House**. For years the family kept the room at the back of the postcard/antique shop open to the public on odd hours. It's worth a visit if the place is still standing; in 1985 the government unveiled a plan to level the left-hand side of the street (preserving the more interesting architecture on the right) to make way for a new residential-commercial complex. Perhaps ironically, Moshe Safdie, the visionary Israeli architect who designed Habitat at the 1967 Montreal World's Fair and several radical plans for the modernisation of Jerusalem, now has his offices in one of the remaining old buildings above the empty store-fronts of Mamillah Road.

Until the 19th century, the Old City walls effectively served as the city limits for Jerusalem's Jews – outside, intolerant Muslims and Bedouin raiders posed a threat to any adventurous stragglers. Opposite the Old City between the Jaffa Gate and Mt Zion, the first Jewish suburb to penetrate this barrier remains *in situ*. Wishfully called **Mishkenot Sha'ananim**, or "Dwellings of Tranquillity", the long, blockish structure was built in 1860 by English philanthropist Sir Moses Montefiore, with the bequest of Judah Touro, a New Orleans Jew.

In the next four years, Montefiore bought an adjoining plot of land and

ontefiore
indmill tops
emin
oshe.

expanded the quarter, calling it Yemin Moshe. In the wake of the 1967 war, Yemin Moshe was revitalised as an artist's colony, and today its serene walkways and stone homes command some of the highest rents of any neighbourhood in the city. Montefiore built the landmark **windmill** at the edge of the quarter to provide flour for the settlement, and in 1948 it served as an important Israeli observation post. It now houses a modest museum.

Between this residential enclave and the Old City walls is the **Sultan's Pool** – long ago a reservoir, today a theatre for outdoor concerts. An ornate Mameluke drinking fountain or "sabil" sits on the roadside bridge nearby. Just below the Jaffa Gate, half-hidden in the greenery, lies the **Khutzot HaYotzer** or Arts and Crafts Lane, which houses the studios and shops of artisans.

**Russians and Prussians:** Jaffa Road has long been the prime entranceway to Jerusalem. It was paved in 1898 for the visiting Prussian Kaiser, Wilhelm II – for whose procession, as well, the wall between the Jaffa Gate and Citadel was rent open. Today **Jaffa Road** remains the main axis for new city traffic, meandering from the gate to the northern bounds of the city.

Leaving the Old City behind, Jaffa Road enters the fabric of the new at **Zahal Square** (Allenby Square until 1948 and afterwards renamed to honour the Israel Defence Forces). The small street to the right hosts another noted crafts area, while behind them to the right loom the massive French hospices of St Louis and Notre Dame d'France. This plateau, overlooking the city walls from the north marks the most vulnerable spot in the city's defensive barrier and over the ages served as the launching spot for most of its assaults, including the Assyrians' in 701 BC and Titus's victorious siege in AD 70.

Further up Jaffa Road is the new City Hall municipal complex and plaza. Nearby is **Gan Auster**, with bronze plaques describing the growth of Jerusalem's population in modern times. On the left-hand side of the street are two

Jaffa Road awaits visit ◀ Kaiser Wilhelm II in 1898.

notable buildings: the city's **Central Post Office**, and, next door, Erich Mendelsohn's Anglo-Palestinian Bank, now **Bank Leumi**. With its torch-like window grilles and airy, cool interior the 1938–39 building marks a graceful union of levantine and Bauhaus themes.

The **Russian Compound**, which covers a territory of several blocks to the right of Jaffa Road ahead, was purchased by Czar Alexander II in the wake of the Crimean War as a refuge for thousands of Russian pilgrims who flocked to the city every year, often dirt-poor and under considerable duress from their trip. Started in 1860, this complex marked the first notable presence outside the Old City; most of the buildings, including the handsome green-domed **Cathedral** and the Russian consulate, were completed by 1864. The compound has been largely bought by the Israeli government, and the buildings now house Law Courts, a Police Station and part of Hadassah Medical School. The **Hall of Heroism** is a small museum at the back of the complex, within what was once a British prison; it is dedicated to the Jewish underground resistance of the Mandate period.

**Downtown:** Continuing towards Zion Square, Jaffa Road begins to take on the bustling atmosphere of an urban centre. On the right, pleasant cafés are interspersed with various stores: a French-language bookstore, a xerox place, a city tourist office, numerous banks. A hop, skip and short walk up Queen Heleni Street takes you to a small **Agricultural Museum** and the Jerusalem offices of the **Society for the Protection of Nature**, whose Hebrew- and English-language tours of the country are widely praised. Nearby are two pleasant evening spots, Home Plus and the Pie House, and numerous second-hand bookshops.

To the left are the winding lanes of **Nahalat Shiva**, Jerusalem's second oldest residential suburb, now delightfully renovated. Founded by Joseph Rivlin in the early 1860s, the enclave grew to hold some 50 families by the end of that decade. Now **Rivlin Street** and **Salomon Street** cross the old neigh-

*Jaffa Road today in mid-winter snow.*

bourhood; despite their decidedly narrow girths, these pedestrian avenues house quite a few of the city's favourite restaurants and much of its nightlife.

At the hub of it all is **Zion Square** – always crowded, always crazy. It was so dubbed for the Zion Cinema, now long gone, a rallying spot for young Zionists in the 1930s. A bulky glass tower stands on the site now.

A block up HaRav Kook Street, on the left, is one of Jerusalem's most unexpected little nooks – the newly restored **Ticho House**. In the early part of the century it was the home and office of Avraham Ticho, Jerusalem's humanitarian eye doctor, and in more modern times of artist Anna Ticho.

The Jerusalem café scene gets into its stride at **Ben Yehuda Street**, the five-block long pedestrian avenue that begins at Zion Square. This is the place that everyone comes to see (and be seen), drink and get drunk, sip cappuccino, sample pastries and mingle with friends and stranger alike. Musicians, young couples and would-be prophets are always out in force, and several local characters have established their reputations here. You either love it or hate it.

Marking the city's main north-south axis, **King George V Street**, too, has its share of hubbub. The contrast between old and new is most vivid at the plaza in front of the City Tower, where the preserved doorway facade of an earlier building stands oblivious to its new surroundings. At 24 King George is another **Government Tourist Office**; just across the street is the American Express office and, further on, in the opening to **Independence Park**, three curvaceous steel columns, by renowned Dadaist Jean Arp. Hillel Street, leading back down towards the Old City from the Tourist Office, is the site of the lovely, ornate **Italian Synagogue**, transported, from Conegliano Veneto, near Venice, in 1952 and dating originally to 1719; it is once more in use today. The **Beit Agron**, or press building, is further on, opposite the park and an ancient reservoir: **Mamillah Pool**.

The **Bezalel Academy** on the other side of the Tourist Office is Jerusalem's premier arts and design college and was founded in 1906.

Religion dominates King George Street further on. The **Yeshrun Synagogue** across from the park is followed down the block by the **Jerusalem Great Synagogue**, which aspires to be a third Temple with its massive entranceway, and adjoining **Hechal Shlomo**, seat of the chief Rabbinate of Israel.

**King David Street:** Between King George and Mamillah Road, Gershon Argon Street rims the final edge of Independence Park; this quiet avenue boasts the world's only **Taxation Museum**.

Nearby **King David Street** hosts two of Jerusalem's most celebrated edifices. The YMCA, constructed 1928–33, came from the firm of Shreve, Lamb & Harmon, who at the same time were designing the Empire State Building. Its 120-ft tower offers an outstanding view of Jerusalem and its environs and with its symmetrical rotundas reflects an elegant harmony of modern Middle-Eastern form. The **King David Hotel** directly opposite was built with old-world

Orthodox Jew and child walk in Mea Shearim.

grandeur by Egyptian Jews in 1930. It served as a British base of command in the Mandate period and the entire right wing of the building was destroyed in a famous raid by the Jewish underground in 1946. The hotel in recent years has become known for hosting Israel's most famous visitors, including Anwar Sadat in 1977.

Below the hotel, Swiss sculptor Max Bill's geometric **cubes** face the Old City and lead to the Khutzot HaYotzer.

Beyond the King David, an airy park holds the cavern of **Herod's Family Tomb**, where the stormy monarch buried his wife Mariamne and two sons after murdering them in a paranoid rage.

**Opposite Mt Zion:** Heading down the road between this park and **Liberty Bell Garden** on the right, the modern city once more opens onto the old. Embedded on the side of the Valley of Hinnom like a rugged gem, the **Cinemateque** is the secular set's favourite new landmark. Its theatres screen a wide variety of foreign films.

Above the cinema, the Scottish **St**

Andrew Church** has a well-regarded hospice, and a memorial for Scottish King Robert Bruce, who on his death in 1329 requested that his heart be taken to Jerusalem (the heart was waylaid en route in Spain and never made it). Around the corner, the **Khan Theater's** atmospheric archways host folklore and jazz performers alike, and the popular Poire & Pomme Restaurant. The **train station** a block further dates from 1892 and still offers a daily service to Tel Aviv and Haifa.

While the area is quite serene today, the **Valley of Hinnom** is historically the site of human sacrifices to idolatrous gods during the reign of King Solomon.

**Tree-lined Boulevards:** Stretching due east from Hinnom are 2 sq. km of tree-lined boulevards and peaceful homes. The area immediately east, called the **German Colony**, was founded in 1873 by German Templars and still has a subtle European air. In the centre of the neighbourhood is an island housing several important institutions: the **Van Leer Foundation**, the **Israel Academy**

ontemporary
nagogue at
Scopus
mpus.

of Arts & Sciences, the **Presidential Residence** and the city's new **Cultural Center**. This complex includes the handsome **Jerusalem Theater**, home to the Jerusalem Symphony Orchestra, and a multi-theatre complex.

Nearby is the **L.A. Mayer Museum of Islamic Art** and some of the city's most expensive addresses. Tucked off in the greenery of a by-street is the modest **Natural History Museum**.

The neigbourhood of **Rehavia**, just across Azza Street, is also lovely. In between the apartment homes is an ancient burial chamber known as **Jason's Tomb**, containing Roman-era inscriptions; it was discovered by chance in 1956. The neighbourhood was the home and haunt of many early Zionist leaders, including Levi Eshkol, Ephraim Katzir, Golda Meir, Menachem Ussishkin and Eliezer Sukenik.

**Religious enclave:** Across Jaffa Street again, the mood is far more intense and unworldly. Over a quarter of all Jerusalem citizens are *haredi*, or ultra-Orthodox, and these neighbourhoods reflect the rigorous religious lifestyles of their inhabitants. The most famous Orthodox community is **Mea Shearim** – literally "a hundred gates" – built as early as 1875 as a refuge for Hassidic families. The neighbourhood has retained much of the intimacy and flavour of a European *shtetl*. The Orthodox who live here wear the traditional styles – *peot* (sidecurls), heavy, black garments for the men and shawls for the women. Signs surrounding the community warn that secular fashions, especially "immodest" female dress, is offensive and not tolerated.

The **Bukharian Quarter**, to the northwest, dates from the 1890s and houses the descendants of this Central Asian Jewish group. Once quite wealthy, the community fell into decline after the Soviet annexation of the territory brought an end to emigration there.

North Jerusalem, arching from here out across the hills, holds one of the city's more contemporary monuments: **Ammunition Hill**, the scene of a bitter five-hour battle between Israelis and Jordanians in 1967. Today, the trenches and bunkers are preserved and a memorial museum honours the soldiers who died here.

In nearby Sanhedria lie the **Tombs of the Sanhedrin**, who were the judges of ancient Israel's highest court. The highway passing by the crypts leads out of the city proper to the village of **Nebi Samuel**, and a mosque marking the spot where the great prophet Samuel is said to be buried. The highway continues to Tel Aviv. The bizzare hexagonal housing units of **Ramot** and clusters of other new apartment homes all around mark Jerusalem's new residential frontier.

**East Jerusalem:** The infamous "green line" that split the city into Israeli and Jordanian sectors wound snake-like across the north of the Old City from just east of the New Gate. While the no-man's land that separated the two areas has officially been cleared away, the gap remains: **East Jerusalem** is still Arab territory at heart and Arabic-language music and mosques grace its streets. Much of the population is Christian by faith, however, and middle-class too, and many of the homes, hotels and

eft, moon
oms over
ew city – the
ussian
athedral is
t centre left,
ith Mount
copus at
p. Right,
med interior
the Shrine
the Book.

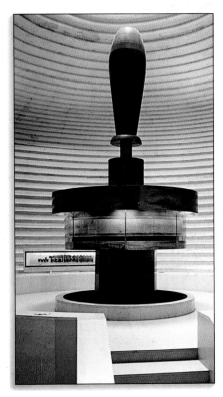

avenues here are lovely, if not ritzy.

Off Chail Handassa Street at the brink of the old border, the **Tourjeman Post** is a fascinating museum documenting the division of the city, within a house that served as an Israeli border post. Nearby is the site of the **Mandelbaum Gate**, since taken down, but from 1948 to 1967 the sole crossing from east to west.

HaNevaim, or **Prophet's Street**, runs from behind the Russian Compound to the Damascus Gate. Off its course lie several religious institutions, including the **Ethiopian Coptic Church**.

The **Damascus Gate**, the grandest entryway to the Old City, marks the hub of the Arab part of the city. Newly landscaped, its plaza offers one of Jerusalem's best forums for people-watching. The **Roman Square Museum** beneath the gate examines the Roman era of the city from the lower-level portal of that period. Also under the Old City walls close by are Solomon's Quarries, an ancient mine which tunnels deep below the alleys to Mt Moriah.

The **East Jerusalem Bus Station** just opposite operates buses to points in the West Bank using an independent Arab line. The **Rockefeller Museum**, further on, boasts a stately octagonal tower, a gracious courtyard and an extensive collection of archaeological finds; battle-scarred from 1967, it is now part of the Israel Museum.

From alongside the Old City, East Jerusalem's two main avenues, **Nablus Road** and **Saladin Street**, lead into a busy cobweb of traffic. Among the best-known restaurants here: the Sea Dolphin on Rashid Street, and Philadelphia, Dallas and Café Europa on Az-Zara Street. The **Garden Tomb**, the Protestant Golgotha (discussed with the Old City), is off Nablus Road.

Golgotha aside, the whole of East Jerusalem is in fact something of a vast necropolis, and is rife with caves and burial crypts. These include **Jeremiah's Grotto**, where the prophet supposedly wrote lamentations over Jerusalem, and the **Tomb of Simon the Just** – a Jewish high priest from the 3rd century BC. The most awesome chamber is the misnamed **Tomb of the Kings**, actually that of Queen Helena of Mesopotamia, who converted to Judaism in 54 BC.

In that part of the eastern city known as **Sheik Jarrah**, the **American Colony Hotel** is a luxurious Arab villa that in times past greeted such travellers as Mark Twain and Herman Melville.

**Potent peaks:** Isolated and aloof atop a ridge north of the city, **Mount Scopus** holds a special place in Jerusalem history. Its prime importance is as the site of the **Hebrew University**, inaugurated here under the vision of Chaim Weizmann in 1925. It was cut off from the rest of Jewish Jerusalem in the 1948 War of Independence, after the massacre of a **Hadassah Hospital** convoy of scientists and staff in April of that year. Re-absorbed into the city since 1967, the university has enjoyed spectacular modernisation, still ongoing, of its campus. Among the most impressive sites here today is the classical **amphitheatre**, which hosts concerts and lectures and, when empty, offers an awesome view of the rolling Judean Hills. Other notable monuments include the modern **pylon** and a **British cemetery** from World War I.

Southern Jerusalem has its own fateful sentinel in the Hill of Evil Council. This overlook is where tradition has it Judas Iscariot received his 30 pieces of silver; the **UN Headquarters** now stands here in the castle that was the seat of the British Mandate government after 1917. The **Peace Forest** and new **Haas Promenade** and **Sherover Walkway** deck the highway leading past here to Talpiot; industrial and commercial **Yad Harutzim Street** is an Israeli Soho, housing many artists' studios. **Kibbutz Ramat Rachel** marks the city's southern tip.

**The Capital:** The open expanse smack west of Central Jerusalem holds the new city's most important landmarks. Ironically, these contemporary forms hover over the eerie 7th-century **Monastery of the Cross**, just below Rehavia, and the juxtaposition of the styles can provide one of the city's most vivid contrasts. (The church marks where the tree for Jesus's Cross was felled.)

The **Israel Museum** is one of those institutions that is so acclaimed it has become beyond reproach. Opened originally in 1965, its boxy structure has allowed it to expand over the years; its collection today bridges ethnography, period rooms, history, Jewish culture, coins and modern art with the Isamu Noguchi-designed **Billy Rose Art Garden**. The nipple-shaped **Shrine of the Book** displays the Dead Sea Scrolls in a chamber nearby. Opposite are two recently opened museums: the Bible Lands Museum and the Bloomfield Science Museum.

The **Knesset**, the nation's Parliament Building, is the symbol of the nation's democratic system. Be sure you take the tour of the interior. The carved **menorah** was presented by Great Britain's Parliament and depicts scenes from Jewish history. The **Wohl Rose Garden** above is sweetest in the spring. Also in the area is the Hebrew University campus of **Givat Ram**, built to substitute for Mt Scopus in 1948–67, and a pyramidal **memorial** to Israel's fallen soldiers.

**Biblical retreat:** Looping westward from the south, you can seek out two unusual sites: a unique scale model of Solomon's Jerusalem at the **Holyland Hotel** and the "**Monster**", a sensuous, creature-faced playground by artist Nikki de Saint Phalle at Kiryat Ha Yovel.

**Ein Kerem**, the biblical townlet nestling in a valley to the west of the city proper, is as timeless as the hills and well worth an afternoon itself. Rich in religious history, its most renowned sites include the Franciscan **Church of the Visitation**, designed by pilgrim-architect Antonio Barluzzi in 1956, where Elizabeth hid John from Herod's soldiers, and the central **Spring of the Vineyard** (also known as Mary's Fountain), which gave the town its name. At the **Church of St John**, mosaics and a grotto mark the traditional birthplace of the Baptist. The **Hadassah Hospital** complex just above the town holds Marc Chagall's famed stained-glass windows depicting the 12 tribes of Israel.

A few kilometres south of Ein Kerem are two contemporary sites: the **Kennedy Memorial**, shaped like a gi-

**A statue expresses grief at Yad Vashem.**

ant tree trunk, and the **Artur Rubinstein Memorial Viewpoint**, shaped like a giant piano keyboard.

**Remembrance:** Remembrance is a key theme of modern Judaism, and Jerusalem has no shortage of memorials. The two most potent of these lie side-by-side on the western ridge of the city, and provide powerful testimony to the two events which altered the course of Jewish history in the 20th century: the Holocaust and the creation of Israel.

**Yad Vashem** is the official memorial to the 6 million Jews who perished in the Nazi-wrought Holocaust in Europe between 1933 and 1945. Prepare to be profoundly moved.

The central chamber, Ohel Yizkor or the **Hall of Remembrance**, sits on a base of rounded boulders; inside, an eternal flame flickers amid blocks engraved with the names of 21 death camps: Auschwitz, Buchenwald, Dachau, Bergen-Belsen, Sobibor, Treblinka… Other structures include the simple shaft of the **Pillar of Heroism**, an **art museum** of the work created by concentration

camp inmates, an extensive archives, the **Hall of Names** in which the personal records of over 2 million of the murdered are preserved, and several works of expressive statuary. The permanent exhibit, "Warning and Witness", documents the horrors of the era. The **Avenue of the Righteous** leading to the memorial is lined with trees planted in honour of individual Gentiles who helped Jews during the Nazi regime.

**Mount Herzl** honours the Viennese journalist who became the founder of the Zionist movement from 1897 to 1904. His remains were transported to Jerusalem in 1949, and his simple black granite tomb marks the summit of the mount. Also buried here are Vladamir Jabotinksy and other Zionist visionaries. A museum about Herzl stands at the entrance to the mount. In the **Military Cemetery** on the northern slope of the ridge lie graves of Israeli soldiers who died defending the Jewish State.

All around them, the stark, rolling Judean Hills and new apartment homes bear mute witness to their sacrifice.

ew
artment
mes at
ench Hill in
rthern
rusalem.

# THE WEST BANK

Hugging the Jordan River to the east and the amber-hued walls of Jerusalem to the west, stretching out over the cities and valleys of Samaria to the north, and the tumbling Judean Hills to the south, the West Bank is perhaps the geographic centre of the Middle East, and the epicentre of all the tensions that area has come to represent in modern times. It lies at the very heart of the Holy Land, holding such revered names as Bethlehem, Hebron, Shiloh and Jericho within its domain.

For centuries, Jews, Christians and Muslims have paid homage here, and today pilgrims from around the world still flock to its shrines. Scattered throughout the region, these places are often claimed by more than one religion, and today such spots lend a physical immediacy to age-old conflicts. More than a millennium has not dissipated the tension in this contested land. The combatants change, the location remains the same.

The current Arab-Israeli discord seems to focuses on the future status of the West Bank and the 1 million Palestinian Arabs who live there. There are myriad assessments of the conflict's implications, but quite simply, both parties fear the other's encroachment on their rights to the land. The issue of the West Bank echoes through the halls of governments and international forums worldwide.

The West Bank is not part of the State of Israel; however it is, being under Israeli administration, accessible from this country and can be reached from Israeli highways with relative ease. Yet the West Bank remains an entity unto itself, and the traveller here is well advised to be aware of current events and local etiquette before entering its boundaries.

**Political history:** In 1948, after Jordan, Egypt, Iraq, Syria and Lebanon promptly declared war on the newly established State of Israel, East Jerusalem and the Arab areas west of the Jordan River fell to Jordan. In 1950, Jordan annexed this region, hence the name "West Bank".

In that same year, the United Nations Relief Works Agency (UNRWA) took on the responsibility of "overseeing and furthering the well-being of the Palestinian refugees until a political solution to the Palestinian displacement could be found."

Over 35 years later, first under Jordanian rule and later under Israeli, this strategic bulge of land has not gained the nation-state status its leaders advocate. Most Israelis, and some Palestinians, will tell you that life under Israeli occupation is better than it had been under Jordan for the Arab inhabitants here. However, there is one principle on which West Bank Arabs agree: an end to Israeli occupation.

The West Bank's location in the centre of Israel made transportation to such Israeli communities as En Gedi, on the Dead Sea, and Tiberius in the Galilee time-consuming and posed a difficult strategic problem. The high hills of the West Bank gave the Jordanians a clear

**Preceding pages:** sheep rush into a pen in the West Bank.

view and access to the lower regions of Israel, and at places along the coast just above Tel Aviv, Israel's territory was a slim 15 km (9½ miles) wide.

On the night following the outbreak of the 1967 War, Tel Aviv was shelled from the Jordanian-controlled town of Kalkilya, just across the border. As a result of the week-long war that followed, Israel gained control of the region. Capturing the former Arab strongholds, the mountains dominating the Jordan River Valley, was a stupendous strategic gain, Israelis agree. But far fewer agree over just what Israel should now do with the territory and the restive Arab population living there.

Aside from an intricate electronic defence system it constructed in the Jordan Valley, Israel's Labour-led coalition installed numerous defence outposts which evolved into settlements. These pockets of Jewish presence quickly became precedents for further settlement based upon religious and nationalistic claims which date back to 1900 BC, when the Patriarchs inhabited

Canaan. More recently, Israelis have been drawn to the area for less ideological reasons: financial incentive. State subsidisation of settlements has made living in this territory substantially more affordable for the inflation-strapped Israeli than housing costs permit within the "green line".

As with most things Israeli, the demographic fate of the West Bank depends on political negotiation. In 1977 when the Likud coalition came into power, its priority was to populate the West Bank, particularly in Samaria, where there are sizeable Arab populations.

When the Labour government took office in 1992, the conception of new settlements was halted, although some already planned or under construction will be completed. However, it is still possible to drive along a road and see, towering over a hill bordering an Arab village, a huge billboard announcing plans for new co-op apartments complete with swimming-pool, tennis courts and a modern shopping centre. In fact, the Israeli settlements are comprehensive residential centres replete with shopping, schooling, recreation facilities and jobs for their residents. Ironically, it is predominantly Arab labourers who construct the very settlements which loom over their own homes.

Predictably, tensions among Palestinians and settlers frequently run high; and before venturing into the West Bank it is advisable to check on the current prevailing political climate. Modest dress (no shorts) is recommended, and single women are advised to bring escorts with them, lest they gain them en route. Several companies offer group tours of the region as well, though these usually express a Jewish nationalistic theme.

Between the army outposts and refugee camps, a trip to the West Bank necessarily provokes political cognisance. But much of the landscape appears unchanged since the days of Abraham, Isaac and Jacob, or David, or Jesus. With the political and spiritual each so firmly entrenched here, your sense of wonder is sure to be heightened one way or another.

# SAMARIA

Leaving Jerusalem along the Jerusalem-Jericho highway, signs of successive civilisations abound in the hills of Samaria, which are stone white by day and gleaming bronze at sunset.

The road winds through the slopes of **East Jerusalem** by the congested quarters of its residents. Women are outside scrubbing clothing; children run up and down stairs and in and out of courtyards. Playing marbles on level slabs of stone is a widely enjoyed game among small Arab boys and a lot of fun to watch.

**Refugees and ruins:** Heading north, a few kilometres from **Ramallah**, **Shofat** is the largest Palestinian refugee camp in the territories. It bustles with activity. Some of the Arab homes here, with their contemporary architecture and well-manicured gardens, are palatial, but for the most part the housing, medical, social and educational aid given by the United Nations Relief Works Agency (UNWRA) is essential. Among its offerings are numerous vocational training centres, such as the Ramallah Women's Training Center, where courses are offered to respond to the demands of the Middle Eastern economy. Ramallah exemplifies the problems of the Israeli presence. For many of the Palestinian Arabs here, it is a hotbed of anti-Israel sentiment. Countless tyre burnings, school closures, and Israeli-imposed curfews have occurred here over the years.

Twelve km (7½ miles) northwest, **Bir Zeit** is the largest of the five major Palestinian universities in the West Bank. Constructed by the Israelis in 1972, it is an active centre of hostility to the Israeli government; Israeli and self-imposed closures occur often.

Travelling north of Ramallah en route to Nablus, limestone terraces climb up and down the hills, retaining all the mineral-rich soil they can. Knotty olive trees edged with flora grace the landscape. These olives are harvested by the local farmers who transport them to the villages for pressing.

Just above the city, two towns atop nearby hills serve as natural land-marks: **Bethel** and **Ai**. Bethel is prominent in early biblical narratives as the site where Jacob dreamed of a ladder ascending to Heaven. At this spot he made an altar and called it Beit El, or House of God. This is also where the Ark of the Law remained until the time of Judges. Ai was one of the earliest cities captured by Joshua and the Israelites during their military conquest of Canaan.

The ancient city of **Shiloh** stood equidistant between Nablus and Bethel. According to the Bible, it was at Shiloh that the land of Israel was divided among the 12 tribes and where the cities were delegated. In the 11th century BC it was the religious centre for the Israelite tribes, and for over 200 years it was the sacred ground for the Ark of the Covenant. And it was in the city of Shiloh that the great prophet Samuel was born, and "grew before the Lord" (I Samuel; 2, 2l). In time, the Philistines defeated the Israelites, captured the ark, and burned Shiloh to the ground. Today, the *tel* of Shiloh spans less than eight acres, although archaeologists have unearthed remnants of civilisations dating to the Bronze Age (1600 BC).

Some 48 km (30 miles) north of Ramallah is **Nablus** (Shechem in Hebrew), which is many things to many people. The largest city on the West Bank, with an estimated population of over 100,000, it is chock-full of sites with biblical resonance. From a distance Nablus resembles a pointilist painting. Innumerable blue doors dot houses neatly spread across a hillside. Within earshot there is a cacophany of sounds emanating from town life: honking car horns, the majestic *mu'ezzin* calling the Muslim faithful to prayer and the provocative ululations of Arab women.

Rich in history, the area just outside today's city centre is mentioned in Genesis as the place where Jacob pitched his tents. **Jacob's Well**, located here, is still in use by Nablus residents. According to the Gospel John (4; 25-26), Jesus stopped here for refreshment, weary from his travels. He spoke to a Samaritan woman who drew water from the

arvesting
heat in
amaria.

well. "I know that the Messiah cometh, which is called Christ," she told him, whereupon Jesus responded: "I that speak unto thee am he." Adjoining this structure is a Greek Orthodox convent built on the remains of a Crusader church.

Nearby, the **Tomb of Joseph** is a Muslim shrine reputed to hold the great man's bones, "in a parcel of ground which Jacob bought of the sons of Hamor the father of Shechem" (Josh; 24,32). (Defying scripture, there is another cenotaph for Joseph at the Tomb of the Patriarchs in Hebron.) Other archaeological discoveries in this proximity include foundations of Canaanite temples, and an ancient *yeshiva*, now guarded by Israeli soldiers.

During the time of the Judges, Abimelech, the son of Gideon, had himself proclaimed king here; some 200 years later, in 928 BC, the 10 northern tribes called on Jeroboam to be king from Dan to Bethel and for several years Shechem served as the capital of the new northern kingdom of Israel.

Going farther back into biblical his-tory, Abraham probably stopped in Shechem just after he arrived in Canaan, and some believe this was the place where he founded the covenant between God and man.

In Roman times, Shechem was re-named Neapolis, or "New City", laying the root of the name it finally gained when it was taken by the Arabs.

**The Samaritans:** Standing like two gate posts at the southeastern entrance to Nablus are two historic sister peaks, **Mount Ebal** and **Mount Gerezim**. Moses spoke of them, blessing Mount Gerezim and cursing Mount Ebal. After the conquest, Joshua built an altar on Mount Ebal and from this point read the law to the people.

Mount Gerezim today is the centre of the Samaritan religion. The sect's origins date back to when Assyria swept through the northern kingdom in 720 BC. Returning from exile in 538 BC, the Jews shunned the Samaritans for their intermarriage with their conquerors, although the Samaritans claimed strict adherence to Mosaic Law. Today, approximately 250 of the remaining 500 Samaritans (they were tens of thousands strong during the Middle Ages) celebrate the Passover holiday.

**Omri's stately capital:** A little over 10 km (6 miles) northwest of Nablus is the site of one of the most impressive ruins of the Holy Land: **Sebastia**. Once called Samaria, it was the capital of the northern Kingdom of Israel upon Omri's accession to power in 887 BC. He and his son, the ill-tempered King Ahab, built magnificent palaces and temples inside a circular protective wall. Ahab also added embellishments and temples to Baal and Astarte, cult figures favoured by his wife and queen, Jezebel, from Sidon. This departure from monotheism incurred the wrath of the Lord and the flight of Elijah, which was to terminate eventually on Mount Carmel.

The remains of Ahab's palace adjoin the impressive steps which led to Herod's Temple of Augustus, constructed in roughly 30 BC. Herod's grandiose style is certainly not lost in the rubble. Many of his massive constructions still stand in part, testimony to the days

Day-to-day life and grandoise pillars at Sebastia.

when he named the city in honour of the Emperor Augustus (Sebaste in Greek) and when he married the beautiful, doomed Mariamne here.

In addition to his work, Sebastia's ruins include an enormous hippodrome, the acropolis, a basilica, and many remains of Israelite and Hellenistic walls. The colonnade-lined street is a majestic reminder of Sebastia's opulence.

In the Arab village of Sebastia just outside the Roman wall lie the ruins of a 12th-century Crusader cathedral. It is reputed to stand over the tombs of the prophets Elisha and Obadiah and St John the Baptist. This site is included in the **Mosque of Nabi Yaya**, in which is a small chamber believed to hold the head of John the Baptist.

Among the parched hills and occasional discarded soda cans that compose the less populated regions of the West Bank, you are likely to spot a Bedouin with his flock sprinkling the hillside. While these nomads usually live in clusters in the Judean Desert and Samaria, it is equally common to see a lone Bedouin tent with an incongruous TV antenna potruding from its centre and a pick-up truck parked outside. Young Bedouin children clad in colourful garments can be affable photographic subjects.

**Hidden hermitage:** On the road southeast to **Wadi Kelt** the silence is so pure that it creates a ringing in your ears. For 1,600 years, since the age of the Patriarchs, monks have inhabited this surrealistic place, where the Wadi Kelt River meanders through a dramatic gorge in the canyon between Jericho and Jerusalem. This 35-km (22-mile) stretch includes ruins on top of ruins, monasteries, eerie hermit caves and surprising watering holes. These sights appear as adornments on the earth's crust, which projects every which way to form hills, cliffs and ravines – a photographer's delight. Honeycombing the rockface are hollowed-out niches which serve as isolation cells for monks, who live off the fruit of the land from a garden by a stream. The Greek Orthodox **Monastery of St George** is just over a century old,

but its community long precedes it. Hasmonean, Herodian and Roman remains line this circuitous course.

South of Jericho, off the Jerusalem-Jericho highway, is the **Mosque of Nabi Musa**, astounding to the eye. It appears out of nowhere in the middle of nowhere. Here, Muslims worship the Tomb of Moses. It is written in Deut; (34, 1-6) that Moses was "buried in a valley in the land of Moab, but no man knoweth of his sepulchre unto this day." But an old tradition dating back to Christian pilgrims places it here. The Mamelukes constructed the mosque in the 13th century, and provided a high cenotaph for Moses.

Today the mosque is open during the times of Muslim prayer, and all day Friday. Only Muslims are admitted during April, when thousands of Muslims make their pilgrimage to Nabi Musa. The Muslims take a route that intersects the procession of Christians making their Easter pilgrimages to al-Maghtes on the Jordan River, and clashes have resulted from the coinciding celebrations.

**The walls of Jericho:** Jericho must have been a prime spot for the earliest city dwellers on earth some 10,000 years ago. Widely considered to have sprouted the first agricultural community, the town today is once more centred on agriculture, although on a less historic scale. Ensconced in an oasis in the midst of barren land, Jericho's greenery is nurtured by underground springs, the secret of its endurance.

In times past, rulers used this spot as a warm-weather retreat. One such vacationer was Hisham, the 10th Ummayid Caliph, who constructed the fabulous **Hisham's Palace** in the 8th century, about 3 km (2 miles) from the city. An enormous aqueduct supplied water from the nearby **Ein Dug Springs** to a cistern which then doled it out to the palace as needed. The carvings and monumental pillars here are awesome, and the palace floors contain examples of the finest in Islamic mosaics.

A few kilometres south of the palace is **Elisha's Spring**, a fountain which the Jews believe was purified by the prophet

Monastery at St George clings to Wadi Kelt.

278

after the populace claimed it was harmful to crops: it is referred to by Arabs today as **Eines-Sultan**.

Nearby is the preserved floor of a 6th-century synagogue, featuring a mosaic *menorah* in its centre, within the walls of a Jericho home.

Ancient Jericho, which lies under **Tel es-Sultan**, is where the walls came tumbling down on the seventh day after they were encircled by Joshua and the Children of Israel. Archaeological excavations confirm that settlements here date to 8,000 BC, when the early population of hunters and gatherers completed here the transition to sedentary life, becoming the earliest practitioners of agriculture and animal husbandry.

Jericho today is a somewhat sleepy town of some 7,000 people, with most of the activity confined to the town's centre. Here, men and women gather to sit on rattan stools, talk, sip coffee, or play backgammon. The markets are ablaze with the earth's fruits and vegetables, and huge bunches of dates and bananas swing from their beams, fresh and delicious. The cafés here offer authentic Middle Eastern foods, refreshment, and a chance to escape the blistering Jericho heat.

In the stark wilderness outside this small town, Jesus encountered the Devil's temptation, on a peak the Bible calls the **Mount of Temptation**. Hinged to the rockface here is a Greek Orthodox monastery, which was constructed in front of the grotto where Jesus was said to have fasted for 40 days and nights.

**Along the river Jordan:** Some 10 km (6 miles) east of Jericho at a ford north of the Dead Sea known as **al-Maghtes**, Jesus was baptised at age 30: "…and it came to pass in those days, that Jesus came from Nazareth of Galilee, and was baptised by John in Jordan," (Mark;1, 6-9). Not surprisingly, this traditional **Site of the Baptism** is favoured today by Christians as a place of christening.

Mark Twain once described the **Jordan River** as "so crooked that a man does not know which side of it he is on half the time. In going 90 miles it does not get over more than 50 miles of ground. It is not any wider than Broadway in New York." Indeed the symbolism attached to this stream – its muddy waters barely flowing in winter – far exceeds its actual size.

The **Allenby Bridge** is the river-crossing from the West Bank to Jordan's Hashemite Kingdom. During the 1967 War, the bridge, reduced to scaffolding, was jammed with Palestinians fleeing the West Bank into Jordan. Since then it has been rebuilt and its traffic is strictly monitored by Israeli security.

Today the Allenby Bridge is the gateway for West Bank produce into the market places of the Arab world. Visits are exchanged by families and friends on both sides of the Jordan, and many West Bank residents go to Amman to do banking and preserve commercial links.

Stationed at the bridge's western side are young Israeli soldiers, who meticulously search the sacks, parcels and personal belongings of all travellers. The armed checkpoints at the border just beyond are potent reminders that the official state of war between the two nations is yet unresolved.

ᵣistian site
d political
ᵒss-way
ᵃre river
d roadsign.

סמן הטבילה

درب المعمودية

PLACE OF
THE BAPTISM

גשר אלנבי

جسر النبي

ALLENBY BRIDGE

# JUDEA

There is no clear boundary marking the transition of the hills of Samaria to those of Judea, as both are part of the same central range of high ground, reaching from above Ramallah in the north through the Judean cities of Bethlehem and Hebron. Yet the **Judean Hills** have sustained an adored body of legend, as a wellspring of both the Old and New Testament. To the east, marking the descent of the range into the Jordan Rift Valley, lies the **Judean Desert**, which over the centuries served as a place of refuge for prophets, monks and kings. Judea is as elusive as it is revered; all around, the arid rolling hills remind you that this is the land of the Bible, and belie the tensions below the surface.

The northern approach to Bethlehem holds **Rachel's Tomb**, where the wife of the Patriarch Jacob and mother of Benjamin is said to be buried. The shrine is one of the holiest in Judaism, and is a place of worship for Jews and Muslims alike. The modest dome over the site was rebuilt by the British philanthropist Sir Moses Montefiore in 1841, at the place where it is said "Jacob set a pillar upon her grave."

**Shrines of Bethlehem:** Centuries after Rachel, during a Bethlehem field harvest, the widowed Ruth fell in love with Boaz. Their great grandson David, chosen from these same fields (and born in Bethlehem), became the famous poet-king of Israel. On the eastern edge of Bethlehem lies the **Field of Ruth**. It is near the Arab village of **Beit Sahur** (House of the Shepherd), and is believed to be the **Shepherds' Field** where the angel appeared before the shepherds "keeping watch over their flock by night," to announce the birth of Jesus.

On Manger Street, which leads directly into the hub of town, up a flight of stairs, you'll find three huge water cisterns hewn out of rock, said to be **David's Well**. When he was battling the Philistines, David was in their garrison here when thirst prompted him to cry "Oh, that one would give me water to drink of the well of Bethlehem, which is by the gate!" But, offered the water drawn from the well of his enemies, "he would not drink thereof, but poured it out unto the Lord." (Sam II; 23, 16).

Today, music, bells and churches grace the town of **Bethlehem**. The area is teeming with pilgrims during the holidays, and the festivities don't stop after Christmas and Easter. The great pomp, ornate decor and beautiful displays continue year round.

Christ was born in Bethlehem. The exact route of the Nazarene in life remains unknown, and the Gospels do not even agree on chronology. But over the ages there has been a broadening consensus on the exact site of His birth. Following the road into **Manger Square**, is the hub of Bethlehem – wide plaza before the **Church of the Nativity**, entered by stooping through a small entranceway, reduced to such scale by the Crusaders for defence purposes, and again made smaller in later years. The original basilica here was built in the year 325 by the Emperor Constantine. The foundation for the structure is the cave revered in Christian tradition as the place where Jesus was born, and which is mentioned in the writings of St Justine Martyr just 100 years after Christ.

Beyond the vestibule is the nave; much of this interior, including the towering wooden beams, dates from the Emperor Justinian's rebuilding the church in the 6th century. At the front of the church, down some stairs, is the **Grotto of the Nativity**, where the altar features a barely discernable 12th-century mosaic. But the eye is riveted to a gleaming silver star on the floor of this small space, inscribed in Latin, "*Hic de virgine Maria Jesus Christus natus est,*" (Here Jesus Christ was born of the Virgin Mary). Next to the ornate and gilded grotto is the **Chapel of the Manger**, where Mary placed the newborn.

Typically, the Church of the Nativity is adjacent, diagonal and adjoined to several churches of varying Christian denominations. The most celebrated on Christmas Eve is St Catherine's Church, from which Bethlehem's annual midnight mass is broadcast worldwide.

Christmas procession at Manger Square in Bethlehem.

A few minutes walk down Milk Grotto Street will take you to the **Milk Grotto Church**. Its milky white colour lends the name; the legend is that while nursing the newborn Jesus, some of Mary's milk splashed to the stone floor and permanently whitened it. Today stone scrapings are sold to pilgrims to empower better breastfeeding. From this spot, the Field of Ruth and the expansive Wilderness of Judah are in clear view.

Outside of the churches and shrines, countless self-appointed tour guides promise to show you all you wish to see. Often, these folk know some interesting tidbits about the history of the town, but expect to pay for this "freely" offered information or be hounded around Manger Square and its environs.

All over town, but particularly in the area of the Square, Bethlehem vendors offer a wide array of religious articles and artifacts. They are freshly minted, but traditionally inspired, often of olive-wood, ceramic or Jerusalem stone. If you are persistent but not too pushy, you can bargain with these people and take care of all your Christmas shopping in one go.

Looking into the town of Bethlehem to the north, steeples rise from the hillside maze of houses, proclaiming the city's continued sanctity to the 20,000-odd Arab Christians who live here. Among the various religious institutions here is an Arabic-language university directed by the Catholic Order of the Brothers of Christian Schools; known as **Bethlehem University**, it was established with Israeli assistance.

**Castles in the wilderness:** Some 8 km (5 miles) east of here is the desert citadel of **Herodian**, perhaps the most outstanding of Herod's architectural conceits. As a result of all his conquests, Herod felt he needed a safe haven from those seeking revenge and Herodian is nothing if not aloof. A monstrous circular protective wall struck with four equidistant watch posts guards Herod's ample living space and bath house; included in the layout were hot baths, arcades, a synagogue, and numerous other luxuries. The banquet hall of the palace is as

**Left**, bas relief at Milk Grotto. **Below**, Herodian.

immense as a football stadium, and the structure caps an elevation of 800 metres (2,500 ft) above sea level or 100 metres above the desert floor.

The view from Herodian is a kaleidoscope of the region; Jerusalem lies north, Bethlehem to the west, while the Dead Sea glistens beyond the Judean Wilderness to the south and east. According to scholars, just as in Masada, the Jewish uprising resulted in this mountain's defenders taking their own lives before the Romans could. But like the zealots of Masada, the bearers of this fortress were among the last to fall.

Even more remote, dug into the canyon walls overlooking the Kidron River to the northeast, is the blue-domed **Mar Saba Monastery**. In years gone by, St Sabas used this serene niche in the desert as a retreat for study and worship and in 492 he established the monastery named after him. In the 7th century, Persians and Arabs ruined the monastery and murdered the monks; it was rebuilt, however, and early in the 8th century John of Damascus came to the site. The

writing he did here was an important contribution to Christianity and representative of Christian/Islamic differences at the time. Today, the most prominent feature of the hermitage, from first approach, is the huge protective wall that surrounds the complex. Among the finds inside are the robed remains of St Sabas himself, returned here from Venice in 1965, where they had been stored for over 700 years for preservation. Also on display are the skulls of the hundreds of monks killed by the Persians in 614. This one's solely for the gentlemen, however. Women are not allowed entrance to the monastery.

The area is inhabited by Bedouin, who claim to descend from the monastery's ancient caretakers, who travelled from Byzantium.

Along the path to Mar Saba is the **Church of St Theodosius**, where the three wise men rested after paying homage to the infant Jesus, and where St Theodosius died in 529 at the age of 105. Back on the road above Bethlehem is another fortress-like monastery, **Mar**

ar Saba
onastery.

**Elias**. Built on a spot where the prophet Elijah slept in fleeing Jezebel, it was restored by the Crusaders in the 11th century and served as an important border post in the years the West Bank was Jordanian – between 1948 and 1967.

Roughly 25 km (15 miles) from Bethlehem, heading south towards Hebron, lie the dark-green cisterns known as **Solomon's Pools**. Tradition attributes them to the workers of the great Jewish king in the 10th century BC; archaeology suggests they date from Roman times. In either case, an aqueduct carried water from here to the population of Jerusalem, and today they still serve as a source of water for the city.

**Passionate Hebron:** Close to 16 km (10 miles) south from Bethlehem lies the ancient city of **Hebron**. While Hebron represents layers of history, its agriculture and urban community is progressive. Farmers, goat and sheep herders, and food packers have made great strides in production by mechanising.

The town also boasts a major Islamic university which enrolls nearly 2,000 Arab students. In existence since 1971, this institution is noted for promoting Palestinian culture and nationalism, much to the chagrin of the Israeli authorities who close the facility every so often, citing anti-Israel activity.

Hebron is definitely not the place to sport your knowledge of Hebrew. In fact, any attempt on your part to speak a few words of Arabic will be appreciated by the local Arabs. It's a good idea to bone up on some friendly phrases before visiting with the town folk. Chances are that you will be beckoned into a web of merchants stalls or to a private home for a cup of tea. Turning down such an invitation is offensive but take care not to enter into a discussion or situation which could turn volatile. Debating the merits of Israel's presence on the West Bank, for example, is ill-advised.

Meander through the criss-cross of alleyways in the Hebron *casbah*. Here you will find a variety of artisans crafting pottery, compressing and sculpting olivewood, and of course blowing the

**Tomb of the Patriarch dominates Hebron.**

colourful glass for which Hebron is widely famed. A variety of fresh fruits can be bought all along the roadsides and in the shuk. Hebron-grown peaches, pale and sweet, are in demand all over the Middle East. Hebron's produce, including dried and fresh fruits as well as different types of vegetables, are transported to Arab countries by way of the Allenby Bridge and Israeli allowance.

Jewish presence in Hebron dates back to when God bestowed upon Abraham the father-role over the descendants of monotheism, Israel and Ishmael. He chose this airy hill as the burial ground for his family, and today the **Tomb of the Patriarchs** dominates the city, and is visited by both Jews and Muslims. According to the Pentateuch, Abraham bought the **Cave of Machpelah** from Ephron the Hittite as the burial site for his wife Sarah. Here, all three Patriarchs and their wives are believed to be buried, and their cenotaphs compose the centre of the edifice: Abraham and Sarah in the centre, Jacob and Leah on the outer side of the enclosure, and on the other side, inside the mosque area, Isaac and Rebecca. More expansive folklore further contends the site to hold the graves of Adam, Eve, Esau, and all 12 sons of Jacob as well (Cain, Abel and the snake not being included).

Standing just outside the structure is **Joseph's Tomb**, at least by name; according to the book of Joshua (24,32) Joseph's bones were laid to rest instead at Shechem (Nablus today) after their transport from Egypt.

The entire rectangular building gives the impression of a massive fortress, and was built with typical architectural confidence by Herod the Great. The Arabs later made a mosque of it, and the Crusaders made it a church during their stay, adding the roof-top crenellations. In 1188 it was taken by Saladin and once more converted into a mosque.

Eight hundred years after Abraham, David was crowned King of Israel in Hebron, and he ruled from the city for several years before making it his capital. Among his sons born here was Absalom, his favourite, who was to lead a futile rebellion against his father years

later. With David's capture of Jerusalem from the Jebusites in 1000 BC the capital was also shifted, although Hebron would remain one of the four holy cities of Israel, along with Jerusalem, Tiberius and Safed.

The city's Jewish community survived the destruction of both Temples, until the year 1100, when it was expelled by the Crusaders. The population resurfaced and dwindled alternately over the centuries. In 1929 and again in 1936, the community was wiped out in anti-Jewish Arab riots, and it was not until 1967 that Jews re-entered Hebron. In 1968, a group of Jewish settlers gained *de facto* rights to settle the area, although not in Hebron's Arab centre. The result today is a suburb called **Kiryat Arba** (Hebron's name in Biblical time), overlooking the city from a nearby hill.

Both Jews and Muslims claim descent from Abraham, and the Hebron area and particularly the Tomb of the Patriarchs, is a centre of separate worship and mutual confrontation. Adding to the friction is the fact that a mosque

Blowing gla at Hebron.

now covers part of the site, which had at one time been a synagogue.

The situation in Hebron has been tense ever since the 1967 War, and Israeli soldiers are on constant patrol in the area. Violent clashes among Jews, Arabs and Israelis have riddled the town. During the summer of 1985, a few Likud-supported Knesset members staged a sit-in at an apartment opposite the Arab *shuk*. They were protesting the halt of settlement expansion and were evicted on the order of Israel's Defence Minister.

Due to sporadic unrest here, it is best to consult the Israeli Government Tourist Office in Jerusalem before travelling to Hebron. Be sure you have your return trip planned before you go, however: Hebron is the one place in the West Bank where you should not spend the night, tourist or not.

On the outskirts of Hebron stands the gnarled but living **Oak of Abraham**, believed to be some 600 years old. It is reputed to be the site where Abraham was visited by three angels who told him of Isaac's impending birth. It is

owned by Russian monks, who have a small monastery here. The ancient name for this place is Mamre; Abraham supposedly built an altar and a well here, and Herod's structure on the site was where Bar Kochba's defeated troops were sold into slavery.

North of Hebron, along the road to Bethlehem, lies the Etzion Bloc, where the agricultural-religious community of Kibbutz HaDati was founded in 1926. Abandoned in the Arab riots of 1929, it was resettled only to be thwarted again in the riots of 1936–39. In 1948 its persistent settlers were wiped out in Israel's War of Independence. The Etzion Bloc and the surrounding Hebron Hills were retaken by the Israeli army on 7 June 1967 and several months thereafter Kibbutz **Kfar Etzion** was resettled by the children of the original *kibbutzniks*. Today, the Etzion Bloc symbolises the perseverance of Jewish settlement in a hostile environment.

From Kfar Etzion, the highway leads directly back to Jerusalem once more, some 14 km (8½ miles) away.

eep dot
dean
lside in
ringtime.

# THE GAZA STRIP

The sandy strip of Gaza, 6 km (4 miles) wide and 45 km (28 miles) long, begins at the Shikma River in the north and extends to the Egyptian border at Rafa. Once a part of the seafaring Philistine federation, it was here that the illustrious Samson met the beguiling Delilah, who turned out to be his nemesis. And it was here that he was brought, when he was captured after numerous battles. "Let me die with the Philistines," he begged the Lord amid his celebrating captors, "And he bent with all his might; and the house fell upon the lords, and upon all the people therein." (Judges; 16, 17-30.)

According to Arab tradition, Samson is buried under the site of the Great Mosque, a structure built by the Crusaders in 1150 and transformed into a mosque by the Mamelukes. Gaza hosted Muslims, Crusaders, Turks, the British, even Napoleon's soldiers, since Samson's time. In 1948 Egyptian soldiers were perched on this gateway to Palestine, and Egypt retained control after Israel attained Independence.

Approximately 20 percent of the 700,000 Palestinian Arabs who were displaced in the fighting before and after 1948 ended up in Gaza. Egypt's President Nasser organised the first Fedayeen and encouraged their terrorism against Israel. Israel responded in 1956 with the Sinai Campaign, during which it briefly occupied the Sinai Peninsula and the Gaza Strip. In 1967 Israel seized the territory from Egypt again.

Now, no one seems to want Gaza; its squalid conditions are an accurate reminder of its hapless history. Gaza's status as the coastal eyesore arises from both Egypt's and Israel's decision not to decide about the territory or its inhabitants. For close to 40 years, Palestinian refugees have lived in UNRWA camps, designed for temporary accommodation. Today there are eight such camps.

Before travelling to Gaza it is important to keep abreast of current political events there and heed Israeli security measures, although the IDF is on constant, vigilant patrol. Meanwhile, white United Nations vans weave through the gleaming Mercedes and battered cars of the city streets. There is little to see by way of pleasing tourist sights, but the street life itself is an attraction here. Arab women in long black robes, plastic baskets balanced atop their heads, walk through the streets and camps, passing by children in crisp school uniforms. The city centres are busy with merchants selling a variety of wares: cotton clothing (the word "gauze" comes from Gaza, which was famous for its fine cottons), terracotta pottery (a local speciality), wicker furniture and mounds of camel-hair carpets.

Surprisingly, some 90 percent of households here have electricity, and the number with refrigerators, washing machines and TVs has increased dramatically during the years of Israeli administration. Still, Gaza falls far short of any promise for vitality. The fishing industry is flagging, due to the dusk-to-dawn curfew, and unemployment remains high.

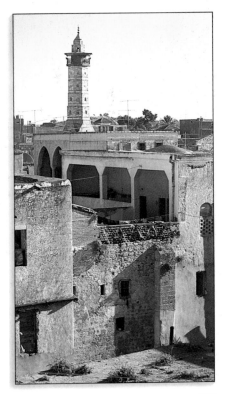

# THE DEAD SEA

Over the centuries, Christian pilgrims travelling here were aghast at the lifelessness they encountered and gave the Dead Sea its name. It's an apt one, for the most saline body of water on the face of the earth contains no life of any sort, and for most of its history there has been precious little life around it either. Yet today it is a source of both life and health: the potash contained in its bitter waters is an invaluable fertiliser, exported all over the world, while the lake and the springs that feed it have cured everything from arthritis to psoriasis since ancient times. Sun worshippers from Scandinavia and health nuts from Germany fill its spas and hotels, seeking remedies and relaxation. Today, many tourists and even Israelis are venturing here to breathe in the abundant oxygen, float on the water's salty surface, and marvel at the rugged panoramas.

Situated some 400 metres (1,300 ft) below sea level, in a geological fault that extends all the way to east Africa, the Dead Sea is the lowest point on the face of the globe, and is surrounded by the starkest scenery that Israel has to offer. Steep cliffs of reddish flint rise sharply to the west, contrasting with beige limestone buffs and the blinding white salt flats of the plain. Across the shimmering gold surface of the water to the east, the mauve and purple mountains of Biblical Moab and Edom are almost indistinguishable in the morning, gaining visibility through the day. In late afternoon, their wadis and canyons are heavily shadowed, forming a spectacular backdrop of ragged earth.

Mild and pleasant in winter time, the Dead Sea basin is an oven in summer. The hot air has an almost solid presence and the glare from the sun makes even the sunglass-wearer screw up his eyes.

The southern part of the Dead Sea has partly dried up, due to the use of the waters of the River Jordan by both Israel and Jordan. On the Israeli side, dykes built for the potash plant form a network of artificial lakes, designed for the extraction of chemicals, but also made use of by bathers.

The **Judean Desert**, the area between the hills of Judea and the Dead Sea, was traditionally a region of hermits, prophets and rebels. David hid there from Saul. The Hasmoneans, who raised the banner of Jewish independence from the Syrian-Greek empire in the 2nd century BC, regrouped there after their initial defeat. Jesus retired to the Judean desert to meditate and the Essenes established their community in its desolate wastes. The Jewish War against Rome of 66–73 AD started with the capture of the Judean desert fastness of Masada.

Israel's pre-1967 border with Jordan ran just north of Ein Gedi, about halfway up the western shore of the Dead Sea, which means that only the southern half of the Judean desert is in Israel proper. Some of the sites described here thus only became accessible to Israelis after the Six Day War of 1967, and may at some future date revert back to Arab administration.

**The scrolls of Qumran:** On the northwest shore of the Dead Sea, is the site of the Essene settlement of **Qumran**, where the famous Dead Sea scrolls were discovered. The Essenes, an ascetic Jewish sect of the Second Temple period, deliberately built their community in this inaccessible spot. It was destroyed by the Romans in AD 68.

In the early summer of 1947, a Bedouin shepherd was looking for a goat which had strayed by the shores of the Dead Sea. He threw a stone into one of the caves in the side of the cliff and heard it smashing pottery. Later, it transpired that he had made the most exciting archaeological discovery of the century: scrolls, dating to the first centuries BC and AD, preserved in earthenware jars.

Some of these documents were acquired by Israel in rather dramatic circumstances. Eliezar Sukenik, professor of archaeology at the Hebrew University, was offered the chance of buying a collection of ancient scrolls by an Armenian dealer. He was shown a fragment briefly and was impressed by its antiquity, but to see the collection, he had to travel to Bethlehem where they were stored. It was the period just prior to the establishment of the State of Israel, and Jerusalem was a war zone; Bethlehem was in the Arab-controlled area, and dangerous for Jews. Sukenik approached his son Yigael Yadin for advice. Yadin, an archaeologist himself, and at that time chief of operations of the new Israel Defence Forces, replied: "As an archaeologist, I urge you to go; as your son, I beg that you do not go; as chief of operations of the army, I forbid you to go!" Sukenik did go to Bethlehem, at considerable personal risk, and managed to buy three scrolls. He could not complete the purchase of the other four, which were eventually taken to the United States and later repurchased for Israel by Yadin.

Subsequent searches of the caves unearthed other scrolls and thousands of fragments, most of which are now on display in Israel, either in the Shrine of the Book, at the Israel Museum in Jerusalem, or at the Rockefeller Museum in the formerly Jordanian part of the city. They have revolutionised scholarship

of the Second Temple period and thrown new light on the origins of Christianity, indicating that Jesus may have been an Essene, or at least was strongly influenced by the sect. The scrolls have revealed the mood of Messianic fatalism among the Jews of that time, explaining both the emergence of Christianity and the fervour of the Jewish rebels in their hopeless war against Rome. The scrolls have also disclosed much about the nature of the Essene way of life and the beliefs of the sect, as well as revealing details of Temple ritual and worship.

The partly reconstructed buildings of Qumran are on a plateau some 100 metres (300 ft) above the shore and worth a visit. Numerous caves, including those where the scrolls were found, are visible in the nearby cliffs, but these are not accessible to the tourist.

The oasis of **Ein Feshkha**, where the Essenes grew their food, is 3 km (2 miles) to the south. Today it is a popular bathing site, where visitors can swim in the Dead Sea and later wash off the salt in the fresh water of the springs. Bathing in the Dead Sea is a unique experience: the swimmer bobs around like a cork, and it is possible to read a paper while sitting on the surface. The salinity of the water – 10 times as salty as the oceans – can make it very painful if the bather has a cut or scratch.

The Emperor Vespasian threw manacled slaves into the sea to test its buoyancy. The modern bather can be expected to show more courage: nonswimmers can float easily, but they must be careful to maintain their balance. The bitter taste of even a drop can linger all day and a mouthful of Dead Sea water is an experience that should be avoided.

Some 19 km (12 miles) south of Qumran is the new kibbutz of **Mitzpe Shalem**. The original site, on a cliff overlooking the sea, has been converted into a field school. Past the school there is access to the steepsided **Murabbat Canyon**, which contains caves where other 1st and 2nd-century scrolls were discovered. The canyon descends to the Dead Sea, but at that point it is sheer and unclimbable. A walk down the canyon from the field school is a memorable

**Qumran Cave**

experience, but not to be undertaken alone. Would-be hikers are advised to go in a group from the school, with expert guides.

Also found in the Murabbat caves were fragments relating to a later revolt against Rome in AD 132–135, led by Simon Bar-Kochba, including a letter written by Bar-Kochba himself to one of his commanders.

**Where David hid from Saul:** Less than 15 km (8 miles) further south is the lush oasis of **Ein Gedi**, site of a kibbutz, a nature reserve and another field school. A particularly beautiful spot, with the greenery creeping up the steep cliffs beside the springs, Ein Gedi is the home of a large variety of birds, and animals, including gazelles, ibex, oryx, foxes, jackals and even a few leopards.

The most popular site for hiking and bathing is **David's Spring**, which leads up to a beautiful waterfall, fringed in ferns, where tradition says David hid from King Saul, when he was the victim of one of the king's paranoid rages. "Then Saul took three thousand chosen

men out of all Israel, and went to seek David and his men upon the rocks of the wild goats." (I Sam; 24, 2) According to the biblical account, Saul went into the very cave where David was hiding and, as Saul slept, David cut off a piece of the king's robe, proving he could have killed him but desisted. A tearful reconciliation followed.

On most days, summer and winter, the area around David's Spring is thronged with visitors, so the more energetic may prefer to hike along the course of **Nahal Arugot**, a kilometre south. This canyon is full of wildlife and has several deep pools for bathing.

Kibbutz Ein Gedi runs a guest house and a spa for bathing in Dead Sea water and nearby sulphur springs. A camping site, youth hostel and restaurant are situated on the shore below the kibbutz.

A little further south is the canyon of **Nahal Hever**. Of particular interest here are the **Cave of Horror**, where 40 skeletons of men, women and children from the time of the Bar-Kochba revolt were discovered, and the nearby **Cave**

atching up
current
ents.

**of Letters**, in which 15 letters written by Bar-Kochba to his commanders were found. As with Murabbat, visitors are not advised to climb to the caves alone.

**Masada:** About 20 km (12 miles) south of Ein Gedi, towering almost 300 metres (1,000 ft) above the Dead Sea shore, is the rock of **Masada**, the most spectacular archaeological site in Israel. Part of the line of cliffs which rise up to the Judean desert plateau, Masada is cut off from the surrounding area by steep wadis to the north, south and west.

It was on this desolate mesa that Herod the Great built an impregnable fortress as a retreat from his potentially rebellious subjects. Visitors to the site can wander through the magnificent three-tiered palace which extends down the northern cliff, the Roman bath house, with its ingenious heating system, the vast storehouses, the western palace with its fine mosaics and the huge water cisterns hewn in the rock. They can appreciate the remarkable desert landscape from the summit, which can be easily climbed from the west via the Roman ramp, ascended by cable-car from the east, or more energetically climbed via the "Snake Path," also from the east.

These features alone make the fortress worth a visit, but it is the story of the epic siege of the fortress in the Jewish War against Rome which has made Masada a place of pilgrimage second only to the Western Wall.

In 66 AD, a group of Jewish rebels called the Sicarii (named after the sica, dagger, their favourite weapon) seized Masada from its Roman garrison, triggering the Jewish War against Rome. Securing their base there, the Sicarii proceeded to Jerusalem, where they took over the leadership of the revolt. In the bitter infighting between the rebel groups, their leader was killed and they returned to Masada to regroup.

The new Sicarii leader, Elazar Ben-Yair, waited out the war at Masada, joined from time to time by other groups. He was still in possession after the fall of Jerusalem in AD 70. In 73, the Roman Tenth Legion arrived to put an end to this last Jewish stronghold.

**Left**, shaft of light punctures cistern at Masada. **Below**, Ibex has free rein at Ein Gedi.

With its auxiliaries and camp followers, the legion numbered over 15,000. Defending Masada were fewer than 1,000 Jewish men, women and children. Herod's store rooms were still well supplied. The Romans destroyed the aqueduct feeding the cisterns from dams in the wadi, but the cisterns had enough water for a prolonged period and were accessible from the summit.

The legion constructed a wall around the rock, reinforced by camps, which blocked the main possible escape routes and then built an earth ramp, reinforced by wooden beams and shielded by stone, which pointed like a dagger at the perimetre wall of the fortress.

The final defences were set on fire, and when the blaze died down, the Romans entered Masada to discover the bodies of the defenders laid out in rows. Repudiating defeat and refusing slavery, the men had first killed their own families and then themselves, drawing lots for a final 10 to carry out the act, one last electee killing the other nine and finally killing himself.

This account in *The Jewish War* by Flavius Josephus has become one of the legends of modern Israel. In recognition of the symbolic importance of the site, young soldiers being inducted into the armored corps today swear their oath of allegiance atop the fortress and vow: "Masada shall not fall again!"

The excavations by Yigael Yadin in the 1960s uncovered the magnificence of Herod's fortress and palaces, but the most moving finds were of the Zealots' living quarters in the casement wall, their synagogue and ritual baths, the remains of the fire, and, in some cases, bits of their final meal. The skeletons of a man, woman and child were uncovered in the northern palace; more were found in a nearby cave, where they had apparently been thrown by the Romans.

The country caught its collective breath when the discovery was announced of a set of inscribed pottery shards, which might have been the lots cast by the defenders to decide which of them would kill the others. One of them was inscribed "Ben-Yai".

The eerie of
Masada rises
above Dead
Sea and
desert.

**Sodom's soothing spas:** Ensconced along the shore just north of biblical Sodom, the resorts of **Ein Bokek** and **Neve Zohar** attract health-seekers from across the globe, with a wide range of accommodations based around their fabled mineral springs. Famous since the 1st century AD, the healing waters are believed to cure a spectrum of ailments, from skin disease to lumbago, arthritis and rheumatism. The clinics, run by doctors and nurses, offer sulphur baths, mineral baths, salt baths, mud baths, massage and exercise programmes; the prices range from fairly reasonable to five-star hotels, where the spas are actually on the premises.

Don't miss the mud if you do stay; Cleopatra is said to have sent slaves here to fetch it for her, and even today Dead Sea Mud has become a sought-after export as a natural moisturiser.

There is a peaceful atmosphere about modern **Sodom**, which despite its oppressive heat, makes it an unexpectedly calm place to swim, stroll or sun. This is in stark contrast with the legendary "cities of sin", Sodom and Gomorrah, which in the Bible were destroyed with fire and brimstone for the decadence and sexual perversion of their inhabitants. The Bible is rather coy regarding the exact nature of these "sins", but homosexuality and buggery are implied (originating the term "sodomite").

According to the story, Lot, Abraham's nephew, pleaded with God to spare the cities and was allowed to escape with his family, but his wife looked back to view the destruction and was turned into a pillar of salt. On the Dead Sea shore there is a cave with a hollow tower. Called **Lot's Wife**, the pillar is said to be remains of that illustrious lady. Take a walk inside, lick your finger, and taste the salt.

Further south, looking like a lunar base against a moonscape, the conveyor belts, funnels and ovens of the **Dead Sea Works** grind and roar day and night. Around it rises an eerie skeletal scaffolding. Huge articulated trucks move ponderously out of the yard, hauling the potash, magnesium and salt down the

Cult basin at Tel Arad.

Arava to Eilat, or up the ridge to the railway and export at Ashdod port.

**Arad, old and new:** Between the spas and the chemical plant, a road wends westward into the mountains, climbing over 1,000 metres (3,280 ft) in less than 25 km (15 miles), to **Arad**, Israel's first planned town.

Arad has a history of human habitation going back 5,000 years, but while modern Arad is constructed on an elevation near the Dead Sea, to ensure a mild climate, the historic settlement is set in farming land, some 8 km (5 miles) further west. The ancient mound of **Tel Arad** has been excavated and partly reconstructed. Sections of a Canaanite town of the third millennium BC have been found, with pottery from the First Dynasty in Egypt, indicating trade between the two nations at that time.

A 10th-century BC fortress of the time of King Solomon was the next settlement. Far smaller than the original Canaanite city, the Israelite enclosure contained a sanctuary modelled on the Temple in Jerusalem, with a courtyard, outer chamber, and Holy of Holies, the only one of its kind ever discovered. Experts say it conforms to the stipulation in the book of Exodus: "Five cubits long and five cubits broad, the altar shall be four square."

Archaeologists found the remains of a burnt substance in two smaller altars inside the Holy of Holies, which analysis showed to be traces of animal fat, indicating sacrifices. This is consistent with the denunciations of the prophets, recorded in the Bible, of continuing sacrifices on the "high places"; King Hezekiah, who ruled Judah from 720 to 692 BC, heeded the advice and "removed the high places and brake the images."

Modern Arad, established in 1961, was the most ambitious "new town" project of its time. It was envisioned as housing health and tourism resorts as well as regional industries. It was well-placed to utilise the natural reserves, archaeological sites and mineral spas at the Dead Sea, and offered dry desert air, suitable for the treatment of asthma.

Architecturally, Arad was conceived as a fortress against the desert: the buildings were grouped around squares; the paved walkways were shaded by houses; greenery was planted in small concentrations which did not require too much water. The six basic neighbourhoods and town centre were less than a mile across. Arad is an interesting example of theory being changed by practice. It was initially assumed that the inhabitants would wish to cluster together in the desert environment, but this did not prove to be the case and the planners were forced to modify their designs to meet demand for more space.

The opposite of improvised Beersheba, Arad is the epitome of planned pioneering: the rational creation of a town, adapted to the desert and utilising its resources.

King Uzziah, the Bible records, "built towers in the wilderness." Constructed only a few miles from where the king built, the apartment blocks of Arad are Israel's new towers in the desert. The two Arads are a symbol of today's Israel: a modern community arising where an ancient one used to exist.

njoying the
ead Sea's
ealing mud.

# NEGEV: THE SOUTHERN DESERT

The very name Negev conjures up an image of the rugged outdoors, jeeps, camels, frontiersmen – an unforgiving expanse of bleak wastes, sunlight and sharp, dry air. In fact, it is every bit as vast and intimidating as it sounds, containing 60 percent of Israel's land area, but holding less than 10 percent of its population. Yet the Negev is far from barren: it supports successful agricultural communities, a sprawling "capital", a complex desert ecosystem, and – since Israel relinquished the Sinai in 1982 – a variety of defence activities.

The Hebrew word means "parched," and the Negev is indeed a desert, with rainfall varying from an annual average of 30 cm (12 inches) in the north to almost zero in Eilat. But don't envisage expanses of white sand and palm trees, like in old Rudolph Valentino movies; Israel's desert is entirely different.

The northern and western Negev is a dusty plain, slashed with wadis, dried-up river beds which froth with occasional winter flash floods. To the south are the bleak flint, limestone, chalk, dolomite and granite mountains, with the Arava valley to the east dividing them from Biblical Edom, today part of Jordan.

Although a desert, the Negev, like the rest of Israel, is saturated with history. In prehistoric times, the area was well watered and settled. It was subsequently dessicated; but by the Chalcolithic period, in the 4th millennium BC, communities had sprung up in the wadis around Beersheba.

At the time of Abraham, around 2,000 BC, the area was inhabited by nomadic tribes. When the Children of Israel left Egypt in the 13th century BC, the warlike Amalekites blocked their path to the Promised Land, setting back their settlement by decades. Joshua eventually did conquer Canaan, and awarded the Negev to the tribe of Simeon, but only the northern part was settled.

King David extended Israelite rule over the entire Negev in the 10th century BC and his son Solomon constructed a string of forts to defend it. Solomon also developed the famous copper mines at Timna, and his southern port of Etzion Geber, today's Eilat. After the division of the kingdom into Israel and Judah, the area was occupied by the Edomites, who were expelled by the Nabateans in the 1st century BC. In the Middle Ages, it was an important Byzantine centre.

In the following centuries the Negev remained the domain of nomadic Bedouin tribes, until the start of Zionist immigration to Palestine in the 1880s. However, it was not until 1939 that the first successful kibbutz, Negba, northwest of Beersheba, was established. Three other outposts were created in 1943, also in the western Negev, and a further 11 were thrown up on a single day in 1946.

The Jews fought hard for the inclusion of the Negev in the new State of Israel, and the UN partition plan of 1947 awarded most of the area to the Jewish state. The rest was won in the War of Independence of 1948, when the Egyptian and Transjordanian armies were expelled in the fighting.

David Ben-Gurion, Israel's first prime minister, was a passionate believer in the development of the Negev, and went to live in what was then a tiny, isolated kibbutz, Sde Boker, in the heart of the desert, when he retired from politics. He was buried there in 1973.

**Capital of the Negev:** Although it has become comparatively civilised, **Beersheba** still possesses something of its old frontier atmosphere: brash, bustling, and bursting with energy. Big trucks park in the main streets; open jeeps drive through the centre; sunburned men with scuffed boots and dust in their hair drink beer in the sidewalk cafés; young soldiers sip their colas, wait for rides and monopolise the public telephones. You don't see too many suits or ties here – even in winter.

Despite planners' efforts to create a new centre further east, the "old city" remains the real centre of town. The unusual rectangular formation of its streets was the work of a German engineer, who served with the Turkish army in the years before World War I. The rest of Beersheba is more spread out, a monument to the great improvisation phase of Israel's development, laid out as if it were an English garden city, without consideration of the special climatic and topographical condition.

But the town, thrown up hastily while Israel was doubling its population with an influx of Jews from Europe and the Middle East, couldn't have been built any other way. There was no time for proper planning. Today, with a population of 150,000, a flourishing industrial base, a university, hospital, medical school, music conservatory, dance school, orchestra and arts centre, Beersheba is Israel's fourth largest city. If it is a mess, it is a triumphant mess.

Beersheba serves as the capital of the Negev, providing services for the surrounding population. The regional offices of the companies extracting potash, phosphates, magnesium, salt and lime are all located here, alongside new factories for everything from ceramics to pesticides.

An immigrant community in every sense of the word, Beersheba holds people from more than 70 countries, the earlier immigrants from Romania and Morocco rubbing shoulders with more recent arrivals from Argentina and the Soviet Union. An Arab town until 1948, it is today a predominantly Jewish community; but several hundred Bedouin have moved here from the surrounding area and form an important part of the population.

Every Thursday morning, there is a **Bedouin market** on the southern edge of town, for which a special structure has been built. The Bedouin still trade their camels, sheep and goats here; but in recent years it has become primarily a tourist attraction, providing opportunity for the purchase of all kinds of Bedouin arts and crafts.

The name Beersheba means "well of the swearing", in memory of the pact sworn between the patriarch Abraham and Abimelech, a local ruler, in which Abraham secured the use of a well to water his flocks. There is a dispute as to the location of the actual Well of the Swearing. The traditional site is at the bottom of the main street in the old town; but more recently archaeologists have suggested it to be the 40-metre (130-ft) well excavated at the site of **Tel Beersheba**, some 6 km (4 miles) east of the modern city.

The **Ben-Gurion University of the Negev**, founded here in 1969, is the only one of Israel's universities to offer courses in humanities, sciences, engineering and medicine. The university has transformed the town from a desert backwater into a modern community, with its own sinfonietta orchestra and light opera group.

The **Beersheba Museum**, housed in a former mosque in the old town, has a good display of archaeological artifacts. The city also boasts a youth hostel, hotels of all standards and several good restaurants, including ones specialising in Moroccan, Romanian and South American cuisine, reflecting the makeup of the population.

About a mile to the east, overlooking the city, is the **Memorial to the Negev**

Spools of thread on offer at Bedouin market in Beersheba.

**Brigade of the Palmach**, which captured Beersheba in the War of Independence. Designed by sculptor Dani Karavan, who spent five years on the project, its trenches, bunkers, pillboxes and tower (through which visitors are encouraged to climb and crawl) create a claustrophobic atmosphere of siege. The sinuous concrete edifice is a worthy commemoration of the bitter battle for the Negev between the Egyptian army and the fledgling Israeli forces backing the kibbutz outposts on the 1948 war.

South of the monument is the country's only animal hospital, which is attached to the life sciences department of Ben-Gurion University. It includes a camel clinic.

Southeast of the hospital, next to ancient Tel Beersheba, is **Tel Sheva**, a modern village built for the local Bedouin. It is the first of five Bedouin villages in the Negev gradually replacing the traditional tented camps of the nomads, which as a rule are spread out over a large area. In the village, high-walled courtyards separate the houses,

in an attempt to preserve as much privacy as possible.

The concept was developed by an Arab architect and its logic seems unassailable; but in fact the Bedouin were not keen on Tel Sheva initially, and subsequent development has encouraged the former nomads to build their own homes. Israel's Bedouin claim large tracts of the desert over which they formerly grazed their herds; but the lands were never registered, and this has led to disputes with the government. In most cases, the Bedouin have been given title to the land around their camps. Where the land has been appropriated by the government, as in the case of the **Nevatim Airforce Base** east of Beersheba, monetary compensation has been awarded in its stead.

There is a Bedouin school at Tel Sheva, and nearly all the children receive elementary education. More recently a Bedouin high school was built and there are a number of Bedouin students at Ben-Gurion University. The first Bedouin doctor to graduate in Israel,

**turistic rary at ersheba's n-Gurion iversity.**

Yunis Abu-Rabia, is now in charge of the region's health services.

There are three main routes leading south from Beersheba to Eilat, Israel's pleasure resort on the Red Sea. The main highway leads down the eastern side of the Negev, through the Arava valley, and that is the one to take if your aim is simply reaching the sunny beaches. A narrow, beautiful, scenic road goes through the middle of the desert; a third road, the most recently constructed, travels along the Sinai border with Egypt to the west.

The traveller may well feel that the Negev between Beersheba and Eilat is a mythical badland dividing Israel from the Red Sea paradise to the south, an impression reinforced by a rapid drive (or flight) to Eilat; but there is plenty to see on all three routes.

**The Arava:** The eastern route takes you past the moshav of Nevatim, settled in the early 1950s by Jews from Cochin in southern India. Even in the Israeli population kaleidoscope, these beautiful, dark-skinned people stood out as "more different" than the others. In the past few years, they have become famous for growing winter flowers, exported by air to Europe. This industry, which takes advantage of the mild desert climate, has been taken up by others and become a major Israeli export.

Further east, the development towns of **Yeroham** and **Dimona**, built in the mid-1950s, were settled primarily by immigrants from North Africa. Yeroham boasts a new park, 10 km (6 miles) south of the road, which should one day become a startling green patch in the arid gray-brown wasteland; but so far the dust tends to dominate the man-high trees. Nearby is an artificial lake, created by a dammed wadi, fed by the winter rains. A huge variety of birds migrates across the Mediterranean coast from Africa to Europe in the spring and returns in the autumn; Israel is one of their favourite way stations.

Between Yeroham and Dimona, the dome of Israel's Atomic Research Station looms in the plain behind its numerous protective barbed-wire fences.

Happy cam■
cluster
quizzically ■
midday drir

Just past Dimona, is the ancient site of **Mamshit**, called Kurnab by the Arabs. A fine example of a Nabatean site of the 1st century it contains the remains of two beautiful Byzantine churches, and a network of ancient dams.

South of the road is the **Machtesh Gadol** (large crater) a spectacular geological fault, and, further east, the **Machtesh Katan** (small crater): less extensive, but more beautiful, with geological layers exposed in some locations like a rainbow cake. Their origin is unknown. One theory ascribes the Negev craters to volcanic activity; another suggests the fall of large meteors in the distant past.

The old road south – today a dirt-track – cuts through the desert south of the small crater, connecting with the Arava valley via **Scorpions' Pass**. The most spectacular road in the southern desert, it plunges down a series of dizzying loops that follow each other with frightening suddenness. To the right are the heights of the Negev, great slabs of primeval rock, slammed together in a

giant's sandwich. Below are the purple-gray lunar formations of the **Valley of Zin**, with the square-shaped hillock of Hor Hahar rising up from the valley floor. Be warned: the rusty metal drums that line the road have not been able to prevent accidents. It should be negotiated slowly with a four-wheel-drive vehicle, or on foot.

The main road reaches the Arava valley south of the Dead Sea, opposite the moshav farming village of **Neot Hakikar**. Situated in the salt marshes and utilising brakish water, it has become one of the most successful settlements in Israel, exporting a variety of winter vegetables to Europe.

In the 1960s Neot Hakikar was settled by an eccentric group of desert lovers, who established a private company. As initial attempts at farming the area proved less than successful, they set up a desert touring company for trips by camel and jeep to the less accessible locations of the Negev. Those initial settlers eventually abandoned the village; but their company (still called Neot

*lds of
*eat ready
* harvest in
*stern
*gev.*

Hakikar) continues to thrive, with offices in Tel Aviv and Eilat.

Similar tours are run by the Society for the Protection of Nature in Israel, which, among its noteworthy spectrum of activities, offers a four-day camel tour starting at Ein Yahav, a *moshav* some 80 km (50 miles) south.

The road through the Arava is bordered by the flint and limestone ridges of the Negev to the west; 19 km (12 miles) to the east tower the magnificent mountains of Edom in Jordan, which are capped with snow in winter. These mountains change colour during the day from pale mauve in the morning, to pink, red and deep purple in the evening, their canyons and gulleys etched in grey.

About 130 km (80 miles) further south, past another dozen *moshavim* and *kibbutzim*, and a small "**snake zoo**," is kibbutz **Yotvata**, with its unique **Hai Bar Nature Reserve**. At this unusual game park, conservationists have imported and bred a variety of animals mentioned in the Bible and which had become locally extinct; wild asses, ostriches and numerous varieties of gazelle included. A holiday village, with modest but comfortable accommodations, swimming pools and mini market is available for visitors. Also at the site is the **Arava Visitors' Center** with a museum and audio-visual display of the desert. **Ketura**, a kibbutz some 16 km (10 miles) to the north, offers riding.

**Timna**, 24 km (15 miles) further south is the site of **King Solomon's Mines**, a little to the south of the modern copper mine. The ancient, circular stone ovens for roasting the copper ore look simple enough, with stone channels to the collection vessels for the metal, but the air channels were skilfully angled to catch the prevailing north wind, which comes down the Arava. The late archaeologist Nelson Gleuck, who excavated the mines, called the ventilation system "an ancient example of automation."

The area surrounding the mines is being developed as a national park, with an artificial lake and a network of roads – including a fine scenic route in the northeast of the park to facilitate tour-

**King Solomon's Mines at Timna.**

ing. Highlights include the massive **Pillars of Solomon**, a natural formation of Nubian sandstone, and the redoubtable **Mushroom Rock**: a granite rock shaped like a mushroom. Also here are the time-worn remains of a settlement, a fortress and two Egyptian sanctuaries used by the ancient mine workers.

**The western Negev:** West from Beersheba the desert is flat and dull, more for settlement than for tourism. It is an area of cotton and potatoes and extensive wheat fields, irrigated by the run-off of the National Water Carrier which ends in this area and Beersheba.

The first Negev kibbutzim were built in this region in the 1940s and after the peace treaty with Egypt, some of Israel's northern Sinai settlements were moved to **Pit'hat Shalom** (the Peace Region) next to the international border in 1982. East of these villages is the **Eshkol Park**, 750 acres of trees, lawns and playing fields with an amphitheatre, swimming pool and a natural pond, surrounded by cattails and cane and stocked with fish.

The Western Negev road, which goes south from this region, is designated as a "military area", as it is right on the Egyptian border and travellers using it have to fill in forms provided by the military. Since the peace treaty with Egypt, it is not regarded as dangerous; but the army wants to know who is using it so that travellers are not stranded there after dark. The southern sector of the road winds attractively through the Negev mountains, providing some spectacular views of Sinai to the west and the Negev to the east.

**The Negev Plateau:** The most interesting route south is also the oldest and least convenient; but it passes a number of interesting sites, the first of which is **Sde Boker**, some 49 km (30 miles) south of Beersheba. The kibbutz was the final home of David Ben-Gurion, Israel's first prime minister, and his wife, Paula. Their simple, cream-coloured tombstones, which overlook the **Wilderness of Zin**, is a place of pilgrimage for Israeli youth movements and foreign admirers. The old man is said to have

e
shroom
k.

personally selected his burial place with its view of beige and mustard limestone hills, the flint rocks beyond, the delicate mauve of Edom in the hazy distance.

The Sde Boker College south of the kibbutz is divided into three sections: the Institute for Arid Zone Research, which coordinates desert biology, agriculture and architecture; the Ben-Gurion Institute, which houses all the first prime minister's papers and records, and the Center of the Environment, which runs a field school and a high school with emphasis on environmental studies.

South of the college is **Ein Avdat**, a steep-sided canyon with freshwater pools fringed with lush vegetation. Rock badgers, gazelles and a wide variety of birds inhabit this oasis, where the water is remarkably cold even in the heat of summer. A swim can be refreshing, but the water is deep and sometimes it is difficult to climb out on the slippery rocks. Lone hikers should not take the risk, and a party of visitors should take it in turns, leaving some out of the water to haul out their companions. There are

paths up the sides of the cliffs, with iron rungs and railings in the difficult parts.

A few miles further south is **Avdat**, site of the Negev's main Nabatean city, built in the 2nd century BC. Situated on a limestone hill above the surrounding desert, Avdat was excavated and partly reconstructed in the early 1950s. With its impressive buildings, burial caves, a kiln, workshop and two Byzantine churches, it is one of the most rewarding sites in the country; but what makes it fascinating is the reconstruction of the Nabatean and Byzantine agriculture.

An Arab tribe, the Nabateans, dominated the Negev and Edom in the first centuries BC and AD. With their capital at Petra (in the Kingdom of Jordan today), their achievements in farming the desert are unsurpassed. Their technique was based on the run-off systems of irrigation. Little rain falls in this part of the desert, but when it does, it is not absorbed by the local loess soil; it cuts gulleys and wadis, running in torrents to the Mediterranean in the west and the Dead Sea and the Arava in the east. The

*Irrigation puⁱ a belt of green vegetation through the Negev.*

run-off system collects this water in a network of fields and terraces, fed by dams, channels and slopes. Variations include gently sloped fields in which each tree has its own catchment area. Botanist Michael Evenari, working with archaeologists and engineers, has reconstructed Avdat and two other farms, growing a variety of crops without the help of piped water: fodder, wheat, onions, carrots, asparagus, artichokes, apricots, grapes, peaches, almonds, peanuts and pistachios among them.

What started as research into ancient agriculture has proved to be relevant to the modern era, as the system could provide valuable foodstuffs in arid countries of the third world using only existing desert resources, thus preserving the delicate ecological balances.

Some 45 km (28 miles) west of Avdat of the Beersheba Nizzana is Shivta, another Nebatean city later rebuilt by the Byzantines in the 5th century. Although less accessible, it is still quite well-preserved with three churches, a wine press and several public areas still intact. **Nizzana** 25 km (16 miles) further west at the intersection of the Western Highway is one of three active border crossings to Egypt.

Further into the desert, and further back in time, lie the venerable walls of some 40-odd strongholds built by King Solomon to guard his route to Timna and his port of **Etzion Geber**. After the peace treaty with Egypt, 20 of these fortresses were partly excavated in a "rescue operation" mounted by the Department of Antiquities, in advance of the redeployment of the army in the Negev. Sustained by Solomon's decisive authority, they were destroyed shortly after his death, and never rebuilt. The one exception is the fort of **Kadesh Barnea**, some 35 km (21 miles) west of the road, rebuilt in the 8th century BC during the temporary resurgence of Judea under King Uzziah.

A number of the strongholds are close to the road, including **Ritma** and **Halukim** north of Sde Boker, and **Mishor Haruh**, further south. In general, it is advisable to visit such sites in the company of a trained guide.

A half hour south of Avdat is the development town of **Mitzpe Ramon**, perched at an elevation of 1,000 metres (3,280 ft) along the northern edge of the **Machtesh Ramon** – the largest of the three craters in the Negev, at 40 km (25 miles) long and 12 km (7½ miles) wide. Despite its enormity, the crater comes into view quite suddenly: an awesome sight. Among the finds here have been fossilised plants and preserved dinosaur footprints, dating back 200 million years to the Triassic and Jurassic periods. The town has an observatory connected with Tel Aviv University, which takes advantage of the dry desert air. In the Ramon crater, a geological trail displays the melting pot of minerals in the area, evident from the patches of yellow, rush, ochre, purple, and even green that tint the landscape.

To the south lies the **Paran Valley**, the most spectacular of the Negev wadis, which runs into the Arava. The road twists through the timeless desert scenery, before joining the southern part of the Arava road on its way to Eilat.

e astro-
servatory
Mitzpe
mon.

# EILAT: GATEWAY TO THE RED SEA

Eilat is remote. It is searing hot and parched dry. The cultural diversions are negligible and a geological fault runs through town. There's neither casino, nor racetrack nor concert hall.

Nevertheless, Eilat is one of Israel's most popular tourist resorts. Vacationers migrate, like tens of thousands of lemmings, instinctively to its sunburnt shores and soothing seas. What's more, a good percentage of these vacationers are Israelis who know the best places in the country for spending a holiday.

Some Israelis going to Eilat claim they're vacationing *hutz l'aretz* – abroad. Others simply say they're off to *sof olam* – the end of the world. And anyone who drives from the populated central part of Israel across that "Great Bald Spot" known as the Negev Desert, might be inclined to agree with them.

Eilat is Israel's southernmost community. It is the Jewish State's flipper-hold on the Red Sea. It is also a Mecca (if such a word might be used in Israel) for snorkellers, windsurfers, water-skiers, swimmers, sailors, sandcastle builders, bikini-watchers, sun worshippers, tropical-fish fanatics, bird watchers and other dilettantes.

Eitlat's single significant industry lies in assisting visitors to do nothing productive. It is a sensual city which caters to people who like magnificent natural beauty, lazy afternoons, spicy food and cold beer.

**First city:** Eilatis whimsically call their town Israel's "First City", because it was the first piece of modern Israel's real estate to be occupied by the Children of Israel after the Exodus from Egypt (Deut; 2, 8). Like most Eilatis, though, Moses was only a tourist; he moved north to find milk and honey soon afterwards.

A few centuries later, King Solomon built a port here and called it **Etzion Geber**. With the help of his friend King Hiram of Phoenecia, the wise monarch sent a fleet of ships eastward, to the land of Ophir, "and fetched from thence gold, four hundred and twenty talents, and brought it to King Solomon." (I Kings: 9, 26). Since there were about 3,000 shekels to the talent, and about a half-ounce to the shekel, those sailors must have lugged something like 20 tons of gold back via Eilat to Jerusalem.

Eilat changed hands many times over the following centuries. The Edomites grabbed it for a while, and then King Uzziah grabbed it back for the Israelites. The Syrians later wrested it away from him. A succession of conquerors marched through – Nabateans, Greeks, Romans, Mamelukes, Crusaders, Ottoman Turks and a bunch of others. (The Crusaders left behind their 12th-century fortress at **Coral Island** just south of Taba.) The celebrated colonel T. E. Lawrence, better known as Lawrence of Arabia, trekked through here after his conquest of Akaba across the bay.

The most recent army to "conquer" Eilat was the Israel Defence Forces which swooped down on this exotic pearl during Operation Uvda in March,

1949, and scared the dickens out of several sleepy lizards and a cranky tortoise inhabiting the ruins of Umm Rashrash – an uninhabited mudbrick "police station" which stood all alone in what is now the centre of town.

Although the United Nations had allocated Eilat to Israel in its partition plan, the War of Independence capture of this corner of the Promised Land was so hastily organised that the Israeli troops arrived without a flag to proclaim the land as part of their new state. Thus a soldier with artistic talent was issued a bed sheet and a bottle of blue ink with which to produce one Israeli flag of appropriate dimension and design.

**Development town:** The new flag didn't fly over very much, but Israeli authorities knew that Eilat was located at a very strategic position and quick steps were taken to create a town.

Eilat's position was strategic because it was Israel's only access to the Indian and Pacific oceans, and trade with Asia, East Africa, Australia and the islands including vital oil supplies from pre-revolutionary Iran. Holding on to Eilat also meant a break in land continuity between Egypt and Jordan, thus offering a military advantage to defence.

In the rush to create a city on the Red Sea, Eilat's builders didn't invest very much in architectural masterpieces. Instead, they wanted fast, simple, sturdy construction of apartments to house immigrants trickling in as survivors of the Holocaust in Europe, and the great waves of Jews who were being expelled by newly created Arab states such as Iraq and Yemen. Visitors to Eilat can see some of the older 1950s apartment buildings still standing like concrete bastions on the hillside. They're still quite serviceable and occupied by Eilati families who have affectionate nicknames for them, such as "Sing Sing" and "La Bastille".

As the city expanded, other neighbourhoods grew further up the slopes of the Eilat Mountains. Improved architecture did not spare them from satirical nicknames. One neighbourhood built about a kilometre up a steep hill west of the centre of town is locally know as the "Onesh" district. In Hebrew, *onesh* means "punishment" and anybody who walks this distance from the centre of town on a hot day will appreciate the appropriateness of this sobriquet. In recent years, prosperity has produced colonies of villas around town, unleashing a new generation of cognomens which are still to stand the test of time.

**Crisis and boom:** Egypt's Gamal Abdal Nasser realised the strategic value of Eilat and its potential for becoming a multi-million-dollar tourist playground. He planned that Eilat would be one of his first conquests in the 1967 War.

In May of that year, he again imposed a blockade on Eilat and shut down its shipping – including the vital oil supplies from Iran. Next, he ordered the UN peace-keeping forces out of Sinai, and moved his own army into the mountains northwest of Eilat, within clear view of Jordan. With one quick push, he could have cut off Eilat, linked-up with the Jordanian Arab Legion, and created a solid, integrated southern front against Israel. Eilat was in an extremely vulner-

Dutch tourist takes in the fun and sun a beachside.

314

able position for a few days, until the Israeli pre-emptive strike against Egyptian air fields deprived Nasser of the vital air cover his troops would need. The following six days witnessed Israel's lightning conquest of Sinai and the removal of military threats against Eilat.

Shortly after the Six Day War, terror infiltration from Jordanian territory near Eilat caused apprehension. There were several incidents. People were killed. Eilat remained unattractive for tourism, immigration and development until the charismatic Moshe Dayan flew there to make a speech intended for the ears of Jordan's King Hussein. Further infiltration of terrorists from Jordan would indicate to Israel that the Jordanian armed forces were incapable of maintaining a secure border, Dayan said. If this became the case, he added, the Israel Defence Forces would have to do the job for them by entering Jordanian territory – including the port city of Akaba if need be – to stem the incursions.

The Jordanian monarch got the message and border security improved tremendously and immediately. Assured of security, Eilat blossomed. The past decade has catapulted the city into success, with an ever-expanding tourist business, a population of close to 50,000 and a busy downtown, its **Modern Art Museum**, a sheltered lagoon and marina, and a shorefront of hotels.

Many of the tourists are Israelis who drive the six-hour trans-desert trek from Jerusalem and Tel Aviv for their autumn, winter or spring holiday. But most are foreigners who have discovered that several charter groups fly directly from major European airports to Eilat, where they discharge their passengers within sight of the beach and its many hotels. Arkia, Israel's domestic airline, also operates several flights a day from here to Israel and the Sinai.

**Plenty of rocks:** An adage grew up among Eilatis: "If we could export rocks, we'd all be millionaires!" The key to Eilat's tourism has been to twist the adage to bring the foreigners to the rocks. Nearly all of these rocks are Precambrian. formed by the forces of the

o ways of
tting the
ter.

earth in the epochs before the beginning of life on the planet. Aeons ago, they were beach-front real estate facing to the north, where the ancient Tethys Sea flowed over what is now the Land of Israel. To the south extended the primordial megacontinent of Gondwanaland. (Gondwanaland eventually drifted apart to form India, Africa, South America, Australia and Antarctica, and the bed of the Tethys Sea was pushed up to form the bedrock of Israel).

Geologists are forever pottering about the Eilat Mountains, picking at chunks of granite, gneiss, quartz-porphyry and diabase. In some places, they are after an attractive rock which they call $CuCo_3.Cu(OH)_2$. Merchants in town call this bluish-green malachite Eilat Ston, a type of copper ore which can be shaped and given a high polish. In fact, this stone has been used in jewellery-making in the region for thousands of years, and is still very evident in many Eilat tourist shops.

For those who like to see their rocks in the rough, Eilat has the **Eilat Moun-** **tains**: spectacular ascents of colourful stone. In some areas, it appears as if their volcanic genesis was quick frozen, and their flowing magmas interrupted in full flood. Erosion here has taken some bizarre and incredibly beautiful courses. In places, it is possible to walk through narrow canyons, with walls towering hundreds of metres vertically, but a mere metre or two apart. The harsh desert wind has carved monumental pillars among the mountains, particularly in the sandstone regions such as the **Pillars of Amran** (named for the father of Moses), some 9 km (5½ miles) north of Eilat and 3 km (2 miles) west of the main highway. The site is laced with lovely ravines and clusters of imposing natural columns.

About 4 km (2½ miles) south of Eilat, along the coast highway leading to Sinai, is the entry to **Solomon's Canyon**, a popular hiking area. A dusty granite quarry at the mouth of the canyon tends to obscure the formations lying beyond, but those following the Nature Reserves Authority path markers will be treated

Etzion Geber King Solomon's port.

to an exotic geological adventure. Entering the canyon, **HaMetsuda** – the Stronghold – rises to the left. This great rock was vital to Eilat's defencees against invasion from the Sinai coast. The path then leads another 16 km (l0 miles) up into the mountains, twisting and turning along the route of the canyon. Hikers pass beneath **Mount (Har) Yehoshafat, then Mount (Har) Shlomo** and next **Mount (Har) Asa**, all of which tower more than 700 metres (2,300 ft) overhead.

Eventually, the trail crosses the paved Moon Valley Highway which leads into central Sinai. Across the highway, the trail continues on to the spectacular cliffs and oasis at Ein Netafim – the Spring of the Drops – which trickles across a barren rock into a picturesque pool at the foot of an imposing cliff. Further along is Red Canyon, another impressive natural wonder of erosion-sculpted sandstone.

**Seaside sojourning:** Beaches are a year-round attraction in Eilat. Even in the summer, when temperatures can range well above baking at 40°C/l05°F, the waters of the Red Sea are cool and soothing. Mid-winter swimming, however, is usually left to the Europeans and Americans, while native Eilatis stare from the shore, bundled up in parkas to dispel the wintery gusts, which usually hover at around 15°C (roughly 60°F).

Eilat offers five distinct, attractive beaches, spanning some 11 km (7 miles), ranging from fine sand to gravel. **North Beach**, close to the centre of town, is the local hangout for sun worshippers. The bay is protected, the swimming is easy and dozens of hotels line the shore. The eastern end of North Beach also affords inexpensive bungalows and even camping facilities for the economy-minded traveller.

About 6 km (4 miles) down the coast – past the navy station and port facilities – is **Shmurat Almogim** – the **Coral Reserve**. This Israeli Nature Reserve includes a fine sandy beach and a truly spectacular coral reef. Here, visitors can rent diving masks, snorkels and flippers from the reserve's office and swim along

*low*, sun *r*shipper. *ght*, *c*mels watch *v*er boats at *m*arina.

any of three marked routes which lead over different parts of the coral reef. Special markers set into the reef itself identify different types of corals and plants growing there, as well as some of the more common fishes. The reserve also has changing rooms, showers, snack and souvenir stands and other tourist amenities. Nevertheless, it is also a strict nature reserve. Removal of any corals will result in the culprit paying a visit to the local judge.

Further south is the **Coral World Underwater Observatory**, an unusual commercial aquarium and undersea observatory. Here, the visitor walks out upon a long pier to the observatory building, which is set into the reef itself. Descending the spiral staircase within the observatory, one emerges into a circular room with windows facing out into the coral reef at a depth of 5 metres (l6 ft). All sorts of fish swim freely about outside the window, and the many colours and shapes of the living reef are astonishing sights which should not be missed. Nothing quite as lovely has been seen since Captain Nemo retired the *Nautilus*.

**Rafi Nelson's Village** lies another kilometre further on, just past the Sonesta Hotel. The village is an Eilat institution of hedonism and easy living. A golden calf stands by, just to prove the point. The late Nelson, who set up the village, was an institution with his wide brimmed hats, shark-tooth necklaces and bush-grey beard *(picture, page 313)*.

Those who abjure actually going into the water might be more inclined to ride on it instead. A large **marina** and **lagoon** at North Beach is mooring for many boats and yachts, from expensive charter schooners to more affordable windsurfing craft. There are also several glass-bottom boats for reef-viewing, and a number of water-skiing speed boats available for charter. Those who really want to get into the swim of things should make contact with any of the licensed diving clubs: Lucky Divers, Red Sea Divers, and Eilat Aqua Sport. All these will rent diving equipment and offer diving courses.

**The view from the Underwater Observatory**

**For the birds:** Birdwatching too, is a year-round attraction in Eilat, and several dozen species of resident birds can be found in the mountains, deserts, by the seashore and among the fields of neighbouring Kibbutz Eilor. The spring migration season, however, is particularly dazzling and the best time to be here. Millions upon millions of migratory birds fly across the Eilat region on their northward journeys from warm wintering havens in Africa to their breeding grounds scattered across Eurasia. Great waves of eagles and falcons often fill the sky – and highly respected ornithologists keep producing reports with figures like 19,288 steppe eagles, 26,770 black kites and 225,952 honey buzzards through a single migration season. Sharp-eyed birdwatchers will also pick out booted eagles, snake eagles, lesser spotted eagles, imperial eagles, marsh harriers, sparrowhawks and osprey. And then come the pelicans and storks in the tens of thousands.

As an assistance to birdwatchers, the Nature Reserves Authority has established special hiking trails and observation hides in the region to help birders. A special information centre is maintained by the Nature Reserves Authority in the King Solomon Hotel to provide up-to-date information for bird watching, registration for tours, rental of field glasses, sale of literature and nightly lectures and nature films about the Eilat region.

For those less adventurous there are scores of restaurants ranging from inexpensive pizza parlours and *felafel* stands to high-priced haute cuisine in the **Eilat Center**, the **New Tourist Center** and the **Hotel District**. Several hotels also have night clubs, discos and other social entertainments.

Eilat is also the jump-off point for several expeditions into the vast and barren waste land of **Sinai**. Most of the tour agencies in town can book arrangements to visit Santa Katarina, Sharm El-Sheikh and other Sinai attractions, and for a moderate fee, the Egyptian consulate in Eilat provides the required visas.

elow, mping out Taba. ght, lone ndsurfer akes a immering houette.

# TRAVEL TIPS

# GETTING THERE

## BY AIR

Ben-Gurion International Airport is situated in Lydda (Lod in Hebrew) near the Mediterranean coast, 20 km (12 miles) southeast of Tel Aviv, 50 km (30 miles) west of Jerusalem and 110 km (68 miles) southeast of Haifa, and is the main hub for international air traffic. Its facilities include a Government Tourist Office, which is open around the clock to provide information and help arrange accommodation, tel: (03) 9711485. It also has a bank and post office, both open 24 hours except for holidays and Shabbat, plus a cafeteria, shopping area and First Aid post. The El Al Lost & Found department, also open 24 hours, can be reached at tel: (03) 9712541. General airport information can be found 24 hours at tel: (03) 9712484.

About half the international flights in and out of Ben-Gurion International Airport are operated by the Israeli government-owned El Al Israel Airlines, which carries over 2 million passengers a year. Other major airlines with regular flights to Ben-Gurion International Airport include Aeroflot, Air France, Air Sinai, Alitalia, Austrian Airlines, British Airways, Cyprus Airways, Czech Airlines, Delta, Iberia, KLM, Lot, Lufthansa, Malev, Olympic Airways, Sabena, SAS, South African Airways, Swissair, Tarom and Turkish Airlines.

There are also regular charter flights to Ben-Gurion International Airport by El Al, by Arkia, another Israeli carrier, and by overseas companies including Monarch and Tower.

**Approximate flying times:**

| | | |
|---|---|---|
| Amsterdam | 4 hrs | 15 mins |
| Athens | 1 hr | 50 mins |
| Beijing | 10 hrs | |
| Boston | 10 hrs | 5 mins |
| Brussels | 4 hrs | 5 mins |
| Bucharest | 2 hrs | 30 mins |
| Cairo | 1 hr | 20 mins |
| Chicago | 12 hrs | 5 mins |
| Cologne | 3 hrs | 55 mins |
| Copenhagen | 4 hrs | 30 mins |
| Eilat | | 35 mins |
| Frankfurt | 3 hrs | 55 mins |
| Geneva | 3 hrs | 45 mins |
| Istanbul | 1 hr | 50 mins |
| Johannesburg | 8 hrs | 50 mins |
| Lisbon | 5 hrs | |
| London | 4 hrs | 35 mins |
| Los Angeles | 5 hrs | 50 mins |
| Madrid | 4 hrs | 45 mins |
| Marseilles | 3 hrs | 45 mins |
| Miami | 13 hrs | 20 mins |
| Montreal | 1 9 hrs | 55 mins |
| Moscow | 4 hrs | |
| Munich | 3 hrs | 30 mins |
| Nairobi | 4 hrs | 55 mins |
| New York | 10 hrs | 30 mins |
| Paris | 4 hrs | 10 mins |
| Rome | 3 hrs | 5 mins |
| Vienna | 3 hrs | 15 mins |
| Zurich | 3 hrs | 40 mins |

## BY SEA

Israel's main ports are Haifa and Ashdod. The stability line and Sol Line offer regular sailings from Europe to Haifa port, and many Mediterranean cruises include Israel in their itinerary. Official ports of entry for foreign yachts and boats in addition to these two cities include Eilat and the Tel Aviv Marina.

## BY ROAD

Car rental firms which have facilities at the airport are Avis, Hertz, Eurocar, Inter-Rent, Budget Rent-a-car, Kopel, Thrifty and Eldan.

## FROM JORDAN

**Allenby Bridge**, near Jericho, some 40 km (25 miles) from Jerusalem, is the crossing-point between Israel and Jordan. Visitors entering Israel via the Allenby Bridge, may re-enter Jordan by the same route. However, tourists crossing from Israel into Jordan via the Allenby Bridge, are prohibited by the Jordanian Government from re-entering Israel.

The visa requirements are the same as those at any other point of entry into Israel. Travellers who need an Israeli visa should obtain it before going to Jordan as it is not possible to get an Israeli visa in any Arab country except Egypt and it cannot be obtained upon arrival at the Bridge. When crossing from Israel to Jordan the tourist must possess a Jordanian visa and a Jordanian permit to cross the Bridge, and pay a transit tax. This is levied in the form of a revenue stamp which can be purchased at any post office in Israel as well as at the Bridge. Private vehicles (including bicycles) may not cross the Bridge. Cameras must be empty of film.

The Bridge is open Sunday–Thursday 8am–1pm and on Friday and eves of holidays 8–11am. It is closed on Saturdays and Jewish holidays. At Allenby Bridge a Tourist Information Office is open at the same time as the Bridge. Other facilities are: currency exchange, post office, public phones, cafeteria, toilets, porters and *sherut* (service) taxis to Jerusalem, Jericho, Bethlehem, Hebron, Ramallah and Gaza.

## FROM EGYPT

Points of entry open between Israel and Egypt are Nizzana, Rafiah, and Taba, open 363 days a year (exceptions are Yom Kippur and the first day of Id el Adha).

Nizzana, which is the main point of entry, is about 60 km (37 miles) southwest of Beersheba, and is open between 8am and 4pm.

Rafiah, 50 km (30 miles) southwest of Ashkelon, is open between 8.30am and 5pm.

Taba, just south of Eilat, is open from 7am to 9pm. Tourists who cross from Taba to Egypt do not need a visa in advance, but can obtain one on presentation of a passport. The Egyptian visa, valid up to 7 days, is free of charge, but there is a $5 tax. Travel is permitted to the tourist sites in Southern Sinai only, and visitors must return to Israel via Taba. The AL-17 entry form into Israel is required.

With the exception of those entering Southern Sinai (through Taba) an Egyptian visa must be obtained in advance. In addition to your valid passport, the AL-17 entry form must be presented. Private vehicles may be driven into Egypt, and documentation must be obtained from the automobile and touring clubs in your country. Rented cars are not permitted to cross. The Egged Bus Co-op has regular buses from Tel Aviv to Cairo. Southern Sinai may also be entered by sea through Sharm el Sheikh only. Free visas are obtainable in advance, for a 48-hour stay, from the Egyptian Consulate in Eilat.

# TRAVEL ESSENTIALS

## VISAS & PASSPORTS

Tourists are required to hold passports valid for Israel. Stateless persons require a valid travel document with a return visa to the country of issue.

An entry visa is also required, except where stated below. This visa is valid for a stay of three months from the date of arrival. American tourists do not need a visa to enter Israel, only a valid US passport.

Citizens of the following countries also do not require a transit or visitor's visa for entry into Israel:

Austria, Bahamas, Barbados, Belgium, Bolivia, Colombia, Costa Rica, Denmark, Dominican Republic, Dutch Antilles, Ecuador, El Salvador, Fiji, Finland, France, Greece, Guatemala, Republic of Haiti, Holland, Hong Kong, Iceland, Jamaica, Japan, Lichtenstein, Luxembourg, Maldive Islands,

Mauritius, Mexico, Norway, Paraguay, Surinam, Swaziland, Sweden, Switzerland, Trinidad and Tobago, the United Kingdom (including Northern Ireland, the Channel Islands and the Isle of Man).

Citizens of the following countries receive the visa free of charge at the port of entry:

Argentina, Australia, Brazil, Canada, Central African Republic, Chile, Germany and citizens of Italy, New Zealand, San Marino, South Africa, Spain and Uruguay born after 1 January 1928.) Citizens of the Republic of Ireland (Eire) also receive the visa at the port of entry but are required to pay the requisite fee.

Citizens of the following countries receive the visa free of charge but must apply for it, before departure, to any Israel Diplomatic or Consular Mission: Cyprus, Germany (Federal Republic of) born before 1 January 1928 – for an unlimited number of visits during the validity of the passport in use and – Yugoslavia.

The citizens of countries not mentioned above must submit the visa application for approval to the nearest Israel Diplomatic or Consular Mission and pay the prescribed fee.

## TRANSIT VISA

A transit visa, valid for five days, is also available from any Israel Diplomatic or Consular Mission. It can be extended following arrival, for a further 10 days, by applying to any district office of the Ministry of the Interior in Israel.

## LANDING-FOR-THE-DAY CARD

If you visit Israel on a cruise ship, you will be given a Landing-for-the-Day card, which permits you to remain in the country for as long as your ship is in port, and you need not apply for a visitor's visa.

This applies only to people wishing to enter Israel for travel purposes. Anyone wishing to enter for work, study or permanent settlement must apply while still abroad to an Israel Diplomatic or Consular Mission for the appropriate visa.

## VISA FEES

The visa fees for those citizens who are required to pay for the Israel visa are as follows:
Individual tourist visa and transit visa $3.

The fee for the extension of a visitor's (tourist) visa, transit or temporary resident's visa is $3 for a year, or part thereof, for citizens of all countries with the exception of those of Belgium, Holland and Luxembourg, who are exempt from payment.

Further information from: The Ministry of the Interior, Immigration and Registration Department, 24 Rehov Hillel, Jerusalem. Tel: (02) 294777.

## MONEY MATTERS

Tourists may bring an unlimited amount of foreign currency into Israel, whether in cash, traveller's cheques, letters of credit or State of Israel Bonds. They may also bring in with them an unlimited amount of Israel shekels but are allowed to take out upon departure only a minimal amount.

They are not required to declare, upon arrival, the amount of foreign currency in their possession and currency exchanges are not recorded.

Tourists who have changed foreign currency (dollars) into Israeli currency (*shekel*), may re-change their money into dollars by presenting the receipt of the transaction up to a maximum of $500. This may be done at any bank in Israel during the course of one's visit. However, upon departure from Israel, only a maximum of $100 may be exchanged at Ben-Gurion International Airport. This can be done after going through customs and passport control.

## LOCAL CURRENCY

The currency is the New Israeli Shekel (NIS) which officially succeeded the old Israeli shekel in 1985. The shekel is divided into 100 agorot. Bills are issued in four denominations: 10 NIS (orange with a portrait of former Prime Minister Golda Meir), 50 NIS (purple, with portrait of Nobel Prize winner Shmuel Agnon), 100 NIS (grey with portrait of former President Yitzhak Ben Zvi), 200 NIS (reddish brown with portrait of former President Zalman Shazar). Change comes in coins of 5 agorot, 10 agorot, ½ shekel, 1 shekel and 5 shekels.

Exchange rates are the same in all banks. The NIS is relatively stable and floats freely agianst the world's major currency, with a revised exchange rate each day according to supply and demand. Vendors are prepared to accept the world's better known currencies but tend to offer inferior exchange rates.

## CARDS & CHEQUES

Visa, Master Card/Euro Card, American Express and Diners Club are honoured virtually everywhere. The cash machines outside almost every Israeli bank will dispense money against these cards (so remember your personal identification number); this can save waiting around in crowded banks. Traveller's cheques are widely accepted, though banks take a commission on each cheque so it is cheaper to bring higher denomination cheques.

## HEALTH

There are no vaccination requirements for tourists entering Israel except if arriving from infected areas. By far the biggest health problem effecting visitors stems from a lack of respect for the sun. Sunburn and sunstroke afflict bathers, while dehydration plagues those who over-exert themselves sightseeing. Tour-ists should acclimatise gradually, apply suntan lotions, keep indoors or in the shade between 10am and 4pm in the spring and summer, wear light comfortable clothes that cover both legs and arms and don a hat and sunglasses.

Most importantly of all, it is vital to drink continually even if you do not feel thirsty. Research has shown that the average person who is exerting themselves in the heat of the day during an Israeli summer needs to drink one litre (over 2 pints) every hour to replace the body liquids lost through sweat. The first symptoms of dehydration are tiredness, headache and lack of appetite. Advanced dehydration can express itself in just about every unpleasant symptom imaginable from migraines and fever, to diarrhoea and vomiting. Medication will not help. Recovery will come about through rest and sipping water, possibly with some salt added, though it is probably best to consult a doctor to ensure that the problem really is dehydration.

Upset stomachs are also common. Here, too, rest and a diet of water are the best medicine. Tap water is as drinkable as anywhere in the developed world, though mineral waters are available everywhere.

AIDS: The incidence of AIDS in Israel is considerably less than in Western Europe, but is nevertheless on the increase. The Ministry of Interior now requires all visitors seeking to extend their stay beyond three months to be AIDS-tested.

(*Also see medical services page 333.*)

## WHAT TO WEAR

Dress in Israel is informal by Western standards. Few people wear jackets and ties in the summer except for business occasions. However, even in the summer Jerusalem can get quite cool in the evenings. You'll want to be sure to bring some conservative clothes, in any case, for visiting religious sites.

Suggested packing lists might include the following:

Summer (April–October): lightweight suit, slacks, shorts and open-neck shirts for men; plenty of light cotton daytime dresses and an afternoon dress for more formal occasions for women; light shoes, sandals and closed shoes for touring; sunglasses, hat, swimsuit and beachwear; a light coat, jacket or sweater for cool evenings in the hills.

Winter (November–March): warm coat, sweaters, raincoat and hat, walking shoes, overshoes; shirts, slacks, sports jacket and formal suit for men; woollen or heavy suit, blouses, skirts and slacks, long dress or evening skirt for women; lighter clothing and swimsuit for Eilat and the Dead Sea coast.

If you forget anything, you will find that the shops in Israel have high quality clothes for all occasions.

## ENTRY & EXIT FORMALITIES

All visitors to Israel, including diplomats, are required to fill an entry form, AL 17, upon arrival. Visitors who intend continuing to Arab countries (except Egypt) after their visit to Israel should ask the frontier control officer to put the entry stamp on this form instead of in their passports.

# CUSTOMS

Every adult tourist may bring into the country without payment of duty the following articles, provided that they are for personal use (gift parcels sent unaccompanied – by post or any other means – are liable to full import duties and Value Added Tax): eau de Cologne or perfume not exceeding ¼ litre (0.44 pint), wine up to 2 litres and other alcoholic drinks not exceeding 1 litre; tobacco or cigars not exceeding 250 grams or 250 cigarettes; gifts up to $125 in value c.i.f. (including assorted foodstuffs not exceeding 3 kgs or 6½ lbs, on condition that no single type of food exceeds 1 kg).

The following articles may be brought in duty free on condition that they are taken out on departure, and that they are portable and actually in use: typewriter; cameras (1 ordinary with 10 plates or 10 rolls of film and 1 movie below 16 mm with 10 reels of cine film); tape recorder with 700 metres (750 yards) of recording tape or 2 cassettes; record-player; battery operated radio; binoculars; personal jewellery; baby carriages; musical instruments; camping equipment; sports requisites (1 set for fishing, skates, 2 tennis rackets); bicycle without engine.

The red-green customs clearance system is in operation at Ben-Gurion Airport. Tourists bringing in goods mentioned above may choose the Green Channel and leave the Airport. Tourists bringing in other goods, even if they are exempt from duty, must use the Red Channel.

The following articles are subject to declaration and deposits of duties and taxes and the Red Channel must be taken: professional instruments (which can be held in the hand during operation) up to a value of $1,650 c.i.f.; boat (rowing, sailing or motor) and a caravan trailer; scuba-diving equipment portable and appreciably used; records in reasonable quantity. A television in the personal use of the tourist may be brought in free of import duty and taxes provided it is portable and used. It is, however, liable to a deposit on the duty.

## CUSTOMS DEPOSITS

The custom authorities are entitled to demand deposits or guarantees on any article brought in by the tourist or sent separately. This is usually enforced only for professional equipment or expensive items. The guarantee or deposit is returned to the tourist when he leaves the country and takes the articles out with him. Since the formalities take some time, it is advisable to make all arrangements a day or two before departure, and preferably at the port of entry of the goods, so that the return of the guarantee can be carried out more conveniently.

Further information from:

**The Department of Customs and Excise**, 32 Rehov Agron, POB 320, 91000 Jerusalem. Tel: (02) 703333.

# PORTER SERVICES

If you are flying El Al, you can check in your luggage at their office in Haifa, Jerusalem and Tel Aviv the evening before departure (except on Friday, holy days and the eves of holy days). It will be taken straight to your plane and you need only arrive at the airport 1 hour before departure.

The following EL AL offices are open for check-in services:
• Tel Aviv Railway Station, North Tel Aviv. Tel: (03) 6917198. Open: 1pm–midnight.
• Center One, Jerusalem. Tel: (02) 383166. Open: 4–11pm.
• 6 Hanamal St., Haifa. Tel: (04) 677036. Open: 6.30–10pm.

# SECURITY CHECKS

These are for your protection. Be prepared to unlock your luggage and submit yourself and carry-on bags to a careful but courteous examination.

To avoid spoiling any precious records of your visit, make sure to empty your camera of film.

# EXTENSIONS OF STAY

Tourists who wish to stay in the country for longer than three months must obtain an extension of stay. This applies also to citizens of those countries which are exempt from entry visas and generally requires the stamping of your passport. The extension may be obtained through any district office of the Ministry of Interior.

The addresses of the main offices are:
**Jerusalem**, Generali Building, Rehov Shlomzion Hamalka. Tel: (02) 290222.
**Tel Aviv**, Shalom Meyer Tower, Visa Department, 9 Rehov Ahad Ha'am. Tel: (03) 651941.
**Haifa**, Government Building (opp. Municipality), 11 Hassan Shukri. Tel: (04) 667781.

# ON DEPARTURE

## CONFIRMING RESERVATIONS

You must confirm your scheduled departure with your airline at least 72 hours in advance. To save inconvenience, check the departure time to make sure that it has not been changed.

## GETTING TO THE AIRPORT

**From Tel Aviv**: By United Tours Bus No. 222 from Railway Station, Rehov Arlosorov to Ben-Gurion Airport every hour, year round, from 4am–12 noon Details: Tel: (03) 7543410.
By Egged Buses, every 15 minutes, 6am–11.30pm.

**From Jerusalem**: By Egged Buses, from 6.15am–7pm, approximately every 20 minutes. By Nesher *sherut* taxi: book in advance at 21 Rehov Hamelech George. Tel: (02) 257227.

**From Haifa**: by Egged Buses, from 7am–6pm, approximately every 45 minutes. By Aviv *sherut* taxi service, at 5 Rehov Allenby, tel: (04) 666333, approximately every hour from 6am–5pm.

## GETTING TO THE LAND EXITS

### TO JORDAN (Allenby Bridge)

**From Jerusalem**: By *sherut* taxi service from Damascus Gate.

**From Jericho, Bethlehem, Hebron, Ramallah and Gaza**: By *sherut* taxi service from the centre of each town. Tourists who wish to leave by other means of transportation must coordinate their departure with the Tourism Staff Officer, Judea and Samaria, tel: (02) 955318 or with the Allenby Bridge Tourist Information Office, tel: (02) 941038.

### TO EGYPTIAN BORDER POINTS

**From Jerusalem**: By *sherut* service from Damascus Gate.

**From Tel Aviv**: By *sherut* service from Central Bus Station.

In addition to these shuttles, practically every tourist agency in Israel offers inexpensive round-trip bus service in air-conditioned buses, which leave daily except on Shabbat (Saturdays).

Both El Al and Air Sinai also offer several flights to Cairo per week, which although much more expensive, cut the travel time down from 10 hours to less than 55 minutes.

Visas for Egypt cost approximately $15 and can be obtained by visiting the Egyptian Consulate in Tel Aviv, at 54 Rehov Basel, Tel Aviv, 62744. Tel: (03) 5464151.

Rented cars are not permitted to cross the border. As with the airport, all visitors leaving through the land borders are expected to pay a transit tax.

## PROCEDURES ON DEPARTURE

Departing passengers should arrive at the airport 2 hours prior to their flight's departure time and prepare the following documents: a valid passport, flight tickets and money (Israeli currency preferred) for payment of the airport tax, which is obligatory for every passenger over the age of two, and which costs the equivalent of $10. This tax is usually included in the price of the air ticket.

Passengers to Egypt pay a tax approximately equivalent to $8. Passengers departing Israel at the Jerusalem and Eilat Airports pay a tax of approximately $5.50.

Visitors departing via the land crossing point to Egypt at Nitzana pay a tax approximately equivalent to $2. The tax is paid at the Bank Leumi branch at the terminal. Visitors departing via Rafiah pay a tax approximately equivalent to $8. It can be paid at any branch of Bank Hapoalim to the order of the Israel Airport Authority, account number 566-05-39710.

## BACKPACKING

Israel is a backpacker's paradise. It is customary for Israelis after completing their army service to spend six months, or even a year, backpacking around the world. Therefore, backpacking is seen as an acceptable, if not conventional, way of seeing the world and backpackers are generally warmly received in Israel and rarely frowned upon as undesirables.

Everything is geared towards the cost cutting tricks of the backpacker. Hitchhiking is as common as catching a bus and hitchhiking stops, rather like bus stops, can be found at every major junction. But competition is tough, especially in urban areas where dozens of Israelis vie for car space, including many soldiers who receive priority. Buses are relatively cheap and there is a 10 percent discount on inter-city routes for holders of international students cards.

Youth hostels abound and their representatives often wait at bus stations to approach backpackers. Sleeping on the beach or in public parks is also usually permitted. Eating is incredibly cheap and healthy at felafel stalls where you can take as much salad as you want along with your pita bread and felafel for less than $2.

Backpackers also like Israel because there is usually plenty of casual employment. Strictly speaking, this is illegal, and wages are poor, but a week or two's pay for washing dishes or working on a construction site can be useful for those travelling around the world on a shoestring budget.

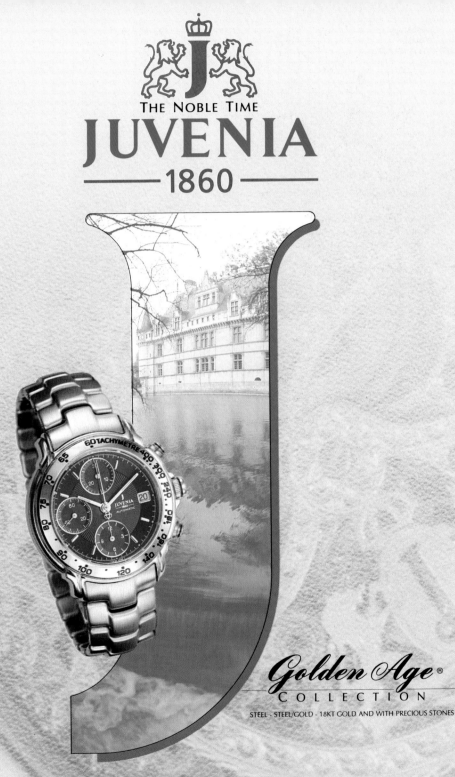

THE NOBLE TIME

# JUVENIA
## —1860—

*Golden Age* ®
COLLECTION

STEEL - STEEL/GOLD - 18KT GOLD AND WITH PRECIOUS STONES

Worldwide list of JUVENIA Agents available on request

**JUVENIA MONTRES SA - 2304 LA CHAUX-DE-FONDS - SWITZERLAND**
Tel. 41/39 26 04 65   Fax 41/39 26 68 00

# GETTING ACQUAINTED

The State of Israel was proclaimed on 14 May 1948. It is a parliamentary democracy with a 120-member single chamber Knesset (parliament) elected every four years by all citizens aged 18 or over. Seats are allocated by proportional representation. Every five years the Knesset elects a President by secret ballot who serves as a ceremonial head of state rather like the British monarch. After each election the President determines which party leader has the best chance of forming a government and thus becoming Prime Minister.

## ECONOMY

Israel's biggest exports are polished diamonds, high-tech and electronic equipment, fruit and vegetables, textiles, petrochemicals and minerals from the Dead Sea. Exports amounted to about $12 billion in 1992. In addition Israel receives nearly $2 billion from tourist income each year, a further $2 billion from donations by World Jewry and other supporters of Israel and over $3 billion from US aid. Israelis receive some $500 million dollars a year from Germany as compensation for Nazi atrocities.

Imports comprise mainly manufactured goods (from cars to compact discs), as well as oil and raw diamonds.

Unemployment has been consistently above 10 percent since the start of mass *aliyah* from the former Soviet Union in 1990. Inflation, which regularly reached over 100 percent a year in the early 1980s, dipped to between 10 percent and 20 percent a year from 1986 onwards. Since 1990 the gross domestic product has been rising by about 5 percent a year.

## GEOGRAPHY

A Middle East crossroads of continents, Israel is bordered by the Mediterranean in the west, the Great Syrian-African Rift in the east and the Red Sea (also part of the Rift) in the south. Israel's immediate neighbours are Lebanon, Syria, Jordan and Egypt.

Israel is a small country, with a total area (including the administered territories) of 21,000 sq. km (8,108 sq. miles).

The northern and central part of Israel, where most of the population is concentrated, is divided into three distinct longitudinal strips: to the west, the coastal plain with the large cities of Tel Aviv and Haifa; to the east, the Jordan and Arava Valleys with the River Jordan linking the two inland seas, the Sea of Galilee and the Dead Sea; and in the centre, the mountain range that includes the hills of Galilee, Samaria and Judea with the capital, Jerusalem. In the northeast rise the Golan Heights and the snow-capped Mt Hermon; and in the south stretches the Negev Desert with Beersheba at the capital and Eilat on the Gulf of Eilat. Altitudes vary from the 1,208 metres (3,962 ft) of Mt Meron in the Upper Galilee, to the −392 metres (−1,286 ft) of the Dead Sea, the lowest spot on earth.

Since 1967, Israel has been in possession of the West Bank, including the hills of Judea and Samaria, and the Gaza Strip, and the status of these areas remains unresolved. They are known alternately as the "administered territories" or the "occupied territories" depending on the speaker. The Golan Heights, which Israel won from Syria in 1967, were officially annexed by Israel in 1981.

## POPULATION

The population of Israel, including the administered territories, is about 5,200,000, of which 4,250,000 are Jews, the rest being Muslims, Christians, Druze and other minorities.

## LANGUAGE

Hebrew, the revived language of the Bible, and Arabic are the official languages of the country. English is also widely spoken. Road signs are in Hebrew, Arabic and English. Tourist information is usually available in French and German as well. Other languages spoken widely include Spanish, Russian, Polish, Yiddish and Hungarian, plus countless others, due to the diversity of immigrants in the country.

## TIME ZONES

Israel is 2 hours ahead of Greenwich Mean Time, and 7 hours ahead of New York's Eastern Standard Time. This means that when it is noon in Tel Aviv, it is:
noon Athens, Cairo
11am Paris, Rome, Madrid
10am London
7am Rio de Janeiro
5am New York, Montreal
4am Chicago
2am Los Angeles
midnight Honolulu
8pm Sydney
7pm Tokyo
5.30pm Singapore
3.30pm Bombay
1pm Moscow

# CLIMATE

Israeli summers are long (from April to October), hot and virtually rainless. During these months, the atmosphere in the hill towns such as Jerusalem and Safed is drier and cooler than in other parts of the country. The winter season (from November to March), is generally mild but quite cold in hilly areas. Spells of rain are interspersed with brilliant sunshine. During this period, the Tiberias area on the Sea of Galilee, the Dead Sea and Eilat, on the Gulf of Eilat, all have ideal warm, sunny weather.

The weather in Israel allows for year-round bathing: from April to October, along the Mediterranean coast and around the Sea of Galilee; and throughout the year, especially enjoyable in the winter, along the Dead Sea shore and the Gulf of Eilat.

## MEAN TEMPERATURES

Minimum–Maximum

| | January | April | July | October |
|---|---|---|---|---|
| **JERUSALEM** | | | | |
| C | 6–11° | 12–21° | 19–29° | 16–26° |
| (F | 43–53°) | (53–69°) | (66–84°) | (60–78°) |
| **TEL AVIV** | | | | |
| C | 9–18° | 12–22° | 21–30° | 15–29° |
| (F | 49–65°) | (54–72°) | (70–86°) | (59–84°) |
| **HAIFA** | | | | |
| C | 8–17° | 13–26° | 20–30° | 16–27° |
| (F | 46–63°) | (55–78°) | (68–86°) | (60–81°) |
| **TIBERIAS** | | | | |
| C | 9–18° | 13–27° | 23–37° | 19–32° |
| (F | 48–65°) | (56–80°) | (73–98°) | (65–89°) |
| **EILAT** | | | | |
| C | 10–21° | 17–31° | 25–40° | 20–33° |
| (F | 49–70°) | (63–87°) | (78–103°) | (69–92°) |

## CULTURE & CUSTOMS

### MEALS

Most Israelis eat a large breakfast, a main "meat" meal at midday and a light "dairy" meal in the evening. The wide variety of restaurants throughout the country naturally cater to this preference, but are also prepared to suit individual tastes. They range from elegant establishments specialising in cooking from many parts of the world, to simple cafés or pizza stands.

### KOSHER FOOD

The Hebrew word "kosher" means food conforming to Jewish dietary laws. Pork and shellfish are prohibited, and meat and dairy foods cannot be served together. While kosher food is the rule in Israel, many restaurants and some hotels and, of course, Arab establishments, are non-kosher.

# ETIQUETTE

After receiving some service or purchase, it is polite to say *toda* – "thanks" or *toda raba* – "thanks very much". Often the response will be *bevakasha* – "please" or – *alo davar* – "it's nothing". The standard hello or goodbye is *shalom*. "How are you?" is *Ma Shlomcha?* to a man or *Ma Shlomayach?* to a woman. "See you" is *lehitra'ot*.

Tipping in better restaurants is along the European standard of 10–15 percent. *Sherut* are not tipped; cab drivers needn't be, but it will be appreciated.

Of obvious sensitivity is religious etiquette. Women should dress conservatively (no legs or shoulders), and men should wear shirts and pants when visiting holy sites. When visiting Jewish shrines or memorials it's also standard for men to cover their heads; if you don't have a *kepah* or hat, a cardboard substitute is often provided.

In certain religious Jewish neighbourhoods, these conservative rules of dress apply as general practice.

While not all Israelis are observant, you should also be aware that religious Jews see the Sabbath as a holy day and smoking or other behaviour can be considered offensive.

# WEIGHTS & MEASURES

Israel uses the metric system.

| | |
|---|---|
| 1 metre | 1.094 yards |
| 1 kilometre | 0.62 miles |
| 1 dunam (1,000 sq. metres) | 0.25 acres |
| 1 litre | 1.76 pints |
| 4.546 litres | 1 gallon |
| 1 kilogramme | 2.2 pounds |

# ELECTRICITY

The electric current in Israel is 220 volts AC, single phase, 50 cycles. Israeli sockets are usually three-pronged, and foreign-made appliances often require an adaptor for the plug. Electric shavers, travelling irons, etc. should be equipped with adaptors to the local current or transformers. These can, of course, be purchased in Israel.

# ASSOCIATIONS

The following Israeli branches have regular meetings and extend a warm welcome to overseas members: B'nai Brith, Freemasons, Rotary, Soroptomists, Lions, Skal, WIZO and Hadassah.

# BANKING HOURS

Sunday, Tuesday and Thursday from 8.30am–12.30pm and 4–5.30pm. Monday and Wednesday 8.30am–12.30pm only. Friday and eves of holy days 8.30am–12 noon.

Branches in the leading hotels usually offer convenient additional banking hours.

Israel observes a lunar year in accordance with Jewish religious tradition, with the New Year occurring in September/October, with the holiday of Rosh Hashana. But the standard Gregorian system is also in daily use everywhere.

The work week runs from Sunday to Thursday, and most businesses are also open Friday mornings. From sunset Friday to sunset Saturday, however, everything is shut down in observance of the Jewish Sabbath, or "Shabbat". This includes all banks and public services, including buses and other forms of transportation.

On Saturday evening, most of these services resume.

Muslims and Christians observe their holy days on Fridays and Sundays, respectively.

## THE SABBATH & JEWISH HOLY DAYS

Saturday, Israel's day of rest and all holy days commence at sundown on the preceding day and end at nightfall. All Jewish shops, businesses, institutions, offices and public places of entertainment (with the exception of a few restaurants and clubs) are closed and most public transport ceases. Some shops and all places of entertainment reopen with the termination of the Sabbath or the holy day, and public transport resumes.

The Hebrew calendar, unlike the Gregorian, is a lunar calendar. Jewish holy days, therefore, fall on different dates in the general calendar each year.

## CALENDAR OF JEWISH HOLIDAYS

| Holy Day | Hebrew Date | Approx. Gregorian Date |
|---|---|---|
| Rosh Hashana Tishri | 1–2 Sept | Oct |
| Yom Kippur Tishri | 10 Sept | Oct |
| Succot Tishri | 15–21 Sept | Oct |
| Simhat Torah Tishri | 22 Sept | Oct |
| Hanukka Kislev 25-Tevet | 3 or 4 Nov | Dec |
| Tu B'Shevat Shevat | 15 Jan | Feb |
| Purim Adar | 14 Feb | Mar |
| Pessah Nissan | 15–21 Mar | Apr |
| Independence Day Iyar | 5 Apr | May |
| Lag Ba'Omer Iyar | 18 Apr | May |
| Jerusalem Liberation Day Iyar | 28 May | June |
| Shavu'ot Sivan | 6 May | June |
| Tisha B'Av Av | 9 July | Aug |

## ROSH HASHANA & YOM KIPPUR

Rosh Hashana (the Jewish New Year) and Yom Kippur (the Day of Atonement) are known as the "Days of Awe". On these days a Jew is called upon to give an accounting of himself before God. These festivals are purely religious in character and are observed principally in the synagogue.

Yom Kippur ends the 10-day period of penitence which begins on Rosh Hashana. For the observant Jew this is a 25-hour period of complete fasting and prayer. On this day the entire country comes to a standstill. All public and commercial services shut down and there is no traffic either public or private. There are no organised tours for tourists on this day. Tourists who do not fast are advised to check with their hotels for arrangements about meals.

## SUCCOT (Feast of Tabernacles) & SIMCHAT TORAH (Rejoicing of the Law)

The Succot Festival has a dual significance – religious and agricultural. Observant Jews dwell, or at least eat, in *succot* (booths) erected near their homes to commemorate the Israelites dwelling in the wilderness after the Exodus from Egypt. Some hotels and restaurants also build *succot* on their premises.

The agricultural significance of the festival is symbolised by the "four species"–the palm branch, the myrtle, the willow and the citron, over which a special blessing is recited on each day of the festival.

Simchat Torah is on the eighth day of the Feast of Tabernacles and on this day the annual cycle of the reading of the Law (Torah) is completed and another cycle begins. This festival is an extremely joyous one and is marked by much singing and dancing in the streets as well as in the synagogues.

## CHANUKAH (Festival of Lights)

Chanukah is an eight-day celebration recalling the successful revolt of the small Jewish community in the Land of Israel in the year 167 BC against the Syrian Hellenistic Empire.

During Chanukah, one light is lit on the first night, two on the second until the eighth night in an eight-branched candelabrum. This is to commemorate the miracle of the burning oil in the Holy Temple which occurred after the revolt. When the victorious fighters came to cleanse and rededicate their temple, which had been polluted by idolatry, they found that the supply of ritual oil, sufficient for one day, miraculously burned for eight days – the length of time needed to prepare a new supply of the special oil.

During Chanukah, large electric lamps are lit outside public buildings and many shops display eight-branched candelabra in their windows. Hotels conduct candle-lighting ceremonies for their guests, after which traditional Chanukah fare, such as doughnuts and potato pancakes, is served.

## TU B'SHVAT (The New Year of the Trees)

On this day, which is also considered the awakening of spring, children all over Israel carry tree saplings which they plant in special planting areas, singing traditional Tu B'Shvat songs. Fifteen species of fruit are tasted and a blessing said over them.

## PURIM

This festival commemorates the events which took place in Shushan in ancient Persia, when the wicked chancellor Haman persuaded Ahasuerus, king of Persia, to kill all the Jews in his domain. Through Queen Esther and her uncle Mordechai, the plot was foiled and the Jews were saved. The festival takes its name from the Hebrew word *purim*, meaning lots, which Haman cast to determine the day to carry out his terrible plan.

On the eve of the festival, the Scroll of Esther, which relates the tale, is read in every synagogue. Throughout the festival children and adults dress up in colourful costumes and masks and eat triangular-shaped pastries filled with fruit or poppy seeds, known as "Haman's Ears".

## PESACH (PASSOVER)

One of the main festivals in the Jewish calendar, joyously commemorating the Exodus of the Jews from Egypt and the miracles that preceded it (including the last plague, which struck the first-born sons of the Egyptians but "passed over" the Israelites).

The centre of festivity is the home, where the ritual Passover meal (Seder) takes place on the eve of the festival, accompanied by the reading of a special text (Haggadah) which recounts the historical events that Passover commemorates through ritual questions and answers, blessings and songs.

During the time of Passover (7 days in Israel and 8 abroad) only unleavened bread (*matza*) is eaten and there is abstention from all fermented foods. Jewish hotels do not serve bread during this period. It is also a time for pilgrimage to Jerusalem, as are Shavuot (Pentecost) and Succot (Feast of Tabernacles). In the Christian tradition, the Last Supper was a Passover meal, and Easter Sunday is determined as the first Sunday in the Passover period.

## SHAVUOT (PENTECOST)

This ancient holiday is mentioned in the Holy Scriptures and the "Feast of the Giving of the Law (Torah)", commemorating God giving Moses the Ten Commandments, which he in turn gave to the Children of Israel; the "Feast of Ingathering", marking the end of the wheat harvest; and the "Feast of the First Fruits", for in ancient days first-fruit offerings were brought to the Temple in Jerusalem as an expression of gratitude to God.

In Israel, Shavuot is observed with prayer and public celebrations. School children can be seen with fresh flower garlands on their heads, carrying baskets of fruit as they parade. The entire night preceding the festival is devoted to the study of the Law (Torah), and the next day special prayers are recited in the synagogues, which are decorated with flowers, fruit and greenery.

It is customary to eat dairy foods and honey during this time.

## TISHA B'A (THE 9TH OF AV)

Commemorating the destruction of the First and Second Temples, and other tragedies that befell the Jewish people in later history, Tisha B'Av is a traditional day of mourning and fasting.

## RELIGIOUS SERVICES

Israel is home to quite a number of religions, including Jews, Muslims, Samaritans, Protestants, Armenians, Catholics, Copts, Eastern Orthodox, Druze, Bahai and Black Hebrews.

All denominations are free to worship in their own ways, maintain their religious and charitable institutions and administer their internal affairs. The inviolability of Holy Places and centres of worship of all faiths is guaranteed by law.

Each religious body has the statutory right to observe its own weekly rest day and holy-days. The Jewish Sabbath (Saturday) and holidays are official holidays in Israel.

## CHRISTIAN HOLY DAYS

These holy days are celebrated on different dates by different denominations – Catholic and Protestant (on same dates), Greek-Orthodox and Armenian.

| Feast | Month |
|---|---|
| New Year (Holy Mother of God) | Jan |
| Epiphany | Jan |
| Miracle of the Wine (Cana) St Joseph | Mar |
| The Sorrows of Our Lady (Calvary) | Mar |
| Bethphage | Mar |
| Palm Sunday | Mar |
| Flagellation (Via Dolorosa) | Apr |
| Gethsemane | Apr |
| Coenaculum (Mount Zion) | Apr |
| Gethsemane (Holy Hour) | Apr |
| Good Friday | Apr |
| Holy Saturday | Apr |
| Easter Sunday | Apr |
| Easter Monday (Emmaus-Qubeibeh) | Apr |
| Invention of the Holy Cross (Holy Sepulchre) | May |
| Ascension Day | May |
| Pentecost Day (Whitsunday) | May |
| Visitation (Ein Karem) | May |
| Procession in Jerusalem | May |
| Corpus & Sanguis Christi (only in Holy Sepulchre) | June |
| St John the Baptist (in Ein Karem) | June |
| St Peter & Paul | June |
| Assumption Day | Aug |
| Nativity of the Holy Virgin (at St Anne's) | Sept |
| Exaltation of the Holy Cross (Calvary) | Sept |
| Immaculate Conception | Dec |
| Christmas Day | Dec |

**Holy Sepulchre Procession**: Daily at noon in the Church of the Holy Sepulchre. Way of the Cross (Via Dolorosa): Procession every Friday at 3pm starting from the Antonia. Protestant holidays, same as above with the exception that Pentecost is called Whitsunday.

A list of churches and times of prayer are available at all Tourist Information Offices.

## MUSLIM HOLY DAYS

Friday is a holy day for Muslims and places of worship are closed during prayers on that day, as they are on all holy days. Muslim holy days are decided on in accordance with the appearance of the new moon, thus falling on different dates in the general calendar each year. The most important are:
Id el Adha, Sacrificial Festival (4 days)
New Year
Mohammed's Birthday
Feast of Ramadan (1 month)
Id el Fitr, Conclusion of Ramadan (3 days)

## DRUZE HOLY DAYS

Id el Adha, Sacrificial Festival
Nabi Shu'eb
Nabi Sablan

# COMMUNICATIONS

## MEDIA

Access to news is very important for Israelis, due to their unique geopolitical situation. Listening to the hourly news updates on the radio in taxis, buses, as well as in private homes is part of the daily routine. There is censorship but only in security matters.

## NEWSPAPERS

Israelis are prolific newspaper readers. With several dozen daily newspapers and countless weekly and monthly magazines, they read more newspapers per head of the population than almost any other country in the world. Most of these newspapers are in Hebrew, the largest being the afternoon journal *Yediot Ahronot*, which sells over 500,000 copies of its Friday (weekend) edition. Remember there are only 5 million Israelis.

It is closely followed by two afternoon papers:

*Ma'ariv* (formerly owned by the late British press baron Robert Maxwell), and *Hadashot*. The most respected daily is *Ha'aretz* and there are four politically aligned dailies: *Davar* (Labor), *Al Hamishmar* (Mapam), *Hatzofe* (National Religious Party) and *Hamodia* (Agudat Yisrael). A further three daily newspapers are devoted to economic and financial news.

The *Jerusalem Post* is published in English six days a week (except Saturdays). Founded in 1932, the paper was originally owned by the Histadrut Trade Union Movement and supported the Labor party. But in 1990 it was sold to the Conrad Black's Canadian-based Hollinger Corporation for $17 million. Hollinger also owns Britain's *Daily Telegraph* group. Under new management, the *Jerusalem Post* supports the right-wing Likud.

The *Jerusalem Report* is an English language biweekly magazine that gives a comprehensive news and features insight into Israeli life.

There is also a dynamic Arab press with over 20 publications including 6 dailies and 6 weeklies. The Israeli Arab press is based in Haifa, while journals printed in East Jerusalem are aimed at a readership in the West Bank and Gaza.

In addition there are several dailies in Russian, as well as weeklies in French, Spanish, Amharic, Hungarian, Romanian and many other languages.

Many of the leading newspapers and magazines from Western Europe and North America are available at Israeli newsagents the day after publication.

## TELEVISION & RADIO

The Israel Broadcasting Authority (IBA) is a government-run organisation modelled on Britain's BBC. Its television channel transmits from 6.30am to 1am and includes a 10-minute news bulletin in English (currently at 5.30pm).

The IBA enjoyed a television monopoly for many years. But now it faces tough competition from cable television which, organised under regional franchises, offers subscribers 30 channels including BBC World Service, CNN and Sky. In addition, Israelis can receive the broadcasts of all its neighbours including two English language stations: Middle East Televsion from Lebanon and Jordan's Channel 6. Israel itself also has a second channel.

The IBA has a comprehensive radio service broadcasting on six networks: news and current events; pop music; classical music; Arabic; foreign-language service; new immigrants. On the foreign language service there are English language news bulletins at 7am, 1pm, 5pm and 8pm.

Other Israeli stations include the army's Galei Zahal and two pirate pop stations: Channel 7 (funded by right-wing organisations), and the Voice of Peace (funded by left-wing bodies) broadcasting in English. The BBC World Service, Voice of America and Jordan's English language radio station mean that listeners are never starved for choice.

# POST & TELECOMMUNICATIONS

## POSTAL SERVICES

Israel's numerous post offices can be identified by a logo of a white stag leaping across a red background. Post boxes are red for out of town and international mail, and yellow for letters within the city. Letters take 7–10 days to reach Europe and America. Express service takes half the time and super Express (very expensive) about one-third of the time.

## TELEGRAMS & FAXES

These services are available from any post office on weekdays. Post office hours are from 8am–12.30pm and 3.30–6pm. Major post offices are open all day. On Friday afternoons, Saturdays and holidays post offices are closed all day.

For Toll Free Information About Postal Services Tel: 177-022-2121

## TELEPHONES

*Golden Pages* classified directories are available in English but otherwise phone books are only in Hebrew. Numbers can be obtained from Information (tel: 144), though callers are charged the cost of one unit for each enquiry.

Public telephone booths can be found throughout the country. Some are operated by tokens (*asimonim*), while others function when telephone cards are inserted. At major tourist sites some telephones accept international credit cards and this can be a convenient way of making overseas calls. Both *asimonim* and cards can be purchased at all post offices, reservation desks of hotels and many shops and kiosks.

Long-distance, international and inter-city calls can be made with both tokens and cards. Many private companies lease out cellular phones, but the costs are high.

Domestic calls are most expensive from 8am–1pm There is a 25 percent reduction from 1–8pm and a 50 percent reduction from 8pm–8am. There is also a 50 percent reduction from Friday at 1pm through Saturday. Telephones in shops and restaurants are often available for domestic calls but will cost you more than public phones.

Israel is divided into the following area codes:
02 – Jerusalem
03 – Tel Aviv
04 – Haifa
06 – The Galilee and north
07 – The South including Eilat, Beersheba (057 until spring 1993) and Ashkelon
08 – Ashdod, Rehovot
09 – Herzlia, Netanya (052 and 053 until 1993)

Overseas calls can be booked through post offices listed below, or the **international operator** 188 or through 03-622881. International phone calls from hotels are often very expensive. Alternatively, using the 177 toll-free number you will be connected to an operator abroad who can replace reverse charge calls or debit your credit card or subscriber account. The numbers to call are:

**Canada**: Tel: 177-430-2727
**UK** (British Telecom): Tel: 177-440-2727
**US AT&T**: Tel: 177-100-2727
**US MCI**: Tel: 177-150-2727
**US Sprint**: Tel: 177-102-2727

To dial abroad first dial 00, then the country code (44 for Britain, 49 for Germany, 1 for the US and Canada and 61 for Australia), then the area code (but omitting any initial zeroes) followed by the number.

International phone calls are most expensive (with the exception of North America) on weekdays from 8am–10pm. There is a 25 percent reduction from 10pm–1am and all day Saturday and Sunday, and a 50 percent reduction from 1–8am. To North America the most expensive rate is from 1pm until midnight. There is a 20 percent reduction from 8am until 1pm and all day Saturday and Sunday, and a 45 percent reduction from midnight until 8am.

Post offices with international telephone call facilities:
**Jerusalem**: 3 Rehov Koresh. Tel: 02-249858
**Tel Aviv**: 13 Rehov Frishman. Tel: 03-5244365
**Eilat**: The Old Commercial Center, Hatamarim Boulevard. Tel: 07-372323
**Tiberias**: Pedestrian Mall. Tel: 06-739218

## USEFUL NUMBERS

**Police** Tel: 100
**Ambulance** Tel: 101
**Fire Service** Tel: 102
**Information** Tel: 144
**Telephone Repairs** Tel: 166
**Overseas Operator** Tel: 188
**Overseas Collect Calls** Tel: 03-622881
**Direct Dialling Information** Tel: 195
**Telegrams** Tel: 171
**Auto Alarm Wake-up Calls** Tel: 174

## RECORDED MESSAGES

By dialing (03) 660259 tourists can receive information on events in the Tel Aviv area. Tourists can also leave a message should they have any questions, and they will be called back the next day. This service operates after 6pm Sunday–Thursday and Friday after 3pm.

Jerusalem has a similar service. The tourist may dial (02) 754863 after 6pm Sunday–Thursday and after 2pm on Friday.

Haifa has a 24-hour telephone service to hear "What's on in Haifa". Tel: (04) 640840.

# EMERGENCIES

## SECURITY & CRIME

Israel has a high rate of non-violent crimes (theft of homes, cars, property, pickpocketing etc.) but little violent crime (mugging, murder and rape). So do not leave valuables in hotel rooms or cars or wallets sticking temptingly out of pockets. Take all obvious precautions.

In terms of violent crime the security situation is the most pressing problem but incidents are few and far between. Under no circumstances leave unattended baggage laying around in a public place. Police sappers will blow it up within a few minutes. You should report all suspicious packages.

Before trips to the West Bank or Gaza you should ask about the prevailing security situation there.

To contact the **police** dail 100.

## LAWYERS

If you need a lawyer there are bound to be many who have emigrated to Israel from your country of origin. Your consulate can probably suggest some names.

## DRUG OFFENCES

Hashish is illegal but prosecutions are rarely brought. Because neighbouring Lebanon supplies much of the world's hashish, the drug is widely available in Israel with peddlers usually frequenting bars. Heroin is also grown in Lebanon but here the Israeli authorities do not turn a blind eye to users.

## MEDICAL SERVICES

Visitors are advised to have medical insurance because in a worst case scenario hospital bills can reach astronomical amounts. Israel has a well developed medical system in which the most advanced techniques from laser surgery to laparoscopic procedures are routine. Even before the recent influx of new immigrants, Israel had the highest ratio of doctors in the world. The Israeli medical system is most commonly compared to Britain's national health system. In other words, health care is well developed but resources are overstretched.

Most Israelis are members of the Histadrut Trade Union's sick fund, Kupat Holim. Hospitals are owned by the government, Kupat Holim or private charitable foundations. There are several private hospitals in the Tel Aviv and Haifa regions.

## EMERGENCY TREATMENT

**Ambulances** can be summoned by dialling 101. If you want to see a doctor urgently, you can go to a Magen David Adom ambulance station at night, or the emergency room of any **hospital** (101 will tell you which hospital is receiving casualty patients).

Most doctors will be happy to see patients privately. The tourist magazines are usually filled with adverts for medical services provided by American and European-trained doctors. Alternatively, you can look up the *Golden Pages* telephone directory. A routine consultation in your hotel room should cost no more than $40.

If in pain, Israelis tend to be expressive. So if you are sitting in the emergency room of a hospital with an appendix that is about to burst, go ahead and yell. If you stoically play the strong silent type, then staff will tend to assume you are not really in pain others will be treated before you, and the severity of your condition will be underestimated.

**Magen David Adom Ambulance Emergency First Aid Stations**: Tel: 101 or
**Jerusalem**: Tel: 02-523133
**Tel Aviv**: Tel: 03-5460111
**Haifa**: Tel: 04-512233
**Eilat**: Tel: 07-72333
**Netanya**: Tel: 053-623333

## DENTISTS

See the *Golden Pages*. Otherwise if you stroll around your hotel you're bound to find dental surgeries.

## PHARMACISTS

Most pharmacists are helpful and used to dealing with tourists. The *Jerusalem Post* will tell you which pharmacy is on all night or weekend duty. Routine prescription drugs like antibiotics are frequently sold over the counter even though this is illegal.

## OTHER USEFUL NUMBERS

**Emotional First Aid:**
Jerusalem: Tel: 02-610303
Tel Aviv: Tel: 03-5461111
Haifa: Tel: 04-672222
Netanya: Tel: 053-625110
**Rape Crisis Centre:**
Jerusalem (24 hours): Tel: 02-245554
Tel Aviv: Tel: 03-234819
Haifa: Tel: 04-660111
Eilat: Tel: 07-31977

## MEDICAL EQUIPMENT

Visitors temporarily in need of such medical equipment as oxygen tanks, wheelchairs, vaporisers, and a large number of other items can obtain them on loan, at no charge, at the Yad Sarah Organization for the Free Loan of Medical Equipment, Jerusalem: 49 Rehove Hanevim, tel: (02) 244242, 244047; Tel Aviv: 14a Rehov Ruppin, tel: (03) 5238974; Haifa: 4a Rehov Mapu, Ahuza, tel: (04) 245286; Rehovot: 31 Rehov Ezra, in addition to numerous other branches throughout the country.

**Dental** emergency treatment is available during weekends and on holy days, in Jerusalem through the Magen David Adom, and in Tel Aviv at 49 Rehove Bar Kokhba.

# GETTING AROUND

## TOURIST INFORMATION

You won't be at a loss for tourist information while in Israel. In fact, you may feel inundated by the many tourist weeklies and the like provided by your hotel.

The Israel Government Tourist Offices (IGTOS) are the only official purveyors of information, however, and will provide you with maps and recommend restaurants or accommodation. They also supply information about free tours and events.

For specific information about different areas in the country, it is best to contact the local IGTO directly:

**Acco**: Municipality Building. Tel: (04) 911764.
**Alleny Bridge**: (Israel-Jordan transit point). Tel: (02) 941038.
**Arad**: Commercial Center. Tel: (057) 954409.
**Ashkelon**: Commercial Center, Afridar. Tel: (07) 732412.
**Bat Yam**: Municipality Information Office, 43 Derech Ben-Gurion. Tel: (03) 5072777.
**Beerscheba**: 6A Ben Zvi St. Tel: (057360010).
**Ben-Gurion Airport**: Lod. Tel: (03) 9711485.
**Bethlehem**: Manger Square. Tel: (02) 741581/2.
**Eilat**: Khan Center, Ophica Park. Tel: (07) 334353.
**Haifa**: (Town Branch), 18 Rehov Herzl. Tel: (04) 666521/2.
**Central Bus Station**: Tel: (04) 512208.
**Jerusalem**: 24 Rehov Hamelech George. Tel: (02) 754888.
**Jaffa Gate**: Tel: (02) 282295/6.
**Municipal Information Office**: 34 Rehov Yafo. Tel: (02) 228844.

**Nahariya**: Central Bus Station. Tel: (04) 879800.
**Nazareth**: Rehov Casanova. Tel: (06) 573003.
**Netanya**: Kikar HaAtzmaut. Tel: (053) 827286.
**Rafiah**: (Israel-Egypt transit point). Tel: (07) 734274.
**Rosh Hanikra**: (Israel-Lebanon transit point). Tel: (04) 927802.
**Safed**: 50 Rehov Jerusalem. Tel: (06) 9230633.
**Tel Aviv**: 5 Shalom Aleichem. Tel: (03) 660259-61.
**Tiberias**: 23 Habanim St. Tel: (06) 722089.

In New York, there is an IGTO branch on the 19th floor of the Empire State Building, 350 Fifth Ave, New York, NY 10118. There are also offices located in Chicago, Houston, Miami Beach, Los Angeles and Toronto.

In Europe, there are IGTOS in London, Paris, Amsterdam, Copenhagen, Stockholm, Zurich, Frankfurt and Milan. There are offices as well in Johannesburg, South Africa, and Cairo, Egypt.

## CHRISTIAN INFORMATION CENTER

The Center, located inside the Old City's Jaffa Gate, opposite the Citadel, welcomes individuals or groups who, on their arrival in Jerusalem, seek help in planning their tours and visits. Services include: information of Christian and general interest, on holy places, Christian hospices, location of churches, times of services, etc; lectures, meetings, exhibitions; books on religious and archaeological subjects; a monthly "Associated Christian Press Bulletin"; guide books and maps.

The Christian Information Center, Omar Ibn El-Khattab Square (Jaffa Gate) P.O.B. 14309 Jerusalem. Tel: (02) 272692.

## FROM THE AIRPORT

An El Al airport bus leaves Ben-Gurion Airport Terminal in Tel Aviv (some 20 minutes away) approximately every hour from 6am–10pm and in accordance with the arrival of planes at other hours. **Egged buses** leave for Tel Aviv every 15 minutes from 5am–11.10pm; for Jerusalem (about 1 hour away) approximately every 20 minutes from 7.15am–6pm; for Haifa (1½ hours) from 7am–6pm approximately every 20 minutes.

**United Tours Bus** No. 222 travels between the airport and the Railway Station, Rehove Arlosorov, Tel Aviv, every hour year round. The service operates from 4–midnight. The bus stops at the Palace, Diplomat, Sheraton and Dan Hotels. For further details tel: (03) 7543410.

*Sherut* **taxis (Nesher)**, in which each passenger pays for his own seat, take less than an hour to reach Jerusalem.

Ordinary taxis are available to almost any point in the country. The fare is fixed and the tourist may ask to be shown the official price list. Cost for taxi service to Tel Aviv is about $10–15, or $22–30 to Jerusalem. *Sherut* service is considerably less expensive. The United Tours bus to Tel Aviv costs approximately $1 to the railroad terminal, or $1.30 to the city.

## INTERNAL FLIGHTS

**Arkia** Israel Airlines Ltd operate the following scheduled flights:
**From Jerusalem** to Tel Aviv, Haifa, Rosh Pinna, Eilat.
**From Tel Aviv** to Jerusalem, Rosh Pinna, Eilat.
**From Haifa** to Jerusalem, Tel Aviv, Eilat.
**From Eilat** to Jerusalem, Tel Aviv, Haifa.

A number of other companies operate charter flights (3–10 passengers) to various parts of the country. Further particulars may be obtained from travel agents or from Government Tourist Information Offices.

El-Rom Airlines operate air taxi services from Beersheba to Tel Aviv, Eilat, Jerusalem and Haifa and from Tel Aviv to Mitzpeh Ramon and Sodom.
For further information:
**Arkia Israeli Airlines Ltd**, Sde Dov Airport, Tel Aviv. Tel: (03) 6992222.
**El-Rom Airlines Ltd**, Sde Dov Airport, Tel Aviv. Tel: (03) 5412554.
Israel's Airports:
**Ben-Gurion International**: Tel: (03) 9710111.
**Eilat**: Tel: (07) 373333.
**Haifa**: Tel: (04) 722084.
**Herzliya**: Tel: (052) 502373.
**Jerusalem**: Tel: (02) 850980.
**Rosh Pinna (North)**: Tel: (06) 936478.
**Sde Dov Tel Aviv**: Tel: (03) 6991058.
**Uvoa**: Tel: (07) 339442.

## TOURING CLUB

The Automobile and Touring Club of Israel (MEMS) is affiliated to the Fédération Internationale de l'Automobile (FIA) and to the Alliance Internationale de Tourisme (AIT), and as such is linked to every Automobile and Touring Club in the world, providing reciprocal services for all tourists who are members of other clubs. Services include: emergency help, towing, legal and technical advice, as well as touring advice.
**Tel Aviv** (Head Office): 19 Derech Petach Tikva. Tel: (03) 5660442.
**Address for corrsepondence**: POB 36144, 61360 Tel Aviv.

## PUBLIC TRANSPORT

**Buses** are by far the most common means of transportation for both urban and inter-urban services. Services are regular and the fares are reasonable though prices have risen substantially in recent years due to the withdrawal of government subsidies.

Most buses in Israel are operated by the Egged Bus Cooperative, the third largest bus company in the world with an annual turnover of $342 million in 1991. Most of its fleet of 4,000 buses are air-conditioned. Egged operates all urban and inter-urban services except within Tel Aviv. Services are punctual and, if anything, impatient drivers tend to leave half a minute before time. If travelling to Eilat, it is advisable to reserve seats several days in advance.

An inter-urban flat fare ticket costs about $1 and a Jerusalem-Tel Aviv ticket costs $4. Jerusalem-Eilat costs $15. Return tickets are cheaper, and there are tickets allowing unlimited travel anywhere in Israel over a period of 7, 14, 21 days or a month.

Buses do not run from Friday before sundown until Saturday after sundown. Inter-urban bus services start around 6am and finish in the early evening except for the Tel Aviv–Jerusalem and Tel Aviv–Haifa lines which continue until midnight. Urban services run from 5am–midnight.
**Toll-free Information** about Egged, tel: 177-022-5555; or at the information window of bus stations.
**Egged Information Offices:**
National Egged Toll free Information Service.
Tel: 177-0225555.

## RAILWAYS

The Israel Railways run from Haifa and Nahariya in the north and from Tel Aviv to Jerusalem, on a daily basis. Fares are considerably lower than bus fares, and seats can be reserved in advance for a small extra charge. Most of the trains are rather old, but all have a buffet car and service, and the trip from Tel Aviv to Jerusalem is particularly lovely, winding through the scenic Sorek valley.

There is no train service on the Sabbath, or on Jewish holidays.
**Main Train Stations:**
**Haifa**: Bat Galim. Tel: (04) 564564.
**Jerusalem**: Kikar Remez. Tel: (02) 733764.
**Tel Aviv**: Central Station, Rehov Arlosorov. Tel: (03) 5421515.
**South Station**: Tel: (03) 822676.
**Student Discount:** On presentation of a student card, a 10 percent discount on all inter-city Egged Bus Company trips and a 25 percent on Israel Railways is available.

## TAXIS & SHERUT

Taxis offer a quick and convenient mode of travel in Israel. You can phone for a taxi in any major city or hail one in the street.

All urban taxis have meters, whose operation is compulsory. If the driver wants to take it off the meter, he might be trying to take you for a ride in more ways than one. Tipping is not compulsory, but often greatly appreciated.

Prices are pre-fixed between cities, and the driver will tell you your fare ahead of time, or show you the official price list if you ask for it.

The *sherut* is Israel's own indigenous mode of transportation, operating in and between main cities every day but Shabbat; some private companies or owners operate on Shabbat as well. In the *sherut*, individuals share a van or cab, which accommodates up to seven people, at a fixed price usually equivalent to the bus fare for the same route.

*Sheruts* between cities leave from near the central bus station, and, in Jerusalem, from near Zion Square. In Tel Aviv and some other cities, local *sheruts* follow the main bus routes, making similar stops in quick time.

## SUBWAY

Israel's only subway, the Carmelit, operates in Haifa. The train runs from Central Mount Carmel to downtown Haifa every 10 miuntes and makes six stops. The trip takes 9 miuntes. It operates Sunday–Thursday 5.30am–midnight. Friday 5.30am to 1 hour before the Sabbath, Saturday from sunset to midnight.

# PRIVATE TRANSPORT

## HIRING A CAR

Many of the world's principal car hire companies, including Hertz, Avis, Euro-Car, Inter-Rent, Budget and Thrifty, have operations in Israel. Israel's largest car hire company, Eldan, also has offices overseas. These companies offer the convenience of supplying you with a car at the airport and allowing you to leave it there on departure. They have a network of offices around. In addition, if you break down a new car is almost immediately at your service.

But hiring a car is expensive (at least $300 a week for a small 1200 or 1300 saloon). Traffic is heavy and parking is difficult in Israel's big cities, so for urban travel it is probably cheaper and more convenient to take taxis.

Hiring a car can be cheaper off-season (October–April) or if you cut a deal with one of the many local, smaller companies. But in general it is much cheaper to book a car as part of a package deal (flight, hotel, car) with your travel agent overseas.

As everywhere in the world, carefully check that there is no damage to the car, that the spare wheel, jack and other equipment is in place and that oil and water are sufficient before accepting a car.

Car hire companies require an international licence or will accept national licences if written in English or French.

## FUEL

Most garages sell 91 and 96-octane gasoline. Higher octanes are difficult to find. Unleaded gasoline and diesel are also available at every garage. As of 1992 virtually all garages are supplied by a cartel of three major companies – Paz, Delek and Sonol – selling gasoline at a fixed price of around 70 cents a litre or $3.20 a gallon, considerably cheaper than Western Europe. In Eilat where there is no VAT, gasoline is 18 percent cheaper. Government deregulation is allowing other companies to sell gasoline and in the near future a price war is expected to break out.

## BREAKING DOWN

Every town has dozens of repair garages. Keep receipts so that car hire companies can reimburse costs. If you break down on the highway put up your hood/bonnet and passers by will be quick to stop. On major inter-urban highways there are emergency telephones every few kilometres.

## DRIVING

Israelis drive with Mediterranean creativity. There is a lot of horn honking, overtaking on the inside and general improvisation. But life on the road is not as chaotic as in many other Mediterranean countries. With well over 1 million vehicles on the roads, Israel has one of the world's densest road systems. There are around 500 fatalities each year from road accidents, which is comparable with death rates on Western Euopean roads.

Laws are strictly enforced and it is necessary to wear seat belts at all times and strap children under 4 into appropriate seats. Speed limits are 90 kph (55 mph) on highways and 50–70 kph (30–40 mph) in urban areas. Keep your passport, driver's licence and other papers with you at all times. Police tend to be lenient with tourists but can take you straight in front of a judge if they wish.

## PARKING

Parking is very difficult in the major city centres and it is best to look for a parking lot. These can cost $1.50 an hour in Jerusalem, and up to $3 per hour in parts of Tel Aviv. If a kerbside is marked in blue and white, you need a ticket which you can purchase in batches of five from many kiosks, lottery kiosks and stores. Each ticket costs about 90 cents and allows you to park for an hour. You must tear out the right time, month and day of the month and display the ticket on the kerbside window. These tickets must be displayed from 7am–7pm. Outside these hours, parking is usually free.

If you fail to display a ticket or the ticket has expired, you are liable for a $20 fine, though this need not be paid for several months.

Do not ignore red and white marked kerbsides or No Parking signs. Here you may be clamped with a "Denver boot" or towed away. In either instance, it will cost you $20 and a lot of wasted time in redeeming your car.

## ON FOOT & BY THUMB

### PEDESTRIANS

Drivers cannot be relied upon to stop at pedestrian crossings. The safest place to cross is at traffic lights when the pedestrian light is green. In Jerusalem, police hand out fines to pedestrians who cross at red lights. Beware at right turn filters where the pedestrian light is green but traffic may still pass.

**Hiking:** Israel is ideal for hiking in the cooler months, October–April, or during early mornings or late afternoons of the summer (*see Nature Trails page 347*).

### HITCHHIKING

Hitchhiking is a conventional form of transport in Israel. There are even hitchhiking stations at major junctions that look like bus stops. But hitchhiking can still be difficult because of the fierce competition and the fact that priority is given to soldiers.

### MOPED RENTAL

Otzma B'Tnua Mehira B.M. (Power Through Speed Ltd) is licensed by the Ministry of Transport to rent mopeds. They may be rented by people aged 18 and over who hold a special licence. For Further information, contact:
**Otzma B'tnua Mehira**, 46 Rehove Ha'aliya, Tel Aviv. Tel: (03) 836894.

### ROAD DISTANCES

| | JERUSALEM | | TEL AVIV | | HAIFA | |
|---|---|---|---|---|---|---|
| | Km | Mi | Km | Mi | Km | Mi |
| Jerusalem | – | – | 62 | 39 | 159 | 99 |
| Tel Aviv | 62 | 39 | – | – | 95 | 59 |
| Haifa | 159 | 99 | 95 | 56 | – | – |
| Arad | 104 | 65 | 158 | 98 | 255 | 158 |
| Ashdod | 66 | 41 | 42 | 26 | 139 | 86 |
| Beersheba | 84 | 52 | 113 | 70 | 210 | 130 |
| Eilat | 312 | 194 | 354 | 220 | 451 | 280 |
| Hebron | 35 | 22 | 97 | 60 | 194 | 120 |
| Metula | 221 | 137 | 196 | 122 | 120 | 75 |
| Nablus | 63 | 38 | 57 | 35 | 93 | 58 |
| Nazareth | 157 | 97 | 102 | 63 | 35 | 22 |
| Netanya | 93 | 58 | 29 | 18 | 66 | 41 |
| Rehovot | 53 | 33 | 24 | 15 | 121 | 75 |
| Rosh Hanikra | 201 | 125 | 137 | 85 | 42 | 26 |
| Toberias | 157 | 97 | 132 | 82 | 69 | 43 |

Distances indicated are measured along the most convenient routes, which are not necessarily the shortest ones.

# WHERE TO STAY

There is a diverse range of accommodation options in Israel including over 300 hotels and dozens of youth hostels. But there is a certain sameness about Israeli hotels, most of which were built between 1960 and 1980, offering modern comfort and convenience without any character.

### KIBBUTZ GUEST HOUSES

Visitors wanting a uniquely Israeli experience should try a kibbutz guest house. The guest house itself usually offers all the facilities of a luxury hotel plus the chance to get acquainted with kibbutz life at first hand. Though many of these guest houses are in isolated rural areas, especially in the northern Galilee, others are located in the country but just 20 minutes or so by bus or car from Jerusalem or Tel Aviv.

For further information, contact Kibbutz Hotels Chain, 90 Rehov Ben Yehuda, 61031 Tel Aviv. Tel: 03-5243358.

### CHRISTIAN HOSPICES

Another unique Holy Land experience is the broad array of Christian hospices. Originally designed principally for pilgrims and owned by churches, these hospices cater for all comers, including many Israeli Jews on vacation, who enjoy the elegance and old-world European charm of these establishments.

The term hospice is misleading. Some like Notre Dame in Jerusalem, owned by the Vatican, resemble luxury hotels. Others reflect the ethnic origins of their founders. The Sisters of Zion in the Jerusalem suburb of Ein Kerem could be a pension in Provence, while St Andrew's Church in Jerusalem could be a guest house anywhere in Scotland.

### HOTELS

Until recently, Israel's Ministry of Tourism graded hotels from ☆☆ up to ☆☆☆☆☆ according to size, service and facilities. This system has now been discontinued, but the ensuing list may refer to the hotel's previous grading to convey an idea of the level of establishment.

Hotels require guests to check out by midday but on Saturdays and holidays guests are entitled to retain possession of their rooms until the sabbath or holiday finishes in the evening.

## PRICES

Hotel prices are high if you simply turn up. It is much cheaper to arrange a package deal before leaving. Whereas a luxury hotel can charge $100 or even $150 a night, two weeks at the Jerusalem Hilton, including a return flight from Britain costs about $1,000. Prices can be even more expensive during high season Easter/Passover, July–August, Jewish New Year and Christmas. But there are hotels catering for every pocket down to youth hostels which charge $10–$15 a night.

Hotel rates are generally quoted in dollars and include a 15 percent service charge. If you pay in foreign currency you are exempt from 18 percent VAT. In Eilat there is no VAT charge.

## ACCO

**Palm Beach Club Hotel**, P.O. Box 2192. Situated on the coastal highway south of Acco with a beautiful view of the old city, this 140-room, 4-star establishment has a swimming pool, private stretch of beach, and was recently renovated after serving as a centre for Ethiopian immigrants. Tel: 04-815815.

## ARAD

**Margoa**, Rehov Mo'av. 100 rooms. Clean, tidy, modern and unremarkable. In tranquil surroundings with superb desert views and swimming pool. 3 stars. Tel: 057-957014.
**Nof Arad**, Rehov Mo'av. Over the road from the Margoa and pretty much the same with 120 rooms and a swimming pool, but costing 10 percent less. Tel: 057-957056.

## ASHKELON

**Dagon**, 2 Rehov Moshe Dorot. Combines comfort and modern facilities with highly personalised service and good food. Has 50 rooms, a swimming pool and is near the sea. Was graded as 4-star. Tel: 07-736111.
**Shulamit Gardens**, 11 Rehov Hatayassim. Also with a 4-star grading, the city's largest hotel is more impersonal. Has 120 rooms and a swimming pool. Tel: 07-736222.
**King Shaul**, 28 Rehov Harekefet. Also unremarkable but a little cheaper. Formerly a 3-star, it has its own swimming pool. Tel: 07-734124.

## BEERSHEBA

**The Desert Inn**, P.O. Box 247. Comfortable but a bit run-down. The hotel, which formerly had a 4-star rating has 164 rooms and a swimming pool. Tel: 057-424922.
**Arava**, 37 Rehov Hahistadrut. Small, clean and tidy. 27 rooms. Tel: 057-278792.

## CAESAREA

**Dan Caesarea Golf Hotel**, Caesarea. Luxurious, in secluded isolated location adjoining Israel's only golf course. Swimming pool; close to the beach and ancient Roman ruins. Tel: 06-362266.

## DEAD SEA

Almost all the Dead Sea's hotels are at Ein Bokek near the southern tip of the sea. High season is during the winter.
**Sonesta**, Ein Bokek. The Dead Sea's newest and most luxurious hotel. Swimming pool, private beach and all mod cons. Tel: 057-584626.
**Moriah Plaza Dead Sea Spa Hotel**, Ein Bokek. Until the Sonesta opened this was the most fashionable and luxurious hotel in the region. Tel: 057-584221.
**Tsell Harim**, Ein Bokek. Unremarkable, clean and comfortable and cheaper than most of the hotels in the region. Tel: 057-584121.
**Ein Gedi Kibbutz Guest House**, Ein Gedi. On the hillside close to the hot water sulphur springs. Tel: 057-584757.

## EILAT

Almost all of Eilat's hotels are to the east of the city. Those wishing to be more isolated should look southwards to Coral Beach.
**King Solomon's Palace**, Northern Beach. Pleasingly designed overlooking the marina, very good service and excellent value buffet meals. Always busy and with its bars and restaurants it is one of the centre's of the city's social life. Tel: 07-334111.
**Lagoona**, Northern Beach. Owned by the same Isrotel group as the adjoining King Solomon's Palace. Offers 4-star prices compared to its neighbour's 5 stars. Tel: 07-332089.
**Neptune**, PO Box 259. Overlooks the Red Sea with its handsome white facade. 5-star hotel with 5-star prices. Tel: 07-335038.
**Moriah Plaza**, Recently renovated and upgraded to 5-star equivalent. Overlooking the sea. Tel: 07-361111.
**Club In**, Coral Beach. Owned by the Hilton chain, located 5 miles (8 km) south of the town at the coral beach. Structured as villas rather than a block. Good facilities for children. Tel: 07-379577.
**Red Rock**, PO Box 306. Located on the beach. More modest and cheaper than most of its neighbours. Tel: 07-373171.
**Moon Valley**, PO Box 1135. Relatively cheap and comfortable with a swimming pool but far from the beach. Tel: 07-333888.
**Etzion**, Sderot Hatamarim 1. Cheap, clean and by the central bus station. Tel: 07-370003.

## HAIFA

Most of the city's hotels are on the peak of Mount Carmel where the air is fresher and the view is invigorating.

**Dan Carmel**, 87 Sderot Hanassi. The city's most fashionable hotel is stylish but expensive. Tel: 04-386211.

**Dan Panorama**, Panorama Center, 105 Sderot Hanassi. A high-rise building with sensational view and all modern conveniences but without the charm of its sister hotel. Tel: 04-352222.

**Nof**, 101 Sderot Hanassi. A poorer man's neighbour to the Dans, but you'll still need plenty of money. Tel: 04-354311.

**Nesher**, 53 Herzl Street. In the centre of town for those on a limited budget. Clean and comfortable 15-room establishment. Tel: 04-640644.

## HERZLIYA

A high-class resort with opulent hotels along the beach.

**Dan Accadia**, Herzliya Pituach. Built in the 1950s as one of Israel's first luxury hotels, this 5-star establishment has more class than most. Tel: 052-556677.

**Daniel Towers Hotel and Spa**, Herzliya Pituach. No expense spared in perhaps Israel's most lavish hotel. For those who like extravagance and don't mind paying for it. Tel: 052-544444.

**Sharon**, Herzliya Pituach. More modest but still up-market. Tel: 052-575777.

## JERUSALEM

Hotels can be found in virtually every corner of the city. High season is the summer, and Jewish and Christian festivals.

**King David**, 23 King David Street. Israel's premiere hotel where political leaders, the rich and famous stay. Built in the 1930s it has a distinctive style but in terms of quality of service and value for money its newer rivals try harder. Tends to rely on its reputation. Has beautiful gardens overlooking the Old City. Tel: 02-251111.

**Hyatt Regency**, 32 Lehi Street, Mount Scopus. Stylish design which blends into the hillside (not easy for a 600-room hotel). Hyatt's usual interior of waterfalls and splendour. Beautiful view but far from town. Tel: 02-323196.

**Jerusalem Hilton**, Givat Ram. Usual Hilton luxury in landmark building by city's entrance. Far from the centre of town but close to central bus station. Tel: 02-581151.

**Ramada Renaissance**, Wolfson 6. Very large and luxurious. Has the country's largest banqueting facilities but little character. Tel: 02-528111.

**Sheraton Plaza**, 37 King George. An ugly concrete block in the heart of Jerusalem, but the lap of luxury and very central for both the Old and New Cities.

Its "Cow on the Roof" (in the basement) is one of the finest and most expensive restaurants in town. Tel: 02-259111.

**Seven Arches**, Mount of Olives. Formerly the Inter-Continental. Built on a desecrated Jewish graveyard by the Jordanians, making it unkosher for Jews. Very stylish with breathtaking view of the Old City. Tel: 02-894455.

**Laromme**, Jabotinsky Street. A lot of character for a hotel built in the 1980s. Excellent location by the attractive Yemin Moshe. Tel: 02-756666.

**Moriah**, Rehov Keren Hayesod. Tranquil atmosphere for such a large hotel. Slightly cheaper than most of the other luxury hotels and conveniently located for New and Old Cities. Tel: 02-232232.

**American Colony**, Nablus Street. Jerusalem's oldest hotel has much character and charm and is favoured by the foreign press corps. Tel: 02-285171.

**Windmill**, 3 Mendele. Opposite the Moriah but less luxurious and less expensive. Tel: 02-663111.

**Jerusalem Tower**, Rehov Hillel. Clean, comfortable and compact and smack in the middle of the New City. 3-star prices. Tel: 02-252161.

**Jerusalem Gate**, Yermiyahu 43. For the budget-conscious but still not that cheap. Right by the Central Bus Station. Tel: 02-383101.

**Lincoln**, 24 King David Street. Formerly the Menorah. Opposite the King David. Pleasant, modern and fairly inexpensive. Tel: 02-234351.

## KIBBUTZ GUEST HOUSES NEAR JERUSALEM

**Mitzpeh Rachel**, Kibbutz Ramat Rachel. Actually within the city limits. Modern attractive setting with superb view of the desert. Tel: 02-702555.

**Kiryat Anavim**, Kibbutz Kiryat Anavim. Seven miles to the west of the city nestling in a forest in the Judean Hills. Tel: 02-342770.

## CHRISTIAN HOSPICES IN JERUSALEM

**Notre Dame**, Opposite the New Gate. Luxurious accommodation, splendid 19th-century architecture and one of Jerusalem's best restaurants–all opposite the Old City walls. Recently taken over and renovated by the Vatican. Tel: 02-281223.

**YMCA**, King David Street, PO Box 294. Stylish 1930s building opposite the King David Hotel. Being refurbished and made more up-market. Reopened Easter 1993. Tel: 02-253433.

**St Andrew's Scots Memorial Hospice**. Intimate guest house offering mulled wine, mince pies and haggis to its Christmas guests. Superb location overlooking the Old City. Tel: 02-732401.

**Our Sisters of Zion**, PO Box 17105, Ein Kerem. Delightful Provence-style pension in the nearby village of Ein Kerem. Spacious gardens filled with olive trees and grape vines. Tel: 02-415738.

## NAHARIYA

**Carlton**, 23 Hagaaton Boulevard. The best hotel in town. Comfortable, fairly unremarkable but quite expensive. Far from the beach but has its own swimming pool. Tel: 04-922211.

**Frank Hotel**, 4 Rehov Ha'aliya. Very neat and tidy like this whole town. Relatively inexpensive. Tel: 04-920278.

## NAZARETH

**Grand New**, St Joseph Road. Not so grand or new but good value and central location. Tel: 06-573020.

## NETANYA

**The Seasons**. Formerly the Dan Netanya, this is Netanya's most luxurious hotel. Overlooking the sea. Tel: 053-618555.

**Yahalom**, 11 Rehov Gad Machnes. Offers a reasonable seaside vacation at reasonable prices. Tel: 053-635345.

## SAFED

**The Rimon Inn**, Artists Colony, PO Box 13110. Very stylish, blending in with the town's historic and artistic image. But you pay for the character. Tel: 06-920666.

**Central**, 37 Rehov Yerushalaim. Less expensive and in the heart of the city. Tel: 06-972666.

## TEL AVIV

Virtually all Tel Aviv's hotels are lined up on the sea front to the north of the city, overlooking the golden beaches.

**Tel Aviv Hilton**, Independence Park. Generally accepted as the city's most luxurious hotel. Very fashionable with Tel Aviv high society, with high prices to match. Tel: 03-5202222.

**Tel Aviv Sheraton**, 115 Hayarkon. Challenges Hilton's claim to being the city's paramount hotel. Tel: 03-5286222.

**Dan Tel Aviv**, 107 Hayarkon. The city's oldest luxury hotel, built in the 1950s. Tel: 03-5241111.

**Dan Panorama**, Rehov Kaufman. Set far away from all the other major hotels, this hotel charges considerably lower prices while offering all the luxuries. Ten minutes walk from Old Jaffa. Tel: 03-5190190.

**Imperial**, 66 Hayarkon. Clean, comfortable and relatively inexpensive. Tel: 03-657002.

**Adiv**, 5 Rehov Mendele. Also clean, comfortable and modestly priced. Tel: 03-229141.

**Shefayim Guest House**, Kibbutz Shefayim (20 minutes from Tel Aviv). Tel: 052-523434.

## TIBERIAS

**Galei Kinneret**, 1 Eliezer Kaplan. The city's oldest luxury hotel for those who avoid modern concrete blocks. Tel: 06-792331.

**Moriah Plaza**, Rehov Habanim. On the lakefront. Modern, luxurious and stylish. Tel: 06-792233.

**Arnon**, 28 Rehov Hashomer. Cheap and quiet. Tel: 06-720181

**Nof Ginossar**, Kibbutz Ginossar. Several miles north of Tiberias on the lake. Tel: 06-792161.

**Beatitudine**, Mount of Beatitudes. Delightfully located in the hills to the north of the lake. Italian atmosphere. Tel: 06-720878.

**Church of Scotland**, PO Box 104. A corner of Scotland in the centre of Tiberias. Tel: 06-790144.

## UPPER GALILEE

This picturesque region has the greatest concentration of kibbutz guest houses including the following:

**Ayelet Hashachar**, The most luxurious of the kibbutz guest houses in the region. Tel: 06-932611.

**Kfar Blum**. The River Jordan flows through this kibbutz, which also has an Olympic-size swimming pool. Tel: 06-943666.

**Hagoshrim**. Also by the River Jordan, and well located for trips to Mount Hermon. Tel: 06-956231.

## CAMPGROUNDS

Israel is good for camping, with camp sites providing an excellent touring base for each region. They offer full sanitary facilities, electric current, a restaurant and/or store, telephone, first-aid facilities, shaded picnic and campfire areas and day and night watchmen. They can be reached by bus, but all are open to cars and caravans. Most have tents and cabins, as well as a wide range of equipment for hire. All sites have swimming facilities either on the site or within easy reach. For full details contact:

**Israel Camping Union**: POB 53 , 221 00 Nahariya. Tel: (04) 923366, 925392.

There is a reception and departure service for campers at Ben-Gurion Airport. By ringing (03) 944524 on arrival, a camping car comes within a very short time to take participants to the reception camping site at Mishmar Hashiva, about 10 km from Ben-Gurion Airport. A similar service is available from Mishmar Hashiva to the airport upon departure, if you stay the last night there.

Arriving campers can obtain assistance from the Tourist Information Office in the Arrivals Hall. At the reception camp at Mishmar Hashiva, campers are given maps and folders and are individually advised on touring the country.

**Reception Site**: Mishmar Hashiva. Tel: (03) 9604185.

Camping sites include Ashkelon, Eilat, Ein Gedi, the Carmel Coast, and Ramat Rachel, just south of Jerusalem, among other locations.

## PRIVATE APARTMENTS

For a longer stay in one place, it can be very economical to rent an apartment, with its own kitchen, bedroom, living room, etc. For families it can mean a cheap way of accommodating the kids; for couples, individuals or groups it can mean a more natural experience of the country, living as the locals do, away from bellhops and room service.

Here, too, options range from the economical to the luxurious.

There are several organisations that offer apartment rentals, either in single buildings, or dispersed.

The one company with the greatest resources at its disposal is Homtel Israel, which has hundreds of apartments throughout Tel Aviv and Jerusalem, on the Mediterranean coast, on the Sea of Galilee, in Eilat, and other places. They also have offices in the US and Europe.
For further information:
**Homtel Israel**, 1170 Broadway, Suite 612 New York, NY 10001. Tel: (212) 6869343.
**Homtel Israel**, Suite 604, Triumph House, 189 Regent Street, London, WlR 7WF.
Tel: (01) 4372892/3.
**Homtel Israel**, 97 Jaffa Street, Jerusalem. Tel: (02) 225062.

## TIME-SHARING

Time-share developments are available in Tiberias, Eilat and Tel Aviv. Swimming pools, sports facilities, restaurants and shops are provided.

## YOUTH HOSTELS

There are nearly 30 youth hostels throughout the country, operated by the Israel Youth Hostel Association (IYHA) which is affiliated with the international YHA. They offer dormitory accommodations and most of them provide both meals and self-service kitchen facilities. There is no age limit. Some hostels also provide family accommodation. Individual reservations should be made directly with the hostel.

The IYHA also arranges individual package tours, called "Israel on the Youth Hostel Trail" for 14, 21 or 28 days. These include nights in any of the hostels with dinner and breakfast, unlimited bus travel, a half-day conducted tour, entrance to 31 National Parks and numerous museums, a map, and other informational materials.
For further information:
**Head Office**–IYHA, 3 Rehov Dorot Rishonim, POB 1075, 91009 Jerusalem. Tel: (02) 252706.
**Acco**, POB 1090, Acre. Tel: (04) 911982.
**Beit Bernstein**, 1 Rehov Keren Hayesod, 94266 Jerusalem. Tel: (02) 258286.
**Beit Binyamin**, POB 1139, Safed. Tel: (06) 921086.
**Beit Noam**, POB 2, Mitzpe Ramon.
Tel: (057) 588443.

**Beit Sara**, Ein Gedi, 86910 MP Dead Sea.
Tel: (057) 584165.
**Beit Yatziv**, POB 7, Beersheba. Tel: (057) 71490/77444.
**Blau Weiss**, POB 34, Arad. Tel: (057) 957150.
**Carmel**, MP Hof Hacarmel, Haifa. Tel: (04) 532516.
**Eilat**, POB 152, Eilat. Tel: (07) 370088.
**Ein Karem**, POB 17013, 91170 Jerusalem.
Tel: (02) 416282.
**Emek Hefer**, Kfar Vitkin. Tel: (053) 666032.
**Haezrahi**, Kiryat Anavim, MP Mate Yehuda.
Tel: (02) 342770.
**Hankin**, MP Gilboa, Ma'ayan Harod. Tel: (065) 531660.
**Havat Hatsofim**, MP Kfar Maccabi, Ramat Yohanan.
Tel: (04) 442976.
**Kfar Etzion**, MP Har Hebron, Kfar Etzion.
Tel: (02) 935133.
**Kiryat Tivon**, 12 Rehov Zeid, Kiryat Tivon.
Tel: (04) 931482.
**Louise Waterman-Wise**, 8 Rehov Hapisga, Bayit Vegan, Jerusalem. Tel: (02) 423366, 420990.
**Ramot Shapira**, POB 7l6, Beit Meir, Jerusalem.
Tel: (02) 342691.
**Taiber**, Poriah, POB 232, Tiberias. Tel: (06) 750050.
**Tel Aviv**, 32 Rehov Bnei Dan, Tel Aviv.
Tel: (03) 5441748.
**Tel Hai**, MP Upper Galilee, Tel Hai. Tel: (06) 940043.
**Yad Labanim**, Rehov Yahalom, Petah Tikva.
Tel: (03) 9226666.
**Y.H. Taylor**, 86901 MP Dead Sea, Massada.
Tel: (057) 584349.
**Yoram**, MP Korazim, Kare Deshe. Tel: (06) 720601.
**Yoseph Mayouhas**, POB 81, Tiberias.
Tel: (06) 721775.
**Youth Center**, Jerusalem Forest, POB 3353, 91033 Jerusalem. Tel: (02)416060/413065.

# FOOD DIGEST

## WHAT TO EAT

Eating is a national pastime in Israel, one engaged in as much and as often as possible. On the street, at the beach, in every public place and certainly in every home, day and night – you'll find Israelis tucking in to food.

The biblical residents of the Land of Canaan were nourished by the fertility and abundance of a land "flowing with milk and honey". But the milk was mainly from sheep and goats, and the honey from dates, figs and carobs. Much depended on the sun, the rains and the seasons. Food was simple; feast predictably followed famine. Times have changed – at least in the culinary sense.

Just as Israel is a blend of cultures from all over the world, so its cuisine is a weave of flavours and textures, contrasts and similarities. There is no definitive Israeli fare, just as there is no definitive Israeli. Rather, there is a unique merging of East and West, and the results are a profusion of culinary delights.

The predominant foodstyle however, reflects the country's geographical location – somewhere between the Middle East and the Mediterranean. Dining out? Don't be led astray by signs telling you that the establishment serves "oriental" food. In Israel, "oriental" refers to the Middle East. "Oriental" Jews are those of Sephardic (Spanish, Italian or Arab) heritage. Each Jewish ethnic group, whether Moroccan, Libyan, Tunisian, Yemenite, Iraqi or native born (sabra) Israeli, has its own special dish and its own holiday fare.

Their food is similar yet distinct from each other. Basic herbs and spices include cumin, fresh and dried coriander, mint, garlic, onion, turmeric, black pepper, and sometimes cardamom and fresh green chili pepper. Dark, fruity olive oil adds further fragrance.

Arabic food is also considered "Oriental" and both Arabic and Jewish meals begin the same way – with a variety of savoury salads. Humus, ground chick pea seasoned with tahina (sesame paste), lemon juice, garlic and cumin – is probably the most popular dip, spread and salad rolled into one. Tahina, prepared likewise, come next. You'll also find the most astounding variety of eggplant salads you've ever seen; eggplant in tahina, fried sliced eggplant, chopped eggplant with vegetables, chopped liver flavoured eggplant and more. Assorted pickled vegetables are considered salads as well.

While the waiters may show some sign of disappointment, you can order the salads as a meal unto itself. Or you can follow it with kebab (grilled ground spiced meat), shashlik (grilled sliced lamb or beef with lamb fat), seniya (beef or lamb in tahina sauce), stuffed chicken or pigeon, chops or fish.

Don't expect pork in either a kosher or traditional Muslim restaurant. Both religions prohibit its consumption. Seafood, while forbidden by Jewish and permissible by Muslim law, is widely available. Shrimps and calamari are the predominant varieties.

Do try the fish, particularly in the seaside areas of Tiberias, Tel Aviv, Jaffa and Eilat (there are no fish in the Dead Sea!). Trout, grey and red mullet, sea bass and St Peter's fish are generally served fried or grilled, sometimes accompanied by a piquant sauce. Authentic North African restaurants will also feature harimeh – hot and spicy cooked fish fragrant with garlic, tomatoes, cumin and hot pepper.

And if you still have room, there's dessert. In Arabic restaurants this may mean baklava (filo dough sprinkled with nuts and sweet syrup), some other rich sweet, or fruit. In typical Jewish oriental restaurants it could mean caramel creme custard, chocolate mousse or an egg white confection laced with chocolate syrup and (for some unknown reason) called Bavarian crème. Turkish coffee or tea with fresh mint seals the meal. If you do not want sugar, tell the waiter in advance.

Yemenite food is characterised by virtually all the same spices as other Sephardic cuisines, just more of them. Genuine Yemenite restaurants offer rather exotic types of soups for the Westerner, including "foot soup", "tail soup" and "udder soup" among others, though more conservative lentil, vegetable, and beef soups are available. All are aromatic and rich in flavour. Several types of bread are served: mallawah (crispy fried, fattening and delicious), lahuh (light and pancake-like) and jahnoon (slowbaked strudel-like dough with copious amounts of margarine). While pitta bread is served automatically with any order, these others must be requested. Eat them with a mixed vegetable salad, humus and/or ful (slow-cooked fava beans), haminados (slow-cooked brown and creamy-yolked eggs), or alone with condiments.

Yemenites have their own special spice mixtures and condiments, and believe them to be generally healthful and a particular aid to digestion. These are hilbe (a bitter-though-interesting fenugreek preparation) thought to be helpful in the treatment of diabetes, and tzhoug (fresh coriander chopped with hot green or red peppers and spices), considered beneficial for blood circulation. In authentic Yemenite restaurants, these are served along with the meal. You may want to end your repast with coffee with hawaiig, a fragrant blend of spices akin to the Indian garam masala.

If it's Askenazic or Eastern European Jewish cooking you're after, you can find traditional gefilte fish, chopped liver, borscht (beet soup), Hungarian goulash (stew) and Russian peroshki (baked or fried piquant filled pastries), but these are not considered day-to-day fare by most of the populace, and are served only by speciality restaurants.

Due to the influx of Vietnamese Boat People, and former residents of Taiwan, Hong Kong, Thailand and the Philippines, Chinese-style restaurants abound and are much beloved by the native population. Ask the locals for recommendations.

Elegant restaurants are also a part of the local scene, and like their counterparts in other countries, offer a rich selection of gourmet foods, some authentic to the cuisine they proffer, some tailored to local tastes. Thanks to a new generation of young Israeli chefs a new movement is growing, based on an intense desire to create an authentic haute cuisine rooted in classic French cookery and personalised with ingredients indigenous to this country.

The results – dishes like "lamb wrapped in bulgar pastry and stuffed with pâté de foie" or "sweetbreads stuffed with avocado and served in an avocado sauce" blend the foreign and the familiar.

For a real understanding of the country's cuisine, visit supermarkets, green grocers and open air

# Our history could fill this book, but we prefer to fill glasses.

When you make a great beer, you don't have to make a great fuss.

# INSIGHT GUIDES

## COLORSET NUMBERS

▶ *What is the significance of the number that appears in a triangle on the spine of each Insight Guide? Each number, in fact, is a color code identifying the background color of the spine. Line up all titles from No. 100 to 300 for a full set of Insight Guides and your book-shelves will radiate a dazzling rainbow of world travel.*

markets, and investigate the little out-of-the way eateries in places like the Old City of Jerusalem, the Yemenite Kerem Hataymanim and Hatikvah quarters in Tel Aviv, the Jaffa port and little villages.

## SNACKS

Since Israelis are major league eaters, snacks play a starring role in the day. Favourite munchies include bagel shaped sesame-sprinkled breads (served with *za'atara* – a wild oregano-based spice mixture available only in "ethnic" settings like the Old City of Jerusalem), nuts and sunflower seeds. Pizza, blintzes, waffles, and burgers all come in and out of vogue. But the ultimate Sabra snack has to be *felafel* (fried chickpea balls served in pitta bread with a variety of vegetable possibilities). Along the side-walks of major streets, you can usually find several adjoining *felafel* stands where you're free to stuff your pitta with salads for as long as your pitta holds out. Tel Aviv's Shuk Betzalel is probably the most famous of the *felafel* centres. Located just near the Carmel market, it features an entire street of *felafel* vendors, with the largest salad selection this side of the Mediterranean.

## FRUIT & VEGETABLES

The country's produce is legendary. Fruits and vegetables arrive at market stalls hours after picking, and a trip to the open-air Mahane Yehudah in Jerusalem or the Carmel market in Tel Aviv, will reveal a sumptuous array of everything from apples to artichokes, kohlrabi to celeriac. Sub-tropical fruits include kiwi, mango, persimmon, loquat, passion fruit, cheromoya and papaya. Fresh dates, figs, pomegranates and the world's largest strawberries are seasonal attractions.

Produce is sold by the kilo or gram, and is most reasonably priced at open-air markets. Avoid supermarket produce because it tends to be second rate. Wash everything well before you eat.

## MEAT & POULTRY

Those who prefer fowl will find the chicken and turkey, and in more elegant restaurants, the goose and mullard duck (an Israeli hybrid) excellent choices. While much beef is imported, all fowl is domestically raised.

## DAIRY PRODUCTS

In days of old, water was scarce and not very palatable, so milk became a major component of the biblical diet. Goat's milk was considered the richest and most nourishing. Next came sheep's milk, cow's milk and finally the milk of camels.

Today's Israel continues the "Land of milk and honey" tradition with a wealth of more familiar cheeses (like Swiss, Camembert, Brie and Gouda), double-rich cottage cheese, and a wide variety of goat and sheep yogurt and cheeses (special types of which are found in some health food stores and Arab villages).

A visit to the supermarket will reveal Israel's range of white cheeses; wrapped in paper or sold in tubs, they are marked with a number signifying fat content. Try Tov Ta'am, a soft spreadable 5 percent fat white cheese wrapped in paper – if you're looking to lower your fat intake. Or taste *leben* or *eshel* – cultured milk products with approximately the same fat content as yogurt.

## HOLIDAY FOODS

If there are jelly doughnuts (*sufganiot*) it must be Chanukah, the occasion also for potato *latkes* (pancakes). On Purim you'll find *oznay haman* (*hamentashen* or filled triangular cookies).

If you're in Israel around holiday time, try to experience some holiday fare. On Passover, it's *matzobrie*, coconut macaroons, and sponge cake. Shavuot is strictly for dairy delights. Sukkot and Tu B'shvat are celebrated with dried fruits and nuts. Every Friday afternoon, there are special braided challahs for the Sabbath. And every Sabbath there is *cholent* (*hamin* if you're Sephardic), a baked bean and meat stew set to bake on Friday for Sabbath lunch.

Throughout the world, bread is considered the staff of life. In Israel eating heartily, and often, is a way of life. *Bon appetit* – or as they say in Israel – *Be'tayavon*.

## DRINKING NOTES

### WATER

You can drink the water in Israel, though plenty of bottled water is also available.

### SOFT DRINKS

All the usual carbonated drinks such as colas are available. As in Britain, "soda" refers to soda water and not a flavoured carbonated drink. Diet and regular soft drinks are available. The most delicious and healthiest drinks to try are the wide range of fruit drinks available. For a few dollars, street vendors will squeeze you an orange, carrot, grapefruit, kiwifruit or a dozen other fruits.

### TEA & COFFEE

Tea connoisseurs will be out of luck. Most Israeli establishments dip a feeble tea-bag into hot water. But, as throughout the Middle East, Israelis take their coffee seriously. Most popular are Middle Eastern coffee (*botz*), Turkish coffee, Viennese coffee (*cafe hafuch*) and filter coffee. Instant coffee western style is known as *nes*. Cafés, like bars in Europe, are often the centre of social life.

## ALCOHOL

Israel has a wide selection of wines, both red and white. During the 1980s many good-quality wines were produced, but they can be expensive. There are several local beers, both bottled and draft, and a range of imported beers – but ale specialists will probably turn up their noses. There are both home-distilled and imported spirits and liquors. The local speciality is *arak*, very similar to Greece's ouzo.

Although Israel has none of the alcoholic inhibitions of its Islamic neighbours, most Israelis consume relatively small amounts of alcohol compared to Europeans and Americans. Excessive drinking is viewed with suspicion by society at large. A person who drinks, say, six bottles of beer (3 pints) every day is likely to be branded an alcoholic.

There are plenty of bars and pubs, and all restaurants and cafés serve alcohol. Israelis will often go to a pub and spend the entire night nursing just one or two drinks. By the same token it is acceptable to sit at a streetside café chatting for several hours over just a coffee and cake.

## WHERE TO EAT

Israel has many worthwhile restaurants; the mini-guide that follows is merely a selection of a few.

### TEL AVIV

#### DAIRY & VEGETARIAN

**Tnuva Cafe**, 30 Ibn Gbriol Street. Tel: 03-268624. Selection of dairy dishes and salads at modest prices.
**Hasifria (The Library)**, 6 Kaplan Street. Tel: (03) 6916079. Dairy foods in a relaxed and comfortable atmosphere. Musical entertainment during evenings. Inexpensive.
**Apropos**, Off Tarsat Street. Tel: (03) 5289288. Chic coffee house/restaurant. Moderately priced.
**Central Bus Station**. Several dozen vendors offer *felafel* with as much salad and chips as you want for less than $2.

#### ORIENTAL & FISH

**Taboon**, Old Jaffa Port. Tel: 03-811176, 816011. Specialises in oven cooked Mediterranean fish. Locals play spot the celebrity. Considering the restaurant's trendiness and charming location in the old port, the food here is inexpensive.
**Babai at the Port**, Old Jaffa Port. Tel: 02-818789. Less glamorous than Taboon's but the food is equally good.
**Pundag**, 8 Frishman Street. Tel: 03-222948. Specialises in fresh sea bass and trout from the Upper Galilee. Plain cooking for fair prices.
**Shaldag**, 256 Ben Yehuda Street. Tel: (03) 5465030/ 5441973. Innocuous atmosphere, wholesome cuisine. Popular for fish and seafood. Moderately priced.
**Bograchof**, On the beach, near the Dan Hotel. Tel: (03) 5280344. Casual atmosphere, fun view, decent food. On the beachfront. Inexpensive to moderate.

### YEMENITE

**Ba-Li**, 8 Ibn Gvirol Street. Tel: (03) 6955661. Inexpensive luncheonette-type place with home-cooked Yemenite food. Authentic Social Yemenite breads and soups. Open for lunch and early dinner.
**Zion**, 28 Peduim Street. Tel: (03) 658714. A classic Yemenite restaurant in the Yemenite Quarter. The 'Exclusive' restaurant is in the back; try the simple workers eatery at the entrance first. Prices from inexpensive to moderate.
**Gamliel**, 38 Hakovshim Street. Tel: (03) 658779 or 661537. Zion's rival. Also good, same as above. Moderate prices.

### HUNGARIAN

**Pirozki**, 30 Yirmiyahu Street. Tel: (03) 457599. Russian, Hungarian and Jewish specialities, including *blintzes*, *piroshki*, *kreplach* and *borscht*. Inexpensive to moderate.
**The Goulash Corner**, On Hayarkon Street, at corner of Frischmann. Has been around for years, serving diplomatic crowd, locals and tourists. Meat is good, cumin-scented fish, and various oriental salads.

### CHINESE

**The Red Chinese Restaurant**, 326 Dizengoff Street. Tel: (03) 448405 or 5466347. Pleasant atmosphere, good selection of food, also Thai dishes. In North Tel Aviv. Moderately priced.
**Yossi Peking**, 302 Dizengoff Street. Tel: (03) 5443687. Very good food, moderate to expensive prices.
**Golden Dragon**, 262 Ben Yehuda Street. Tel: (03) 455070. Like Red Chinese – good food, North Tel Aviv location. Moderately priced.
**Yin Yang**, 46 Rothschild Blvd. Tel: (03) 621833 or 5604121. Excellent food, expensive prices, in an exclusive location.

### ITALIAN

**Casamia**, 72 Frishman Street. Tel: 03-5239856. All the Italian favourites including spaghetti, canelloni, tagliatelle and, tortellini.
**La Italiana Di Montefiori**, 17 Montefiori Street. Tel: 03-623732. Specialises in Tucany-style delicacies as served in Florence and Bologna.

### ROMANIAN

**Mon Jardin**, 186 Ben Yehuda Street. Tel: 03-5238694. An inappropriate French name for a restaurant that serves traditional Romanian and Eastern European Jewish fare at reasonable prices in a homely atmosphere.

### OTHERS

**L'entrecote**, 195 Ben Yehuda Street. Tel: (03) 230726. Price fixed meal, including salad, fries, and butter-soft steak. Intimate if slightly cramped. Moderate prices.
**Casba**, 32 Yirmiyahu Street. Tel: (03) 449101. Good food, famous for duck. A variety of continental offerings. Piano. Fairly expensive.

**Piltz Café**, 81 Hayarkon Street. Tel: (03) 652778. Pseudo-Art Deco atmosphere, near hotels, overlooking beach. Variety of continental and local entrées, desserts. Music, often dancing on Thursday, Friday, Saturday evenings. Moderate prices.

**Kumkum**, 42 Rokach Blvd. Tel: (03) 6990688. Casual atmosphere, local hangout in Yarkon Park, near sports centre, pub/café. Parking. Inexpensive to moderate.

**Pubs Bonanza**, 17 Trumpeldor Street. Tel: (03) 5285803. Quiet, relaxed atmosphere, except Friday afternoons, when regulars come to carouse. Bar and varied menu.

**The Stagecoach (Hakirkara)**, 216 Hayarkon Street. Tel: (03) 5241703. Near the hotels and waterfront. Live music every evening except Friday. Drinks, snacks, light meals.

## HAIFA

### FISH

**Dolphin**, 13 Bat Galim. Tel: 04-523837. Well-established restaurant serving fresh fish at inexpensive prices.

### FRENCH

**Entrecote**, 52 Moriah Avenue. Tel: 04-372594. Good steaks but strictly unkosher. Even serves shrimps.

### CHINESE

**Nof Chinese**, 101 Hanassi Avenue. Tel: 04-354311. Chinese and Thai cuisine and a good view of the bay.

## JERUSALEM

### ORIENTAL & FISH

**Mesadonet**, 74 Derech Bethlehem. Tel: 02-720825. Kurdistani home cooking at inexpensive prices.

Agrippas Street near the Mahane Yehuda market has about 30 good oriental steak bars to choose from. Local speciality is a Jerusalem Mixed Grill comprising various parts of the cow's anatomy. Sima's Restaurant produces excellent steaks at breakneck speed, while Shipudei HaGefen is to be recommended if you want to sit and eat a more leisurely meal.

**Sea Dolphin**, In East Jerusalem, 21 Al Rashadiah Street. Tel: (02) 282788. An almost legendary fish restaurant, popular among Jerusalemites for years. Moderate prices.

**Philadelphia**, In East Jerusalem, Azzahara Street. Tel: (02) 289770. One of the most famous restaurants in the capital. Oriental food. Moderate prices.

### HUNGARIAN

**Csardas**, 11 Shlomzion Hamalka St. Tel: 02-243186. Classic Hungarian. Wholesome tasty food with gypsy violinist thrown in.

**Europa**, 42 Jaffa Road. Tel: (02) 228953. Unpretentious atmosphere, central location at Zion Square, variety of Hungarian specialities including stuffed chicken and goulash. Popular with locals, moderate prices.

### ETHIOPIAN

**Sheba**, Off 63 Jaffa Road. Tel: 02-249138. Very authentic and enjoyable for those who like something completely different. Modest prices.

### CHINESE

**Ten Li Chow**, Ramban 8. Tel: 02-665956. Reasonable food in upmarket windmill mall location.

### ITALIAN

**Mama Mia**, 18 Rabbi Akiva Street. Tel: 02-248080. Jerusalem institution for lovers of Italian food. Inexpensive but sometimes very, very busy.

### DAIRY AND LIGHT MEALS

**Anna Ticho House**, Off Harav Kook Street. Tel: (02) 244186. Garden restaurant/café on first floor of Ticho House Museum. Quiet, youthful atmosphere. The house salad with crushed nuts and cheese is recommended. Inexpensive.

**Café Alno**. Tel: (02) 253821. Another well-liked Ben Yehuda Street institution, featuring many pleasant pastries.

**Café Atara**, 7 Ben Yehuda Street. Tel: (02) 251141. Light meals as well as coffee.

**Four Seasons**, 54 Haneviim Street. Tel: 02-244220. Good value salads and dairy.

**Pie House**, 5 Hyrkanos Street. Tel: (02) 242478. This popular Jerusalem hang-out proffers full meals, salads, etc., in its own low-rise house near Zion Square, across the street from Home Plus. Moderate prices.

**Rimon Café**. Tel: (02) 252772. Next to Hepner's Deli, off Ben Yehuda, on Luntz Street No. 4. A popular hang-out, with a variety of cakes and cookies. Spills out across pavement into street on warm days.

### FRENCH & CONTINENTAL

**Alla Gondola**, 14 King George Street. Tel: (02) 225944. Elegant dining with Italian cuisine. Downtown. Moderate prices.

**Cow On The Roof**, At the Jerusalem Plaza Hotel. Tel: (02) 228133. Elegant Western dining by reservation only. Expensive.

### MOROCCAN

**Au Sahara**, 17 Jaffa Road. Tel: (02) 233239. Reliable Moroccan cuisine and atmosphere, with a variety of North African specialities. Downtown. Moderate to expensive.

### TIBERIAS

**The House (Habayit)**, Opposite 'Lido Beach'. Tel: (06) 792353. Chinese cuisine. Considered to be one of the best restaurants in Israel, located in a 19th-century landmark. Moderately priced.

### SAFED

**Rimonim Hotel**, In Kiryat Omanim. Tel: (06) 920666. One of Israel's loveliest hotels, with excellent European food. Moderately priced.

## EILAT

### FRENCH & CONTINENTAL

**Au Bistro-Chez Michel**, Eilat Street. Tel: (07) 374333. A French family business. Moderate prices.
**La Bohéme**, Almog Beach. Tel: (07) 374222. French food with an accent on seafood. Moderate prices.

### CHINESE

**Lotus**, Next to Caesar Hotel. Tel: 07-376389. Excellent Szechuan and Cantonese food at reasonable prices.

### AMERICAN

**Eddie's Hideaway**, 68 Almogim. Tel: 07-331279. Thick inexpensive steaks.

# THINGS TO DO

## HEALTH RESORTS

Israel has a number of special health resorts which take advantage of its unique geography and geology. For information, see the "Further Reading" section of this guide.

A rare combination of unique therapeutic factors – the mineral-rich Dead Sea, therapeutic mud, sulphur-thermo-mineral springs and a mild, sunny and extremely dry climate – have made certain areas of Israel excellent year-round health resorts, internationally famous since antiquity.

Most of the health resorts are centred in two areas: the Sea of Galilee (-220 metres/-665 ft) and the Dead Sea (-392 metres/-1286 ft). Offering a wide range of accommodation facilites and equipped with modern installations, they provide a choice of treatments for a variety of ailments and conditions.

Hamme Teverya (Tiberias Hot Springs) – in city of Tiberias (Teverya) on Sea of Galilee, for treatment of muscular and joint diseases, traumatic disturbances and sinusitis.

Hammat Gader – ancient Roman spa 20 km (12 miles) from Tiberias, for treatment of muscular and joint diseases.

Hamme Zohar (Zohar Hot Springs) – three therapeutic centres at Newe Zohar on Dead Sea, for treatment of muscular and joint diseases, traumatic diseases, allergies (especially of breathing passages) and skin diseases.

Hamme Yesha (Yesha Hot Springs) – on Dead Sea, south of Kibbutz En Gedi, for treatment of muscular and joint diseases.

En Boqeq – on Dead Sea, international centre of treatment of psoriasis.

Arad – desert town in Judean Hills, 620 metres (2,034 ft) above sea-level, about half an hour from the Dead Sea. The cool, dry and pollen-free air, make this an ideal resort for people suffering from asthma, allergies and breathing difficulties.

A special booklet and further information are available at IGTOs abroad and at
**Health Resorts Authority**, 24 Rehov Hamelech George, 94262 Jerusalem. Tel: (02) 231248/9.

## TREE PLANTING

Visitors wishing to plant trees, for a nominal contribution, may do so on their own or as part of tours organised by the Jewish National Fund. Each planter will receive a certificate and a badge to commemorate the event.

Further information from: "Plant a Tree With Your Own Hands", Meir Malca Jewish National Fund, 7 Rehov Shmuel Hanagid, Jerusalem, tel: (02) 258620 or Visitors Department, Jewish National Fund, 96 Rehov Hayarkon, Tel Aviv. Tel: (03) 234449, 234367.

## DESERT TOURS

Neot Hakikar/Jabaliya runs a variety of tours for those who want to get off the beaten track. These include hiking, sailing, cycling, camel riding, mountaineering, camping, trekking and backpacking in all parts of Israel. Research and study tours focusing on special subjects can be tailored to the interests of individual groups.

A special attraction is the Neot Hakikar/Jabaliya desert safaris in the Negev and the Sinai. Transportation is by 12-seater 4-wheel drive vehicles open at the sides to permit direct contact with the awesome desert scenery. The tours combine driving and hiking with visits to some of the most exciting archaeological sites in the desert. Some nights are spent in organised campsites, some in the homes of local villagers and nomads. Camel trekking and challenging rock climbing are a feature of many tours.
For details contact:
**Neot Hakikar/Jabaliya**, 36 Rehov Keren Hayesod, 92149 Jerusalem. Tel: (02) 636503.

## NATURE TRAILS

For those visitors searching for the unusual, the Society for the Protection of Nature in Israel (SPNI) offers some fascinating tours which combine unique learning experiences in natural settings with touring, hiking and swimming.

These Nature Trails leave the main roads and penetrate into little-known and relatively inaccessible areas. Experienced guides explain the natural and human history of the region and point out hidden places of beauty and interest. All of the tours include some walking. Depending on the interests and abilities of the group, this can range from a few hours per day to difficult hikes for experienced trekkers. There are a number of English-guided trips to all parts of the country suitable for individuals as well as the entire family (children over 12 years old).

Their shops also have a selection of publications and accessories regarding natural Israel. Their main offices are at:
**Jerusalem**, 13 Rehov Helene Hamalka. Tel: (02) 232936.
**Tel Aviv**, 4 Rehov Hashfela. Tel: (03) 375063.
**Haifa**, 8 Rehov Menachen. Tel: (04) 664136.
SPNI has a network of field schools charging about $30 per room per night.

## NATURE RESERVES

There are over 160 Nature Reserves in Israel, extending over some 150,000 acres. Although Israel is a comparatively small country, it has an unbelievable range of different landscapes and natural phenomena.

It is possible to see, side by side, hills of 1,000 metres (3,280 ft) or more and plains and valleys, among which is the lowest depression in the world, some 400 metres below sea-level; thick maquis and arid and barren zones; cliffs up to a height of several hundred metres, and desert gravel surfaces extending over tens of kilometres; narrow canyons and streams, with waterfalls, facing widespread dry riverbeds.

Owing to its geographical location and its particular topographical structure, Israel is a climatic meeting place. There are more than 3,000 different species of plants, 350 species of birds, 100 mammals and 100 reptiles.

The following are some of the principal Reserves.

### NORTHERN AREA

#### TEL DAN RESERVE

There is no other place in Israel with so plentiful a supply of water – about 240 million cubic metres flow annually from the River Dan, the largest of the three sources of the Jordan River. This has determined the character of this Reserve. Here one can find water vegetation of the north, plane trees and Syrian ash, ferns and mosses, together with the giant terebinth. The laurel, known elsewhere as a shrub, appears here as a tall-branching tree.

### SOUTHERN AREA

#### EIN GEDI

Ein Gedi is a unique desert oasis, lying between the Dead Sea shore (the lowest place on earth) and the empty, arid Judean desert. The abundance of plant and animal life concentrated here is due to the many fresh-water springs and waterfall. There is a tropical water-dependent vegetation that cannot be found anywhere else in Israel. This includes moringa, thick-leaved maerua, desert sebestene and salvadora. There is rich fauna, including large herds of ibexes, hyrexes, Black Tristams' Grackles and desert partridges.

#### HAI BAR RESERVE, YOTVETA

Off the Eilat Highway, in the Southern Rift Valley, lies the unique Hai Bar Biblical Wildlife Reserve. Here animals that were in the past indigenous to the area, or still live under the threat of extinction, are kept under conditions of an open zoo. There are also some animals of desert origin threatened by extinction in North Africa and in the desert areas of East Africa. Gazelles, ibexes, wild asses, Saharan oryxes, ostriches, addexes, caracals, wolves, foxes and hyenas are some examples of the fauna to be found here.

Other Nature Reserves range from Banias and the Hula Valley in the north to Mount Carmel and Nahal Poleg on the coast to the many parks outside Jerusalem in the Judean Hills and around Eilat.

The Nature Reserves Authority has recently introduced the new Visit-All Ticket System for overseas visitors, which enables them to visit 10 nature reserves throughout the country. It is valid for one month. Tickets are available at:
**Nature Reserve Authority**, 78 Rehov Yirmiyahu, 94467 Jerusalem. Tel: (02) 387471.

## NATIONAL PARKS

The national parks can include nature sites and sites of historical and archaeological interest. They include Hazor, Achziv, Nimrod Fortress, Caesarea, Ashkelon, Megiddo, Herodian, Masada, Qumran, Jericho, Tel Arad and Ein Avdat.

Visitors to sites and parks can buy a ticket for multiple entrance at the site or park, permitting them to visit all of the sites or parks within a period of 14 days. In the case of groups the ticket can be used for 21 days. It can also be purchased from the National Parks Authority.

For further information, contact:
**National Parks Authority**, 4 Rehov Aluf M.Makleff, Hakirya, 61070 Tel Aviv. Tel: (03) 6902281.

## VOLUNTEER PROGRAMMES

### KIBBUTZ

The kibbutz is a communal or collective settlement governed by the general assembly of its members. All property is jointly owned and work is organised on a cooperative basis. Members receive no salary, but in return for their work, get housing, clothing, food, medical services, education for their children and other social amenities. Most kibbutzim are agricultural but many also have sizeable industrial enterprises. There are over 200 kibbutzim in all parts of the country and the number of members ranges from 90 to over 2,000.

Most kibbutzim accept volunteers for varying lengths of time. Volunteers must be between 18 and 32 years of age. Neither children nor pregnant women are accepted. For further information contact any Israel Government Tourist Office or the following organisations:

**Hakibbutz Ha'artzi**, 13 Rehov Leonardo da Vinci, 64733 Tel Aviv. Tel: (03) 435222.
**Hakibbutz Hadati**, Zipi Romen Volunteer Department, 7 Rehov Dubnov Tel Aviv. Tel: (03) 6957231.
**Ikhud Hakvutzot Vehakibbutzim** and **Hakibbutz Hemeyuhad**, Ben Baor, 10, Rehov Dubnov Tel Aviv. Tel: (03) 5452622.

It's best to plan ahead of time as far as possible if you are serious about volunteering. In New York, you should direct inquiries to:
**The Jewish Agency**, Kibbutz Aliyah Desk, 515 Park Ave. New York, NY 10022. Tel: (212) 688-4134.

In Europe and elsewhere:
**Ichud Habonim-Dror**, POB 154, Waverley, 2024, Sydney, N.S.W. Tel: 389-4993.
**Kibbutz Representative**, 1A Accommodation Rd., London NW1 1, BEP. Tel: 01-450-9235.
**Sochnut**, 17 Vue Forunay, Paris 75017. Tel: 766-0313.
**Ichud Habonim**, John Wermeer –Straat 22, Amsterdam. Tel: 020-719123.
**Haus des Kibbuzes**, D-6000 Frankfurt/Main, Falkensteinerstr. 1. Tel: 0611/556963.

## MOSHAV

There are other forms of agricultural settlements – Moshav Ovdim and Moshav Shitufi. Moshav Ovdim is set up on principles of mutual aid and equality of opportunity and Moshav Shitufi is based on cooperative economy and ownership, as in the kibbutz, but with each family owning its own house and accepting responsibility for its own domestic arrangements.

For further information contact:
**Volunteer Department**, 19 Rehov Leonardo da Vinci, 64733 Tel Aviv. Tel: (03) 6958473.

## ARCHAEOLOGICAL EXCAVATIONS

There is generally no fee paid but food and accommodation are often provided. Transport to and from the site is generally paid by the volunteer. Persons over the age of 18 can apply. There is a minimum participation time. The Israel Department of Antiquites and Museums publishes the Archaeological Excavations Booklet containing information concerning excavations being conducted as well as precise information for prospective volunteers. For further information, contact:
**Marta Retig**: Department of Antiquities and Museums Ministry of Education and Culture, POB 586, 91004 Jerusalem. Tel: (02) 292627/3.

## ULPAN

Ulpan Akiva is a Hebrew-language school where Hebrew is taught as a living language in everyday conversation at all levels: reading, writing, speech patterns, drama and idioms. Courses are from 4–20 weeks, for families and individuals of 12 years and up. The school is located at the Green Beach Hotel near Netanya and facilities include a swimming pool, tennis and basketball courts and the beach.

The programme consists of: four or five hours of Hebrew study a day, lectures on the Bible, Jewish history, Hebrew literature, current affairs; cultural activities that include folk singing and dancing and meetings with local personalities. Study side by side with Israelis and new immigrants and experience the culture of Israel. Tours can be arranged to archaeological sites and other places of interest in the area. Courses are run on a residential, full-board basis. For further information, contact:
**Ulpan Akiva**, International Hebrew Study Center, POB 6086, 42160 Netanya. Tel: (053) 352312/3. Fax: 053-652919.

Many kibbutzim offer courses which cost $50 in return for participants' part-time work on the kibbutz. The courses last for 5½ months and are open to Jews between the ages of 17½ and 35. Students may arrive at the kibbutz a week before the course begins. Participants must be physically fit for work. For further details, contact:
**The Ulpanim's Kibbutzim Department**, The Jewish Agency, 12 Rehov Kaplan, Tel Aviv. Tel: (03) 5423423.

## ZOOS

The Jerusalem Biblical Zoo houses animals mentioned in the Bible. Other zoos are located in Tel Aviv, Eilat and Haifa.

In Haifa the zoo is in Gan Ha'em. It houses animals indigenous to Mount Carmel and Northern Israel. Tel: (04) 81886.

There is a Safari Park, a 250-acre wildlife sanctuary in Ramat Gan near Tel Aviv, where hundreds of animals roam freely. At the Hai Bar Reserve, north of Eilat, many of the animals mentioned in the Bible can be seen. Visitors to the Safari Park and Hai Bar Reserve may tour in closed vehicles only.

In Eilat, there is an underwater observatory for watching exotic aquatic life.

## TOURS

If you have no fixed agenda, travelling alone and want to see more of the country, there are scores of travel agencies and tour companies that would help show you around. The tours range from half-day excursions to round-trip weekends to Egypt or the Sinai, to all-out visits around the country.

Most of their offices are located near the densest tourist areas—Ben Yehuda Street in Tel Aviv, and Jaffa and King George streets in Jerusalem.

## TOUR GUIDES

If you can afford the price, you can hire a private tour guide, with car, to take you around independently. Israel has a special school for tour guides, who must complete a two-year programme. By the time they graduate, they have a firm command of landscape and history, and most have their own unique angle.

Although many of the best guides are recommended through word-of-mouth, the IGTO will also be able to provide recommendations.

## MEET THE ISRAELIS

The best way of getting to know the people of Israel is to meet them in their homes. Israeli families from all walks of life are happy to extend hospitality to tourists. Arrangements can be made (through Tourists Information Offices) for tourists to meet members of their own professions and/or Israelis with similar interests.

## BAR & BAT MITZVAH

For arrangements for bar mitzvah and bat mitzvah ceremonies at the Western Wall, please contact, no later than six weeks prior to the date:
**Naomi Rosenberg**: The Ministry of Tourism, 24 Rehov Hamelech George, Jerusalem. Tel: (02) 754811.

# CULTURE PLUS

Israel has a wealth of cultural and artistic entertainment. Ticket Agencies in each city or town sell tickets for concerts, plays and other events. Calendars of Events are available at the Tourist Information Offices.

## MUSEUMS

The museums of Israel are a mirror of their country: a land both ancient and modern, a crossroads of civilisations and a "melting pot" of a people returning to its homeland from a hundred countries with different cultures and traditions. They are treasure-houses of archaeology, folklore and ethnology, of art ancient and modern, of crafts primitive and sophisticated.

Some of the country's museums are unique in the world, witness the Shrine of the Book, repository of the Dead Sea Scrolls, and the Museum of the Jewish Diaspora. Some of the principal ones are listed below. For visiting hours of specific museums, see the Ministry of Tourism Museums brochure.

### ACCO

**The Municipal Museum**, Old City. Tel: (04) 910251 354. Regional archaeology from the Early Bronze Age to the Ottoman period; Persian ceramics; Arab and Druze ethnology in Eretz Israel; weapons from Crusader to Turkish times; folk art from Turkish times; the history of the Jewish community through the ages in Acre; library. Housed in 18th-century bath-house – Crusader fortress with crypt adjacent.

### BEERSHEBA

Memorial of the Negev Brigade Symbolises the liberation of the Negev by the Negev Brigade.
**The Negev Museum**, Rehov Ha'atzmaut. Tel: (057) 39105. Local archaeology and history of the city.

### EILAT

**The Museum of Modern Art**, Rehov Hativat Hanegev. Tel: (059) 74972.

### EIN GEDI

**Beit Sefer Sade (field school)**. Tel: (057) 91008. Exhibition on the flora and fauna of the area.

### HAIFA

**Clandestine Immigration and Naval Museum**, 204 Derech Allenby. Tel: (04) 536249. The ship *Af-Al-Pi*, which ran the British blockade during the Mandate period, houses most of the museum devoted to clandestine immigration and to the history of Israel's navy.
**Dagon Silo**, Plumer Square (by the port). Tel: (04) 664221. Grain storage and handling in ancient Israel and the Near East, including working models. Guided tours are held Sunday–Friday at 10.30 a.m. or by appointment.
**Haifa Museum**, 26 Rehov Shabbetai Levi. Tel: (04) 523255
consists of:
**Museum of Ancient Art**. Israel's large collection of Greco-Roman sculptures, items recovered from Haifa Bay, terracottas, rare coins and finds from Shikmona, part of ancient Haifa.
**Museum of Modern Art**. Interesting works and exhibitions of Israeli and non-Israeli artists.
**Tikotin Museum of Japanese Art**, 89 Sderot Hanassi. Tel: (04) 383554. Large collection of the Orient – paintings, ceramics, graphics, jewellery and handicrafts.
**Mane Katz**, 89 Rehov Yefe Nof. Tel: (04) 383482. The late world-renowned Jewish artist bequeathed

his home, paintings, and other artworks to the city.

**Music Museum and Amli Library**, 23 Rehov Arlosoroff. Tel: (04) 644485. Folk instruments, ancient and modern, from all around the world. A library of Jewish music and recorded Yiddish folk songs.

**National Maritime Museum**, 198 Derech Allenby. Tel: (04) 536622. Thousands of models and exhibits of sailing crafts, maps and maritime lore from the seas in and around the Middle East.

**Prehistory Museum, Sderot Hanassi**, in Gan Ha'Em, (Mother's Park). Tel: (04) 371833. The Museum, adjacent to the lovely zoo of Haifa, houses archaeological finds from the Carmel and northern Israel, demonstrating the life of prehistoric man in the region. Entrance to municipal museums is free on Saturday.

---

## JERUSALEM

**Artists House**, 12 Rehov Shmuel Hanagid. Tel: (02) 252636. Exhibition of local arts and crafts.

**Cable Car Museum**, Derech Hebron (near Cinematheque). Orginal works of cable car used to transfer wounded in Old City from Mt Zion during War of Independence.

**Chamber of the Martyrs**, Mount Zion. Memorial to the victims of Nazism.

**Givat Hatahmoshet**, (Ammunition Hill). Tel: (02) 829132. Memorial Museum. Ammunition Hill was the scene of the battle for Jerusalem during the Six Day War.

**Herzl Memorial Museum**, Mount Herzl. Tel: (02) 531108. Exhibits documents, books, photographs and the study in which Herzl wrote his famous work, *Altneuland*.

**Hechal Shlomo**, 58 Rehov Hamelech George. Tel: (02) 635212. Museum of Jewish ceremonial exhibits and an Italian Synagogue.

**The Israel Museum**, Hakirya. Tel: (02) 708811. Comprises:

**Bezalel National Art Museum**, Jewish ceremonial art; ethnography of the Jewish communities and the Arabs of Eretz Israel; European painting and sculpture, 15th-20th centuries; contemporary Israeli art; prints room; art from Asia, Japan, India, Far East, Oceania, Africa and Pre-Columbian Americas. Billy Rose Art Garden modern sculpture. Design pavilion. Library.

**Samuel Bronfman Biblical and Archaeological Museum**, Archaeological objects and ancient art from Prehistoric periods to Crusader times; coins; neighboring cultures.

**Youth Wing**, Children's displays. Exhibitions and varied activities and courses. One of the most advanced of its kind in the world.

**Zacks–Abramov Pavilion**, New wing for modern art opened in late 1985.

**Shrine of the Book**. Tel: (02) 633231. The "Dead Sea Scrolls"; Massada scroll fragments; the Bar Kokhba letters and associated archaeological discoveries.

**Rockefeller Museum**, East Jerusalem. Tel: (02) 282251. Israelite archaeology of Israel of all periods.

**Schoken Institute**, 6 Rehov Balfour, 92102 Jerusalem. Tel: (02) 631288. Displays of rare Hebrew and Jewish works.

**L.A. Mayer Memorial Institute for Islamic Art**, 2 Rehov Hapalmach. Tel: (02) 661291. Islamic art of the various periods and lands, including metal work, ceramics, jewellery, carpets, miniatures, textiles, graphics on Islamic lands. Outstanding collection of antique European and Ottoman watches, clocks and music-boxes. Archives and library.

**Museum of Taxes**, 32 Rehov Agron. Tel: (02) 245951. History of taxation in Israel and among the Jewish communities of the Diaspora.

**Ticho House**, Rehov Ticho (near Harav Kook). Art and literature library, museum shop, coffee shop and examples of Anna Ticho's paintings.

---

## TEL AVIV

**Beth Hatefutsoth – Museum of the Jewish Diaspora**, Rehov Klausner, Ramat Aviv. Tel: (03) 6462020. Permanent thematic exhibit of Jewish life in the Diaspora, from the destruction of the Second Temple until today, including photography, models, multimedia presentations, closed circuit television, library and computer reference bank. Chronosphere exhibit of Jewish Diaspora. Also temporary exhibits on Jewish communities in the Diaspora. International guest lecturers and study forums.

**Ha'aretz Museum**, Ramat Aviv. Tel: (03) 6415244/8. Some sections of the museum are:

**The Alphabet Museum**. The history of writing, its spread and development: pre-alphabetic, alphabetic, Hebrew alphabetic: copies of important inscriptions. Libraries:

**Ceramics Pavilion**. History of glass production, methods of styles, especially in Mediterranean lands in antiquity, from Late Bronze Age onwards.

**The Kadman Numismatic Pavilion**. Greek, Jewish, Near Eastern, Roman, Byzantine, Arab, Crusader, British Mandatory and Israeli coins; banknotes; scales and weights of various periods. Library and reading room.

**Man and His work**. Tools and implements for hunting, agricultural industries, energy, light, writing, measuring, in various materials; eight traditional workshops; steam-power in agriculture, oriental market and craftsmen's stoves of last century recreated.

**Nehusthan Pavilion**. Archaeological finds from temple at ancient copper mines at Timna in the Negev, illustrating copper production in various periods.

**The Tel Aviv Museum**, 27–29 Sderot Shaul Hamelech. Tel: (03) 257361.

**Helena Rubinstein Pavilion**, 6 Rehov Tarsat. Tel: (03) 287196. Collections include European and American art from the 17th century until the present, with an emphasis on modern and contemporary art. The collection also includes works by Jewish artists. The collection of Israeli art consists of works from the beginning of the 20th century up to the present time. Temporary exhibitions of modern and contemporary art. Activities: concerts, lectures, gallery talks, cinema, art films and art education.

## HOLOCAUST MEMORIALS

The following are memorials to the six million Jews who perished in the Nazi Holocaust:

### NORTHERN AREA

**Lohamei Hageta'ot** (Kibbutz), Ghetto Fighters' House, Holocaust and Resistance Museum. Tel: (04) 820412. Photographs, documents, models, maps. Exhibits: Vilna, Ulkinieki (a Jewish village); Nazi camps; Nazi conquests: ghettos and deportations; Warsaw Ghetto Uprising; Janus Korczak, a ghetto educator. Art of the Holocaust. Archives, library, reading room.
The museum is open:
Sunday to Thursday 9am–4pm
Friday, eve of holidays 9am–1pm
Saturday, holidays 10am–5pm
Admission is free

### JERUSALEM AREA

**Yad Vashem, Martyrs' and Heroes' Remembrance Authority**, Har Hazikaron (near Mt Hezl), Jerusalem. Tel: (02) 751611. The central museum and monument to the memory of the Holocaust of European Jewry (1933–1945). Exhibition and Hall of Remembrance. Archives and library.

### SOUTHERN AREA

**Yad Mordechai** (Kibbutz), Yad Mordechai Museum for the Heritage of the Holocaust and Heroism. Tel: (051) 20529. Exhibition of photographs and objects relating to Jewish townlets in Europe; the ghettos and concentration camps; the Jewish Resistance and the "illegal immigration"; the camps in Cyprus; statue of Mordechai Anilevitz, leader of the Warsaw Ghetto Uprising. Open daily 8am–5.30pm.

## ART GALLERIES

### JERUSALEM

**Israel Museum**, Hakirya. Tel: (02) 708811.
**Cinematheque**, Gan Wolfson, Derech Hebron. Tel: (02) 724131.
**Jerusalem Theater**, 30 Rehov Marcus. Tel: (02) 667167.

### TEL AVIV

**Tel Aviv Museum**, 27–29 Sderot Shaul Hamelech. Tel: (03) 257361.
**Cinematheque**, Municipality, Kikar Malkhei Israel. Tel: (03) 243311.

### HAIFA

**Cinematheque**, Rothschild Center, Sderot Hanassi 142. Tel: (04) 83424.
**Other Galleries:** There are scores of other museums, small and large, in towns and in kibbutzim. They display archaeological finds, ancient glass, coins, folk costumes, natural science collections as well as contemporary art.

In addition, groups of artists have formed "colonies" in the village of Ein Hod on Mt Carmel (near Haifa), at Safed and in Jaffa, with picturesque studios open to the public. In Tel Aviv, the gallery scene is centered around Gordon Street, also known as "Gallery Street". In Jerusalem, visiting artists from abroad are housed at the Mishkenot and from time to time give performances or speeches for the public. The Aika (Ariel Brown) Gallery in the gritty industrial zone of Talpiot, Jerusalem's artists' work-region, displays contemporary art work at their room at 6 Yad Harutzim St.

Jerusalem also holds a great abundance of public art; the booklet "The City As Museum: Modern Art & Architecture in Jerusalem", published by the Jerusalem Foundation, available in some bookstores, is the best guide.

## FESTIVALS

The Israel Festival of Music and Drama takes place in May of each year, with the participation of the country's leading musical and dramatic talent and world-famous visiting companies and artists. The Festival is centered in Jerusalem, Tel Aviv and the restored Roman Theaters in Caesarea and Beit Shean. Performances also take place in other towns and some kibbutzim.

The annual Ein Gev Music Festival, presenting classical and folk music, is held during the Passover festival at this kibbutz on the Sea of Galilee. Other local festivals include the **Acco Fringe Theater Festival** (September/October), the **Red Sea Jazz Festival** (August), the **Jerusalem Film Festival** (June) and the **Haifa International Film Festival** (October). The **Jerusalem International Book Fair** is held every two years in March. An International Harp Contest takes place every three years, drawing young musicians from all over the world, while the Zimriya, an international choir festival, is another well-established triennial event. Spring in Jerusalem and Spring in Tel Aviv, annual festivals, include music, drama and dance, and the Rubinstein Piano Competition brings talented young artists from all over the world to the country.

Events in Haifa include the International Flower Show (Floris), when hundreds of thousands of flowers from all over the world, typical of their countries of origin, adorn the city, and the International Folklore Festival, in which the best folklore groups from all over the world participate, meeting in dance and music.

## OUTDOOR EVENTS & PERFORMANCES

During July and August there are many outdoor events and performances: Bands, puppet shows, dance, disco, mime, sports activities, etc.

Contact the Ministry of Tourism for their various country-wide locations and times.

## CONCERTS

There are several orchestras, of which the most famous is the Israel Philharmonic, playing under the baton of the great conductors of the world and featuring distinguished guest artists. The Jerusalem Symphony Orchestra gives a weekly concert in Jerusalem during the winter season. There are frequent performances by the Haifa Symphony Orchestra, the Rishon Le Zion Symphony Orchestra, the New Israel Opera, the Ramat Gan Orchestra and Israel Sinfonietta Beersheba, the Israel Chamber Ensemble, and some outstanding trios and quartets.

## DANCE

There are live professional dance companies in Israel, the Israel Classical Ballet, the Batsheva Dance Company, the Bat-Dor Dance Company, Kol Hademana and the Kibbutz Dance Company. Batsheva and Bat-Dor are both modern dance groups. All perform regularly in the three main cities, as well as in other towns and kibbutzim.

## FOLKLORE EVENINGS

Folklore programmes, which portray the spirit of ancient and modern Israel in song and dance, are presented regularly at main hotels in the following towns. For further information contact:
**Ashkelon**: Tel: (07) 732412.
**Haifa**: Tel: (04) 640840, 671645.
**Herzliya**: Tel: (03) 223266.
**Jerusalem**: Tel: (02)241281, 282295.
**Bat Yam**: Tel: (03) 589766.
**Netanya**: Tel: (053) 27286.
**Tel Aviv**: Tel: (03) 223266.

## CINEMAS

There are cinemas in all the big towns; most have three showings a day, one at about 4pm and two evening shows.

For about $7 you can see the latest Hollywood epics. Also on current release you'll find the best latest movies from France, Germany, Italy, Hungary and elsewhere. These films usually have English subtitles but ask at the box office first.

Israel itself produces a dozen or so films a year and these offer an insight into the local culture. These, too, have English subtitles. The local cinematheques show golden oldies as well the more recent movies.

## THEATRES

The theatre is very popular in Israel and there are many companies performing, in Hebrew, a wide range of classical and contemporary plays, including original works by Israelis. The best known are the Habimah and Cameri Theatres in Tel Aviv and the Haifa Municipal Theatre, which take their productions all over the country. Smaller companies often stage productions in English, Yiddish and other languages.

## ARCHAEOLOGY

Archaeology is one of Israel's best-loved national pastimes, and the opportunities for archaeological exploration here are rich and varied.

There are dozens of major archaeological sites – within the country's borders, spanning all time periods of recorded history. The most important sites – such as Caesarea, Ashkelon, Jericho or Masada – are national parks and are open to the public on a regular basis for a modest admission fee. Often these sites include English-language signposts and have informative brochures to explain the history and design of the site. More information on the National Parks system is available from:
**National Parks Authority**, 4 Rehov M. Makleff, Hakirya, Tel Aviv 61070. Tel: (03) 252281.

Other sites, however, are more out of the way or unmarked. Quite a few are closed to the general public without special permission or appointment. For more information on these sites, or to get contacts for permission, contact the Department of Antiquities and Museums.

Numerous museums feature special displays on archaeology, among them the Ha'aretz Museum in (northern) Tel Aviv, and Jerusalem's Israel Museum, which includes the controversial Dayan Collection and the numerous findings housed within the Rockefeller Museum.

## EXCAVATIONS

In any given year there are usually over two dozen separate archaeological sites undergoing excavation, many of which accept volunteers during the summer. Perennial favourites include Tel Dan, near Kibbutz Dan and Banias, in northern Israel, which contains ruins ranging from the Canaanite to the Israelite to the Roman, and Tel Dor, on the Carmel Coast near Kibbutz Nasholim and Caesarea, an erstwhile Phoenician port and multi-layered *tel*. Other sites that have accepted volunteers over the years include Emmaus, Hammat Gader, Horvat Uza, Sepphoris (2 sites), Capernahum, Tel Arad and Timna.

Usually, volunteers must be over 18, (occasionally only 16 years old). Applications should be made (early in the year) to individual excavation directors, who are usually connected to universities in Israel and abroad. These names and addresses, and further

information, can be obtained from any IGTO or:
**Department of Antiquities & Museums**, Ministry of Education & Culture. POB 586, Jerusalem. Tel: (02) 292627.

## NIGHTLIFE

Nightclubs abound in the main cities and resort towns. Many have regular floor shows, while others offer more informal entertainment. Rock, jazz, folk and pop music is the usual fare.

# SHOPPING

## WHAT TO BUY

Shops in Israel offer a wide variety of merchandise and gifts. These include exclusive jewellery and diamonds; oriental carpets and antiques; fashionable ladies' wear and elegant furs; leather goods; paintings and sculptures; ceramics; silverware and copperware; embroidery and batiks and religious requisites. Several hundred shops are approved by the Ministry of Tourism. These shops display a sign stating "Listed by the Ministry of Tourism" and the Ministry's emblem (two scouts carrying a bunch of grapes on a pole between them), which is the symbol of quality merchandise.

In addition, colourful oriental markets and bazaars are found in the narrow alleyways of the old cities of Jerusalem, Bethlehem, Acco, Nazareth, Hebron and Druze villages. These sell handmade arts and crafts – including olive wood, mother-of-pearl, leather and bamboo items, hand-blown glass and clothing, vegetables and fruit.

Duty-free shops are located at Ben-Gurion and Eilat airports and at most of the leading hotels. Foreign-made articles such as watches, cameras, perfumes, tobaccos and liquors as well as many fine Israeli products may be purchased with foreign currency for delivery to the plane or ship prior to departure.

## SHOPPING AREAS

In the Old City of Jerusalem and other Arab market places bargaining is a standard practice. Usually you can buy an item at 25 percent off by starting to haggle at half the quoted price. Avoid haggling if you are not interested in buying or if an item is cheap. Brassware, carvings and fabrics are among the more popular finds.

Other popular shopping places include the weekly Bedouin market in Beersheba Thursday mornings, and the Druze markets in the north.

### JUDAICA

Besides these items, Israel has a unique variety of traditional crafts and Judaica for sale, ranging from religious articles like Menorahs, mezzuzot and spice boxes to wall hangings and statuary. They range from loving reproductions to stark minimalism.

Centres for buying fine crafts include several locations in Jerusalem, among them the House of Quality, the Khutzot Hayotzer Arts & Crafts Lane, Yochanan Migush Halav Street, and the Mea Shearim area.

## SHOPPING HOURS

Most stores in Israel are open daily 8am–1pm and 4–7pm. Shops in the hotels are often open till midnight. On Friday and the eve of Jewish holy days, the stores close around 2pm. Jewish stores are closed on Saturday and holy days. Muslim shops are closed on Friday, and Christian shops on Sunday.

## EXPORT OF ANTIQUITIES

It is forbidden to export antiquities from Israel unless a written export permit has been obtained from the Department of Antiquities and Museums of the Ministry of Education and Culture, Jerusalem. This applies also to antiquities which accompany tourists who are leaving the country. Antiquities proven to have been imported to Israel after 1900 are exempted. Antiquities are defined as objects fashioned by man before the year 1700. A 10 percent export fee is payable upon the purchase price of every item approved for export.

The articles must be dispatched by post, with an accompanying check for the appropriate amount, or taken in person to: The Department of Antiquities and Museums Rockefeller Museum, opposite Herod's Gate, POB 586, Jerusalem. For personal visits, it is advisable to phone (02) 278627 for an appointment.

### VAT

After being stamped by customs, apply to Bank Leumi BN in the exit hall. A refund of VAT (value-added tax) of 18 percent is made at the point of your departure. However, you must make sure that:
1. The total net sum (after the 18 percent reduction) on one invoice is not less than $50. The following items are not included in this scheme: tobacco products, electrical appliances and accessories, cameras, film and photographic equipment.
2. The purchased items are packed in a plastic bag with at least one transparent side.
3. The original invoice (white) is placed inside the bag in such a manner that the entries on it can be read.

4. The bag is sealed or glued shut.

5. The bag must remain sealed during your entire stay in Israel.

6. When arriving at the departure hall on leaving the country, you present the sealed bag with the purchased goods to the Customs Official for approval of refund.

After checking and placing the stamp of approval on the invoice, the customs official will direct you to the bank counter where the refund will be made in us dollars.

# SPORTS

Israel is an ideal place for sports enthusiasts. Here they will find excellent facilities and an opportunity to combine interests such as skin and scuba diving, riding, tennis, golf, swimming and skiing with a general tour of the country. The Mediterranean climate guarantees most outdoor sports year round (the exception being snow skiing, which is available only in winter).

## PARTICIPANT

The Mediterranean shoreline and the Sea of Galilee are ideal for water sports: swimming, surfing, sailing and water skiing. The Tel Aviv Marina offers yachting as well as sailing. All the large hotels have swimming pools and there are municipal or private pools all over the country. Skin and aqualung diving are especially popular along the Gulf of Eilat; centres at Eilat will rent equipment and provide instruction.

Fishing equipment, both angling and under water, can be hired along the Mediterranean and the Red Sea, though the latter is a protected area, with fishing permitted only in certain places.

Tennis courts are available at a number of hotels and the Tennis Centre at Ramat Ha-Sharon, near Tel Aviv, is putting Israel on the international tennis circuit. There is a fine 18-hole golf course at Caesarea. You can find riding clubs in Arad, Beersheba, Caesarea, Eilat, Netanya, Vered Hagalil and other places. Bicycles can be rented in most cities and cycling tours of the country can be arranged. During the winter, there is skiing on the slopes of Mt Hermon. Marches, races, and swimming competitions are organised by the HaPo'el and Maccabi sports organisations. The highlight of the year is the annual Jerusalem March, a highly organised event, in which thousands of Israelis from all over the country, as well as overseas visitors, both individually and in groups, make a colourful and high-spirited pilgrimage to the capital. This event is held during the spring, usually in April.

A programme of events is published monthly and can be obtained from the **Israeli National Sports Association**, 5 Rehov Warburger, Tel Aviv. Tel: (03) 5281968.

Tourists in sports-related professions or those contemplating such careers will be interested in the Wingate Institute for Physical Education and Sport, near Netanya. Under the auspices of the Israeli Ministry of Education and Culture, the Institute consists of the College for Physical Education Teachers, the School for Sports Coaches and Instructors and the School of Physiotherapy. The Institute also houses the Department of Research and Sports Medicine and the National Archives of Physical Education and Sport.

## GOLF

Israel's golf course is located on the Mediterranean coast by the ancient seaport of Caesarea. Halfway between Tel Aviv and Haifa (40 minutes by car from either city), the Caesarea Golf Club welcomes tourists. The full-sized 18-hole, 72 course measuring 6,200 metres is open all year round. A driving range is also available. Professional lessons are given and clubs and other equipment can be rented at the Club's shop. Lockers and changing rooms are at the players' disposal. Restaurant on premises.

For further information, contact:

**Caesarea Golf Club**, POB 1010, 30660 Caesarea. Tel: (06) 361174.

## SQUASH

**Haifa** Squash Center. MP Hof, Kfar Zamir, Hacarmel. Tel: (04) 539160.

**Herzliya** Squash Center. Tel: (052) 357877.

**Ramat Gan**, Kfar Hamaccabiah, Sport Center. Ramat Chen. Tel: (03) 715715.

## TENNIS

Tennis is one of Israel's most rapidly growing sports. Courts are available at many major hotels and other tennis centres. Lessons are offered at several courts.

The Israel Tennis Center, in Ramat Hasharon, just north of Tel Aviv, is the hub of Israeli tennis. Facilities include 16 all-weather, floodlit courts, training walls and educational facilities. Both national and international tournaments are held in the 5,000-seat Spectator's Stadium.

**Israel Tennis Center**, Ramat Hasharon. Tel: (03) 481803, 485223.

For further information, contact:

**Israel Tennis Association**, 79 Rehov Maze, 67137 Tel Aviv. Tel: (03) 613911.

# SKIING

Israel's only snow skiing resort is located on the northeastern slopes of the Hermon range, 1,600 to 2,100 metres (5,249 ft to 6,890 ft) above sea level. The highest peak offers a stunning panoramic view of the Golan Heights, Upper Galilee, the Hulah Valley, the Birket Ram Lake, the Qalat Nimrod Crusader Fortress and the Banyas Spring. The ski resort is 30 km (18 miles) from Kiryat Shmona and 65 km (40 miles) from Tiberias.

The skiing season begins in December or January and ends in mid-April. The heavy and wet snow ranges from 2-3 metres (6-9 ft) on the highest slope to 1 metre (3 ft) at base level. There may be days when the roads are closed due to heavy snow.

Skiers may phone the ski site between 9am and 3pm or Moshav Neve Ativ, the holiday village which runs the ski site, throughout the day. The site is open daily from 8.30am until 3.30pm, subject to weather and security conditions. The last ride on the chairlifts is at 3.30pm. It is advisable to make the visit on weekdays when the site is less crowded.

Runs are available for all levels of skiers; the longest run is about 2½ km (1½ miles). Other facilities include a shop for the hire of ski equipment and the sale of ski accessories, a buffet and a cafeteria.

Lodgings relatively close to the site include the kibbutz guest houses of Hagoshrim, Kfar Giladi and Kfar Blum, hotels in Metulla and Kiryat Shmona and the youth hostel of Tel Hai. Other accommodation within travelling distance include the Ayelet Hashachar and Nof Ginosar kibbutz guest houses, hotels in Safed and Tiberias and youth hostels in Rosh Pinah, Kare Deshe, Poria and Tiberias.
For further information, contact:
**Hermon Ski Site**. Tel: (06) 981339.
**Moshav Neve Ativ**, 12010, MP Ramat Hagolan. Tel: (06) 981331.
**Israel Ski Club**, POB 211, Givatayim.

# RIDING

Riding schools and stables can be found throughout the country. Horse lovers who are interested in more than just riding can contact the Israel Horse Society, which occasionally sponsors horse shows and concentrates on horse breeding in Israel. For those wishing to explore, there are riding facilities which specialise in trail riding.

Among the larger riding stables are:

### CAESAREA
**Herod's Stables**, Dan Caesarea Golf Hotel. Tel: (06) 389065.

### EILAT
**Sunbay Hotel**, Lagoon Beach. Tel: (059) 73145.

### JERUSALEM
**Havat Amir**, Atarot. Tel: (02) 852190.

### NAHARIYA
**Bacall's Riding School**, Sderot Ben Zvi. Tel: (04) 920534.

### RISHON LE ZION
**Havat Hadar Riding Center**, POB 307. Tel: (03) 941088.

### TIBERIAS
**Vered Hagalil Ranch**, Mobile Post Korazim. Tel: (067) 35785.

# HANG GLIDING

The Agur Hang Gliding School in Bat Yam (Tel Aviv Area), offers courses in hang gliding. Duration of the course is 18 hours (5 meetings).

Equipment can be rented from the company for a fee upon presentation of an authorised hang gliding certificate.
For further information, contact:
Mr Arnon Har Lev
**Agur Hang Gliding School and Club**, 124 Rehov Balfour, Bat Yam. Tel: (03) 867467.

# WATER SPORTS

Israel is truly a diver's paradise. Its mild climate ensures year-round diving in the crystal clear waters of both the Mediterranean and Red seas, where hundreds of miles of easily accessible coral reefs and spectacular seascapes await the diving enthusiast. A variety of diving experiences unequalled anywhere in the world include underwater photography, archaeological diving, grotto and cave diving. It should be noted that unless the diver has a 2-star licence, he must take a special diving course.

**In the Mediterranean Sea**
The Mediterranean has two good diving seasons – autumn (September–December) and spring (March–May), although there are also fine periods during the summer and winter when diving is possible. Visibility on good days averages 10 metres (33 ft), with calm waters. Tides are never a problem as their average fluctuation is only 40 cm (18 ins) even on rough days. Water temperatures range from 16°C (61°F) in February to 29°C (84°F) in August.

**In the Gulf of Eilat**
The Gulf is one of the most interesting diving centres in the world, containing an underwater nature reserve with especially exquisite coral.

Diving can be carried out every day of the year. The area is usually free of large and strong waves; currents and tides are moderate, with variations of up to 80 cm (2½ ft) between high and low tides. These variations do not in any way affect the diver's movement. Visibility is generally excellent, ranging from 15–40 metres (50–130 ft) and even more. Water temperatures range from 21°C (70°F) in

February to 27°C (80°F) in August.

**Snorkeling**: At the Nature Reserve on the Coral Beach, Eilat. Snorkels are available for renting on premises. Underwater paths are marked.

### Skin and Scuba Diving Courses

The courses for beginners last about five days and cover the theory of diving, lifesaving, physiology, physics and underwater safety. The only qualifications necessary are the ability to swim, a certificate from a doctor confirming fitness to learn diving, and a chest X-ray. Beginners can also go out on individual introductory dives, lasting from one to 1½ hours, accompanied throughout by an instructor.

It is possible to rent all the necessary skin and scuba diving equipment at the following centres:

**AHZIV**

**Ahziv Scuba Diving Center**. Regional Council Sulam Zor, MP Western Galilee. Tel: (04) 926785.

**EILAT**

**Aqua Sport**. Red Sea Diving Center, Coral Beach. Tel: (07) 334404.
**Lucky Divers**. Moriah Hotel. Tel: (07) 332111.
**Red Sea Divers**. Caravan Hotel. Tel: (07) 373145/6.

**NAHARIYA**

**Skin Diving Center**. Galei Galil Beach. Tel: (04) 924424.

**TEL AVIV**

**Aquamarine International Diving Club**, 23 Rehov Hissin. Tel: (03) 284206/7.
**Andromeda Yachting Club**, 83 Rehov Salame. Tel: (03) 824725. (Diving for groups).
**Water Sports Center**, Marina POB 16285. Tel: (03) 282972. For further information, contact: **The Federation for Underwater Activities in Israel**, POB 6110, 61060 Tel Aviv. Tel: (03) 5467968.

**Water Skiing, Wind Surfing or Board Surfing**
These sports are available at the following centres:

**EILAT**

**Aqua-Sport Red Sea Diving Center**, Coral Beach, POB 300. Tel: (07) 334404.

**NORTH BEACH**

**Rafi Nelson's Village**

**NETANYA**

**Blue Bay**, 37 Rehov Hamelachim. Tel: (053) 37131-8.
**Kontiki**, 11 Rehov Usishkin. Tel: (053) 32954.

**TEL AVIV**

**Aquamarine International Diving Club**, 23 Rehov Hissin. Tel: (03) 284206/7.

## SWIMMING

Israel's mild climate allows year round swimming at all of its coasts – the Mediterranean, the Gulf of Eilat, the Dead Sea and the Sea of Galilee. Qualified lifeguards are in attendance at all beaches and pools.

Swimming is free at many beaches: Ahziv, Acre, Ashdod, Ashkelon, Eilat, Ein Gedi, Haifa, Herzliya, Nahariya, Netanya, Rishon Lezion, Tiberias and Tel Aviv. Most hotels have swimming pools, to which guests of the hotel are generally granted free entry, and many allow use by visitors, for a fee.

## SPECTATOR

Soccer is the number one spectator sport with several matches every week. Israelis are especially proud of the Tel Aviv Maccabi basketball team, which has won the European championship twice. There are many international matches during the winter season at stadiums in the Tel Aviv area.

# SPECIAL INFORMATION

## DOING BUSINESS

Business customs are essentially European. Israel exports to survive and has a free trade agreement with the US and is an associate member of the European Community. Everybody speaks either English or French, but bureaucratic red tape can sometimes hamper commerce.

## USEFUL ADDRESSES

**Israel Export Institute**, 29 Mered Street, Tel Aviv. Tel: (03) 5142830.
**Israel Chamber of Commerce**, Ben-Gurion Airport. Tel: (03) 9711984.
**Ministry of Trade and Industry**, Agron Street, Jerusalem. Tel: (02) 750111.

## CHILDREN

Israelis love children who are expected to be seen and heard. Restaurants, hotels and cafés are very flexible in meeting children's fussy food needs and many hotels operate baby-sitting services.

Children under five travel free on the buses. Children under four must be harnessed into special seats when travelling in cars (except taxis).

## GAY

Homosexuality is illegal in Israel, but no prosecution has ever been brought for relationships between consenting adults. Independence Park in Tel Aviv is the country's main gay pick-up point and the city abounds with gay clubs.

## ESCORT AGENCIES

Tourist magazines are filled with adverts for escorts. The organisations that run them are thinly veiled prostitution services. Prostitution is legal in Israel providing customers are not solicited. If you want a free erotic show, drive north to Tel Aviv's Tel Baruch beach where the cheaper courtesans hang out.

## DISABLED

**At the Airport:** For disabled passengers, particularly those confined to wheelchairs, there are improved facilities in all sections – widened doorways to the duty-free shops, lowered public phones, widened access in public restrooms, lowered tables in the snack bar, free parking at the terminal entrance and strategically located ramps. There is a specially constructed lift for the boarding and disembarking of wheelchairs. Ben-Gurion is the only airport in the world with such a device.

## HIRE OF WHEELCHAIRS

Folding wheelchairs can be hired – subject to availability – from:
Jerusalem
**The Alyn Orthopaedic Hospital for Crippled Children**, Rehov Shemaryahu Levin, Kiryat Hayovel. Office Hours: Sunday–Thursday, 9am–1pm. Tel: (02) 412251.
**Yad Sarah**, 43 Rehov Hanevi'im. Yad Sarah operates over 30 lending stations in Israel.

## DIALYSIS SERVICE FOR TOURISTS

**Elisha Private Hospital**, Mount Carmel, Haifa. Tel: (04) 81419.

## STUDENTS

**Youth Tours**: The Israel Student Tourist Association (ISSTA) arranges low-cost flights to and from Israel and offers young visitors a variety of tours including safaris and work camps. The association also issues and renews International Student Identity Cards. The ISSTA representative at Ben-Gurion Airport answers queries on kibbutzim, archaeological digs, hotels and hostels, buses, taxis, inland flights, and discounts.
Its offices are located in Israel's three main cities:
**Tel Aviv**: 109 Rehov Ben Yehuda. Tel: (02) 247164/5.
**Jerusalem**: 5 Rehov Elishar. Tel: (02) 225258.
**Haifa**: Hakranot, Rehov Herzl. Tel: (04) 669139.

## SPECIAL PROGRAMMES

The following universities hold special summer courses for students from abroad:
**Ben-Gurion University**, Beersheba. Tel: (057) 461104. Summer course for studying Hebrew.
**Hebrew University of Jerusalem**. Mr Weinberg, Department of Summer Courses; Overseas Students Admission Office. Goldsmith Building, Mount Scopus, Jerusalem. Tel: (02) 882604, 882624. Summer vacation programme – six-week intensive course in Hebrew or Arabic; three-week intensive course in the following fields: archaeology; Jewish thought; Jewish history; Middle East studies; Israel studies; contemporary Jewry; international relations; folklore; Holocaust studies; art history; psychology; environmental studies.
**University of Haifa**. Ruth Moskovitz, Overseas Students, Derech Abba Khoushi, Haifa. Tel: (04) 240111. Summer vacation programme, Intensive Hebrew course.
**Technion, Israel Institute of Technology**, Technion City, Haifa. Tel: (04) 292287. Summer vacation programme; summer seminar for science-oriented youth; folklore seminar.
**Tel Aviv University**, Amos Gilboa University Campus, Ramat Aviv. Tel: (03) 242111.

The Youth Department of the Jewish Agency also helps to place volunteers as workers on kibbutzim. The Head Office is located at 49 Rehov Hamelech George, Jerusalem. Tel: (02) 639261.

The Youth Section of the Ministry of Tourism provides maps and other printed information and helps youth visitors to join archaeological digs, many of which are open to student participants from abroad.

Volunteers must be over 17 years of age and physically fit. They are expected to pay their own fares to and from Israel and to take care of all of their accommodation and other arrangements not connected with their work on the dig.

For further information, contact David Sandovsky, The Ministry of Tourism, Youth and Student Division, 23 Rehov Hillel. Tel: (02) 240141, 240951 or if writing: 24 Rehov Hamelech George, 94262 Jerusalem, POB 1018, Jerusalem.

## PILGRIMAGES

While Israel has much to offer every tourist, for the Christian pilgrim, a trip to Israel is more than just a journey because here the pilgrim has the unique opportunity of tracing the footsteps of Jesus and the early Christians visiting sites significant to the life and teaching of Jesus: Bethlehem, His birthplace; Nazareth, the town of His boyhood; the Sea of Galilee, scene of miracles and his ministerial teaching; Mount Tabor, site of the Transfiguration; the Garden of Gethsemane and Jerusalem, where He spent his last hours of prayer and agony; and Latrun, now the site of a Trappist monastery, where Jesus appeared before His disciples after the Resurrection.

## JERUSALEM

**Armenian Cathedral of St James**. Tel: (02) 284549. Monday–Friday 3am–3.30pm, Saturday–Sunday 2.30am–3.15pm.

**Armenian Museum**. Monday–Saturday 10am–5pm. Tel: 282331.

**Bethany St Lazarus**. Tel: (02) 271706. 7am–noon, 2–6pm.

**Bethphage**. Tel: (02) 284352. 7am–5.30pm. Ring bell.

**Cenacle** (Last Supper). 8.30am–sundown.

**Cenacle Chapel Franciscans**. Tel: (02) 713597. 7am–noon, 3pm–sundown. Ring bell.

**Christ Church** – Office. Tel: (02) 282082. 8–10am, 4.30–6pm.

**Christian Information Center**. Tel: (02) 287647. 8.30am–12.30pm and 3–6pm (Sunday closed 3pm, 5.30pm in winter).

**Dominus Flevit**. Tel: (02) 285837. 6.45–11.30am; 3–5pm.

**Ein Karem: St John's**. Tel: (02) 413639. 5.30am–noon, 2.30–6pm (winter 2.30–5.30pm).

**Ein Karem: Visitation**. Tel: (02) 417291. 9am–noon, 3–6pm.

**Flagellation**. Tel: (02) 282936. 6am–noon, 2–6pm (winter 2–5.30pm).

**Garden Tomb**. Tel: (02) 283402. 8am–1pm, 3–5pm. Sunday closed (winter 8am–12.30pm, 2.30–4.30pm).

**Gethsemane, Church of Agony and Grotto**. Tel: (02) 283264. 8.30–noon, 3pm–sundown (winter 2pm–sundown).

**Holy Sepulchre**. Tel: (02) 273314. 4am–8pm (winter 4am–7pm).

**Lithostrotos-Ecce Homo**. Tel: (02) 282445. 8.30am–4.30pm. Sunday closed (winter 8.30am–4pm).

**Lutheran Church of the Redeemer**. Tel: (02) 282543. 9am–1pm, 2–5 pm, Friday 9am–1pm. Sunday for services only.

**Monastery of the Holy Cross**. Tel: (02) 634442. Irregular hours – phone ahead.

**Paternoster Church**. Tel: (02) 283143. 8.30–11.45am, 3–4.30pm.

**Russian Cathedral**. Tel: (02) 284580 by appointment.

**St Mary Magdalene**. Tel: (02) 282897. Irregular hours – phone ahead.

**St Alexander Excavations**. Tel: (02) 284580. 9am–1pm, 3–5pm ring the bell.

**St Ann's – Bethesda**. Tel: (02) 283258. 8am–noon, 2.30–6pm (winter 2–5pm).

**St George's Cathedral**. Tel: (02) 282253 or 282167. 6.45am–6.30pm.

**Tomb of Mary (Gethsemane)**. 6.30am–noon, 2–6pm.

**St Mark's (Syr. Orth.)**. Tel: (02) 283304. 9am–noon, 3.30–6pm (ask for the key). (winter 2–5pm).

**St Peter in Gallicantu**. Tel: (02) 283332. 8.30–11.45am, 2–5pm. Sunday closed.

**St Stephen's Church**. Tel: (02) 282213. 7.30am–1pm, 3–6pm.

**Dormition Abbey**. Tel: (02) 719927. 7am–12.30pm, 2–7pm.

**Abu Gosh Crusader Church**. Tel: (02) 539798. 8.30–11am. 2.30–5pm.

## BETHLEHEM

**Bethlehem Nativity Church**. 6am–6pm.

**Bethlehem St. Catherine**. Tel: (02) 742425. 8am–noon, 2.30–6pm.

**Bethlehem Shepherd's Field**. Tel: (02) 742423. 8am–11.30am, 2–6pm. (winter 2–5pm).

**Cana: Wedding Church**. Tel: (067) 55211. 8am–noon, 3–6pm (winter 3–5pm).

**Capernaum "City of Jesus"**. Tel: (067) 21059. 8.30am–4.30pm.

**Emmaus Qubeibeh**. Tel: (04) 952495 ext: 4. 6.30–11.30am, 2–6pm.

**Latrun Monastery**. Tel: (08) 420065. 7.30–11.30am, 2.30–5pm.

**Jacob's Well: Nablus**. 8.30am–noon, 2.30–5pm.

**Mar Saba Monastery** (men only), only with permission of the Greek-Orthodox Patriarch.

**Mount of Beatitudes**. Tel: (067) 20878. 8am–noon, 2–4pm.

**Mount Carmel Stella Maris**. Tel: (04) 523460. 6am–noon, 3–6pm (winter 3–5pm).

**Muhraqa: Sacrifice of Elijah**. 9–11am, 1–5pm.

## NAZARETH

**Nazareth: Basilica of the Annunciation & St Joseph's**. Tel: (06) 572501. 8.30–11.45am, 2–6pm. Sunday: 2–6pm (winter 2–5pm).

**Nazareth Synagogue**. 8.30am–5pm (ring bell).

**Nazareth St Gabriel's (Well)**. 8.30–11.45am, 2–6pm.

**Tabor Transfiguration**. Tel: (06) 567489. 8am–noon, 3–5pm.

**Tabgha: Primacy St Peter**. Tel: (06) 771062. 8am–sundown.

**Tabgha: Multiplication of the Bread**. Tel: (06) 721061. 8am–4pm.

**Temptation Monastery Jericho**. 8am–noon, 3–4pm.

**Good Samaritan Inn in the Judean Desert**. 8am–1pm. Closed Friday.

# THE ISRAEL PILGRIMAGE COMMITTEE

An inter-ministerial body which functions in close cooperation with representatives of foreign and local trade organisations, as well as Christian bodies. It has the following aims: to establish conditions which will enable Christian pilgrims and visitors who arrive in Israel, singly or in groups, to come into closer contact with the citizens of the country and to be made aware of its achievements and problems; to establish fruitful cooperation with clerical and other Christian bodies resident in Israel for joint promotional pilgrimage activities; to enable pilgrim groups to summarise their impressions and discuss them in their own language. Israeli personalities in various fields are available to reply to questions concerning the biblical, cultural, economic and political life of Israel. The panel for this forum can easily be adapted according to the professional and/or religious composition of each group. The Israel

Pilgrimage Committee will offer, free of charge, lectures of a general nature on such specific topics as: the remaking of a nation; the conquest of the desert; Israel and the Arabs; the revival of the Hebrew language; biblical archaeology; Judaism in modern Israel; films.

For more information contact: **Ministry of Tourism Pilgrimage Division**. POB 1018, Jerusalem. Tel: (02) 247962.

## FRANCISCAN PILGRIMS OFFICE

Located at the Christian Information Centre, inside the Old City's Jaffa Gate, opposite the Citadel. The office makes arrangements for Catholic priests who wish to celebrate a Mass. Reservations can be made at the office, free of charge, for shrines in Jerusalem, Bethlehem, Bethany, Ein Karem, Emmaus (Qubeibeh) and Jericho. The office also issues certificates of Christian pilgrimage.

## BAPTISMAL SITES

An organised baptismal site has been erected at the mouth of the River Jordan, 8 km (5 miles) south of Tiberias. There are three levels of platforms in the water and descent is by steps or a wheelchair-accessible ramp. There is ample space for groups. The site is open during daylight hours. Entry is free.

# LANGUAGE

Hebrew is the most widely spoken language in the country, and Hebrew and Arabic are the official languages of the country. Although other languages, especially English, are also fairly widely spoken it is a good idea to know some basic Hebrew words and phrases before coming to the country. Here are 60 basic words which may help you find the language a little less daunting:

| | |
|---|---|
| all-purpose greeting (literally "peace") | *shalom* |
| good morning | *boker tov* |
| good evening | *erev tov* |
| yes | *ken* |
| no | *lo* |
| please | *bevakasha* |
| thank you | *toda* |
| very much | *raba* |
| good | *tov* |
| bad | *ra* |

| | |
|---|---|
| big | *gadol* |
| little | *katan* |
| more | *yoter* |
| less | *pahot* |
| I | *ani* |
| you (singular) | *m/f ata/at* |
| (plural) | *m/f atem/aten* |
| we/us | *anahnu* |
| them | *m/f hem/hen* |
| want | *m/f rotseh/rotsa* |
| how much? | *kama?* |
| too dear | *yakar midai* |
| cheaper | *yoter zol* |
| bank | *bank* |
| restaurant | *mis'ada* |
| post office | *do'ar* |
| hotel | *malon* |
| shop | *hanut* |
| taxi | *monit* |
| train | *rakevet* |
| bus | *autoboos* |
| station/bus stop | *tahana* |
| Where is? | *eyfo?* |
| right | *yemin* |
| left | *smol* |
| when? | *matai?* |
| white | *lavan* |
| black | *shahor* |
| red | *adom* |
| blue | *kahol* |
| right, correct | *nahon* |
| wrong | *lo nahon* |
| straight | *yashar* |
| one | *ehad* |
| two | *shtayim* |
| three | *shalosh* |
| four | *arba'* |
| five | *hamesh* |
| six | *shesh* |
| seven | *sheva'* |
| eight | *shmoney* |
| nine | *taysha'* |
| ten | *esser* |
| hundred | *me'a* |
| thousand | *elef* |
| many | *harbey* |
| stop, wait a minute! | *rega!* |
| cinema | *kolno'a* |
| newspaper | *iton'* |
| water | *mayim* |
| food | *okhel* |
| bill | *heshbon* |

## SPELLING

As of yet, there is no standardised spelling of Israeli place names. Thus one has: "Acre", "Akko" and "Acco"; "Nathanya" "Natanya" and "Netanya"; "Elat", "Elath" and "Eilat"; "Ashqelon" and "Ashkelon"; "S'fat", "Zefat", "Tzfat" and "Safed", etc. As if to purposely confuse the visitor, all are used freely.

# USEFUL ADDRESSES

## EMBASSIES

Most embassies are closed on Sunday.

**Embassy of The United States of America.** 71 Rehov Hayarkon, 63903 Tel Aviv. Tel: (03) 5174338.

**Embassy of The Republic of Argentina.** 112 Rehov Hayarkon, 2nd Floor, 63571 Tel Aviv. Tel: (03) 5271614.

**Australian Embassy.** 185 Rehov Hayarkon, 63405 Tel Aviv. Tel: (03) 6950451.

**Embassy of the Republic of Austria.** 11 Rehov Hermann Cohen, 64385 Tel Aviv. Tel: (03) 5246186.

**Embassy of The Kingdom of Belgium.** 266 Rehov Hayarkon, 63504 Tel Aviv. Tel: (03) 454164/5/6.

**Embassy of The Federative Republic of Brazil.** 14 Rehov Hei Be'lyar, Kikar Hamedina, 5th Floor, 62093 Tel Aviv. Tel: (03) 219292/4.

**British Embassy.** 192 Rehov Hayarkon, 63405 Tel Aviv. Tel: (03) 5249171.

**Embassy of The Socialist Republic of The Union of Burma.** 19 Rehov Yona, 52376 Ramat Can. Tel: (03) 783151.

**Embassy of Canada.** 220 Rehov Hayarkon, 63405 Tel Aviv. Tel: (03) 5272929.

**Embassy of The Republic of Chile.** 54 Rehov Finkas, Apt. 45, 11th Floor, 62261 Tel Aviv. Tel: (03) 5662123.

**Embassy of The Republic of Columbia.** 52 Rehov Finkas, 6th Floor, Apt.62, 62261 Tel Aviv. Tel: (03) 449616.

**Royal Danish Embassy.** 23 Rehov Bnei Moshe, 62308 Tel Aviv. Tel: (03) 5442144.

**Embassy of The Dominician Republic.** 32 Rehov Zamenhoff, Herzliya B. Tel: (052) 72422.

**Embassy of The Republic of Ecuador.** Asia House, 4 Rehov Weizmann, Room 231, 64239 Tel Aviv. Tel: (03) 258764.

**Embassy of The Arab Republic of Egypt.** 54 Rehov Basel, 62744 Tel Aviv. Tel: (03) 5464151.

**Embassy of The Republic of El Salvador.** 16 Rehov Kovshei Katamon Jerusalem. Tel: (02) 633575.

**Embassy of Finland.** Beit Eliahu, 8th Floor, 2 Rehov Ibn Gvirol, 64077 Tel Aviv. Tel: (03) 250527/8.

**Embassy of France.** 112 Tayelet Herbert, Samuel, 63572 Tel Aviv. Tel: (03) 5101415.

**Embassy of The Federal Republic of Germany.** 16 Rehov Soutine, 64684 Tel Aviv. Tel: (03) 5421313.

**Embassy of Greece.** 35 Sderot Shaul Hamelech, 64297 Tel Aviv. Tel: (03) 6959704.

**Embassy of The Republic of Guatemala.** 1 Rehov Bernstein Cohen, Apt. 10, 47227 Ramat Hasharon. Tel: (03) 490456.

**Embassy of Haiti.** Asia House, 4 Rehov Weizmann, Room 230, 64239 Tel Aviv. Tel: (03) 252084.

**Embassy of Hungary.** 18 Pinkas. Tel: (03) 5466860.

**Embassy of Italy.** Asia House, 4 Rehov Weizmann, 64239 Tel Aviv. Tel: (03) 264223/5.

**Embassy of Japan.** Asia House, 4 Rehov Weizmann, 64239 Tel Aviv. Tel: (03) 257292/4.

**Embassy of the United States of Mexico.** 14 Rehov Hei Be'lyar, Kikar Hamedina, 62093 Tel Aviv. Tel: (03) 5230367.

**Royal Netherlands Embassy.** Asia House, 4 Rehov Weizmann, 64239 Tel Aviv. Tel: (03) 6957377.

**Royal Norwegian Embassy.** 10 Rehov Hei Be'lyar, Kikar Hamedina, 62093 Tel Aviv. Tel: (03) 5442030.

**Embassy of The Republic of Panama.** 28 Rehov Hei Be'lyar, Kikar Hamedina, 62998 Tel Aviv. Tel: (03) 5412090.

**Embassy of The Republic of Peru.** 52 Rehov Finkas, 8th Floor, Apt. 31, 62261 Tel Aviv. Tel: (03) 5441081.

**Embassy of The Republic of the Philippines.** 12 Rehov Hei Be'lyar, Kikar Hamedina, 62093 Tel Aviv. Tel: (03) 5102229.

**Embassy of Portugal.** Weizmann 4. Tel: (03) 6956373.

**Embassy of The Socialist Republic of Romania.** 24 Rehov Adam Hacohen, 64585 Tel Aviv. Tel: (03) 247379, 242482.

**Embassy of The Republic of South Africa.** 2 Rehov Kaplan, 9th Floor, 64734 Tel Aviv. Tel: (03) 6956147.

**Embassy of Spain.** 3 Daniel Frisch. Tel: (03) 265217.

**Royal Swedish Embassy.** Asia House, 4 Rehov Weizmann, 64239 Tel Aviv. Tel: (03) 6958111.

**Embassy of Switzerland.** 228 Rehov Hayarkon, 63405 Tel Aviv. Tel: (03) 5464455.

**Embassy of Turkey.** 34 Rehov Amos, 62495. Tel Aviv. Tel: (03) 454155/6.

**Embassy of The Oriental Republic of Uruguay.** 52 Rehov Pinkas, 2nd Floor, Apt 10, 62261 Tel Aviv. Tel: (03) 440411/2.

**Embassy of The Republic of Venezuela.** Asia House, 4 Rehov Weizmann, 5th Floor, 64239 Tel Aviv. Tel: (03) 656287.

**United Nations Truce Supervision Organization.** POB 490, 91400 Jerusalem. Tel: (02) 716223/6.

## CONSULATES IN JERUSALEM

**Austria.** 8 Hovevei Zion St. Tel: (02) 630675.

**Belgium.** 5 Biber St. Tel: (02) 828263.

**Denmark.** 5 Bnei Brit St. Tel: (02) 258083.

**France.** 5 Emil Botta St. Tel: (02) 259481.

**Greece.** 31 Rachel Imenu. Tel: (02) 619583.

**Italy.** 29 November St. Tel: (02) 518966.

**Spain.** 53 Rambam St. Tel: (02) 633473.

**Turkey.** Sheikh Jarrah. Tel: (02) 828238.

**UK** 19 Nashabibi St. Tel: (02) 828281.

**US** 16 Agron St. Tel: (02) 255755.

## OTHER USEFUL ADDRESSES

**American Cultural Center**. Kcpsn Hayrod St. 19, Jerussalem. Tel: (02) 255755.
**British Council Library**. 3 Zthidpia St., Jerusalem. Tel: (03) 250153.
**British Council Library**. Hayarkon St. Tel Aviv. Tel: (03) 222194.

# FURTHER READING

## OTHER INSIGHT GUIDES

Apa Publications' companion volume, *CityGuide: Jerusalem*, leads the reader step by step through the Holy City. In 240 pages, expert writers and photographers provide a comprehensive guide to the sites and entertainments of "the centre of the earth".

# ART/PHOTO CREDITS

# INDEX